Drugs in America

Sociology, Economics, and Politics

Ansley Hamid, PhD
Associate Professor
Department of Anthropology
John Jay College of Criminal Justice
New York, New York

AN ASPEN PUBLICATION®
Aspen Publishers, Inc.
Gaithersburg, Maryland
1998

The author has made every effort to ensure the accuracy of the information herein. However, appropriate information sources should be consulted, especially for new or unfamiliar procedures. It is the responsibility of every practitioner to evaluate the appropriateness of a particular opinion in the context of actual clinical situations and with due considerations to new developments. The author, editors, and the publisher cannot be held responsible for any typographical or other errors found in this book.

Library of Congress Cataloging-in-Publication Data

Hamid, Ansley.
Drugs in America: sociology, economics, and politics/Ansley Hamid.
p. cm.
Includes bibliographical references and index.
ISBN 0-8342-1060-6
1. Drug abuse—United States.
2. Drug abuse and crime—United States.
3. Drug traffic—United States.
4. Narcotics, Control of—United States. I. Title.
HV5825.H213 1998
362.29'1'0973—DC21
98-25990
CIP

Orders: (800) 638-8437
Customer Service: (800) 234-1660

About Aspen Publishers • For more than 35 years, Aspen has been a leading professional publisher in a variety of disciplines. Aspen's vast information resources are available in both print and electronic formats. We are committed to providing the highest quality information available in the most appropriate format for our customers. Visit Aspen's Internet site for more information resources, directories, articles, and a searchable version of Aspen's full catalog, including the most recent publications: **http://www.aspenpublishers.com**
Aspen Publishers, Inc. • The hallmark of quality in publishing
Member of the worldwide Wolters Kluwer group.

Editorial Services: Kathy Litzenberg
Library of Congress Catalog Card Number: 98-25990
ISBN: 0-8342-1060-6

Printed in the United States of America

1 2 3 4 5

Table of Contents

Introduction: Drugs and Humans

Objectives

The destinies of drugs and humans are so intertwined that outright prohibition is an unattainable and ill-advised goal. Instead, the relationship should be investigated and negotiated more.

As a social phenomenon, the human use of psychoactive drugs is both primordial and nearly universal. In almost every human culture in every age of history, the use of one or more psychoactive drugs was featured prominently in the contexts of religion, ritual, health care, divination, celebration (including the arts, music, and theater), recreation, and cuisine. Through these multiple institutions these drugs heavily conditioned the life of the individual person. Inuit societies, adapted to the frigid temperatures of the North Pole, are the only exceptions. They were prevented by the climate from harvesting psychoactive plants in the wild or from cultivating them, and they found that their environment did not harbor animal sources either, such as toads in Haiti or the fugu fish in Japan.

Because of their ubiquity, therefore, some anthropologists have speculated that drug use is a basic human activity, and that the first human users were "mimicking the behavior of other animals through the millennia. . . . Throughout our entire history as a species, intoxication has functioned like the basic drives of hunger, thirst, or sex. . . . Intoxication is the fourth drive" (Siegel, 1989, p. 10).

The historical record might even indicate that the meeting between psychoactive plants and psychoactive animals was destined to occur. Scholars have speculated that altered states of consciousness, reached through drug use, first prompted humans to acquire an inner life, mentality, memory, language, and self-consciousness (Furst, 1972; Tart, 1969; Wasson, Kramrisch, Ott, & Ruck, 1986). Others, appealing to the notion of a consciousness-at-large, or one that transcends individual nervous systems, believe that these plants are repositories of knowledge about the universe and existence that humans incrementally access when needed. Far from delusional, experiences encountered in the psychedelic state connect the user to a more fundamental, or spiritual, reality (Bennett, Osborn, & Osborn, 1995; Devereux, 1997; Harner, 1973).

Of course, drugs having psychoactive, therapeutic, or other desirable effects can still be dangerous. As they are no different from poisons except in dosage, most cultures have regarded them as Janus-faced: from this angle smiling benignly, from the other side ugly, ominous, and even lethal. Many other cultural objects or social activities are characterized by the same duality. Even insofar as drug taking is risk taking, however, anthropologists have asserted that both are necessary for human evolution and progress. The species could not have advanced if pioneers had not abandoned the comforts of the safe and familiar and ventured into the hazardous unknown (Leary, 1968; Weil, 1972).

Traditional societies achieved balanced relationships with psychoactive drugs because typically drug seeking and drug use were completely circumscribed by rules. Recognizing the potential for harm, they reduced it. While cherishing them, they were not indiscriminately permissive regarding drugs and did not tolerate all drug use under any circumstances. On the contrary, elaborate customs, rituals, and belief systems combined to limit and define the appropriate settings, behaviors, and attitudes for acceptable drug use. These tightly interrelated patterns of cultural life imposed a compelling set of social controls that averted drug abuse. Indeed, drug-using traditional cultures effectively maintained remarkable social cohesion, and some, surviving genocidal assaults against them in the modern age, have endured for thousands of years. These include the Yanomamo of the Amazon and Orinoco basins, who blow a powder prepared from ayahausca, or *caapi*, into one another's nostrils; Andean Indian groups, who chew coca leaves and drink potions prepared from the San Pedro cactus; tribal groups of Laos, Cambodia, Vietnam, Burma, and northern Thailand, such as Karen, Mien, Hmong, Akha, Lahu, and Lisu, who cultivate opium poppies for recreational and ceremonial use; several North American and Mexican Indian tribes, who eat peyote; the Hopi and the Navajo, who consume food and beverages made with datura; Mexican Huichol and Tarahumara Indians, who eat psychoactive mushrooms; the Kuma of New Guinea, who eat the local psychoactive mushrooms; natives of the Horn of Africa (Somalia, Yemen, Djibouti, Eritrea, Ethiopia, and Kenya), who chew qat; Siberian reindeer herdsmen who drink the urine of their shamans after they have eaten fly agaric mushrooms; Australian aborigines who hallucinate after swallowing pituri; southeast Asians who swallow the juices of the betel nut or areca; and Pacific

Islanders who drink kavakava (de Rios, 1984; Schultes, 1972; Schultes & Hoffman, 1992).

Additionally, the socially accepted drugs in traditional societies were almost always locally grown plants from the nearby habitat, such as the coca plant for the indigenous tribes of the Andes mountains, or the fruits and grains used for wine and beer in many areas of the globe. Naturally diluted by other, nonpsychoactive, ingredients, the drugs in these plant or liquid forms were usually less potent than the refined powders and pills that chemists now extract from them.

Finally, and most important, youth were initiated into drug use under the personal supervision of respected elders, whether their own fathers, uncles, female relatives, or the shaman of the tribe. These experts determined the hour and circumstances of use (often preceded by preparatory ritual cleansing or abstinences from certain activities and substances), the eligibility of participants, and the appropriate dosages. They participated during the drug-using session itself, giving practical guidance and alerting their charges about what effects to expect and how to deal with them. These ceremonies were frequently communal, attended also by one's closest kin, intimates, and co-workers, a circumstance that by itself fostered control and decorum.

Diverse traditional societies thus furnish a treasury of examples of how human actors can deliberately mold and craft the effects that drugs will have upon them. Cross-cultural comparisons, for example, demonstrate how the same drugs have encountered contrastive responses in different local contexts. Even chocolate, as harmless as it appears to modern Americans, was proscribed in some places as a dangerous, habit-forming aphrodisiac (Weil & Rosen, 1983).

Communities varied most in their responses to the introduction of "foreign" innovations, such as imported drugs:

> The approval of some drugs for some purposes usually goes hand in hand with the disapproval of other drugs for other purposes. For example, some early Muslim sects encouraged the use of coffee in religious rites, but had strict prohibitions against alcohol. On the other hand, when coffee came to Europe in the seventeenth century, the Roman Catholic Church opposed it as an evil drug but continued to regard wine as a traditional sacrament. . . . Many North American Indians who use peyote and tobacco in religious rituals consider alcohol a curse. (Weil & Rosen, 1983, p. 11)

Administered with these restraints, therefore, psychoactive drugs have been highly valued, and human populations have ingested them safely and confidently since prehistoric times. In the past 100 years, however, their reputations have plummeted. In that brief period alone, the seal of approval that had sufficed for thousands of years was replaced by obloquy and condemnation. Regarded only yesterday as sacred substances to be approached respectfully, they have been demonized today and function as emblems of the worst excesses of contemporary society, especially urban society.

This turnabout was the accomplishment of a handful of American policymakers. Even though the peoples of nations across the globe, including the majority of Americans, have continued their centuries-old relationships with their favorite drugs, a small but powerful and influential number of their fellow citizens have declared their intention to make America and the world drug free (Gusfield, 1986; Musto, 1973; Walker, 1989).

The antidrug prohibitionist movement in the United States formed in the 1900s. Prior to it, only opium had been regulated (Kane, 1882). The movement combined sincere concerns about drug addiction with the political agenda of professionals, such as licensed doctors and chemists, who aimed to monopolize the lucrative businesses of diagnosing illness and prescribing cures. In reaction to an age before Americans had systematically regulated health care services, when careless distinctions were sometimes made between real and imagined diseases and the public was being aggressively encouraged to consume a myriad drug preparations to relieve them, the professionals founded the American Medical Association (and the Association of Chemists), which launched a political campaign to eliminate untrained and unlicensed competitors. The Pure Food and Drug Act of 1906, inspired by Upton Sinclair's *The Jungle*, a novel exposing the unhygienic conditions of the meat-packing industry (Sinclair, 1905/1960), and recommended by President Theodore Roosevelt as a passionate statement against interstate commerce in mislabeled or bogus foods and drugs, was a first fruit of these efforts. The act also responded to the indiscriminate use of cocaine and opiates in prepared foods and beverages.

The mighty industrialists of the day supported the movement (Rumbarger, 1989). Previously, employers had encouraged drug use as a boost to productivity, as they had in preindustrial economies. For example, a hallowed place for alcohol in particular was found in negotiations between employees and employers, who agreed to pay wages as well as liquor and either set aside hours for drinking or encouraged it in the workplace itself. Obliged to rely on a motley work force, however, which included disorderly elements among urban, Catholic, working-class immigrants, African Americans in the segregated South, and immigrant Mexicans, factory owners and capitalists used the enforcement of drug and alcohol prohibition by police to discipline and control workers.

The movement was joined by the contemporary ranks of the religious objectors who had been fighting against "demon alcohol" since colonial times, such as the Anti-Saloon League, Women's Christian Temperance Union, and other organized groups of Protestant, middle-class, and rural outlook. They were greatly empowered by developments in the mid–19th century, such as the replacement of the small workshop by factories, an attendant shift from informal work norms to the more structured shop-floor regimen, increased working-class incomes, shorter work days, and a more rigid separation of the workplace from leisure-time or domestic pursuits. Instead of occurring on the job or at home, drinking was diverted to such new establishments as saloons and recreational lounges (Rosenzweig, 1991; Sante, 1992). By 1877, Louise Hayes, a Methodist, had banned serving alcoholic drinks in the White House, and cartoonists surprised President Rutherford B. Hayes as he allegedly sneaked out with cronies to drink at these "trendy" public venues.

These combined forces scored their first victory with the Harrison Act in 1914, which was the first comprehensive federal legislation to prohibit the distribution and use of opium, morphine, heroin, and cocaine. Marijuana was added to the list in the Marijuana Tax Act of 1937 through the almost single-handed efforts of Harry Anslinger, a discredited customs officer who was looking for another, more successful career when he formulated his campaign to convince Congress that Mexicans (and other "social undesirables") were routinely driven mad by it (Musto, 1973).

Their next major victory was the prohibition of alcohol by a constitutional amendment of 1919, which remained in effect until its repeal in 1933. Prohibition resulted especially from the culmination of efforts by the religious campaigners. The nation was preoccupied with war and approved of postponing pleasure for the greater national good; it distrusted the Germans, who financed the alcohol lobby; and it questioned the good faith of saloonkeepers who disregarded public health concerns. The war also placed a premium on efficiency at the expense of due process, "red tape, counter-arguments, comfort or convenience" (Allen, 1931/1964, p. 206). But the outcomes of the legislation—crime and illegal alcohol production and use—led other Americans to oppose it.

Briefly stated, subsequent drug policy was less sweeping. The Food, Drug and Cosmetic Act of 1938, which applied principally to the pharmaceutical industry, restricted the availability of some drugs to "by prescription only" and established guidelines for the testing and manufacture of new drugs. The Humphrey-Durham and Kefauver-Harris amendments, of 1951 and 1962, respectively, strengthened them (Mintz, 1967). The Comprehensive Drug Abuse Prevention and Control Act (The Controlled Substances Act) of 1970 divided drugs into five schedules, each carrying its specific regulations and penalties. Although it was lenient toward drug users, it targeted organized-crime distributors (Stimmel, 1991).

Nonetheless, prohibitionists have rallied again. Starting with the passage of the Anti-Drug Abuse Act of 1988 by the Reagan administration and the appointment of the conservative William Bennett as the nation's first "Drug Czar," they are waging a "war on drugs," not only in the United States, but globally. They have (sometimes forcibly) exported the policy of drug prohibition and reliance on law-enforcement agencies to eradicate drugs and criminalize their users, producers, and distributors worldwide (Belenko, 1993; Nadelmann, 1989; Reuter, 1992).

Prohibitionists have added powerful weapons to their antidrug arsenal. One is the significant psychosocial harm attributed to drugs in contemporary societies. For example, while drug use at the turn of the century in America had become rather more widespread than many authorities cared to tolerate, and although rates of addiction alarmed doctors, addicts were not suspected as yet of being prone to criminality, violence, or neglect of family, job, and community responsibilities. Only alcohol was blamed for such outcomes. Indeed, that age's portrait of the American drug addict depicted a genteel, hard-working, nurturing European-American housewife becoming dependent on the opiates her doctor freely prescribed. Pharmaceutical companies were then the leading manufacturers and distributors of opiates and other drugs currently outlawed. For example, heroin was first manufactured and distributed in the United States by Bayer, in a box that was identical to the one that contains Bayer aspirin today.

By the late 1960s, however, drug use was construed as both cause and symptom of urban disorder and decay. The popularity of marijuana and the psychedelics among young European Americans at the height of mobilization for the Vietnam War also hardened attitudes against drugs. The American addict was now portrayed as an overly indulged European-American middle-class student, recklessly and ungratefully rebelling against cherished American values.

In the heroin-injecting epidemic of 1964–1972 among young minority males in the inner cities of New York, San Francisco and Los Angeles, the evolving image of American drug addiction acquired even more somber tones. The face was now that of the completely "disinhibited," violent, minority male driven to commit atrocious crimes not only to support his drug misuse, but also to satisfy an insatiable libido that drugs had unleashed. The amoral, violent, criminal, minority female, supplying drugs to "addicted" neonates through the placenta and in breast milk, completed the family picture during the cocaine smoking epidemic of the 1980s (U.S. Public Health Service, 1992).

Despite these embellishments, however, it is not likely that this born-again, minority American prohibitionist crusade will ever prevail. Drug use has been too persistent through the ages. In the meantime, however, it has succeeded in perilously aggravating these same adverse personal and societal consequences of drug misuse. Indeed, some scholars believe that they are directly caused by it. Drug prohibition, they argue, has perverted all preexisting drug-use patterns. It has spawned criminal drug distribution, which has artificially increased demand and provokes violence and other criminality. It has replaced safe means of administration by riskier ones. And it has spawned the search for more compact, potent chemicals that distributors can adulterate more before they reach the consumer.

Drug prohibition has also had societal impacts in its own right that rival the worst misfortunes it has attributed to drugs. In the war on smokable cocaine, or crack, in the 1980s, for example, over a million young men and women were incarcerated. As they were disproportionately from the poor, African-American and Latino inner cities, their already disadvantaged communities bore the price of losing them as workers, kinsmen, and neighbors. American race relations worsened appreciably as a result (Kennedy, 1994; Szasz, 1974).

This book was written at a potential crossroads in American drug policy. In December 1996, the electorates of Arizona and California voted to allow doctors to prescribe marijuana for medical reasons. The federal government has since determined to reinforce federal sanctions and Drug Enforcement Administration operations against doctors who follow this mandate.

Given their "addictive" potential and other drawbacks accompanying their use, could or (should) modern societies entirely ban drugs? The majority of humans in the modern age do not want drugs, which is an enormous consolation. But individuals do run a gauntlet with the fact and idea of society. They do so necessarily, both in the process of individuation and also to affirm communal values by challenging and eventually restoring them. In the latter process, they may even modify societal conventions, contributing to ongoing evolution of the species.

Humans in all cultures have reserved the use of drugs for an occasion to be merry, to celebrate the ceremonial and heraldic aspects of life, to be introspective, and to be productive. On the whole, and unlike infanticide, female subjugation, war, and other inveterate practices that societies might well outgrow, drug use has been good for humans. Drugs create solidarity, distinguish one group from another, and supply anticipated and desired effects such as fortitude, aggressivity, creativity, effort, and relaxation. Drug-using sessions usually recreate the group and reinforce group norms and understandings. In America, however, drug use has polarized society by pitting prohibitionist and liberal, policeman and user, against one another.

Freud (1890/1974) has argued that drugs have an important function in the chemical economy of the brain. Because human life is so fragile and so much at the mercy of external forces, because happiness can never be sustained but is always only episodic, drugs deliver individuals from an inherently frustrating condition. Like the shamans of premodern societies, some modern theologians and religious thinkers have urged that drugs are valuable as an aid in the religious quest for self-transcendence. Initiation and subsequent drug use may resemble religious conversion and the life of a devotee, surrendering completely to the Beloved (James, 1902/1958).

More recently, drug economies have served overall economic life so well that it appears as though some of us are predetermined to be addicts and distributors, in order to generate and sustain the flow of those billions of indispensable dollars. In some phases of the global and national economies, the dollars are used to support local-level capital accumulation and reinvestment; in another phase, they are extracted from hitherto unrecognized values, aggregated and removed to few powerful centers (Hamid, 1990, 1992).

Drugs are so deeply, anciently, and usefully embedded in so many aspects of human societies that their extinction is virtually unthinkable. At the same time, the benefits that drugs bring can be gained by alternative means, with a greatly reduced possibility of adverse outcomes. For example, the arts and music (although notorious as worlds in which illicit drug use thrives) provide some of the same gratifications, and success in these fields gives a person the bonus of self-fulfillment and the satisfaction of achievement. Exercise, yoga, and meditation are other fruitful means for altering consciousness or mental and physical functioning. Perhaps there is too little awareness of these options, and systematic efforts to introduce them on a wide scale could be made.

It will help the reader to know at the outset that the author believes, like the voters of Arizona and California, that national drug policy may be more effectively redesigned if the harm caused by the Harrison Act is reversed, criminal sanctions against drug use are removed, and drug misuse or addiction are prevented by drug education, by the medical monitoring of users, and through informal controls (which can be identified, described precisely, and strengthened). Disgusted by the absurdities and excesses of the drug war, the author craves "drug peace."

The achievement of this goal cannot lie, however, in a simple resurrection of the balance enjoyed by traditional societies. Present-day societies, after all, are qualitatively different from the latter: the entire globe is their reference and they represent the continuous (often unsuccessful) striving by heterogeneous and competing populations to unite in single polities. In them, the adjustment between individual rights and social obligation is more complexly negotiated. The author hopes that readers will find in this book materials that will help them master this difficult task and contribute usefully to the urgent and widening national debate on drugs.

Discussion Questions

1. Read several ethnographies or other accounts of drug use in traditional societies or in different periods of history. Describe and discuss the various functions drugs performed in them. Make notes of the ways in which the potential dangers of drug use are avoided.
2. Discuss how the rights of individuals (life, liberty, and the pursuit of happiness) are to be balanced with those of the group (to endure). Make a chro-

nology of American drug policy, giving details of the movements and persons who were its chief architects.

3. Comment on the quest for altered states of consciousness and transcendent experience. Could these serve evolutionary purposes? What is their relation to a purpose in life? Where did they originate? Does our culture encourage their pursuit? Discuss the arts, meditation, yoga, or other technologies as means to arrive at self-transcendence.

4. What are the impacts of the war on drugs in the reader's community? How are different agents affected—users, distributors, public officials, police, hospitals, and the community at large?

REFERENCES

Allen, F.A. (1931/1964). *Only yesterday: An informal history of the 1920's* (Perennial Library ed.). New York: Harper & Row.

Belenko, S.J. (1993). *Crack and the evolution of anti-drug policy.* Westport, CT: Greenwood Press.

Bennett, C., Osborn, L., & Osborn, J. (1995). *Green gold, the tree of life: Marijuana in magic and religion.* Frazier Park, CA: Access Unlimited.

de Rios, M.D. (1984). *Hallucinogens: Cross-cultural perspectives.* Albuquerque: University of New Mexico Press.

Devereux, P. (1997). *The long trip: A prehistory of psychedelia.* New York: Penguin/Arkana.

Freud, S. (1890/1974). In R. Byck (Ed.), *Cocaine papers.* New York: Stonehill.

Furst, P.T. (1972). *The flesh of the gods: The ritual use of hallucinogens.* New York: Praeger.

Gusfield, J.R. (1986). *Symbolic crusade: Status, politics and the American temperance movement* (2nd ed.). Urbana, IL: University of Illinois Press.

Hamid, A. (1990, Spring). The political economy of crack-related violence. *Contemporary Drug Problems, 17,* (1).

Hamid, A. (1992). The developmental cycle of a drug epidemic: The cocaine smoking epidemic of 1981–91. *Journal of Psychoactive Drugs, 24,* 337–349.

Harner, M., (Ed.). (1973). *Hallucinogens and shamanism.* New York: Oxford University Press.

James, W. (1902/1958). *The varieties of religious experience: A study in human nature* (Mentor Book ed.). Markham, Ontario: Penguin/New American Library.

Kane, H.H. (1882). *Opium-smoking in America and China.* New York: Putnam.

Kennedy, R. (1994). The state, criminal law and racial discrimination: A comment. *Harvard Law Review, 107,* 1255–1278.

Leary, T. (1968). *The politics of Ecstasy.* New York: Putnam.

Mintz, M. (1967). *By prescription only.* Boston: Benson Press.

Musto, D. (1973). *The American disease: The origins of narcotic control.* New Haven, CT: Yale University Press.

Nadelmann, E.A. (1989, September). Drug prohibition in the United States: Costs, consequences and alternatives. *Science,* pp. 939–947.

Reuter, P. (1992). Hawks ascendant: The punitive trend of American drug policy. *Daedelus, Journal of the American Academy of Arts and Sciences, 121*, 314–336.

Rosenzweig, R. (1991). The rise of the saloon. In C. Mukerji & M. Schudson (Eds.), *Rethinking popular culture: Contemporary perspectives in cultural studies* (pp. 121–157). Berkeley and Los Angeles, CA: University of California Press.

Rumbarger, J.J. (1989). *Profits, power and prohibition: Alcohol reform and the industrializing of America, 1800–1930.* Albany, NY: State University of New York Press.

Sante, L. (1992). *Low life: Lures and snares of old New York* (Pt. 2, pp. 71–177). New York: Vintage Departures.

Schultes, R.E. (1972). An overview of hallucinogens in the Western Hemisphere. In P.T. Furst (Ed.), *Flesh of the gods: The ritual use of hallucinogens* (pp. 3–54). New York: Praeger.

Schultes, R. E. & Hoffman, A. (1992). *Plants of the gods.* Rochester, VT: Healing Arts Press.

Siegel, R.K. (1989). *Intoxification: Life in pursuit of artificial paradise.* New York: Dutton.

Sinclair, U. (1905/1960). *The jungle* (Signet Classic ed.). New York: New American Library.

Stimmel, B. (1991). *The facts about drug use: Coping with drugs and alcohol in your family, at work, in your community.* Yonkers, NY: Consumer Union of the United States.

Szasz, T. (1974). *Ceremonial chemistry: The ritual persecution of drugs, addicts and pushers.* Garden City, NY: Anchor Books.

Tart, C. (Ed.). (1969). *Altered states of consciousness.* New York: Wiley.

U.S. Public Health Service. (1992). *Dispelling myths, restoring hope.* Washington, DC: Author.

Walker, W.O. (1989). *Drug control in the Americas* (rev. ed). Albuquerque, NM: University of New Mexico Press.

Wasson, R.G., Kramrisch, S., Ott, J., & Ruck, C.A.P. (1986). *Persephone's quest: Entheogens and the origins of religion.* New Haven, CT: Yale University Press.

Weil, A. (1972). *The natural mind: An investigation of drugs and the higher consciousness.* Boston: Houghton Mifflin.

Weil, A. & Rosen, W. (1983). *From chocolate to morphine: Understanding mind-active drugs.* Boston: Houghton Mifflin.

CHAPTER 1

Historical Overview

Chapter Objectives

Drug use in the modern age is unlike that in traditional societies. It symbolizes and expresses all the important themes, complexities, antagonisms, and contradictions of contemporary life. To think critically about drugs, students must forget much of what they have learned in drug education classes, which do not situate drug use and drug users in these actual, dynamic, real-life contexts. Some assertions that users and distributors of drugs make are also misleading. As a methodology, ethnography implies an emphasis on social, economic, cultural, and political parameters. Ethnographers respect and report the knowledge of users and distributors of drugs in their own words, but subject it to a disciplined scrutiny. The chapter also introduces the principal drugs to be discussed in subsequent chapters—alcohol, marijuana, cocaine, and heroin.

The purpose of this book is to provoke critical thinking about "the drug problem" in the United States and in modern societies generally. It is not to persuade readers to adopt any single point of view, even that of its author, on a matter that some leaders have identified as the "No. 1 national security threat." Rather, if this book succeeds in its intention, readers will acquire a much better understanding of how and why drug use has been construed as problematic in the contemporary world.

DRUGS AND MODERNITY

Some features of drug use in traditional societies, and in the United States until recently, were sketched in the Introduction. Drugs, however, make their way in a different world in modern societies. The particulars by which the latter are differentiated from traditional societies have profoundly altered the drug experience. The market economy, with its emphases on earning and spending money; the formation of nation states and the conflicts between them; American hegemony in the late 20th century, the emergence of a global economy, the polarization of wealth; ethnic divisions and cultural strife; and the threat of environmental collapse, overpopulation, and nuclear disaster have forged modern humans who have vastly complicated their relationship to psychoactive drugs.

Since the waning of the Middle Ages and the triumphant emergence of a market-based economy, Europeans have gradually spread their own restlessly expanding civilization outward over the entire planet, by an often violently disruptive historical process which undermined—and sometimes abruptly shattered—all the previously cohesive local communities with their age-old customs. Capitalism thus steadily developed into a world system, eventually forcing all areas of the planet into its interdependent web of production and consumption (Amin, 1974; Wallerstein, 1974).

Modern society connotes especially the replacement of traditional social classes and the relationships among them. This substitution especially modified the human-drug interaction. For example, the western European consumption of exotic and intoxicating substances in the medieval era was linked with changes in labor, class structure, and leisure, through which the shift from feudal, agrarian economies to bourgeois, industrial economies was mediated. At first, upwardly mobile western Europeans clamored for exotic "oriental" and tropical goods, and the consumption of intoxicating substances was particularly associated with status. The nobility were demarcated by their fondness of "oriental" spices, tobacco in various forms, and coffee. Eventually, tea was favored by the emerging industrial bourgeoisie in England, chocolate by the leisure class, and alcohol by the working masses. While serving thus as indicators of the metamorphosing class structure, these intoxicants or stimulants also "tie the individual into society more effectively because they give him pleasure" (Schivelbusch, 1992, p. 192). By satisfying desire and supplying pleasure, they helped to acculturate and socialize individuals to the new order. Other imported luxuries—spices, fabrics, furniture—and (sometimes) whole systems of thought—mathematics and philosophy—were adopted and conferred or confirmed status (Schivelbusch, 1992).

Indeed, it could be argued that the appetite for spices created the modern world. The ability to purchase and exhibit them in the preparation and presentation of extremely "spiced" foods functioned as an important marker of wealth and prestige in medieval Europe. A middle class of importers formed to finance the costly and difficult trading expeditions to Asia, but the overland routes used at the time soon proved inadequate to supply the huge demand in Europe. Status items frequently exert a driving force in history when they are in short supply, and the craving for spices prompted Columbus and others to seek a maritime route to India. Thus spices, after Columbus had inadvertently discovered America, facilitated the crystallization of the new global society and economy. Their use eventually spread to the middle classes, growing devalued and "common" in the process. Finally they were dropped from *haute cuisine* (Schivelbusch, 1992).

The enthusiasm for all exotic goods, however, soon turned to distaste and condemnation. The colonial relation into which European nations now entered with the territories they had penetrated elsewhere in the world created a source of ambivalence. Tropical countries with their native populations, flora, and fauna turned especially disquieting. Their initial appeal had to be subordinated to the trade in slaves and the justification of slavery. The colonial ideology eventually reduced the actual diversity of the tropics and projected the darker elements of experience—greed, lack of control, incivility, ignorance, crude intoxication, barbarism, and inhumanity—onto subjugated, tropical peoples, reserving their opposites as the virtues of the colonizing Europeans. Drugs—heroin, cocaine, marijuana, tobacco, tea, coffee, chocolate, and peyote buttons are all tropical in origin—were thus drawn into a brutal political drama. King James of England lashed out against tobacco and the Spaniards against coca because they represented the Devil, another increasingly tropicalized folklore figure.

The formation of nation states and national economies, and the strife that continues to characterize relations among them, are also fundamental constituents of the modern quotidian, pervading every aspect of individual behavior. National identities, for example, were frequently fabricated as business elites sought to secure loyal clienteles for their products. As French bakers or the Spanish sherry-producing nobility relied on "Frenchmen" or "Spaniards" to buy their bread or wine, a "France" and a "Spain" took shape, with governments that made sure—through taxes, tariffs, and wars—that they did. As nations defined themselves as communities and polities written large (Anderson, 1983), they dictated how the bodies of their representative citizens should appear, what was permissible to put into them, how they should behave, and whether they were to be mortified or celebrated (Bordo, 1993; Brumberg, 1988; Chernin, 1985; Turner, 1984). In one stage of national development, therefore, women might be admired for an ample girth; in another, they are driven to anorexia, or to embrace a "heroin chic," as in the early 1990s (Hamid et al., 1997). Caloric intake ranged from the Edwardian, when British nobility munched unceasingly from dawn to bedtime, to the current anxiety to eliminate fat from diets. Whether or not to enjoy pleasure and the rights of individuals versus the community in its pursuit were also puzzles, which societies resolved by alternating periods of license and prohibition. "Inordinate pleasure caused by drugs was seen to provide youth with a poor foundation for character development, and a resulting loss of independence and productivity" (Musto, 1973, p. 244).

When drugs were converted into money-making commodities, the cleavage in the human experience with drugs in opposing traditional and modern societies was complete. Drugs figured prominently in the great struggles by which nations consolidated themselves and sought to dominate others. In Europe, taxes were imposed on wines and other alcoholic products to protect and strengthen national economies. Later, the trade in rum was crucial (Kenney & Leaton, 1991). West Indian molasses was made into rum at distilleries in New England and Great Britain, and the rum was exchanged in West Africa for slaves, who were then sold in the Americas. Similarly, tobacco cultivation and sales undergirded the survival of Virginia and the Carolinas.

The most notorious examples of "drug imperialism" were the Opium Wars waged by Britain against Imperial China at the turn of the century, when Lord Palmerston, the British War Secretary, invaded Chinese ports to declare Britain's right to sell its Burmese opium to the Chinese (Beeching, 1975). The Chinese were again besieged by plentiful supplies of opium in the 1930s, when the Japanese aimed not only to addict them but, like the British, to pay for their military machine with the resulting drug revenues.

Nor were Americans exempt from wartime promotion of drugs. During World War II, U.S. armed forces engaged priests to shower servicemen with free rations of cigarettes and beer (Buckley, 1994; Warner, 1990). Amphetamine was dispensed to both Japanese and American soldiers to overcome combat fatigue, elevate spirits, and improve endurance (Brecher, 1972). A few decades later, during the Vietnam War, the U.S. military experimented with lysergic acid diethylamide (LSD) and other psychotropic drugs as potential mind-control drugs. They gave the drugs to unsuspecting persons without their knowledge or consent. One, a government scientist, confused by what was happening to him, jumped to his death from the window of a hotel in New York City (Lee & Shlain, 1985).

Drug use figured in the political struggles within countries. These hostilities framed emerging drug policy, which in turn further complicated the behavior of drug users and distributors. Thus, more so than in Europe, where public health concerns preoccupied lawmakers, drug policy in America was formulated less with regard to the drugs themselves than in deference to power struggles between various contending interests and elites in the political process that would lead America eventually to world dominance (Musto, 1973). Several professional or special-interest groups—police, doctors, chemists, churches, philanthropists, politicians, pharmaceutical companies, and tobacco companies—gained definition and consolidation as they jousted over drugs.

In particular, drugs played important roles in several countries in confrontations between capital and labor and in the assimilation of immigrant laboring masses. Within Europe, there had long been the "racism" of Protestant northwestern Europeans, such as Germans or the British, who constructed a national character around the habits of punctuality, cleanliness, and orderliness, and who disdained the emotionalism, demonstrativeness, and populism of Catholic Mediterraneans, such as Italians, Spaniards, and Portuguese. British imperialists castigated the Irish and other Celtic peoples for being poetic, musical, overly sentimental, lazy, shiftless drunks who could only be made to work by what Malthus called "the lash of hunger!" In the United States, the campaign for prohibition against alcohol had been animated by the small-town nativist American of northern European descent who contrasted his sobriety and industriousness with the "license" of the later immigrant waves of "hard-drinking," contentious Irish, Italian, and Latino proletarians. The task of molding them into a reliable and productive work force encouraged repressive social policies.

Since the mid-1970s, business elites in western nation states have been eager to reimpose austerity programs. They fear that they will be overtaken by the "miracle" growth economies of the Pacific Rim, such as Japan, South Korea, Singapore, Malaysia, Indonesia, and Taiwan, where citizens are socialized to work uncomplainingly for long hours as team players for the Corporation and the Nation, and where the slightest deviancy is heavily penalized. For example, managers in the American automobile industry, selling fewer cars than their Japanese competitors, had decried the use of marijuana, Quaaludes, or other drugs by young, rebellious, assembly-line workers as a major cause of rising absenteeism, sabotage, constant strikes, and mediocre workmanship (Aronowitz, 1973).

The will to make Americans work harder is not disguised. Several decades of cumulative progress in labor-saving technologies have not resulted in a much shorter average workday, workweek, and working lifetime for American workers. Instead, they seem to be pressured into working even longer, just to maintain the same standard of living of a generation ago (Schorr, 1997). No "peace dividend" has resulted from the end of the Cold War. Employers have sought to extract more profits by pressuring workers to accept less income for more labor, whether at the point of production or in the battle to shrink the "social wage" of government-mediated transfer payments (health care, scholarship grants, pensions, rent and utility subsidies, and welfare). They have supported legislation and contract negotiations to defeat (or co-opt) the legal gains won during previous decades by trade unions, ethnic minorities, "nontraditional" women, and those with "deviant lifestyles" (i.e., centered around nonprocreative sex and recreational drug use). And they have sought to squeeze out or eliminate "alternative social spaces," such as the underground economy and the various subcultural scenes in which it had been possible to survive outside the system. "It's not 'Fun City' anymore," a Giuliani aide declared at a public hearing, voicing the motivation behind a recent ordinance to crack down on sex shops/adult video stores. The postaffluent society is also the postpermissive one (Weeks, 1981).

These trends contextualize and inform the latest attempts to intensify drug prohibition. They are also nourished by a specific authoritarian backlash against the "permissive" 1960s in the United States that aims to restore "old-fashioned discipline" at schools and workplaces. Characterizing the "permissiveness" of the recent "consumer society" phase of post–World War II America as a state of affairs that the ruling class surely could not tolerate indefinitely, one of its chroniclers remarked, "It will prove to be nothing but a long drunken furlough from the iron disciplines of war, FBI and church" (Mailer, 1961, p. 420). In the same vein, laws are being drafted to make divorce more difficult to obtain; V-chip censorship has been imposed; public universities are being restructured to operate like their expensive Ivy League competitors; school uniforms and curfews on teenagers are recommended; "quality of life" transgressions, such as drinking in public, merit arrest and incarceration; welfare has been dismantled; and plans are being made to raise the retirement age and to reform Social Security guarantees.

In the late 1990s, while some American entrepreneurs are excelling in such areas as computer technology and international finance, others in more traditional manufacturing enterprises are being squeezed by international competition in global markets. The decade witnessed a frenzy of downsizing and mergers, and more recently manufacturers have bypassed domestic workers and relocated abroad to take advantage of lower-paid, better-disciplined work forces.

The drug experience in the modern world is fragmented to a degree impossible in traditional societies. The powerful issues enumerated above, contested in local arenas shaped by very specific historical and social conditions, have resulted in a wide range of variations in drug-related behaviors and effects. Struggles between labor and capital or over competing cultural orientations have had divergent outcomes in a country's many regions or even in the different neighborhoods of the same city, producing contrastive drug or other phenomena. The various age groups and males and females have also been differentially affected, guaranteeing unique encounters with drugs.

Finally, greater and increasingly sophisticated global migration is a defining feature of the modern age that has transformed the human-drug union. The arrival of immigrants from different parts of the world and at specific junctures in the nation's history has repeatedly redefined the tenor of American life, not the least in the ways in which Americans relate to drugs. The temperance movement and the Anti-Saloon League of the late 1800s formed as much in opposition to the general way of life of Irish and Italian laborers as to their alcohol use. When Chinese immigrants were viewed as competitors for jobs rather than as a useful, underpaid laboring force, Americans turned xenophobic and were alerted to the dangers of Chinese opium use. Antiopium laws and those restricting Chinese immigration were passed hand in hand, and the former hardened attitudes toward drugs. Mexicans and marijuana were next to bear their brunt. Subsequently, other ethnicities were scapegoated.

For example, an enduring theme of drug distribution in New York City is that, as the drugs or methods of administration succeeded one another in vogue, control over distribution shifted from one ethnic population to another. Before the 1960s, Jewish, Irish, and Italian mobsters monopolized this criminal undertaking. From the mid-1960s to 1981, as the appeal of heroin declined in popularity and cocaine remained rare and prohibitively expensive, marijuana-selling organizations proliferated in inner-city neighborhoods. Caribbean Africans (and especially Rastafarians) organized the marijuana market, orchestrating not only street-level sales but also cultivation on the Caribbean islands and import into the United States. Bulk and retail buyers from Latino and European-American communities sought them out for the drug (Hamid, 1997b).

In the 1980s, when sales of Colombian cocaine overtook marijuana, Cubans, Jamaicans, and eventually Colombians themselves vied for control of the drug's domestic distribution. At the street level, Rastafarians ceded their dominance of drug markets to African-American and Puerto Rican youth. The latter in their turn were eclipsed by Dominicans.

As heroin use rises in the late 1990s in New York City, Colombian exporters are supplying it to their Dominican cocaine distributors. Ecuadorian and other Andean exporters, who depend on powerful Mexican or Central American intermediaries, have also debuted. Meanwhile, Chinese, Nigerians, Afghanis, and Russians, sometimes using Midwest housewives as "mules," import southeast Asian heroin. Nationally, many other ethnicities are active.

The ethnicities or identities of drug users also rotate. Once, the portrait of opiate users in America showed Chinese males, followed by adult European-American workers; next, young African-American and Latino males replaced them. Their place has been taken in the 1990s by young, urban European Americans. There appear to be ethnic preferences in drug use as well. Peyote and mushrooms (and alcohol) are esteemed by some Native Americans, datura by others, and khat by Somalis and immigrants from the Horn of Africa.

The struggles between these groups for power, influence, and affluence in America determine not only their use or other engagements with drugs, but those of Americans as a whole.

DRUG EDUCATION

Access to the full range and complexity of the social, cultural, economic, and political dimensions in which drug use is represented is necessary if readers are to think critically about it and form considered opinions about its appeal or the dangers it may pose. It is prevented, however, by the barrage of "noise" with which certain sources of misinformation on these topics have confused minds.

The abstinence-oriented drug education curriculum that is offered in most American schools is one. Many readers have taken these courses, which are often taught by police officers and prominently reported in community newspapers and radio and television programs.

Prior to the mid-1960s, there was little perceived need for drug education for students younger than the university level. But then, in a hastily improvised response to a youth "counterculture," which popularized marijuana and psychedelics such as mushrooms, peyote, and LSD (see later), drug education programs were implemented at the high school level. Largely because there was little credible scientific research then available, these curricula resorted to an old staple—unfounded (and transparent) fearmongering. In the conflict of generations at that time, young persons' faith in their elders had ebbed generally. Their pronouncements on drugs were further undermined by their "hypocritical" acceptance of alcohol and tobacco misuse.

By the early 1970s, the continued growth of illicit drug use mandated the search for a more effective strategy. The findings of the Nixon Administration's inquiry (U.S. National Commission on Marijuana and Drug Abuse, 1972), as well as the publication in 1972 of Edward Brecher's landmark study, *Licit and Illicit Drugs*, indicated a reorientation. New drug education programs for adolescents reflected it: "The programs of the early 1970s carried a more ambivalent message, that the mere use of addictive drugs was not necessarily bad, that children had to be encouraged to learn all they could about the favorable and unfavorable effects of drugs in order to be able to make their own decisions about drug use" (Rosenbaum, 1996, p. 4). Indeed, the White House Special Action Office for Drug Abuse Prevention (SAODAP) explicitly called for "an end to all scare tactics."

Illicit drug use climbed steadily throughout the 1970s, however, and policy soon reverted to the more unyielding antidrug position. When Dr. Peter Bourne, President Carter's Special Assistant for Health Issues and an outspoken advocate against criminalizing drug offenders, was forced to resign in 1978 under suspicion of having improperly written a prescription and personal cocaine use, the Carter White House could not afford to appear as though it condoned drug use (Musto, 1987).

In addition, beginning in the late 1970s, well-orchestrated grassroots pressure from the new "parent power" movement forced the return to a national policy of abstinence, as the housewives who organized the National Federation of Parents for Drug-free Youth (NFP) "began to monitor federal publications with the goal of weeding out comments . . . that could be interpreted as anything other than firmly against drug use. . . . This group and others like it were warmly received by the Reagan administration . . . an outspoken member of the parents' movement, Dr. Ian MacDonald . . . rose to become the administration's top spokesman on drug issues . . ." (Musto, 1987, p. 8).

Partly, therefore, the battle over drug policy was only one aspect of the larger "cultural war" waged by those conservatives who emphasized "moral issues" and the reaffirmation of "traditional values." Aligning themselves with these interests, educators redesigned their drug curricula, as Rosenbaum (1996) describes:

> Drug education in the U.S. begins with young children, often starting as early as the third grade or approximately age eight. . . . One of the most popular and prevalent school-based drug education programs is DARE (Drug Abuse Resistance Education). Since 1990, DARE has received over $8 million in direct federal funding plus millions more in state and local funds. Approximately 20,000 police officers have delivered drug education to an estimated 25 million youth as part of the DARE program. A five-year study tracking DARE students and published in 1994 has shown ". . . no long-term effects for the programs in preventing or reducing adolescent drug use." (p. 6)

Rosenbaum (1996) further states:

> Drug education in the U.S. is based on several questionable assumptions about adolescence and drug use: 1) total abstinence is a realistic goal; 2) the use of illegal substances necessarily means abuse; 3) one form of drug use inevitably leads to other, more harmful forms; 4) understanding the risks inherent in drug use will deter children from experimentation; and 5) children are incapable of making responsible decisions about an issue as serious as drug use.
>
> Championing abstinence has thus led to the inevitable failure of programs that have made this their primary goal because some form of drug use is nearly universal, and certainly integral to American culture. . . . A problem with the blurring of distinctions between use and abuse is the inconsistency with students' observations or experiences. When young people are told once-a-month use of a substance is abuse, they often snicker. They see others, and often themselves, as people who have used an illegal substance without any of the addictive or deleterious effects that would constitute "abuse." . . . In the effort to encourage abstinence, "risk" and "danger" messages are often exaggerated. Aside from glaring falsehoods and ridiculous analogies (e.g., the fried egg commercial) these messages are often inconsistent with children's actual observations and experiences. (p. 8)

DRUG USERS' FOLKLORE

Another obstacle to balanced thinking on drug issues is the contentiousness of drug users themselves. Some groups, patterning themselves after the *junkiebonden* or "addicts' unions" of Europe, have recently attempted to create forums for their opinions, not only so that they may be heard, but also to encourage self-criticism and to promote more impartial knowledge (Edney, Bowman, & Lober, 1997).

Drug folklore among drug users themselves is often quite as misleading as state-sponsored drug education, albeit in different ways. For example, many heroin injectors do not know how to inject safely even after many years of doing it several times a day. They inject in improper body sites, needles may be blunted by repeated use, or tourniquets may be left tightly strapped around an arm. Infections, sores, and gangrene follow. Drug users frequently rely on superstitions rather than sound knowledge in the lethal matter of acquired immunodeficiency syndrome (AIDS) transmission. The most damaging is the conviction that the human immunodeficiency virus (HIV), like other bulletins from officialdom targeted at drug users, is an "establishment fiction." Others are the belief that heterosexual intercourse is not a route of HIV infection, that males are virtually immune, that visually inspecting one's partner will reveal sexually transmitted diseases, or the disbelief that persons can "look healthy" for many years while carrying the HIV virus.

Often, drug users simply accept the despicable roles that the prevailing ideology allots to them. They convince themselves that they are impaired in multiple ways, that drugs are evil, and that the inevitable consequences of drug use include crime, morbidity, and further immorality.

Ethnography is a powerful corrective against both sources of error. In the field, anthropologists respect and preserve the interpretations that drug users and distributors (and their neighbors) have of their own behavior and motives. At the same time, open-ended questioning facilitates self-examination and sophistication. By providing users with theoretical schemas and stimulating the study of comparisons and contrasts, ethnographers show them ways to interpret and explain their directly lived and directly observed personal experiences. Freed by this methodology from prejudice or propaganda, they arrive at a richer appreciation of the complexity and diversity of behaviors and outcomes that "the drug problem" encompasses. In the same stroke, the nonusing public and policymakers are better informed too.

DRUGS IN AMERICA

It will help the reader to have brief biographies of the drugs that have concerned the American public and that will be considered in this text. Since colonial times, Americans have used all kinds of psychoactive substances and have revised their relationship to them continuously in the course of national development.

Alcohol

Alcohol was the first of the drugs that Americans would eventually find problematic. The only one of European and nontropical origin, it was native, in wine, beer, and liquors, to the European peoples who vanquished the original Americans and colonized the continent (Pittman & Snyder, 1962). Indeed, when introduced to the Native Americans, alcohol disrupted preexisting social controls (see Introduction), and provoked drunkenness, violence, greed, betrayal, and internecine warfare. It thus proved to be a major instrument in their demise. As Benjamin Franklin chillingly observed: "If it be the design of Providence to extirpate these savages to make room for the cultivators of the earth, it seems not improbable that rum may be the appointed means" (Cunningham, Sobell, Freedman, & Sobell, 1994, p. 220).

Per capita consumption of copious amounts of alcohol, however, was the norm among early European Americans and was measured in barrels. They used it not only recreationally, but as medicine and in food preparation. It was applied externally as a salve, solvent, astringent, and antiseptic (Howland & Howland, 1978). The production and sale of spirits sustained economies. After Congress passed an excise tax on whiskey in 1791, President Washington was obliged in 1794 to send federal troops into the state of Pennsylvania to crush the Whiskey Rebellion that farmers and distillers had staged in response. Nevertheless, despite its manifold usefulness, excessive drinking was condemned: "Although alcohol use was socially acceptable, however, drunkenness was not, and the sanctions against it ranged from congregational confessions to fines, flogging and public display in stocks" (Peele, 1985, p. 36).

As America industrialized in the early 20th century, attitudes against drunkenness and alcohol itself stiffened and resulted in Prohibition (see Introduction). Since its repeal, however, most Americans have willingly complied with numerous regulations on the legal sale of alcohol (pertaining to hours and days of sale, or the number and locations of alcohol outlets) and, over the past 20 years, have voluntarily reduced the amount and potency of their alcoholic drinks. Health and dietary concerns, as well as the premium placed on sobriety, advance them in this trend. Drunken drivers have faced stiffer penalties. Indeed, the successful crusade against drunken driving is a good example of a sensible, carefully targeted harm-reduction approach, which, without prohibiting the enjoyment of alcohol, makes irresponsibility accountable. One heartening result is that from 1982 to 1987, the number of teenage traffic fatalities dropped from 2,187 to 1,494. The number of intoxicated drivers, bicyclists, and pedestrians killed in accidents is also declining (National Highway Traffic Safety Administration, 1988).

Despite its dwindling appeal, alcohol continues to be implicated in the incidence of murders, domestic violence, rapes, reprehensible behaviors on campuses and at conventions, and in a wide range of health problems. Outbreaks of popularity, as the craze for malt liquors in the late 1980s among inner-city youths and for "microbrews" and specialty beers in the early 1990s among more affluent European Americans exacerbate these effects, but they are quickly exhausted. Most Americans who drink do so socially; therefore, problem drinking seems to be confined to specific subgroups, such as segments of unemployed men and women, some Latino ethnicities, and some Native American tribes.

The alcohol lobby in the United States is well organized, contributes to both major political parties, is ever mindful of the period of Prohibition in the 1920s, and is determined that it will not be repeated.

Marijuana

The Spanish conquistadors brought the two plants, *cannabis indica* and *cannabis sativa* from the Old World, where they had been native to India and China, to the New World (Abel, 1980; Bennett, Osborn, & Osborn, 1995). *C. indica* is the smaller plant, which thrives in cooler climates, as in the upper slopes of mountains. The potent modern *sinsemilla* varietals (literally, "without seed," or intensively cultivated marijuana, requiring careful tending and the separation of female plants), are grown from strains of *C. indica*. *C. sativa* is a tall, bushy lowland plant, better adapted to tropical heat and rain. Until the 20th century, it was apparently grown in America for hempen fibers, cloths, and seeds. Americans for the most part ignored the tinctures, gums, and other medicinal preparations of the plant described in European pharmacopeias.

Marijuana smoking for recreational purposes or as a religious sacrament and its use as a food were brought in the mid-1840s to the Americas via the Caribbean by Indian laborers, who had been indentured to replace emancipated African labor in the region's sugar cane plantations (Hamid, 1980, 1997a; Morton, 1916; Weller, 1972). The differential reception of the drug on the various islands is described and investigated in Chapter 4. For example, while its cultivation and use were routinized among (mostly African) Jamaican peasants, they were rejected by the Africans of Trinidad, and eventually by the Indians themselves.

Elsewhere in the Americas, marijuana smoking was diffused by Jamaicans to Mexicans and other "invisible" populations. Thus, until the mid-1960s, it was restricted in the continental United States to Caribbean and Mexican immigrants, a few segments of the African-American population, and criminal or bohemian circles in major cities (Burroughs, 1958). In the 1950s, African-American jazz musicians and artists favored it, and a fledgling distribution system formed (Brown, 1965; Haley, 1965).

In the mid-1960s, marijuana use among young European Americans climbed from 3% of the 18- to 25-year age cohort to over 50% (Gitlin, 1987; Goode, 1970;

Kandel, 1988). Disseminated by them to youth populations across the globe, it reached the Caribbean Africans, whose stories are retold in Chapter 4. Marijuana enjoyed a worldwide efflorescence in the 1970s and was cultivated everywhere, from hothouses in Alaska to windowsills in New York City. Major American harbors and airports were centers of a global exchange of marijuana and marijuana products, which encompassed producing regions or units in nearly every country on earth.

After it was replaced in popularity and newsworthiness in the 1980s by smokable cocaine, use is rising once more in the 1990s (Hamid et al., 1997). The present demand is being catered mainly by domestic U.S. producers, who furnish expensive high-grade *C. indica* exotics from greenhouses and indoor gardens in every state, or who grow plantations of cheaper *C. sativa* in Kentucky, Texas, Mississippi, and other states with favorable climates (Weisheit, 1992).

The destiny of the marijuana plant may change in the near future. Voters medicalized its use in Arizona and California in 1996. Although the federal government has declared its intention to prosecute physicians who prescribe it, Californians and Arizonans are devising methods for making it available to those who need it. In one initiative, proposed and directed by a former San Francisco police detective, marijuana confiscated for use in criminal trials will be redistributed to terminally ill patients under tightly controlled conditions. The Cannabis Cultivators Club of San Francisco already supplies marijuana to patients with prescriptions.

Campaigns elsewhere in the United States are seeking to promote marijuana's health benefits. Advocates for decriminalization or legalization of cultivation, possession, and use, such as the National Organization for the Reform of Marijuana Laws (NORML), the Drug Policy Foundation (DPF), and countless local groups, have gained substantial new financial support. Although the federal government declines to fund research on its medical uses, and while local administrations, such as Mayor Giuliani's in New York City have applied strict programs of "zero tolerance" and included public marijuana smoking among its more serious "quality of life" offenses, a groundswell of noncompliance is building.

The marijuana plant itself is likely to evolve further. The cultivation of *sinsemillas* in the 1970s has spurred innovation among cultivators, who now use hydroponics and other advanced agricultural techniques to grow it (Boyle, 1984). An annual growers' fair, held in Amsterdam, facilitates the diffusion of techniques, the exchange of information, and, most important, the seeds of impressive hybrids.

The conventions of users also evolve continuously in response to availability, the form in which the drug is offered (oils, smokable buds, hashish, foods), potency, and the prevailing attitudes toward recreational drug use. In 1997, for example, when many American youths have grown circumspect and wary of criminal or "deviant" conduct, they share marijuana in *blunts* (or cigars emptied of their tobacco filling and repacked with the domestic product currently being distributed). Sharing blunts regulates dosage, discourages individual use while promoting it in groups, and applies group norms and informal controls to the activity.

Cocaine

Erythroxylon coca grows in the moist and woody regions of the eastern Andes, at altitudes of 2,000 to 10,000 feet, and has been cultivated for thousands of years by local Native American populations who chewed the leaves to relieve fatigue, cold, and hunger (Antonil, 1978; Freud, 1890/1974). A lowland variety of the plant was also cultivated in the Amazon basin (Plowman, 1981; Weil, 1972). After they were enslaved by the Spaniards, the Andeans claimed that chewing the leaves gave them the fortitude and endurance to perform as coerced labor in tin mines high in the thin air of the mountains. Coca chewing also functioned as an integrative institution of the beleaguered indigenous society and religion. Suspicious and fearful of these effects, the conquistadors condemned it as a type of devil worship, destroyed coca plantations, and forbade their slaves to consume it. Nevertheless, coca chewing and the cultivation of the plant for that purpose have persisted in the Andes to the present day, despite repeated attempts to eradicate them (Henman, 1990).

Coca and its derivatives were introduced to European societies in 1860, when the alkaloid cocaine was isolated by Albert Neimann in a German laboratory (Grinspoon & Bakalar, 1985). By the 1880s, medical practitioners in Europe and America lauded it as a miracle drug, and it was prescribed to treat a wide variety of medical problems (Courtwright, 1982).

In the United States, spurred by the medical profession, suppliers offered the drug in such a variety of forms that it was nearly impossible for an American to avoid using it. It was contained in elixirs, extracts, infusions, pastilles, wines, cordials, tonics combined with beef and iron, cheroots, cigarettes, inhalants, and prepared solutions (cocaine citrate, cocaine hydrobromate, cocaine muriate, cocaine salicylate), some injectable. Ulysses S. Grant, Sarah Bernhardt, Pope Leo XIII, Thomas Edison, Emile Zola, Henrik Ibsen, Jules Verne, and Albert, Prince of Wales, were among the devoted international patrons of *vin Mariani*, a wine infused with coca leaves. Its use was truly universalized when it was added to medicated soft drinks, such as Coca Cola, Koca Nola, Celery Cola, Wiscola, Pillsbury's Koke, Kola-Ade, Kos-Kola, Cafe-Coca, and Koke.

As the prohibitionist movement gained strength, articles appeared in the newspapers which drew attention to yet another, "more sinister" pattern of use:

E.R. Waterhouse, a St. Louis physician, remarked that few people knew the true extent of the cocaine habit in the lower walks of city life. He described a local drug store that was in reality a "cocaine joint" where pulverized cocaine crystals were wrapped in paper and sold to prostitutes for 10 cents a piece. . . . A woman reporter who managed to peek into the room spied a dozen lower-class prostitutes, black as well as white, Waterhouse commented, lost in a sort of dreamy intoxification, not unlike the Chinaman "hitting the pipe" in Dope Alley. . . .

No point was more stressed than the growing popularity of cocaine among blacks, who would purchase a nickel's worth of the drug and go on a "coke drunk." Editorials in two leading professional journals, pointed to increased black cocaine use, as a justification for restricted legislation. "I am convinced," declared Colonel J.W. Watson of Georgia in 1903, "that if some stringent law is not enacted and enforced against [cocaine sniffing] the habit will grow and extend to such proportions that great injury will result; in fact, great injury has already resulted, for I am satisfied that many of the horrible crimes committed in the Southern States by the colored people can be traced directly to the cocaine habit." (Courtwright, 1991, p. 3)

At least two "epidemics" of intranasal cocaine use occurred among African Americans by the 1900s. Indeed, the equipping of policemen with .38-caliber weapons at that time was inspired by the belief that the smaller bore weapons (.25s) then in regular service were unable to bring down a "cocaine-crazed Negro" (Musto, 1987, p. 52)

In 1914, the prohibitionists' war against drugs climaxed in the passage of the Harrison Act. Its provisions subjected cocaine to the same regulations that prevented the sale and use of morphine and heroin. By 1915, so many restrictions had been enacted against its distribution and use that availability decreased, causing prices to rise. The plentiful (mostly harmless) forms in which the drug had been supplied disappeared. Only illegal cocaine hydrochloride powder for intranasal use or injecting remained. By the 1940s, amphetamine had replaced cocaine both in medical practice and in illicit drug markets (Grinspoon & Bakalar, 1985; Musto, 1987).

Although legal restrictions on amphetamine in the 1970s have been held accountable for again promoting cocaine use, especially among middle-class, European-American users (Puder, Kagan, & Morgan, 1988), such a monocausal explanation is rarely satisfactory to social scientists. Rather, the story of how cocaine was transformed from a benign recreational intranasal drug, the accompaniment of champagne and lobsters in fashionable society, into a compulsive item in the "crack and Olde English" (a cheap malt liquor popular in the inner cities in the 1980s) era casts a powerful light on the diverse drug culture in many American cities that drug prohibition has created and sustained, demonstrating that one of its principal features is repeatedly to foster newer, perhaps riskier, drug fashions that have adversely and incrementally affected more and more Americans since 1914.

As it was in scarce supply and very expensive, cocaine persisted as a luxury drug that only very wealthy persons, such as higher-level heroin distributors, could afford. Nevertheless, periodic upswings of substantial intranasal use of cocaine hydrochloride powder in minority communities were again reported in the 1920s and 1950s by African-American writers, when it acquired a widespread following as a pain and fatigue reliever, as well as a mild hallucinogen, among African-American workers. The novels of Claude McKay, *Back to Harlem*, and *Banjo* (McKay, 1928, 1929), described these beneficial effects among African-American and Caribbean-African ex-servicemen, who had found jobs after the Great War in the merchant marine or on the Pullman trains. In *Back to Harlem*, for example, a young Martiniquan medical student, working on the trains during his vacations, sniffed cocaine to overcome the annoyance the famous fleas of the Chicago railroad yards were causing him. The drug promptly lulled him to sleep, the parasites notwithstanding, amid a serene reverie of his native island! Malcolm X, recalling the 1950s when he had been, as "Detroit Red," a young daredevil and drug distributor in Harlem, also spoke admiringly of the drug (Haley, 1965).

The cocaine smoking epidemic of 1981–1991 is the first ever to have occurred in the United States and in the world. Although chemists and others probably knew how to prepare a smokable precipitate ever since the manufacture of cocaine hydrochloride powder, smoking the drug (except in cheroots and cigars made of the natural coca leaf) had never been popular. In 1885, the Cocabacco Company of St. Louis marketed Cocarettes, a combination of Virginia tobacco and Bolivian coca leaves wrapped in rice paper, which it advertised as a delicious tonic and brain stimulant, but sales lagged (Siegel, 1982). Indeed, when it was first brought to public notice in the mid-1980s, smokable cocaine was regarded as a completely new drug, and some researchers and policymakers had speculated whether it was a cocaine product at all (Chitwood, Rivers, & Inciardi, 1996). The drug was offered to smokers either as *freebase* or *crack*.

It required a rudimentary knowledge of chemistry to prepare smokable cocaine from cocaine hydrochloride powder. Some methods, however, proved too cumbersome and dangerous to have become widespread. For example, the comedian Richard Pryor suffered third-degree burns over much of his face and body while freebasing when the ether used in one method exploded into flames (see below).

Freebase and *crack* are two names for the same identical pharmacological substance. Each term denotes, however, a particular time period, a different set of marketing conditions, a distinct clientele, and (sometimes) contrastive use patterns. Freebase was the name given to smokable cocaine in 1979–1981, when the distributor prepared it in a tiny cooking bottle sale by sale for each successive customer, or when the customer prepared it for herself or himself. Crack referred to the period following 1984 or 1985, after the notorious cocaine cartels had formed in Medellín and Cali, Colombia. Their efforts quadrupled the production and export of cocaine, causing street prices to plummet. A poorer clientele was attracted and the number of distributors serving them surged. They prepared the precipitate ahead of time in large quantities (in saucepans, teakettles, and microwave ovens), packaged it in thousands of vials, and presented it ready to use to the terminal consumer. Crack signified separation of use from sales, and marks the determination distributors had at that time to separate themselves from their clientele by offering a preprepared, prepackaged item. In the mid-1990s, as the popularity of smokable cocaine began to wane, users were buying cocaine hydrochloride powder instead of crack and self-preparing freebase once more.

Cocaine smoking, as opposed to intranasal use, allows for a more immediate and direct absorption of the drug into the bloodstream and "beams up" [intoxicates] the smoker more rapidly. Some researchers maintain that these pharmacological actions carry an increased risk of dependence and acute toxic reactions, such as brain seizure, cardiac irregularities, respiratory paralysis, paranoid psychosis, and pulmonary dysfunction (Inciardi, 1987, 1992; Wallace, 1990).

Originating in 1979–1981 in South America, cocaine smoking spread first to the Caribbean and then to major cities in the United States (Hamid, 1992b; Inciardi, 1987). In 1985, Jane Brodie, a reporter for the *New York Times*, published the first newspaper article nationally on cocaine smoking (in the form of crack). She claimed that the practice was a "plague" that was destroying inner-city communities in New York City. An outpouring of sensationalistic media reports followed. They were greeted with a curious perversity on the part of many individuals in the author's study neighborhoods in Brooklyn. The more diabolical the depiction of the drug, the more eager they were to try it. When they viewed the film, *This Is Your Life, Jo-Jo Dancer*, which was screened in the early 1980s and portrayed the tragicomedy of comedian Richard Pryor's personal freebase smoking, they rushed in droves to experiment with it, although Richard Pryor had doused himself with ether and set himself aflame at the end of the film out of frustrations the drug had caused him. Subsequent research has indicated a correlation between the volume of media attention and onset to the drug (Levine & Reinarman, 1987).

By the late 1980s, crack misuse had afflicted at least a million souls in low-income, minority neighborhoods in major American cities (National Institute on Drug Abuse [NIDA], 1990). In the Andean nations of South America, where the fashion had started, and in Latin America and the Caribbean islands, to which it had been diffused next, persons undone by misuse of the drug had become a fixture of low-income settlements, slums, and shanties. More socially prominent misusers were exposed in the local press. In the early 1990s, cocaine smoking was reportedly the trend in the Yemeni-Jewish quarters of Israel, and threatened to gain footholds in eastern Europe, countries of the former Soviet Union, South Africa, and Asia. In 1997, it was arriving in rural America and yet other parts of the world.

The age and gender of cocaine smokers have been disputed among researchers. Some give the impression that very young persons—children and adolescents, or persons under the age of 18—and females were the majority (Fullilove & Fullilove, 1989; Wallace, 1987). A review of several studies supports this researcher's actual field observations that, although some youngsters experimented (and fewer persisted) with the drug, the typical user was older than 23 years at onset in the early 1980s. In fact, middle-aged persons were the most numerous experimenters and confirmed users, and they continued to predominate in subsequent cocaine phenomena. While many more women became cocaine users than had succumbed to heroin injecting in the late 1960s, men dominated both use and sales (Morningstar & Chitwood, 1987; Ratner, 1993).

While cocaine in all its forms or modes of administration had been valued by its admirers of the 1980s as an energizer that banished sleep and rest, it has earned a reputation for directly opposite effects among long-term or chronic cocaine smokers in New York City. Researchers observing them in 1997 found that, after at least 10 years of use, cocaine smoking or injecting visibly calms them (Hamid et al., 1997). As in the cocaine-inhaling outbreaks of the 1920s, even their voices soften and slow down.

Heroin

The products of the opium poppy, or *papaver somniferum* (from Virgil's *Aeneid*, Book IV: the "sleep-bringing poppy"), revered among the ancients of Asia and the classical world, have been used in Europe for many centuries and since colonial times in America. Opium was imported from Turkey and southeast Asia, and substantial amounts were added to workers' daily rations of beer on both sides of the Atlantic (Berridge & Edwards, 1981). Morphine was self-administered extensively in European wars and by American soldiers during the Civil War to relieve pain, diarrhea, and dysentery. When the hypodermic needle was developed in 1854, the use of opium skyrocketed. Consumers did not require a prescription to buy these substances in pure form, and they were ingredients in thousands of patent medicines recommended for the treatment of headaches, toothaches, coughs, and pneumonia. The mail-order service of Sears, Roebuck and Company dispatched both hypodermic syringe kits and laudanum, a form of opium, to its customers. The latter were primarily respectable citizens, including legions of genteel, European-American middle-class housewives. State laws and the Pure

Food and Drug Act of 1906 reduced the availability of these medicines, and finally the Harrison Act of 1914 outlawed them.

Synthesized by a German chemist in 1874, heroin had been marketed legally in the United States by both foreign and domestic pharmaceutical companies, which advertised it widely as a cure-all. Physicians endorsed the claim, and Bayer's heroin became a leading seller. Very many Americans—housewives, factory workers, laborers—habitually swallowed heroin pills as they built the cities, the bridges, the railroads, the industries, and the temples of finance that would magnify the United States among the world's nations. Their numbers, however, were dwindling steadily, as physicians changed their prescribing practices in response to public concern about the dangers of addiction (Courtwright, 1982; Musto, 1987). Its consumption was also associated with "Asians" (Chinese immigrants, for example, were alleged opiate users who were bent on seducing Caucasians into the practice) and was often portrayed as "un-American" (Musto, 1987).

Heroin was the first drug to which prohibition had given an unusual (and menacing) prominence. Because heroin was less bulky, easier to adulterate, and more potent and more rapidly ingested than opium (for smoking), cocaine hydrochloride powder (for intranasal use), or morphine (for injecting), it was preferred by the criminal drug distributors then surfacing internationally (Courtwright, 1982). Their adoption of it made heroin the rage, and turned its users into the architects and trendsetters of "deviant" drug subcultures. The circumstances in which they were placed after 1914 have proved to be a fertile ground for generating several more drug rages, which arguably have culminated in smokable cocaine.

As in the case of cocaine, an immediate result of prohibition was to reduce the many modes of administering the drug to one. Pills, tinctures, tonics, and smoking were replaced by injecting, which maximized the cost-effect ratio, but also rendered users more vulnerable to impurities or adulterants. It became compulsive, and put users at risk of contracting infections. Fortunately, the very act of injecting was repugnant to so many potential users that a sort of "natural" boundary was drawn around intravenous heroin use.

Prohibition, however, did allow illegal heroin distribution to be established successfully: even if it made use unpleasant, hazardous, and more addictive, it created nevertheless a motivation and a method for making large sums of cash rapidly, which continue to exert a powerful influence, independent of the seductions of the drugs themselves, on many to the present day. Thus, by 1960, a small bohemian heroin injecting subculture, still predominantly European American and including musicians, artists, and writers, grew in New York and Los Angeles but not in other cities (Hentoff, 1964; Robins, 1980; Winick, 1959). Their heroin use, and that of fellow bohemians, figured prominently in the works of William Burroughs (1958), Allen Ginsberg (1956), and Herbert Huncke (1990).

It was not primarily drug use, however, but their interest in money via illegal drug distribution that drew the most recent generation—the inner-city enthusiasts of the 1964–1972 heroin injecting epidemic—into involvement with heroin at all (Boyle & Brunswick, 1980; Johnson et al., 1985; O'Donnell, Clayton, Slatin, & Room, 1976).* After remaining stable in the preceding decades, heroin use rose because continuing prohibition had opened up new opportunities in criminal distribution. When minority American soldiers went to Vietnam, they discovered cheap, high-quality heroin that could be sold for handsome profits to the older users in the United States. Distribution would be undertaken willingly by other young people in low-income, minority neighborhoods who were experiencing continuing difficulty throughout the 1960s in finding decent jobs. But after becoming distributors, they often became users. The resulting scourge was immortalized in Piri Thomas' *Down These Mean Streets* and films such as *Panic in Needle Park.*

The legacy of the 1964–1972 "heroin injecting epidemic" in the mid-1990s has been a stable heroin market serving a multiethnic cadre of aging users. Their fortune has been an unrelenting round of methadone maintenance, imprisonment, homelessness, AIDS, and mental illness. Their restless experimentation and polydrug use was a crucible in which cocaine smoking was diffused to American populations. They persisted during the "cocaine smoking epidemic" of the 1980s, adding some initiates to their number. Most of the extant American social scientific research on AIDS (Chaisson, Moss, Onishi, Osmond, & Carlson, 1987; Des Jarlais et al., 1994; Feldman & Johnson, 1986; Schilling et al., 1989), AIDS risk behaviors (Becker & Joseph, 1988; AIDS Community Research Group, 1988; Dolan, Black, DeFord, Skinner, & Robinowitz, 1987), treatment for AIDS/substance misuse (Eldred & Washington, 1975; New York City Department of Health, 1989; Singer et al., 1990), needle sharing among injectors (Battjes & Pickens, 1988), needle exchanges (AIDS Community Educators, 1989; Selwyn, 1988), drug law enforcement (Sviridoff, Sudd, & Grinc, 1992), and the lifestyles of heroin users (Chein, Gerald, Lee, & Rosenfeld, 1964; Friedman, Kleinman, & Des Jarlais, 1992; Hanson, Beschner, Walters, & Bovelle, 1985; Rosenbaum, 1981; Singer et al., 1990; Taylor, 1993; Waterston, 1993) has engaged them almost exclusively as study participants.

Since 1989, however, there have been indications of change in the status of "junk" once again. As the market for smokable cocaine stabilized (Hamid, 1997b), some cocaine smokers switched to heroin (Hunt & Rhodes, 1993), some heroin users switched to smokable cocaine, and many used both. As the purity of heroin rose and prices fell, surviving street-level markets have been reinvigorated as retail "supermarkets" for drugs (Curtis & Maher, 1992). Washington Heights,

---

*The following 11 paragraphs were adapted with permission from A. Hamid, 1997 heroin epidemic, Vol. 29, No. 4, pp. 375–382, © 1997, *Journal of Psychoactive Drugs.*

for example, while enduring as the heart of citywide wholesale cocaine/crack distribution, has been transformed overnight into a major source for heroin also.

There are other indicators of change. While officials estimate that there are between 500,000 and 1 million "hard-core, chronic" heroin users nationwide (Rhodes, 1993), evidence of supplemental users heralding another heroin era includes more overdoses and overdose deaths, greater demand for treatment, larger seizures of heroin at all levels of distribution and related arrests, and broader media coverage. Other signals come from abroad. Cultivation of opium poppies is presently undertaken not only in Southeast Asia, but in other parts of the world, including Mexico, Colombia, Morocco, and Afghanistan (Gamella, 1994; Griffiths, Gossop, & Strang, 1994; Grund, 1993; McCoy, 1991; Sabbag, 1994). Use of the drug has followed in these countries and along the trading routes by which it travels from field to processing plant and to consumers abroad.

Many new heroin users are reclusive and hard to detect. Among them are young, upper- and middle-class European-American males and females (Carroll, 1987; Yablonsky, 1997). In their late 20s and 30s, they have constructed a world around their heroin use that diverges sharply from that of the "hardcore" group. Younger Puerto Rican users express another variant of recent hidden heroin use. Their lifestyles are in contrast with those of both the veterans and the young European-American users. Another separate group is formed by recent, or first-generation immigrants, such as Russians and Haitians. Heroin structures unusual behavior as users aspire to updated versions of the "American Dream." Other new users include Chinese Americans, Hasidic Jews, suburban European-American youngsters, underground homeless, gay men in single residence occupancy (SROs), "club kids" (teenagers and young adults who haunt raves and dance clubs), European-American runaway adolescents, squatters, and Native American injectors (Hamid et al., 1997).

The most incognito new users, however, may be the most numerous. Mindful of the addictive potential of the drug, but powerfully attracted to its stimulant, tonic, and narcotic properties, they maintain a stable pattern of lifetime use consisting of small dosages administered occasionally in the course of a year. Such a user's annual expenditure on heroin, therefore, never exceeds approximately $200 and annual consumption is never greater than a couple of grams.

While the inner-city injectors of 1964–1972 universally experienced heroin as a narcotic drug that induced "nodding" and sleep, the new users of the 1990s, who are chiefly sniffers, are excited and made alert by it. Heroin rewards them with deep sleep only after they have expended energy briskly in multiple tasks over several hours. Heroin even wakes up those chronic cocaine smokers whom cocaine has lulled to sleep (Hamid et al., 1997)!

Young African Americans are strictly avoiding heroin in the late 1990s. Despite rigorous searches in African-American neighborhoods, ethnographers have yet to identify more persons than a single female in Central Harlem who are under 30 years of age and have undergone onset recently. Her husband, a sniffer for the past 20 years, had inducted her in 1995. African-American youths in New York City generally avoid both heroin and cocaine. They consume only marijuana. They view even cigarettes and malt liquor, which have been aggressively marketed in their neighborhoods (Marriott, 1993), with disfavor. Equally profound changes have occurred simultaneously in other aspects of their lives. For example, they commit far fewer crimes or acts of violence than formerly, contributing to the fall in the city's crime rate to the lowest in 30 years. At the same time, they have redoubled their efforts to complete their education, find jobs, and participate in communal activities.

The indifference toward heroin shown by young African Americans is more curious when viewed in an international context. For example, in the United Kingdom, young Britishers of Caribbean-African ancestry have also eschewed heroin, although they share the same (or a worse) socioeconomic situation as their patrial British neighbors and age-mates. The latter, however, have been identified, in films and novels such as *Trainspotting*, as trendsetters in the current global upsurge of heroin use. Surinamese in Amsterdam who lead high-risk, user-dealer lifestyles are apparently the only immigrants of African descent in Europe who like it (Grund, Kaplan, Adriaans, & Blanken, 1991). A few Haitians in New York City have also adopted it of late (Hamid et al., 1997).

Striking too is the contrast in America between privileged young European Americans, who affect a heroin-veiled, anorexic, impoverished, "thin" appearance (see below) and young African Americans, considered by some to be a truly endangered group (Gibbs, 1988), who, avoiding heroin and dressed in expensive, oversized, designer clothes, compliment themselves for looking "phat" (fat) and "butter" (Hamid et al., 1997).

While the content of heroin bags has always mystified users and researchers, it is particularly problematic in recent times. First, the drug now originates not only in Turkey, Pakistan, and southeast Asia, but in many other regions worldwide, such as Morocco, Mexico, and Colombia. Quality thus ranges from "China White" to "Mexican brown tar." Also, the Drug Enforcement Administration (DEA) has found that, unlike the previous era of heroin use when purity on the streets of New York City fluctuated between 1% and 10%, it now reaches 98% (DEA, 1996). The "cut" used to dilute heroin is a third uncertainty: once heroin leaves the producing countries and arrives in the United States, kilograms are subdivided and may be cut, the purchasers may adulterate it further and package it with a brand name and logo, and the operations may be repeated many times before the drug arrives at street level. As a result, samples within a single neighborhood, city or country may differ greatly in composition. In an assay of 40 bags of street-level heroin bought on 9 days over a 3-month period in New York City in 1996, purity ranged from 6% to 90% and at least 27 types of adulterants and cuts had been added (Strategic Intelligence Section, Domestic Unit, 1996). They included both psychoactive and inert substances, such as Valium, cocaine, lidocaine, quinine, mannitol, starch, and dextrose. Since many heroin users also consume other drugs, it is hard to say which has what effects on them (Hamid et al., 1997). Investigators studying heroin purity in Spain found that it was dissimilar in the 17 parts of the country from which samples were taken. Street samples, which were expected to be less pure than the kilos police had interdicted at points of entry into the country, sometimes were not (de la Fuente et al., 1996).

A review of heroin use in America would be incomplete without a discussion of methadone. A presidential commission was appointed in 1972 by President Nixon to consider heroin maintenance for the treatment of heroin addicts. It was not recommended, and methadone was promoted instead. The latter has proved useful to many persons in recovery from heroin misuse, especially when they have enduring family and job ties. But for the unemployed and marginalized, methadone maintenance translated into dependence on the clinic, further disempowerment, continued polydrug misuse, and criminality. Another complaint is that dosages are frequently too low to maintain patients adequately. Despite these adverse aspects, however, methadone maintenance still remains the major treatment option open to American heroin misusers.

After facing much opposition, needle exchanges now feature prominently in the lives of heroin injectors in many European and American cities. They have reduced needle sharing appreciably (Stimson, 1989) and served as a conduit to other treatment services (Gostin, Lazzarini, Jones, & Flaherty, 1997; Heimer & Lopes, 1994). Studies have shown that HIV seroprevalence and the spread of hepatitis decreased in cities with needle exchange programs and increased in those without, and that many infections could have been avoided had they been implemented nationally (Hurley, 1997; Lurie & Drucker, 1997; Normand, Vlahov, & Moses, 1995). No evidence for the fear that needle exchanges encouraged drug use was found (Heimer & Lopes, 1994).

In the mid-1990s, other options are becoming available. Acupuncture is a standard offering at many hospitals, clinics, and needle exchanges. Another is ibogaine treatment, which functions on the historically questionable premise that use of one chemical will cure addiction to another. (The history of drug treatment in America contains many a scandal in which "magic bullets" were offered as cures. Heroin was once prescribed as a cure for morphine addiction. In the early 1900s, Rev. Clarence Downs was one of several who offered chemical potions and a patented program of self-improvement to suppress addiction [Musto, 1973]). Others include the use of naloxone, naltrexone (O'Malley et al., 1996), nalmefene (Mason et al., 1994) and other newly developed medicines to effect cures within 24 hours. Little is known about the effectiveness of these treatments. Meanwhile, many continue to quit using heroin of their own volition soon after experimenting with it, or at different stages afterward.

Other Drugs

Every drug currently in use in the world is probably (or potentially) available in the United States, and Americans use many more than the four most discussed in subsequent chapters. Compared with tobacco chewing and smoking, cigarette smoking, begun after the invention of the Bonsack cigarette-rolling machine in 1880, was a virtually unstoppable cultural innovation that was diffused rapidly worldwide. John Wayne, Gary Cooper, Humphrey Bogart, Lauren Bacall, Marlene Dietrich, Joe DiMaggio, Ted Williams, Stan Musial, Mickey Mantle, Edward Murrow, Franklin Roosevelt, and Ronald Reagan were a few of the icons of the American screen, sports, and public life who popularized it. Sales were boosted by manipulative and relentlessly aggressive advertising ("Marlboro Man," "Joe Camel," "the cool, Newport gang," "You've come a long way, baby— Virginia Slims"), often targeted at specific groups in turn (such as women or young minority persons). Cigarette smoking is very prevalent and incurs heavy personal and societal costs:

> Cigarette smoking causes more premature deaths than do all the follow-
> ing together: acquired immunodeficiency syndrome, cocaine, heroin,
> alcohol, fire, automobile accidents, homicide and suicide. Attainment of
> a tobacco-free society ultimately would produce a life-expectancy gain
> comparable with that that would accompany the elimination of all can-
> cers not caused by tobacco use. In particular, each year 350,000 indi-
> viduals who would have experienced tobacco-related deaths would real-
> ize a life-expectancy gain of 15 years. Reflecting their higher smoking
> prevalence and rates of smoking-related diseases, blacks would benefit
> more than whites. By altering the mix of morbid conditions and fatal
> diseases, the end of tobacco-related disease would shift the need for par-
> ticular medical specialties and health facilities. The tobacco industry
> implies that demise of tobacco consumption would wreak havoc with
> the economy. By contrast, some anti-tobacco activists suggest that the
> end of tobacco use would yield a multibillion dollar fiscal dividend.
> Each argument is fundamentally flawed. The economic impacts of a to-
> bacco-free society would be modest and of far less consequence than the
> principal implication: a significantly enriched quality and quantity of
> life. (Warner, 1987, p. 2080)*

In 1997–98, secret industry documents that were leaked to the press disclosed that the tobacco companies were very much aware that nicotine was addictive and

---

Source: Reprinted with permission from K.E. Warner, Health and Economic Implications of a Tobacco-Free Society, *Journal of the American Medical Association*, Vol. 258,
No. 15, p. 2080, Copyright 1987, American Medical Association.

that they deliberately manipulated the dosage in cigarettes to addict consumers. All the while, they had denied the practice, and maintained staunchly that cigarettes were nonaddictive and mostly harmless. Public opinion turned against them, and currently harsh regulations, compensatory repayments, and price increases are being designed for the industry. While facing these penalties at home, however, the industry is proceeding with "business as usual" abroad.

Coffee drinking is the quintessential American drug experience, as tea drinking is England's, China's, or India's. More than 80% of Americans consume more than two cups a day (Heller, 1987), thereby imbibing a powerful stimulant, caffeine, which has, in addition to its pleasurable effects, serious adverse health consequences, such as convulsions, respiratory failure, nausea, birth defects in neonates, and even death (Dranov, 1987; MacMahon, Yen, Trichopoulos, Warren, & Nardi, 1981; NIDA, 1983). Most young Americans drink caffeine at an early age in soft drinks (Paterson, 1988).

The ordinary neighborhood health food store contains foods and other preparations from which moderately competent chemists can extract mind-altering substances of staggering potency (Shulgin & Shulgin, 1991). American lay chemists have produced amphetamine (Brecher, 1972), LSD (Hoffman, 1980; Solomon, 1966), ketamine (Dotson, Ackerman, & West, 1995; Hansen, Jensen, Chandresh, & Hilden, 1988), Ecstasy (Eisner, 1994; Welsh, 1996), and many other psychoactives in their homes. Other illegal drugs such as peyote or khat are restricted to the small ethnic populations that have used them traditionally, such as Native Americans or Africans from the Horn of Africa. Mushrooms are gathered and consumed by rural Americans and exported to cities or are grown in basements (Riedlinger, 1990).

The pharmaceutical industry tirelessly produces mind- and mood-altering drugs that make their way to the consumer over the counter, by prescription, or in illegal markets. Ritalin, a stimulant, is administered to an alarmingly large number of children diagnosed with attention deficit/hyperactivity disorder (Bonn, 1996). Antidepressants such as Valium, Halcyon, Prozac, and Zoloft have been abused (Breggin & Breggin, 1994). A sedative-narcotic synthetic, flunitrazepam (Rohypnol), is notorious as the "date-rape pill" (Smith, Wesson, & Calhoun, 1996).

No significant drug-using subculture has formed among consumers of these drugs. In the 1960s, amphetamine was an emblem of motorcycle gangs such as Hell's Angels, who also distributed it nationwide. It still appeals periodically to students staying up late to study, to persons trying to maintain a strict diet, and more recently, to some gay circles in California preoccupied with sexual performance.

The Extent of Drug Use in America

Drug studies are seriously hampered by researchers' inability to furnish credible estimates of the number of drug distributors, users, and misusers in a local site or the nation. Since, for example, the casual user is probably the most prevalent but hardest to detect, misusers, who are not only known to authorities but are highly visible in their neighborhoods, assume an unnatural prominence, and their misfortunes erroneously define the human drug experience.

Because drug use and distribution are illegal activities, random samples of telephone listings or addresses are not feasible. Most substitutes devised by epidemiologists such as the Drug Abuse Warning Network (DAWN), Drug Use Forecasting (DUF), the National Household Survey on Drug Abuse (NHSDA), and Monitoring the Future (MTF) have strengths as well as serious defects.

In a typical survey, for example, the researcher administers a standardized, fixed-choice questionnaire. The ease with which these can be reproduced, administered to large groups of people, and analyzed through a computerized process is of great value, and allows researchers to get an overview of trends, patterns, and characteristics. The questionnaire format is flexible, and it permits the researcher to investigate several topics or multiple hypotheses. The reliability and validity of the findings can usually be guaranteed by the method's internal consistency.

On the other hand, most surveys use samples drawn from prisons and other criminal justice institutions where persons often have little reason to tell the truth or to trust in procedures that guarantee confidentiality. Such samples ignore the nonincarcerated. When surveys are made by telephone, only subscribers are sampled; but, as everyone knows, many drug users dispense with that service. The fixed-choice questionnaire is also a straitjacket that confines the researcher to the words and concepts with which he or she began the work.

Surveys have often been very wrong about the extent of use, how users are initiated, how they switch between drugs, their different use patterns, how much they use, how they quit, and who their drug distributors are and how they operate. Surveys illuminate very little about the contexts of social life, its complexity and situational aspects, and its economic, cultural, and political dimensions.

The best figures derived from these sources are therefore subject to question. According to them, 12.8 million Americans, or 6.1% of the population over 12 years old, used illicit drugs in 1995, down from a high of 25 million or 14% in 1979 (SAMSHA, 1996). In 1996, 24.6% of high school seniors had used them (Johnston et al., 1997). By contrast, unofficial estimates count at least 64 million Americans as marijuana smokers alone! European-American males formed the largest group of users, and misuse was more prevalent among the unemployed and poorly educated (SAMSHA, 1996). Fifty-two percent of the population, or 111 million, used alcohol, of whom 32 million were binge drinkers, including 11 million alcoholics. They accounted for 100,000 deaths a year and for most deaths by traffic accidents (Doyle, 1996). Twenty-five percent of these 11 million also used illicit drugs. Generally, however, consumers of alcohol are better educated and better employed than users of illicit drugs. Twenty-nine percent of Americans, or 61 million, smoked tobacco, while 6.9 million used smokeless tobacco

(SAMSHA, 1996). If an American avoids the use of any of these substances until the age of 20, she or he is likely never to use them (Chen & Kandel, 1995).

Moral panics created by opinion makers, powerful interest groups, and the media have exaggerated these figures with an implausibility that is sometimes ludicrous. For example, in Caribbean islands that grow marijuana, police routinely claim credit for destroying crops that exceeded the capacity of the small acreages most have. Such "plantations" would have crowded out every other living species and would have left no room for rivers, beaches, or tourist resorts!

A fact that the conservative or prohibitionist ideology has obscured is that only a minority of persons in modern societies *want* to use drugs. It is not true that punitive measures have kept the majority from using them. The steep increases in use and societal problems they anticipate simply will not occur, even if drugs are legalized or decriminalized.

The proof is in the inner city, where the worst scenarios for legalization or decriminalization are forecast. Even in a "drug-infested" low-income study site in Central Harlem where both open-air and curbside drug markets (as well as indoor selling locations) flourished, an exhaustive ethnographic head count, made at the peak of the cocaine smoking epidemic of the 1980s, found only 17% of the local population having any engagement at all in either use or distribution of marijuana, cocaine, or heroin or in the consumption of alcohol (Hamid, 1992a). Only a very small proportion of them misused these substances or had adverse psychosocial outcomes (other than breaking drug laws) on account of them. Sometimes, problematic drug use occurred in only one stage of a person's career in drug use, and may have been preceded and followed by longer periods of more moderate consumption. Eventually many were released entirely through "spontaneous remission." The drugs stopped having any appeal. They had never appealed to most persons in the neighborhood, despite extraordinary accessibility, some community tolerance, and relative impunity. A consumer could employ a "runner" to buy the drugs, or distributors might make home deliveries. Drugs were sold from some units in many apartment buildings and were thus available indoors with minor risk to residents. But even when drugs could be acquired at no risk simply by knocking at the neighbor's door, most Harlemites ignored them, their users, and their distributors.

A comparison of the different drug markets is also suggestive. For example, of the three curbside markets for smokable cocaine discussed in Chapter 4, the business nickels market, the crack sellers coop, and the free-lance nickels market, the second was the most regulated (through an informal "agreement" between sellers and buyers to decrease buying episodes to a minimum) and least attended by violence or crime. Workers who never lost their jobs on account of cocaine smoking patronized it. Regulated by the threat of violence by "owners," both distributors and customers conform to strict rules of conduct in business nickels markets, in which predictable crimes occur. They catered to many "binge" users who preferred to buy a weekend's supply of drugs only from a reliable or "reputable" market. But in the least regulated market, the free-lance nickels market, a thousand pathologies bloomed! The three markets may be viewed as better or worse attempts to impose order on the chaos (of both sales and use) which the condition of illegality had created.

Several databases have indicated a marked downward trend in the use of all drugs, including alcohol and cigarettes in the 1990s (Kandel, 1991). For example, NIDA (1990) figures from a national survey of 9,000 households, released on December 18, 1990, are as follows:

- Occasional users of cocaine dropped from 5.8 million (1985) to 2.9 million (1988) to 1.6 million (1990). Overall, this is a 72% decline.
- There were declines in once-a-year users of cocaine, from 6.2 million (1985), and in once-a-week users, from 900,000 (1985) to 662,000 (1990).
- Daily cocaine users increased from 292,000 (1988) to 336,000 (1990).
- Population of crack misusers remained stable at 500,000.
- Alcohol users dropped from 113 million to 102 million.
- Cigarette smokers dropped from 60.3 million to 53.6 million.
- Marijuana smokers dropped from 22.5 million (1979) to 10.2 million (1990).
- Hospital drug-related mentions declined in 1990, from 8,000 in the first quarter to 7,000 in the last quarter.
- In the age group 18–25, 14.9% are users of illicit drugs. In the African-American population, 8.6% are; 7.3% of individuals in large cities are users.

The results of different studies, including studies carried out in Canada (Smart & Adlaf, 1989), converge in documenting that throughout the 1980s there have been downward trends in the prevalence of licit and especially illicit drug use in all age groups in the population, although these appear to have slowed down over the past 2 years (1989 and 1990) compared to prior years (Kandel, 1991). The use of Ice, phenylcyclohexylpisperidine (PCP), and amphetamine has declined (Kandel, 1991). Ecstasy and designer drugs still remain the privilege of young middle-class European Americans (Rosenbaum & Dobler, 1991).

Using groups, however, may be "flying below the radar" and are as yet undetected. For example, some young middle-class youths in American and European capitals and elsewhere have initiated heroin use. Still confined to these experimenters, heroin use could "break out" and enlist consumers in other ethnic groups.

One of the most heartening developments since the late 1980s is that young African Americans are avoiding "hard" drug use. Young persons under the age of 23 in low-income, minority neighborhoods have not discontinued illicit drug use, but they have avoided smokable cocaine and any form of heroin so far. A party of 11 young African-American males (18–21 years of age) told a newspaper reporter in a Chinese restaurant in Flatbush that they liked to drink 40-oz bottles of malt beer and to smoke marijuana in *blunts* (a cheap, 10-cent cigar, usually the Phillies brand, that is hollowed out and refilled with marijuana). They emphasized, however, that sexual adventures ranked equally with the drugs (Hemphill, 1990). Some mentioned the acquisition and display of guns as a rival passion. Young African Americans are still strictly avoiding heroin in the late 1990s.

American drug users thus appear to be approaching the mid-1990s with extreme caution. They are opting for milder drug-using patterns that greatly reduce whatever harm may be caused by drugs, such as health problems, irresponsible behavior, addiction, and arrest. Former heroin injectors have taken advantage of the greater purity and cheaper price currently available and have switched to intranasal use (Hunt & Rhodes, 1993). New users have followed their lead (Hamid et al., 1997). They rush to treatment centers whenever they have misgivings at the first hint of alarm. Similarly, new users of marijuana seek professional assistance at the emergency rooms of hospitals instead of relying exclusively on the nostrums of friends or older users in the drug culture.

Many reasons can be proffered to explain this ethos of circumspection, learning, self-discipline, and resistance in regard to drugs. Mementos remain in the inner-city of the scourges of injectable heroin and smokable cocaine, which deter young persons from trying them. The campaign of public education that has linked drugs and sex-for-drug encounters to such undesirable outcomes as unwanted pregnancy, sexually transmitted diseases, AIDS, and other pathology has reduced the number of drug experimenters and sends them to the emergency room at the first sign of discomfort:

> The implementation of numerous school- and community-based drug-prevention programs, drug-treatment initiatives, extensive media interventions, the simple JUST SAY NO campaign, the formation of parent groups against drinking and illicit drug use, the mobilization of communities against the use of drugs by young people, the AIDS epidemic and associated national educational efforts linking it to drug use, a general emphasis in our society on health and diet, and the dynamic processes of the spread and constriction of epidemics all may play a role. (Kandel, 1991, p. 404)

As the prevalence of drug use has declined, the perceived harmfulness and the risks associated with using drugs have increased sharply (Johnston, O'Malley, & Bachman, 1997; Kandel 1991).

Of course, the world has also changed. Just as marijuana was a medium of local-level capital accumulation in the 1960s and smokable cocaine the instrument of capital depletion in the 1980s (see Chapter 6), drug use in the 21st century will be adapted to the evolution of an unfolding global society.

In the early 2000s, the American population will again become more youthful, and a mass of persons in the age range of 16–25 years of age may be tempted to experiment with drugs and crime. In New York City, the at-risk youthful popula-tions include not only minorities (Latinos, African Americans, Caribbean Afri-cans) in inner-city neighborhoods, but also European Americans in formerly pros-perous middle-class communities, such as Bay Ridge, Bensonhurst, and Howard Beach.

The general conditions of life in their communities have also worsened since the 1960s. Rising rates of poverty, chronic unemployment, political apathy, and pathology will have affected young persons born in the late 1970s more acutely and cumulatively than earlier age cohorts. For example, they report more fre-quently that childhood sexual abuse or codependency on parental drug abuse were factors in their drug use or criminality. More so than their predecessors, young persons in the late 1990s will be apparently able to tolerate in their personal and communal lives high levels of violence and criminality, and of individual, domes-tic, and societal dysfunction. Treatment and prevention strategists must have de-tails of these differences in order to redesign outdated approaches.

A combination of epidemiological and ethnographic methods (see Chapter 2) will probably yield more reliable figures. Several street-based samples could be drawn, the proportion of known/unknown users could be calculated, and then used to improve official statistics. (For example, if only 5 out of every 10 in street-based samples are known to the police or treatment personnel, a researcher may conclude that the "true" number of users or distributors is twice the police or treat-ment record.) In 1990, the Census Bureau commissioned ethnographers to deter-mine the undercount in neighborhoods where drug use and distribution (by fright-ening away enumerators or because mail-in questionnaires had not reached addressees) may have compromised census taking. Relying on extensive prior knowledge of their sites, the ethnographers completed an exhaustive head count and reported undercounts of up to 50%. In one neighborhood in Harlem, New York City, where it had been 49%, the ethnographer counted 71 occupied housing units out of a total of 132, of which 5, or 7%, were locales for either drug use or distribution. Of 143 persons enumerated, 25, or 17%, had been drug users or dis-tributors (Hamid, 1992a). This Harlem neighborhood resembled many others in similar low-income, minority sections of New York City. Multiplying by the num-ber of the latter and compensating for the (probable) dearth of drug activity in other neighborhoods, statisticians might generate a more accurate citywide aggre-gate. Regional and national totals could be estimated by the same procedure.

Good sense strongly advocates combining survey methodology with qualitative techniques to arrive at the best possible estimates. Obviously, surveys are the ap-propriate instrument for gaining a rapid overview of trends, characteristics, and patterns when populations are too large to allow for more direct observations. But ethnography can make them far more effective by correcting their several faults.

THE SCOPE OF THIS BOOK

In the chapters that follow, the "drug problem" has been deconstructed into its constituent parts. The methodology by which this is accomplished is outlined in the Introduction, in which pharmacological or clinical research and epidemiological surveys are contrasted with anthropological investigations of drug users in their actual social environments. In Chapter 3, drugs are recognized as commodities, the symbiosis between corporate capitalism and informal economies is explored, and drug distribution is identified as a sector of the latter, affording a view of drug users and distributors as laboring populations who perform vital functions for the maintenance of the community by earning and spending money as they do. Chapter 4 assesses law enforcement initiatives and the responses of the criminal justice system to "the drug problem." Chapter 5 explores the drugs-crime connection, and Chapter 6, that between drugs and violence. In Chapter 7, the impact of drugs upon families, women, and the parenting process is measured. A major rationale of the "war on drugs," the destruction of inner-city neighborhoods by drugs, is addressed in Chapter 8. In Chapter 9, facts and theories of addiction are reviewed.

In each chapter, the aim is to replace a simplistic, monocausal explanation of social problems—drugs "cause" crime, violence, sexual promiscuity, dangerously emancipated women, abusive or neglectful parenting, addiction, and neighborhood deterioration—with a more comprehensive, better-informed perspective that emphasizes the numerous, interrelated social, economic, cultural, and political processes in modern societies that impinge upon human-drug interactions. Finally, Chapter 10 outlines an enlightened drug policy for the 21st century.

Discussion Questions

1. Give examples of how drugs brought prosperity to various regions and nations, including the United States.
2. How did modern consumer societies and consumerism arise? Research and discuss the examples given in this chapter of Europe in the medieval era and in the 18th and 19th centuries, when great strides were made toward this outcome. What was the role of drugs in transforming social stratification and the ethos of societies?
3. Reconstruct and research the periods in America when the commodities multiplied and there was a rise in consumerism. Was there a link to drugs?
4. Comment on and illustrate the observation that, because they give pleasure, drugs and other commodities "tie in" the consumer to his or her community.

5. Give details of how the colonial situation and, later, non–European migration to the United States affected the reception of tropical drugs in Western societies. Discuss drugs as an instance of a culture absorbing foreign and "different," in this case Europe accepting the tropics.
6. Describe changes in American perceptions of the male and female body. Relate them to dietary prescriptions or the use of different (legal and illegal) drugs.
7. Discuss examples of wartime use of drugs in both traditional and modern societies (see also Chapter 6).
8. Describe prevailing expectations of drug use in the reader's community, specifying the drugs associated with different segments (age, gender, ethnicity, neighborhood) of the local population.
9. Recall and discuss the political uses of drugs in American history.
10. Describe and discuss drug education classes the reader may have attended. Who taught them? What was the content? How did students respond? Evaluate their impact on the reader and classmates.
11. Discuss the histories of the principal drugs Americans use: caffeine, nicotine, alcohol, marijuana, cocaine, amphetamine, and heroin. How are they used in the reader's community? What other drugs are available and what is known about them?
12. Describe attitudes toward drunkenness or drug addiction in the reader's community.
13. Enumerate and discuss the difficulties an observer would encounter in attempting to get accurate figures in the reader's community about what kinds of drugs are used, in what quantities, how many used them, and how much they cost.
14. Give examples and discuss how the supply of (any) goods affects the demand for them, or their consumption.
15. Discuss immigration to the United States, the arrival of different ethnic groups, ethnic relations in America, and the part the different drugs—alcohol, marijuana, heroin, and cocaine—played in these arenas. Discuss ethnic occupational stereotyping: "Jews are lawyers, Irish are police, Italians are construction workers, Dominicans and Jamaicans sell drugs."
16. Recall and discuss Prohibition (1919–1933).
17. How are identities in modern societies shaped by consumption?

REFERENCES

Abel, E.R. (1980). *Marihuana: The first twelve thousand years*. New York: Plenum.

AIDS Community Educators. (1989). *A report from the underground: A report on the current status of the unauthorized needle-exchange program in New Haven, CT*. New Haven, CT: Author.

AIDS Community Research Group. (1988). *AIDS, knowledge, attitudes and behavior in an ethnically mixed urban neighborhood*. Hartford, CT: Connecticut State Department of Health Services.

Amin, S. (1974). *Accumulation on a world scale: A critique of the theory of underdevelopment*, 2 vols. (B. Peare, Trans.). New York: Monthly Review Press.

Anderson, B. (1983). *Imagined communities: Reflections on the origin and spread of nationalism*. New York: Verso.

Antonil. (1978). *Mama coca*. London: Hassle Free Press.

Aronowitz, S. (1973). *False promises: The shaping of American working class consciousness*. New York: McGraw-Hill.

Battjes, R., & Pickens, R. (1988). *Needle sharing among intravenous drug abusers: National and international perspectives*. Rockville, MD: National Institute on Drug Abuse.

Becker, M., & Joseph, J. (1988). AIDS and behavioral change to reduce risk: A review. *American Journal of Public Health, 78*, 394–410.

Beeching, J. (1975). The Chinese opium wars. New York: Harcourt, Brace, Jovanovich.

Bennett, C., Osborn, L., & Osborn, J. (1995). *Green gold—the tree of life: Marijuana in magic and religion*. Frazier Park, CA: Access Unlimited.

Berridge, V., & Edwards, D. (1981). *Opium and the people: Opiate use in nineteenth century England*. New York: Saint Martin's Press.

Bonn, D. (1996). Methylphenidate: Are U.S. and European views converging? *Lancet, 348*, 255.

Bordo, S. (1993). *Unbearable weight: Feminism, western culture and the body*. Berkeley, CA: University of California Press.

Boyle, J., & Brunswick, A. (1980). What happened in Harlem?: Analysis of a decline in heroin use among a generational unit of urban black youth. *Journal of Drug Issues, 10*, 109–130.

Boyle, T.C. (1984). *Budding prospects: A pastoral*. New York: Viking/Penguin.

Brecher, E.M. (1972). *Licit and illicit drugs: The Consumer's Union report on narcotics, stimulants, depressants, inhalants, hallucinogens, and marijuana—including caffeine, nicotine and alcohol*. Boston: Little, Brown.

Breggin, P.R., & Breggin, G.R. (1994). *Talking back to Prozac: What doctors won't tell you about today's most controversial drug*. New York: St. Martin's Press.

Brown, C. (1965). *Manchild in the promised land*. New York: Macmillan.

Brumberg, J.J. (1988). *Fasting girls: The emergence of anorexia nervosa as a modern disease*. Cambridge, MA: Harvard University Press.

Buckley, C. (1994). *Thank you for smoking*. New York: Random House.

Burroughs, W. (1958). *Junky*. New York: Harcourt, Brace, Jovanovich.

Carroll, J. (1987). *Basketball diaries*. New York: Penguin.

Chaisson, R., Moss, A., Onishi, R., Osmond, D., & Carlson, J. (1987). Human immunodeficiency virus infection in heterosexual intravenous drug users in San Francisco. *American Journal of Public Health, 77*, 169–172.

Chein, I., Gerald, D., Lee, R., & Rosenfeld, E. (1964). *The road to H: Narcotics, delinquency and social policy*. New York: Basic Books.

Chen, K., & Kandel, D.B. (1995). The natural history of drug use from adolescence to the mid-thirties in a general population sample. *American Journal of Public Health, 85*: 41–47.

Chernin, K. (1985). *The hungry self: Women, eating and identity*. New York: Harper & Row.

Chitwood, D.D., Rivers, J.E., & Inciardi, J.A. (1996). *The American pipe dream: Crack cocaine in the inner city*. Fort Worth, TX: Harcourt Brace.

Courtwright, D.T. (1982). *Dark paradise: Opiate addiction in America before 1940.* Cambridge, MA: Harvard University Press.

Courtwright, D.T. (1991). The first American cocaine epidemic. Rockville, MD: National Institute on Drug Abuse, C/CRWG Newsletter, No. 1, pp. 3–5

Cunningham, J.A.L., Sobell, C., Freedman, J.L., & Sobell, M.C. (1994). Beliefs about the causes of substance abuse: a comparison of three drugs. *Journal of Substance Abuse, 6,* 219–226.

Curtis, R., & Maher, L. (1992). Highly structured drug markets on Williamsburg's southside. In J. Fagan (Ed.), *The social ecology of drugs.* New York: Social Science Research Council. Unpublished manuscript.

de la Fuente, L., Saavedra, P., Barrio, A., Royuela, L., Vincente, P., & the Spanish Group for the Study of the Purity of Seized Drugs. (1996). Temporal and geographic variations in the characteristics of heroin seized in Spain and their relation with route of administration. *Drug and Alcohol Dependence, 40,* 185–194.

Des Jarlais, D., Friedman, S., Sotheran, J., Wenston, J., Marmor, M., Yancovitz, S., Frank, B., Beatrice, S., & Mildvan, D. (1994). Continuity and change within an HIV epidemic: Injecting drug users in New York City, 1984 through 1992. *Journal of the American Medical Association, 271,* 121–127

Dolan, M., Black, J., DeFord, H., Skinner, J., & Robinowitz, R. (1987). Characteristics of drug abusers that discriminate needle sharers. *Public Health Reports, 102,* 395–398.

Dotson, J., Ackerman, D.L., & West, L.J. (1995). Ketamine abuse. *Journal of Drug Issues, 245,* 751–757.

Doyle, R. (1996). Deaths due to alcohol. *Scientific American, 275* (6), 30–31.

Dranov, P. (1987). Caffeine redeemed? *Health, 19,* 70.

Drug Enforcement Agency. (1996). *Drugs of abuse.* Washington, DC: U.S. Department of Justice, DEA.

Edney, H., Bowman, M., & Lober, B. (1997). *Junkphood.* San Francisco: Santa Cruz Needle Exchange.

Eisner, B. (1994). *Ecstasy: The MDMA story.* Berkeley, CA: Ronin.

Eldred, C.A., & Washington, M.M. (1975). Female heroin addicts in a city treatment program: The forgotten minority. *Psychiatry, 38,* 75.

Feldman, D. & Johnson, T. (Eds.). (1986). *The social dimensions of AIDS.* New York: Praeger.

Friedman, S.R., Kleinman, P.H., & Des Jarlais, D.C. (1992). History, biography and HIV infection. *American Journal of Public Health, 82,* 125.

Freud, S. (1890-1974). *Cocaine papers* (R. Byck, Ed.). New York: New American Library.

Fullilove, M., & Fullilove, R. (1989). Intersecting epidemics: Black teen crack use and sexually transmitted diseases. *Journal of the American Medical Women's Association, 44* (7), 151–153.

Gamella, J.F. (1994). The spread of intravenous drug use and AIDS in a neighborhood in Spain. *Medical Anthropology Quarterly, 8,* (2), 131–160.

Gibbs, J.T. (Ed.). (1988). *Young, black and male in America: An endangered species.* Dover, MA: Auburn House.

Ginsberg, A. (1956). *Howl & other poems.* San Francisco: City Lights Books.

Gitlin, T. (1987). *The sixties: Years of hope, days of rage.* New York: Bantam Books.

Goode, E. (1970). *The marijuana smokers.* New York: Basic Books.

Gostin, L.O., Lazzarini, Z., Jones, T.S., & Flaherty, K. (1997). Prevention of HIV/AIDS and other blood-borne diseases among injection drug users: A national survey on regulation of syringes and needles. *Journal of the American Medical Association, 277,* 53–62.

Griffiths, P., Gossop, M., & Strang, J. (1994). Chasing the dragon: The development of heroin smoking in the United Kingdom. In J. Strang & M. Gossop (Eds.), *Heroin addiction and drug policy: The British system*. London: Oxford University Press.

Grinspoon, L., & Bakalar, J.E. (1985). *Cocaine: A drug and its social evolution* (rev. ed). New York: Basic Books.

Grund, J. (1993). *Drug use as social ritual: Functionality, symbolism and determinants of self regulation*. Dissertation. Rotterdam: Instituut Voor Verslavingsonderzoek (IVO).

Grund, J.-P.C., Kaplan, C.D., Adriaans, N.F., & Blanken, P. (1991). Drug sharing and HIV transmission risks: The practice of "front loading" in the Dutch intravenous drug using population. *Journal of Psychoactive Drugs, 23*(1), 1–10.

Haley, A. (1965). *The autobiography of Malcolm X*. New York: Grove Press.

Hamid, A. (1980). *A precapitalist mode of production: Ganja and the Rastafarians in San Fernando, Trinidad*. Dissertation, Columbia University/Ann Arbor, MI: University Microfilms.

Hamid, A. (1992a). *Ethnographic follow up of a predominantly African-American population in a sample area in central Harlem, New York City: Behavioral causes of the undercount of the 1990 census/final report #11 for joint statistical agreement 89-28*. Washington, DC: Bureau of the Census/Center for Survey Methods Research.

Hamid, A. (1992b). The developmental cycle of a drug epidemic: The cocaine smoking epidemic of 1981–1991. *Journal of Psychoactive Drugs, 24*, 337–347.

Hamid, A. (1997a). *The political economy of drugs*, Pt I: *Ganja and Rastafarians in Trinidad and New York*. Unpublished manuscript.

Hamid, A. (1997b). *The political economy of drugs*, Pt II: *The cocaine smoking epidemic in New York City's low-income minority neighborhoods, 1981 to 1991*. Unpublished Manuscript.

Hamid, A., Curtis, R., McCoy, K., McGuire, J., Conde, A., Bushell, W., Lindenmayer, R., Brimberg, K., Maia, S., Abdur-Rashid, S., & Settembrino, J. (1997). The heroin epidemic in New York City: Current status and prognoses. *Journal of Psychoactive Drugs, 29*, 375–391

Hansen, G., Jensen, S.B., Chandresh, L., & Hilden, T. (1988). The psychotropic effect of ketamine. *Journal of Psychoactive Drugs, 20*, 419–425.

Hanson, B., Beschner, B., Walters, J., & Bovelle, B. (1985). *Life with heroin*. Lexington, MA: Lexington Books.

Heimer, R., & Lopes, M. (1994). Needle exchange in New Haven reduces HIV risks, promotes entry into drug treatment, and does not create new drug injectors. *Journal of the American Medical Association, 271*, 1825–1826.

Heller, A. (1987, September). Caffeine and your health. *Shape*, p. 58.

Hemphill, C. (1990, October 11). Turning a corner on crack: Statistics show decline in drug's use. *Newsday*, p. 1.

Henman, A. (1990). Coca and cocaine: Their role in the traditional cultures of South America. *Journal of Drug Issues, 20*, 577–588.

Hentoff, N. (1964). *The jazz life*. New York: Pantheon.

Hoffman, A. (1980). *LSD: My problem child*. New York: McGraw-Hill.

Howland, R.W., & Howland, T.W. (1978). 200 years of drinking in the United States. In J.A. Ewing & B.A. Rouse (Eds.), *Drinking: Alcohol and American society—issues and current research*. Chicago: Nelson-Hall.

Huncke, H. (1990). *Guilty of everything*. New York: Paragon House.

Hunt, D.E., & Rhodes, W. (1993). *Tracking the incidence of heroin use: Is there a possible epidemic?* Washington, DC: Office of National Drug Control Policy.

Hurley, S.F. (1997). Effectiveness of needle-exchange programmes for prevention of HIV infection. *Lancet, 349,* 1797.

Inciardi, J.A. (1987). Beyond cocaine: Basuco, crack and other coca products. *Contemporary Drug Problems, 14,* 461–492.

Inciardi J.A. (1992). *The war on drugs 11: The continuing epic of heroin, cocaine, crack, crime, AIDS and public policy.* Mountain View, CA: Mayfield.

Johnson, B., Goldstein, P., Preble, E., Schmeidler, J., Lipton, D., Spunt, B., & Miller, T. (1985). *Taking care of business: The economics of crime by heroin abusers.* Lexington, MA: Lexington Books.

Johnston, L.D., O'Malley, P.M., & Bachman, J.G. (1997). *National survey results on drug use from the monitoring the future study, 1975–1996.* Ann Arbor, MI: Institute for Social Research, University of Michigan.

Kandel, D.B. (1988). Issues of sequencing adolescent drug use and other problem behaviors. *Drugs and Society, 3,* 55–76.

Kandel, D.B. (1991). The social demography of drug use. *Milbank Quarterly, 69,* 365–414.

Kenney, J., & Leaton, G. (1991). *Loosening the grip: A handbook of alcohol information.* St. Louis: Mosby.

Lee, M.A., & Schlain, B. (1985). *Acid dreams: The CIA, LSD and the sixties remembered.* New York: Grove.

Levine, H.G. & Reinarman, C. (1987). *The crack panic.* San Francisco: Institute for Scientific Analysis.

Lurie, P., & Drucker, E. (1997). An opportunity lost: HIV infections associated with lack of a national needle-exchange programme in the USA. *Lancet, 349*: 604–608.

MacMahon, B., Yen, S., Trichopoulos, D., Warren, K., & Nardi, G. (1981). Coffee and cancer of the pancreas. *New England Journal of Medicine, 304,* 630–633.

Mailer, N. (1961). *Advertisements for myself.* London: Flamingo (HarperCollins).

Marriott, M. (1993, April 16). For minority youths, forty ounces of trouble. *New York Times,* p. A1.

Mason, B.J., Ritvo, E.C., Morgan, R.O., Salvato, F.R., Goldberg, G., Welch, B.,& Mantero-Atienza, E. (1994). A double-blind, placebo-controlled pilot study to evaluate the efficacy and safety of oral nalmefene HCI for alcohol dependence. *Alcohol and Clinical Research 18,* 1162–1167.

McCoy, A. (1991). *The politics of heroin: CIA complicity in the global drug trade.* Brooklyn, NY: Lawrence Hill Books.

McKay, C. (1928). *Home to Harlem.* New York: Harper and Bros.

McKay, C. (1929). *Banjo: A story without a plot.* New York: Harcourt, Brace, Jovanovich (Harvest Book).

Morningstar, P.J., & Chitwood, D.D. (1987). How women and men get cocaine: Sex-role stereotypes and acquisition patterns. *Journal of Psychoactive Drugs, 19,* 135–142.

Morton, S. (1916). *John Morton of Trinidad: Journals, letters and papers.* Toronto: Westminister.

Musto, D.F. (1973). *The American disease: Origins of narcotic control.* New Haven, CT: Yale University Press.

Musto, D. (1987). *The American disease: Origins of narcotic control* (expanded ed.) New York: Oxford University Press.

National Highway Traffic Safety Administration. (1988). *Drunk driving facts.* Washington, DC: NHTSA, National Center for Statistical Analysis.

National Institute on Drug Abuse. (1983). *Stimulants and cocaine.* Rockville, MD: National Institute on Drug Abuse.

National Institute on Drug Abuse. (1990). *National household survey on drug abuse: Main findings 1988.* Rockville, MD: National Institute on Drug Abuse.

New York City Department of Health. (1989). *The pilot needle-exchange study in New York: A bridge to treatment: A report on the first ten months of operation.* New York: New York City Department of Health.

Normand, J.D., Vlahov, & Moses, L.E. (Eds.). (1995). *Preventing HIV transmission: The role of sterile needles and bleach* (pp. 240–243). Washington, DC: National Academy Press.

O'Donnell, J., Clayton, R., Slatin, G., & Room, R. (1976). *Young men and drugs: A nationwide survey.* Rockville, MD: National Institute on Drug Abuse.

O'Malley, S.S., Jaffe, A.J., Chang, G., Rode, S., Schottenfeld, R., Meyer, R.E., & Rounsaville, B. (1996). Six-month follow-up of Naltrexone and psychotherapy for alcohol dependence. *Archives of General Psychiatry, 53*: 217–224

Paterson, B. (1988, March). Caffeine, villain or victim?" *Consumer Research*, pp. 16–19.

Peele, S. (1985). *The meaning of addiction.* Lexington, MA: Lexington Books.

Pittman, D.J., & Snyder, C.R. (Eds.). (1962). *Society, culture and drinking.* New York: Wiley.

Plowman, T. (1981). Amazonian coca. *Journal of Ethnopharmacology, 3*, 195–225.

Puder, K., Kagan, D., & Morgan, J. (1988). Illicit methamphetamine: Analysis, syntheses, and availability. *American Journal of Drug and Alcohol Abuse, 4*, 463–473.

Ratner, M.S. (Ed.). (1993). *Crack pipe as pimp: An ethnographic investigation of sex-for-crack exchanges.* New York: Lexington Books.

Rhodes, W. (1993, Spring). Synthetic estimation applied to the prevalence of drug use. *Journal of Drug Issues, 23*, 297–321.

Riedlinger, T. (Ed.). (1990). *The sacred mushroom seeker.* Portland, OR: Dioscorides Press.

Robins, L. (1980). The natural history of drug abuse. In D.J. Lettieri, et al. (Eds.). *Theories on drug abuse: Selected contemporary perspectives.* Washington, DC: National Institute on Drug Abuse.

Rosenbaum, M. (1981). *Women on heroin.* New Brunswick, NJ: Rutgers University Press.

Rosenbaum, M. (1996). *Drug education: A report.* San Francisco, CA: National Council on Crime and Delinquency.

Rosenbaum, M., & Dobler, R. (1991). Why MDMA should not have been made illegal. In J. A. Inciardi (Ed.). *The drug legalization debate.* Newbury Park, CA: Sage.

Sabbag, R. (1994, May 5). The cartels would like a second chance. [Special issue on drugs in America] *Rolling Stone, 681*, 35–38.

SAMSHA. (1996, August). *Preliminary estimates from the 1995 national household survey on drug abuse. Advance report No. 18.* Rockville, MD: Office of Applied Studies, Substance Abuse and Mental Health Services Administration.

Schilling, R., Schinke, S., Nichols, S., Zayas, L., Miller, S., Orlando, M., & Botvin, G. (1989). Developing strategies for AIDS prevention research with black and Hispanic drug users. *Public Health Reports, 104*, 2–11

Schivelbusch, W. (1992). *Tastes of paradise: A social history of spices, stimulants, and intoxicants.* New York: Pantheon.

Schorr, L.B. (1997). *Common purpose: Strengthening families and neighborhoods to rebuild America.* New York: Anchor Books.

Selwyn, P. (1988). Sterile needles and the epidemic of acquired immunodeficiency syndrome: Issues for drug treatment and public health. *Advances in Alcohol and Substance Abuse, 7*, 99–105.

Shulgin, A., & Shulgin, A. (1991). *Pihkal: A chemical love story.* Berkeley, CA: Transform Press.

Siegel, R.K. (1982). History of cocaine smoking. *Journal of Psychoactive Drugs, 14*, 277–299.

Singer, M., Flores, C., Davidson, L., Burke, G., Castillo, Z. Scanlon, K., & Rivera, M. (1990). SIDA: The economic, social, and cultural context of AIDS among Latinos. *Medical Anthropology Quarterly, 4*: 73–117.

Smart, E.F., & Adlaf, R.G. (1989). *The Ontario alcohol and other drug survey, 1977–1987.* Toronto: Addiction Research Foundation.

Smith, D.E., Wesson, D. R., & Calhoun, S. (1996). *Rohypnol (flunitrazepam).* San Francisco, CA: Haight-Ashbury Free Clinic, Inc.

Solomon, D. (Ed.). (1966). *LSD: The consciousness-expanding drug.* New York: Berkeley Medallion Book.

Stimson, G. (1989). Syringe exchange programs for injecting drug users. *AIDS, 3*, 253–260.

Strategic Intelligence Section, Domestic Unit. (1996). Domestic monitor program. Washington, DC: United States Department of Justice, Drug Enforcement Administration, Intelligence Division.

Sviridoff, M., Sudd, R., & Grinc, R. (1992). The neighborhood effect of street-level drug law enforcement: Tactical narcotics teams in New York, an evaluation. New York: Vera Institute of Justice.

Taylor, A. (1993). *Women drug users: an ethnography of a female injecting community.* New York: Oxford University Press.

Thomas, P. (1967). *Down these mean streets.* New York: Knopf.

Turner, B. (1984). *The body and society: Explorations in social theory.* Oxford, England: Blackwell.

U.S. National Commission on Marijuana and Drug Abuse. (1972). *Official report.* Washington, DC: U.S. Government Printing Office.

Wallace, B.C. (1987). Cocaine dependence treatment on an impatient detoxification unit. *Journal of Substance Abuse Treatment, 4*, 85–92.

Wallace, B.C. (1990). Crack cocaine smokers as adult children of alcoholics: The dysfunctional family link. *Journal of Substance Abuse Treatment, 7*, 89–100

Wallerstein, I. (1974). *The modern world system: Capitalists, agriculture and the origins of the European world economy in the sixteenth century* (Vols. 1–2). New York: Academic Press.

Warner, K.E. (1987). Health and economic implications of a tobacco-free society. *Journal of the American Medical Association, 258*, 2080–2086.

Warner, K.E. (1990). Till death do us part: America's turbulent love affair with the cigarette. *Medical and Health Annual, Encyclopedia Britannica*, pp. 60–79.

Waterston, A (1993). *Street addicts in the political economy.* Philadelphia: Temple University Press.

Weeks, J. (1981). *Sex, politics and society: The regulation of sexuality since 1800.* London: Longman.

Weil, A. (1972). *The natural mind: A new way of looking at drugs and the higher consciousness.* Boston: Houghton Mifflin.

Weisheit, R. (1992). *Domestic marijuana: A neglected industry.* Westport, CT: Greenwood Press.

Weller, J.A. (1972). *The East Indian indenture to the Caribbean.* Rio Piedras, PR: Institute of Social and Economic Research.

Welsh, I. (1996). *Ecstasy: Three tales of chemical romance.* New York: W.W. Norton.

Winick, C. (1959). The uses of drugs by jazz musicians. *Social Problems, 7*, 119–126.

Yablonsky, L. (1997). *The story of junk.* New York: Farrar, Strauss & Giroux.

SUGGESTED READING

Collison, M. (1996). In search of the high life: Drugs, crime, masculinities and consumption. *British Journal of Criminology, 36*, 428–444.

Des Jarlais, D., Friedman, S., & Hopkins, W. (1985). Risk reduction for the acquired immunodeficiency syndrome among intravenous drug users. *Annals of Internal Medicine, 103*, 755–759.

Goodman, J. (1993). *Tobacco in history: The culture of dependence.* London: Routledge.

Levine, H.G., & Reinarman, C. (Eds.). (1997). *Crack in America: Demon drugs and social justice.* San Francisco: University of California Press.

Moskowitz, H., & Burns, M. (1990). Effects of alcohol on driving performance. *Alcohol and Health Research World, 14*, 12–14.

Singer, M., Flores, C., Davidson, L., Burke, G., Castillo, Z., Scanlon, K., & Rivera, M. (1990). SIDA: The economic, social, and cultural context of AIDS among Latinos. *Medical Anthropology Quarterly, 4*, 73–117.

Stephens, R.C. (1991). *The street addict role: A theory of heroin addiction.* Albany, NY: State University of New York Press.

Waldorf, D. (1973). *Careers in dope.* Englewood Cliffs, NJ: Prentice Hall.

Williams, R. (1991). The dream world of mass consumption. In C. Mukerji & M. Schudson (Eds.), *Rethinking popular culture: Contemporary perspectives in cultural studies* (pp. 198–235). Berkeley, CA: University of California Press.

CHAPTER 2

Writing about Drugs: Ethnographic versus Psychopharmacological Approaches

---

Chapter Objectives

Humans have been telling stories about drugs ever since they first encountered them. But their focus has shifted over the centuries. Many drugs, such as marijuana, were first noted in pharmacopeias, liturgies, and travelogues. A tradition of literary writing and commentary followed, in which both the pleasurable and terrifying aspects of drug use were described. It has been sustained today not only in drama and literature, but also in popular music and the arts. Another influential narrative is antidrug propaganda. The most powerful today, however, is science. Within the latter, ethnographic and psychopharmacological approaches challenge and complement each other. The methodologies are thus presented as two among several discourses about drugs.

The aim of this textbook—to locate the phenomena of drug use and misuse (as well as the opposing sides in an ongoing debate on drugs) in their social, economic, political, and cultural contexts or in their relationships to urbanization, consumerism, technological progress, and the other characteristic features of modern societies, such as advanced social stratification, the division of wealth, the struggle between competing interests, labor markets, the diacritics of local neighborhoods (housing, domestic and community organization, education, the physical plant), the global power structure, the efforts of law enforcement, the news media, and academic research (see Chapter 1)—is derived from a unique method of studying these topics.

In this chapter, ethnography is contrasted with the psychopharmacological approach, which has prevailed thus far in drug studies in America. Federal funding agencies and private sources of research support, however, have recently recognized ethnography as a valuable, indispensable scientific methodology for the study of drugs in modern societies. Until 1960, all funding was for biochemical research. In the 1960s, under Dr. Eleanor Carroll of the National Institute on Mental Health (NIMH), some funding was awarded to anthropologists to study marijuana use in Jamaica and Costa Rica. A few ethnographic studies of cocaine smoking were funded during the 1980s. In 1997, under the leadership of Dr. Alan Leschner, Director of the National Institute on Drug Abuse (NIDA), and Dr. Richard Needle, Branch Chief, several projects have been funded.

The two methodologies, defined and discussed below, have bred radically opposing outlooks. They are introduced as two among the many discourses on drugs.

WRITING ON DRUGS

Writing about drugs (or passing down thoughts and folklore about them orally) is almost as ancient a human practice as consuming them. The Chinese were among the first to set down their drug-related thoughts in pharmacopeias and treatises. The first medical uses of cannabis, for example, were documented in China, in an herbal text of the second century A.D., which chronicled oral traditions passed down from prehistoric times. At about the same time, the extensive use of cannabis in India was recorded in the *Atharva Veda*. The texts proved the antiquity of cannabis as a cultivated species in China and India and attested to its multitudinal uses. Pharmacopeias, compiled by herbalists and medical practitioners, remained the chief repository of knowledge about drugs until quite recently.

The religious texts, epic poetry, and dramatic works of several ancient civilizations offer another rich source of information about drugs and how different kinds of persons related to them. The Bible, which is crammed with references to wines and liquors, witnesses to the fondness that Hebrews, Egyptians, Persians, Greeks, Romans, Ephesians, and other contemporaries had for alcohol. Opium was also well known, and is mentioned in Homer's *Odyssey* as well as Virgil's *Aeneid*. The great Egyptian, Greek, Roman, and Arab physicians, such as Galen, Hippocrates, and Avicenna, wrote treatises about its use in medicine and as food.

It should not be forgotten that these ancient medical and literary references to drugs were supplemented by the other arts. Surviving stone tablets, pottery, statues, scrolls, drawings and paintings, mandalas, and embroideries, as well as actual drug paraphernalia (some very ornate) testify to the use of alcohol, cannabis, opium, coca leaves, tobacco, and other psychoactives in Asia, Africa, Europe, and the Americas since at least 5000 B.C.

Herodotus, the Greek traveler credited with being the "father of history," reported his sojourn among marijuana users in the fifth century B.C. The Scythians he had observed were nomads originating in Central Asia who inhabited areas near the Black and Caspian Seas at the time of his visit. They purified themselves during funereal rites by bathing in the smoke of burning cannabis seeds. Marijuana made the Scythians shout with joy:

> I must mention that hemp grows in Scythia, a plant resembling flax, but much coarser and taller. It grows wild as well as under cultivation, and the Thracians makes clothes from it very much like linen ones . . . and now for the vapor bath: on a framework of three sticks meeting at the top, they stretch pieces of woollen cloth, taking care to get the joins as perfect as they can, and inside this little tent they put a dish with red-hot stones in it. Then they take some hemp seed, creep into the tent, and throw the seeds on the hot stones. At once it begins to smoke, giving off a vapour unsurpassed by any vapour-bath one could find in Greece. The Scythians enjoy it so much they howl with pleasure. (Herodotus 515 B.C./1954, IV: p. 73)

Ibn Khaldun, the Arabic historian, also took a keen interest in marijuana and hashish. Suspicious of intoxification, the Koran had warned strictly and explicitly against all alcohol use, but because cannabis had long been cultivated in the Middle East, the birthplace of Islam, the eating or smoking of hashish and marijuana was usually tolerated, although not encouraged, throughout the Arab world. Ibn Khaldun commented on the customs and mores of this extensive Muslim demimonde.

In the 13th century, Marco Polo, the Venetian whose family had opened trade routes between Italy and China, drew attention to the relationship among drugs, crime, and violence. Apparently sensationalizing some accounts of his travels, he wrote of the threat posed by "hashishiyya," or thugs who robbed and killed under the influence of cannabis (Abel, 1980).

Tobacco was the great drug excitement of the 15th century, and Sir Francis Bacon was perhaps among the first to pen a modern antidrug tract, which warned against its pernicious effects. Columbus's helmsman, Rodrigo de Jerez, was probably the first modern drug felon, after he was imprisoned for tobacco smoking, which his prosecutors identified as "possession by the devil" (Doweiko, 1993).

In the 16th and 17th centuries, the works of sufis and poets, such as *The Rubáiyát* by Omar Khayyám, extolled alcohol, opium, and cannabis preparations. The Mughal art of India portrayed their use, while styles of music and dance were associated with them. In England, the English physician, Thomas Sydenham, wrote advertisements about laudanum, a tonic he had prepared from opium, which ensured its widespread adoption. In the same period, coffeehouses flourished, especially in England and France, and attracted a clientele of so many literary and artistic personages, who declaimed or exhibited their works-in-progress, that they were known as "penny universities," the penny being the cost of a cup of coffee (Meyer, 1954).

In Europe in the 18th and 19th centuries, yet another consumer revolution (see Chapter 1) enormously multiplied the number of commodities persons or households required for self-definition and status display (McCracken, 1988; McKendrick, 1982). The aristocratic, leisure classes of Britain and France especially craved to be thrilled and stimulated by perceptions that marvelously transformed drab, ordinary surroundings. They had both disposable income and time, in amounts surpassing what earlier generations had enjoyed, to invest in them. Invoking aristocratic privilege and revolting against the unremitting duties of the bourgeois moral code, they glorified the pursuit of "rare and exquisite pleasures." Defiantly labeling themselves "the decadent," they celebrated luxury and beauty instead of the virtues of the age, such as utility and efficiency. They re-created the euphorias to which they had been transported by their plentiful experiments with opiates, hallucinogens, and other psychoactives in sensuously detailed novels, poems, and paintings. An "opium eater," Thomas De Quincey (1856/1960) enthused:

> I was stared at, hooted at, grinned at, chattered at, by monkeys, by paroquets, by cocatoos. I ran into pagodas, and was fixed for centuries at the summit, or in secret rooms; I was the idol; I was the priest; I was worshipped; I was sacrificed. I fled from the wrath of Brama through all the forests of Asia; Vishnu hated me; Seeva lay in wait for me. I came suddenly upon Isis and Osiris. I had done a deed, they said, which the ibis and the crocodile trembled at. Thousands of years I lived and was buried in stone coffins, with mummies and sphinxes, in narrow chambers at the heart of eternal pyramids. (p. 241)

Arthur Rimbaud, J. K. Huysmanns, and Samuel Taylor Coleridge were other leading lights of 19th-century European literature who attributed part of their inspiration to the altered states to which hashish and opium had transported them. Coleridge composed the famous poem, "Kubla Khan," which children throughout Britain and the Commonwealth learn by heart, while in an opium trance. Sensibilities today echo with his images of "Xanadu," "treasure domes," "the sacred River Alph," and "bottomless caverns measureless to man!"

Two celebrated Parisians, the poet Charles Baudelaire and the novelist Theophile Gautier, formed Le Club des Haschishins (The Hashish Eaters Club), where they could convene like-minded fellows for joint experimentation with cannabis and opium. In his exhaustive, carefully observed, account of his first experience with hashish, Gautier (1845/1967) guides the reader through the sensations the club most valued—jeweled visions, a fantastic bestiary and fauna, synesthesia, out-of-body ideation, timelessness, and a noetic quality that climaxes in art:

> At the end of several minutes, a general numbness spread through me! It seemed to me that my body dissolved and became transparent. In my

chest I saw very clearly the hashish I had eaten, in the form of an emerald which gave off millions of tiny sparkles. . . . Around me streamed and rolled precious stones of all colors. In space, flower patterns branched off ceaselessly in such a way that I know nothing better with which to compare them than the play of a kaleidoscope. At certain moments, I saw my comrades again, but they were distorted, they appeared half-men, half-plants. . . . One of these gentlemen began to converse with me in Italian, but which the hashish by its omnipotence translated into Spanish for me. (p. 35)

Baudelaire and Gautier were at pains to keep their Club exclusive, and they cautioned their general readers about the risk of bizarre hallucinations or grotesque nightmares. Baudelaire's "artificial paradise" (1851/1995) contained many pitfalls for the unwary and the unworthy. Baudelaire and Gautier felt that only an elite of the most refined spirits deserved admission:

Take a piece as big as a walnut, fill a small spoon with it, and you possess happiness; absolute happiness with all its frenzies, its youthful follies, and also its infinite beatitudes. . . .

I forgot to say that as hashish causes an exaggeration of the personality at the same as a very sharp feeling for circumstances and surroundings, it is best to use it only in favorable circumstances and surroundings. . . . As far as possible, one should have a beautiful apartment or landscape, a free clear mind, and some accomplices whose intellectual temperament is akin to your own; and a little music too, if possible. . . .

The hallucinations begin. External objects take on monstrous appearances. . . . Sounds have a color, colors have a music. . . . Clear enchanting water flows. Nymphs with radiant flesh look at you with large eyes clearer than water and the sky. . . .

I do not say that hashish produces all the effects I have just described on all men. The phenomena I have described usually took place, with a few exceptions, among people of an artistic and philosophic spirit. But there are temperaments upon which the drug only develops a noisy insanity, a violent gaiety that resembles vertigo, dances, leaps, stamping, bursts of laughter. It can be said that their hashish is entirely materialistic. They are intolerable to those of a spiritual nature, who have great pity for them. The ugliness of their personalities becomes obvious. (p. 74)

The tradition of drug-enhanced literary and artistic expression continues to grow. Indeed, it is a striking observation that in the periods of popularity of the various drugs, each was accompanied by an art, letters and music that it had often directly inspired and that spilled over into dress, appearance, the argot and the areas of culture. Thus, in Europe, the enthusiasm for cocaine in the late 1800s and early 1900s found voice in the writings of Sir Arthur Conan Doyle and Oscar Wilde. Later in the century, Aldous Huxley, Jean Cocteau, Antonin Artaud, and Jean Genet, describing the inner journeys they undertook with the help of mescaline, morphine, opium, and heroin, articulated a Europe upturned by the savagery of two world wars and more influenced by Marxism, psychoanalysis, fascism, the persistence of contentious inequalities in society, and surrealism and the other great modern art movements. In the 1960s, as marijuana and the psychedelics replaced other drugs in popularity, the Beatles and other British and European bands produced a music that promoted non–Western philosophies, a pacifist ethic, sexual experimentation, and a countercultural lifestyle for youth. Young Jamaican immigrants, experiencing onset to marijuana in both Jamaica and the United Kingdom, converted to Rastafari, a religio-political movement, and invented reggae music. Rastafari distinguished themselves by wearing their hair in long, matted locks, by affecting African-style clothes, and by their speech (Hamid, 1980; Hebdige, 1979).

In America, the strong prohibitionist ethos marked but did not stem the same outpouring of expressions. A signer of the Declaration of Independence, Dr. Benjamin Rush, had published *An Inquiry into the Effects of Ardent Spirits upon the Human Body and Mind* in 1784, but that did not prevent Fitz Hugh Ludlow from publishing *The Hasheesh Eaters*, one of the earliest writings on American recreational marijuana use, in 1870; nor did it prevent Edgar Allan Poe from consuming opium and writing about it. In America, the sunny, drug-drenched utopias of the earlier European tradition were replaced by dread, difference, and terror. While the alcoholic and opiate worlds of William Faulkner, Ernest Hemingway, F. Scott Fitzgerald, and their peers were ribald, they were corroded by cynicism. For the next wave of writers and artists such as Allen Ginsberg, Ken Kesey, William Burroughs, Hunter S. Thompson, (and later) Andy Warhol and Jean-Michel Basquiat, heroin addiction and drug use had been the "angry howl" of a generation confronting racial segregation in the American South and the civil rights movement, battles on American streets between citizens and the police, the Vietnam War, and major realignments in the American economy and politics. Issues of women's and gay rights also wracked them (Farber, 1994). Not surprisingly, the postwar or "beat" generation concentrated on the darker or more dangerous aspects of experimentation with drugs.

In his landmark 1956 poem, "Howl," Allen Ginsberg, "saw the best minds of my generation destroyed by madness, starving, hysterical, naked, Dragging themselves through the negro streets at dawn looking for an angry fix . . . " (p. 126)

His "angelheaded hipsters burning for ancient heavenly connection to the starry dynamo in the machinery of the night," smoked marijuana, drank turpentine, alcohol, "ate fire in paint hotels," contemplated jazz (another suspect form) "in the supernatural darkness of cold-water flats floating across the tops of cities" and "bared their brains to Heaven." Their drug experiences ushered them through universities "with radiant cool eyes hallucinating Arkansas and Blake-light tragedy among the scholars of war." Expelled from academe and released in New York, they cowered "in unshaven rooms in underwear, burning their money in wastebaskets and listening to the Terror through the wall." (Ginsberg, 1956/1984, pp. 126–131).

For many of Ginsberg's friends, however, drugs also had a liberating and revolutionary side. For Hunter S. Thompson, the drugs which had produced his book, *Fear and Loathing in Las Vegas*, were also a guarantee of the omnipotence of his generation and had been taken in the absolute conviction that revolutionary ideas would prevail, ushering in an American age ruled by the young, purged of hypocrisy, imperialism, and the onus of "white supremacy." For Timothy Leary and Andrew Weil, drugs had played important roles in evolution thus far, and contemporary drug use would advance men and women beyond the hurtful contradictions of their times. Advising his students to "Turn On, Tune In, Drop Out," Leary (1965) explained: "When I first learned about psychedelic drugs I tried to apply them in a humanist context, not in a medical context, or a psychiatric context or a CIA brainwashing context, but as a tool for the individual to activate and operate his or her own brain. I was never advocating LSD [lysergic acid diethylamide]. I was advocating something much more subversive: think for yourself!" (p. 19)

Besides the "angry howl," therefore, drugs indicated hitherto uncharted realms of possibility for a new class of young middle class consumers. Instead of seeking the aesthetic rewards for which middle classes with access to disposable capital had yearned a generation before, these young Americans felt challenged by an incomplete social contract, which permitted indifferent elites to enjoy guilty pleasures, while the disenfranchised majority, in America and the rest of the world, was denied the basic requirements for productive, self-fulfilling lives. Drug users made concrete utopian dreams with actual grass-roots mobilization, identified the personal as also the political, stiffened the resolve to struggle, forged interpersonal ties across the barriers of social class and ethnicity, and helped propagandize radical and revolutionary agendas. The anti-war and civil rights movements furnished a platform for their coalition. Psychedelic drugs, prized above opiates for their properties of mind- and consciousness-expansion and as stimuli of social and cultural innovation and invention, were the preferred "sacraments," as Timothy Leary called the substances and practices which exercised minds and propelled them into what they considered more efficient, better adapted planes of functioning.

The "heaven and hell" of drugs, or these specific interpretations of them, soon engaged wider audiences. American drug commentary departed its restriction to middle-class literary, academic, and artistic circles in the 1960s but proliferated in a more plebeian and heterogeneous milieu when popular music, jazz, and pop art were legitimized as artistic expressions. The opiate indulgences of the great maestros and divas of jazz—Billie Holiday, Charlie Parker, John Coltrane, Dexter Gordon, and Miles Davis—were disclosed, and pop musicians such as Jimi Hendrix, Jim Morrison, Jerry Garcia, Paul McCartney, John Lennon, and Mick Jagger assumed their mantle and the advocacy of drugs. Their lyrics (whether the original San Francisco bands of the "psychedelic scene," heavy metal and punk rockers, or "grunge" from Seattle in the 1990s) evoked the same imageries, both the brilliant glories and the dark abysses of the drug-altered consciousness, but reached a more global audience than the somewhat arcane works of their original exponents. The greater mass appeal of rock music and the insatiable appetite of rock musicians for a smorgasbord of drugs (illegal heroin, cocaine, pills, and alcohol have contributed to many untimely deaths) made crusaders against drugs equally hostile to them. An irony of the age was the spectacle of President Nixon presenting Elvis Presley, who later died of an overdose of prescription drugs, with an award for protecting youth against the dangers of illegal drugs.

Thus, as the discourse on drugs was shifted during the 1960s to a dimension resting on very different premises than before, and as the Vietnam War polarized national political debate and gave it wartime stridency and urgency, the pro–war forces and the federal government rallied with a scientific assault on "drugs, sex and rock'n'roll."

PSYCHOPHARMACOLOGICAL AND EPIDEMIOLOGICAL APPROACHES TO DRUGS

The language of the sciences proved to be more persuasive than even the most popular artist. Sometimes an iconoclastic societal force (Sagan, 1997; Silver, 1998), as when Galileo battled with the Vatican, or later, as the discoveries of Darwin and Freud undermined the Christian orthodoxy, "scientific rationality" was enthroned as the ideological basis of the triumph of capitalism over feudalism (Butterfield, 1965). It scored decisive victories as scientists explained and vanquished mankind's hoary scourges: polio, tuberculosis, malaria, anthrax, and smallpox and cholera. These medical successes were based on the availability of the technologically advanced methods of laboratory science, such as microscopy, which enabled researchers to observe the actions of microorganisms, to isolate the pathogens that caused various diseases, and thus to devise effective antidotes. As Peele (1985) observed: "This approach has worked best in medicine with bacteria and some viruses in which a single disease agent could be identified and assaulted. Discoveries by such legendary microbe-hunters as Robert Koch, Louis Pasteur, and Joseph Lister led to the rout of many longstanding disease scourges through the sciences of bacteriology and immunology and the techniques of vaccination and sterilization." (p. 7)

At the same time, its origins and instrumentality in the struggle between social classes (for example, the bourgeoisie versus the *ancien régime*; or, today, between "modern" or Westernized elites and the representatives of other cultures) have justifiably engendered skepticism toward the claims of science (Feyerabend, 1993). In the case of medical research on psychoactive drug use, which flourished in a decade of revolutions, independence movements, and riots worldwide, and of unprecedented unrest in the United States, it was easy for scientists to surrender, or to be suspected of having surrendered, their professed ideal of disinterested, value-free objectivity. The mere pressure of economic dependence on the government for research funding could compromise scientists.

Thus, although the application of the "microbe-hunter model" to drug-related problems or to behavioral problems generally was problematic, substantial federal funding in the 1960s paid for the attempt. As the use of marijuana and psychedelics climbed from 3% to 50% among young middle-class European Americans, the National Institutes of Health, in a division reorganized as the National Institute on Drug Abuse (NIDA), began financing research on illegal drug use. Supporting 85% of all the research done in the world on drug abuse and addiction, the emphasis of NIDA-funded research is the study of precisely how specific drugs affect the brain and nervous system. Its stated goal was to find science-based prevention and treatment methods, ideally in the form of "chemical blockers" for the various drugs. NIDA funded medical researchers, epidemiologists, pharmacologists, clinicians, psychologists, psychiatrists, and survey takers to study the problem and provide solutions. Thus, writing on drugs took a new political, ideological, and theoretical departure.

The immediate drug threat to which the new thrust was applied and that preoccupied policymakers and researchers in that decade was marijuana. Several hundred studies of the drug were undertaken by NIDA-funded experts. Not surprisingly, given their preoccupation with disease and pathology, these studies found that marijuana smokers were deviant and sick. Some of the pathologies they discovered have extensively informed policy, media, public opinion, and drug education to this day. These disorders include those described below.

Amotivational Syndrome

The hallmarks of the syndrome are said to be "distressed awareness of self, apathy, confusion and poor reality-testing. . . . Many of those we observed were physically thin and often appeared so tired that they simulated the weariness and resignation of some of the aged; they all appeared older than their chronological age. This seemed to imply some form of organic change in the brains of chronic marijuana users" (Kolansky & Moore, 1971, p. 488).

In an influential study in the midst of the Vietnam War, Chopra and Jandu (1976), two Indian social scientists, frightened Americans with the intensity of the disaffection, rebellion and the "amotivational syndrome" that they had discovered among American marijuana smokers—hippies and "flower children"—traveling in India:

> Chronic cannabis use in heavy doses affects the central nervous system. The changes are related to the type of dose and the setting in which the drug is taken. Overall, the picture is one of depression and apathy. . . . Subjects who take smaller doses tend to be quiet, apathetic and disinterested in their surroundings; these changes are followed by permanent behavioral alterations, which are more marked under stress, starvation, poor health, and so on, resulting in an "amotivational syndrome." . . . Eighty-two (29.81%) individuals showed behavioral changes concerning lack of interest in work and family, a happy-go-lucky attitude, and other personality traits. In addition, 30 (10.9%) individuals, who mostly belonged to lower social strata, such as religious mendicants and other beggars, exhibited an "amotivational syndrome." They were generally ill-nourished and neglectful of personal hygiene. Excessive use is associated with personality inadequacies. Persons who exhibit emotional immaturity, low frustration tolerance, and failure to assume responsibility tended to be overrepresented in groups I and II, the heavy cannabis users. In behavioral terms, these traits are manifested in an unrealistic emphasis on the present as opposed to the future, a tendency to drift along in a passive manner, failure to develop long-term abilities or skills, and a tendency to favor regressive and magical rather than rational thinking processes. (p. 100)

Cannabis Psychosis

Some studies proposed that marijuana smokers were unpredictable and mentally unstable, as proposed further by Chopra and Jandu:

> . . . prolonged marijuana use in larger doses may induce psychosis in individuals with low psychotic thresholds. It may also produce hallucinations and psychomimetic effects, as seen in the stage of acute intoxication. . . . The effects were mostly of a mental nature that simulated toxic psychosis. . . . In India, there has always been a popular belief that prolonged and excessive use of these drugs leads to certain

types of mental disorder and crimes of a violent nature. In previous studies, we have discussed the relationship between hemp habituation and mental disease and crime. It became evident in these studies that excessive indulgence in these drugs by unstable and susceptible individuals was likely to produce states of confusion, characterized by hallucinations, delusions, and disorientation. Prolonged excessive use also appeared to lead to the development of toxic psychosis. (p. 101)

Mental and Physical Deterioration

Researchers were also convinced that, attending the "amotivational syndrome" and "cannabis psychosis," marijuana caused mental and physical deterioration. They warned that mental, affective, and behavioral changes were the most easily recognized consequences of marijuana use, and that concentration, motor coordination, and memory were adversely affected. For example, the ability to perform complex tasks such as piloting a plane was impaired even after the acute intoxication phase. The association of marijuana use with trauma and intoxicated motor vehicle operation was also thought to be well-established (Voth, 1994).

Brain Damage

In the aftermath of the Tet Offensive in 1968, when North Vietnamese troops routed the armies of the Saigon regime and the United States, the domestic battle over the advisability of the war reached unprecedented intensity. A beleaguered administration sought to discredit spokespersons against continued engagement. Thus it pleased supporters of the war to have scientific evidence that the growing ranks of protesters were in fact brain damaged:

> Critics state that marijuana has been shown to damage brain cells and that this damage, in turn, causes memory loss, cognitive impairment, and difficulties in learning. The original basis of this claim was a report that, upon post-mortem examinations, structural changes in several brain regions were found in two rhesus monkeys exposed to THC [tetrahydrocannabinol]. . . . However, to achieve these results, massive doses of THC—up to 200 times the psychoactive dose in humans—had to be given. In fact, studies employing *100 times* the human dose have failed to reveal any damage. . . .

> No post-mortem examinations of the brains of human marijuana users have ever been conducted. However, numerous studies have explored marijuana's effect on brain-related cognitive functions. . . . While there is general agreement that, while under the influence of marijuana, learn-

ing is less efficient, there is no evidence that marijuana users—even longterm users—suffer permanent impairment. (Zimmer & Morgan, 1995, p. 9)

Other pathologies included chromosomal loss, proneness to violence and criminality, amorality, and abusive and neglectful parenting.

Escalation/Gateway Drug

Finally, even if marijuana were acquitted on all other charges, it remained a "deceptive weed" (Nahas, 1975) that, while in it itself causing little harm, led invariably to other drugs, which did terrible damage: "The theory here is that marijuana is a 'gateway' to other drugs. That isn't Reefer Madness alarmism: reliable research shows that virtually all heroin and cocaine addicts started out with pot" (Bai, King, & Klaidman, 1997, p. 43). Of course, of the 64 million marijuana smokers in the United States, less than 4 million have ever experimented with heroin, cocaine, or other drugs, and less than 1 million have serious adverse consequences from using them (see Chapter 1).

ANTHROPOLOGICAL AND ETHNOGRAPHIC APPROACHES TO DRUGS

The conservative political bias of these studies and their lack of scientific rigor did not go unremarked. They frequently employed atypical samples, such as captive animal and human study populations, and investigated the effects of unusually large dosages in artificial, often hostile, settings to arrive at the foregoing results. The "gateway drug" theory simply contradicted the observations of the ordinary citizen:

Most users of heroin, LSD and cocaine have used marijuana. However, most marijuana users never use another illegal drug. Over time, there has been no consistent relationship between the use patterns of various drugs. As marijuana use increased in the 1960s and 1970s, heroin use declined. . . . Cocaine use increased in the early 1980s as marijuana use was declining. During the late 1980s, both marijuana and cocaine declined. During the last few years, cocaine use has continued to decline as marijuana use has increased slightly. . . . In short, there is no inevitable relationship between the use of marijuana and other drugs. In the Netherlands, for example, although marijuana prevalence among young people increased during the last decade, cocaine use decreased—and remains considerably lower than in the United States. Whereas approximately 16% of youthful marijuana users in the U.S. have tried cocaine, the comparable figure for Dutch youth is 1.8 percent. (Zimmer & Morgan, 1995, p. 14)

In his theory of set and setting, Zinberg (1984) argues that drug effects are mediated by society and culture. Drugs identical in form and potency may be administered to the same human stock, but with strikingly dissimilar results. Thus, the sociopolitical identities of the users, and the social and economic circumstances in which the drug was used, assumed prominence.

Becker (1963), for example, dismissing studies that purport to show cannabis-related brain damage or chromosome damage, has argued:

> Sociologists are unlikely to accept such an a-social and uni-casual explanation of any form of complex behavior, whatever the findings of pharmacologists and others. . . .
>
> What interests the social scientist is the problem of the drug-induced experience, taken in its own right. This interest reveals the following facts: (a) that "drugs" are accompanied by a wide variety of effects, only one or few of which the user may choose to experience. Thus the same drug may induce different experiences in different populations. And, (b) to say that users are seeking experiences not ordinarily available to them, is to say they will choose effects which are unconventional, or deviant; e.g. distortions in space and time, shifts in judgements of the importance and meaning of ordinary events. (p. 61)

Becker contends that "how a person experiences the effects of a drug greatly depends upon the way others define those effects for him." In other words, the "drug experience" and associated behaviors are intelligible only in an interactionist framework: that is, in a sociological framework as opposed to a biochemical one. Citing Mead, Becker writes:

> Objects have meaning for the person only as he imputes that meaning to them in the course of his interaction with them. The meaning is not given in the object, but is lodged there as the person acquires a conception of the kind of action that can be taken with, by, toward, and for it. Meaning arises in the course of social interaction, deriving their character from the consensus participants develop about the object in question. (p. 62)

Anthropological research has been a useful corrective to psychopharmacological studies. It differs from these approaches principally because it is the only scientifically rigorous method that observes drug users (and drug traffickers) in their naturalistic settings. Following the pioneering work in Jamaica, in which heavy marijuana smokers were observed in six rural communities (Rubin & Comitas, 1975), anthropological research on this drug has been undertaken in Costa Rica (Partridge 1980), Trinidad (Hamid, 1980), and Greece (Comitas, 1983).

Anthropology emphasizes the social, economic, cultural and political parameters of the phenomena being studied. A discipline that is also concerned to demonstrate that all human beings are fundamentally alike, share the same basic instincts, and have common obligations to one another, it relates patterns of individual behavior and belief to the environments in which human groups live, and documents how these adaptations have evolved since the primate past and may change in the future. A holistic science, it focuses on the study topic as it manifests among humans taken as whole organisms who adapt to their environments through a complex interaction between biology and culture. Its investigation of social problems in modern societies draws on a wealth of experience and theories about human conduct derived from the exhaustive studies the discipline's pioneers had performed on a myriad topics in small-scale, homogeneous, preindustrial groups in many parts of the world (Harris, 1968). The techniques of inquiry fashioned for small groups proved ideal for the study of special and hidden modern populations, such as drug users and distributors.

These methods of inquiry, or ethnographic fieldwork, are unique and central to anthropology. Direct participant observation is paramount. Its aim is to present an authentic and coherent grasp of the cultural system in which drug users and distributors participate. While relying on the concepts and words of informants, however, the anthropologist incessantly matches observed behavior with its spoken or other symbolic representation. A dialectic between eye and ear and the (always) different worlds they unveil contributes to the richness of ethnographic reporting. Meanwhile, adding to the complexity, the ethnographer herself or himself is not unmoved by what she or he sees and hears.

The most important result of ethnographic research is to reinsert the drug user in the ordinary walks of everyday life, and to seek the meanings of his or her behaviors in those contexts. The user is first seen as sister, brother, kinsperson, neighbor, co-worker, political/cultural agent, and fellow citizen. Drug use and distribution are viewed in the web of relationships engendered by these statuses. Whereas many studies had focused exclusively—and thus misleadingly—on those who have had severe problems with drugs, such as hospitalization and arrest, ethnographers take note of the full range, including the many users who have *never* encountered such problems and have remained invisible to researchers employing other methodologies.

The validity and reliability of ethnographic research lies in its thoroughgoing empiricism. It uses indigenous informers, speaking in their own language, framing thoughts with familiar concepts, and analyzing them with a native intelligence. Ethnography relies on four core features:

1. *Ethnography is always a community study.* The first task the ethnographer undertakes is to get to know the patterns of life in a local community (Arensberg & Kimball, 1972). The information puts the phenomena under

study in a general perspective and contextualizes the study's final results. In Chapter 8, drug phenomena, such as use, distribution, effects, and psychosocial outcomes, are seen to differ by neighborhood, and it is argued that neighborhoods form a proper unit for observing and analyzing them.

Continued residence in the study community is the ideal research situation. Whereas anthropological fieldwork originated in 1-year to 2-year stints abroad, however, prolonged stays are difficult in working with hard-to-reach urban populations. The ethnographer, usually with academic and other professional obligations herself or himself, strives to sustain as much continuity and contact in the field as possible through daily visits. Many rent a local storefront or apartment for interviews, from which they also recompense study participants with what services they can provide. Ethnographic work is labor intensive, but probably does not cost more than surveys (see Chapter 1).

2. *The ethnographer's principal research tool is her/himself—body, mind, spirit, and training.* Anthropologists are very specially trained to have an apperception of the social or cultural dimensions of behavior, and to cultivate holistic thinking. A kind of tension builds in this person: the phenomena resonate off it. This is the reading an ethnographer makes—on a scale of inner struggle, rather than on a stethoscope—the results of a battery of tests, analyses of dreams, or a statistical correlation.

As a rule of thumb, an ethnographer is ready to make useful statements about the study sample when no one any longer takes much notice of her or his presence in their midst. From this hard-earned position, the ethnographer can observe and listen with minimal interference of the data.

3. *The ethnographer uses informants, rather than subjects, patients, clients, and respondents.* Realistically, ethnographers can enjoy an in-depth relationship with only a few key informants, and they must take great care to ensure the latter's representativeness. An intimate bond eventually unites them, and the informant performs frequently as a parent, guiding the ethnographer through the social and cultural field, pointing out noteworthy features, teaching the names of entities, and explaining them. The inverse of the power relation between subjects, patients, clients, respondents and their respective professionals obtains between informant and ethnographer: the latter pays and says "thank you."

4. *The ethnographic research program is multivariate, developmental, and recursive.* If a line of inquiry does not account for a sufficient number of facts, or does not entirely consume the ethnographer's curiosity about the objects under study, its lack of rigid structure permits her or him to pursue others.

Finally, a special kind of analytic thought process is required of anthropologists—*abduction*, as outlined by Agar (1996):

> First of all, new concepts have to exist at the end of the study that did not exist in the original research problem. Often people describe research as inductive or deductive, with ethnography said to exemplify the former and hypothesis-testing the latter. What this split leaves out is the concept of *abductive* research.
>
> Ethnography is abductive, a term invented by Charles Pierce, one of the founders of American pragmatism, around the turn of the century (Hookway, 1992). Abduction is about the imaginative construction of a *p* that implies an observed *q*, or, to put it in our terms, about the modification of frames that explain rich points. . . . Rich points are problems in understanding when an ethnographer learns that his or her assumptions about the world and the way it works, usually implicit and out of awareness, are inadequate to understand something that had happened. . . . *Frame* names knowledge structures [which allows the ethnographer] to link up different kinds of knowledge in different kinds of way at different levels . . . and its goal is to set up expectations rather than concrete predictions. *Participant observation* makes the research possible; *rich points* are the data you focus on and *coherence* is the guiding assumption to start you off on the research that those rich points inspired. . . . Abduction is a research logic that features the development of new theoretical propositions to account for material the new propositions didn't map onto. Ethnography is theory generating, a strength realized some time ago in the Glaser and Strauss (1967) term, or *grounded theory*.

With deductive research, one starts with concepts, derives hypotheses, and then measures the variables in that hypothesis to test it. With inductive research, one gathers some data, then asks what the data tell us about the prior system of concepts. That's why they call it inductive statistics.

Both of these approaches are *closed with reference to the original of concepts*. In one case the data are controlled by the hypothesis; in the other case, they aren't. But the final results are dressed up in the same concepts, come what may.

This is one reason, incidentally, why anthropology-type ethnographers often have problems with ethnographic studies from other disciplines. Sociologists, for instance, tend to work within the same theoretical systems as their more deductive colleagues. They start their work ethno-graphically, in the sense that they make plenty of room for the people they are interested in to talk and act in their own way. But then in the analysis of those materials, the sociologists often jump in and classify data in those of prior theoretical concepts.

Anthropological ethnographers don't like this much. They see data as containing their own patterns, their own concepts, and they view analy-sis as a long-term effort to figure out what those concepts might be. Maybe the events do eventually map onto some available theory; but if they don't, so much the better. The new concepts bring you closer to the world of the people you worked with than available theoretical concepts ever could have.

That's how abduction works. Instead of, from p we derive q, or from q we derive p, the logic changes to, what kind of p do I need such that this new and interesting q makes some kind of order.

So, *necessary condition number one*: if a piece of research doesn't pro-duce new concepts, concepts that take you closer to the world that is the object of research than previous understandings could have, then it isn't ethnographic. No abduction, no ethnographic.

A good ethnography will overwhelm the reader with the way new con-cepts and patterns account for this variety of information in surprising and unexpected ways. . . . *Strips* are ethnographic data, strips of experi-ence, be they segments of an interview or sequences of behavior en-countered in participant observation or even passages in a novel or film or archival document. . . . The more the number and variety of strips that the pattern accounts for, the more *massively determined* that pattern is. When the number and variety of strips escalates to some level—I have no idea how to tell when you reach it—the pattern is *over-determined* as well. (pp. 31–40)

Overdetermination supplies one kind of proof of ethnographic findings. This book draws heavily on the *overdetermined* patterns the author has uncovered as an anthropologist researching drugs for the past 20 years and on those articulated by other ethnographers.

Discussion Questions

1. Make a list of films, novels, videos, or other media treatments of drugs. Review them and report on themes, attitudes, portrayals of behavior and character, and understandings.

2. Collect and review some of the religious and literary texts mentioned in the chapter and analyze the references to drugs: uses, justifications, beliefs, recommended behaviors, and effects.
3. Make a list of popular ballads and songs that mention drug use. Recall the succession of popular musical styles since the 1940s and discuss their relation to the use of particular drugs.
4. Discuss the relationships among art, altered states of consciousness, and drug use.
5. Persons tell stories—including scientific ones—for definable social reasons. Stories help the storyteller to present herself or himself; they are meant to make specific impressions on listeners, and their contents are one kind of cultural inventory. Relate the different types of writing on drugs to the specific types of society in which they occurred. Why do persons tell these drug stories?
6. Contrast and explain the two tendencies in drug-related literary and artistic expression: dread, difference, and terror on the one hand; utopias and paradises on the other. Identify artists of both schools and discuss their works.
7. What is science?
8. Review and discuss the scientific literature on a variety of drugs, such as nicotine, alcohol, cannabis, cocaine, the opiates, amphetamine, or Ecstasy. Comment on samples, research settings, hypothesis generation and testing, data collection procedures, analysis, inference making, and theory and results.
9. Make a chronology of anthropological works on drugs. Where were studies conducted? Who formed the sample? How were the drugs investigated and what were the conclusions? Specify what the ethnographers did to obtain data.
10. Make an inventory of "common knowledge" about drugs in the reader's community. How does it differ from the scientific understandings? How would the latter improve the communal debate about drugs. How could it be brought to the local public's attention?
11. Do some research on the principles of ethnography and read some actual ethnographic monographs. Discuss the uses of ethnography for exploring a variety of social problems: drug use, other criminal behavior, health care, housing and homelessness, or employment.

REFERENCES

Abel, E.R. (1980). *Marihuana: the first twelve thousand years*. New York: Plenum

Agar, M. (1996). *The professional stranger: An informal introduction to ethnography*. San Diego, CA: Academic Press.

Arensberg, C., & Kimball, S. (1972). *Culture and community.* Gloucester, MA.: Peter Smith.

Bai, L., King, C., & Klaidman, B. (1997, February 3). Cocaine and kids. *Newsweek,* p. 43.

Baudelaire, C. (1851/1995). *Du vin et du hashish (Artificial paradises).* New Brunswick, NJ: Citadel Press.

Becker, H.S. (1963). *Outsiders: Studies in the sociology of deviance.* London: Free Press of Glencoe.

Butterfield, H. (1965). *The origins of modern science: 1300–1800.* London: G. Bell and Sons.

Chopra, G., & Jandu, B. (1976). Psychoclinical effects of long-term marijuana use in 275 Indian chronic users: A comparative assessment of effects in Indian and USA users. *Annals of the New York Academy of Sciences, 282,* 95–108.

Comitas, L. (1983). *Opprobrium and persecution: Hashish users in urban Greece.* Unpublished manuscript.

De Quincey, T. (1856/1960). Confessions of an English opium eater. London: Dent.

Doweiko, H.E. (1993). *Concepts of chemical dependency.* Pacific Grove, CA: Brooks/Cole.

Farber, D. (Ed.). (1994). *The sixties: From memory to history.* Chapel Hill, NC: University of North Carolina Press.

Feyerabend, P. (1993). *Against method.* New York: Verso.

Gautier, T. (1845/1967). Hashish. In G. Andrews, & S. Vinkenoog (Eds.). *The book of grass.* (pp. 56–60). New York: Grove Press.

Ginsberg, A. (1956/1984). Howl. In A. Ginsburg, *Collected poems, 1947–1980.* New York: Harper & Row (Perennial Library).

Glaser, B., & Strauss, A. (1967). *The discovery of grounded theory.* Chicago, IL: Aldine.

Hamid, A. (1980). *A precapitalist mode of production: Ganja and the Rastafarians in San Fernando, Trinidad.* Dissertation, Columbia University/Ann Arbor, MI: University Microfilms.

Harris, M. (1968). *The rise of anthropological theory: A history of theories of culture.* New York: Harper.

Hebdige, D. (1979). *Subculture: The meaning of style.* New York: Methuen.

Herodotus. (515 B.C./1954). *The histories.* Harmondsworth, U.K.: Penguin Books.

Hookway, C. (1992). *Pierce.* London: Routledge.

Kolansky, L., & Moore, W. (1971). Effects of marijuana on adolescents and young adults. *Journal of the American Medical Association, 216,* 486–492.

Leary, T. (1965). *The politics of Ecstasy.* London: Paladin.

McCracken, G. (1988). *Culture and consumption.* Indianapolis, IN: Indiana University Press.

McKendrick, N. (1982). *The birth of a consumer society: The commercialization of eighteenth century England.* Bloomington, IN: Indiana University Press.

Meyer, H. (1954). *Old English coffee houses.* Emmaus, PA: Rodale Press.

Nahas, G. (1975) *Marijuana: The deceptive weed.* New York: Raven Press.

Partridge, W. (1980). Cannabis and cultural groups in a Colombian municipio. In V. Rubin (Ed.), *Culture and cannabis,* (pp. 147–172). The Hague, Netherlands: Mouton.

Peele, S. (1985). *The meaning of addiction.* Lexington, MA: Lexington Books, D.C. Heath.

Rubin, V., & Comitas, L. (1975). *Ganja in Jamaica: A medical anthropological study of chronic marijuana use.* Paris: Mouton.

Sagan, C. (1997). *The demon-haunted world: Science as a candle in the dark.* New York: Ballantine.

Silver, B.L. (1998). *The ascent of science.* New York: Oxford University Press.

Voth, E. (1994). Should marijuana be legalized as a medicine? No, it's dangerous and addictive. In *The world and I*. Washington, DC: The Washington Times Corporation.

Zimmer, L., & Morgan, J. (1995). *Exposing marijuana myths: A review of the scientific evidence*. New York: The Lindesmith Center, Open Society Institute.

Zinberg, N.E. (1984). *Drug, set, and setting: The social bases of controlled drug use*. New Haven, CT: Yale University Press.

CHAPTER 3

Drugs and Labor

Chapter Objectives

In order to use drugs in the modern age, one can no longer climb a tree and reap them. The user must earn and spend dollars first. "Earning" and "spending" are structures of behavior that exist independently of drugs. "Dollars" exchanged in drug worlds have a necessary affinity with other dollars in the community, and behave according to a logic that governs dollars. It does not originate in the drug experience. From this outlook, drug users and distributors are identified as special types of laborers who earn and spend money; they labor in the informal economic sector, which has been tied indissolubly to the capitalist corporate economy since the 13th century; drugs are commodities that are exchanged for money.

In the field of drug studies, one of the most innovative results of the ethnographic reinsertion of the drug user into the quotidian life of communities is the view of her or him as a worker, who, like the remainder of the laboring population, sustains the community by earning and spending money. Although they may deviate from the majority in the uncommon ways by which they generate and dispose of their income, drug distributors, users, and misusers nevertheless perform those same vital functions.

In the traditional psychopharmacological approach to drug studies described in Chapter 2, the conviction that drug users or misusers are "losers" who are incapable of working is deeply entrenched. Some scholars add that a penchant for violence and lawbreaking, which disqualifies them for other employment, attracts individuals to drug distribution. In that chapter, a link was established between the emerging field of government-funded drug research and the fright of middle-class Americans confronting the alienation of their youth. Also reflected in it was the anxiety of American businessmen competing in newly forming global markets. Authorities, reacting to "drugs, sex and rock'n'roll," feared that an "amotivational syndrome" would infect the work force, cripple business, and disable the armed forces in Vietnam.

As "anthropological" ethnographers try to reconstruct the total, social life of a specific community, however, they usually find it nearly impossible to identify an idler among the able-bodied and firm of mind, even in populations having high rates of "unemployment." For the most part, persons keep their eyes open and are very busy!

An outstanding exemplar of the methodology, *Ganja in Jamaica* (Rubin & Comitas, 1975) focused its findings to refute the claim that marijuana users damaged their productive capability. The study found that most rural Jamaicans who smoked ganja (marijuana) were extraordinarily diligent peasants who invested impressive amounts of time and energy in multiple income-bearing schemes every day of the year. Starting before sunrise, they tended livestock and poultry; farmed gardens; hired out their labor for wages; exchanged goods and services in an indigenous marketing system; maintained churches, self-help associations, political parties, guilds, schools, and households; and sometimes, at night, clandestinely cleared acres of forest to cultivate marijuana. They listened to the radio, watched television, and read newspapers to perform better as citizens in a modern democracy. These active, clearsighted economic strategists and community builders depended on a heavy daily intake of ganja for nourishment as "brain food," and relied on it specifically to improve production. Adult Jamaican marijuana smokers consumed some six or more large "spliffs" (hand-rolled cigars) of ganja a day, or a few ounces. They also consumed it in teas, tisanes, and tonics. As employers, they preferred to pay their employees ganja rather than money and encouraged its use in the workplace (Rubin & Comitas, 1975).

In their preoccupation with hard labor, Jamaican marijuana smokers were reviving one of the essential features of the ganja complex, which had been diffused from India to them by Indian indentured laborers in the mid-1800s. In a remarkable case of survival over some 5,000 years and across multiethnic national boundaries, this culture of marijuana use had been built around the drug's religious and sacramental properties and its beneficial effects on labor and productivity, as the Indian Hemp Drugs Commission noted in 1894:

> The use of these drugs to give staying power under severe exertion or exposure or to alleviate fatigue is very largely in evidence. Hence it is ganja especially which is credited with these beneficial effects. For ganja [for smoking] is far more extensively used than bhang [a beverage] among the laboring classes. The latter is mainly used by persons like the Chaubes of Mathra, who are frequently referred to, and profes-

sional wrestlers. Gymnasts, wrestlers, musicians, palki-bearers [rick-shaws] and porters, divers and postal runners, are examples of the classes who use the hemp drugs on occasions of especially heavy exertion. Fishermen and boatmen, singhara cultivators working in tanks, dhobis [washers] and nightwatchmen, mendicants and pilgrims, are named among those who use them under severe exposure. All classes of laborers, especially such as blacksmiths, miners and coolies, are said more or less generally to use the drugs as a rule in moderation to alleviate fatigue. (Kaplan, 1969, pp. 181–182).

During the 1970s, in a later period of extensive marijuana use in the Americas, and when in the Caribbean it had slipped out of its confinement to Jamaica, young Caribbean Africans on the other Caribbean islands and in immigrant communities abroad, whom unemployment had left restive and frustrated, were introduced to the drug. Not only had they been denied access to jobs in the formal corporate economy, but the modernization and development plans had commoditized and thus discontinued prosperous lines of indigenous production (see the Informal Economic Sector below), which had gainfully occupied their parents and even earlier generations.

Marijuana smoking exploded their inertia. Responding to a growing demand for the drug among the salaried working and middle classes, they briskly organized and dominated cultivation, street sales, and export of the drug. An international trading network formed rapidly, through which they exchanged other contraband as well as legitimate goods, such as electronics and designer clothes. Reinvesting profits according to the Rastafari ideology, a religion to which many marijuana distributors had converted and that emphasized spiritual and material self-sufficiency, they launched a substantial program of grassroots, indigenous renewal, funding schools, newspapers, farms, residential and commercial properties, health food stores and restaurants, groceries, transportation services, and other lucrative, legitimate enterprises. One was marijuana centered—Rastafari music, or reggae—which not only bequeathed millions of dollars in sales of recordings, but also introduced world-renowned cultural icons, such as Bob Marley and Peter Tosh.

By rescuing individual lives and reintroducing them to meaningful, profitable work, marijuana also built up communities as a whole. By emulating the Rastafari marijuana distributors, their nondistributing but marijuana-smoking co-religionists modeled a myriad enterprises on the self-reliant ganja economy (Hamid, 1980, 1991a, 1997a).

Nevertheless, the myth of the feckless drug addict has persisted. Thus, in the heroin-injecting epidemic of 1964–1972 among minority, inner-city males in New York City, Los Angeles, and San Francisco, social scientists claimed (falsely) that street gang members avoided heroin use because they were resourceful, aggressive, well-integrated boys who were "reality-oriented" in their street environment. Instead, passive, anxious, inadequate boys who could not adapt to street life injected it (Chein, Gerald, & Rosenfeld, 1964). Others branded them "retreatist" and "double failures," who qualified neither for legitimate nor illegitimate pursuits (Cloward & Ohlin, 1960).

This same cohort of drug users, however, were championed by two outstanding ethnographers in East Harlem, who specifically discredited an additional imputation of cowardice and ineffectuality:

> It is often said that the use of heroin provides an escape for the user from his psychological problems and from the responsibilities of social and personal relationships—in short, an escape from life. . . . [Our study] contradicts this widely held belief. Their behavior is anything but an escape from life. They are actively engaged in meaningful activities and relationships seven days a week. (Preble & Casey, 1969, p. 1)

In more recent times, drug users typically have not stopped working, but their duties have grown more onerous, more risky, and less rewarding.* For example, in the cocaine smoking epidemic of the 1980s, the laboring lives of users and misusers, far from being terminated, worsened: they worked harder, for less remuneration and under mortal threat. The most observable new feature of existence into which they were ushered, when cocaine had replaced marijuana as their preferred drug, was their altered income-generating capability (Hamid, 1991a, 1991b, 1992a). All the African-American, Caribbean-African, and Latino persons in the low-income neighborhoods of New York City who participated in research on the drug experienced marked transformations of their laboring lives after onset to smokable cocaine.

Consider, for example, the young woman who, before 1984, might have spent a typical day moping about the house, half-stupefied by Olde English Ale (a cheap, popular brand of malt liquor popular at the time) and a nickel bag ($5.00) of reefer (marijuana). Past her boosting (shoplifting) years, she might expect to get drunk with friends during the day, or to play cards and listen to music or watch the soaps, or to entertain the man (or men) from whom she receives sporadic supplements to her public transfer income. Once in several years she may participate in a welfare fraud operation (organized by a male relative), or hit the numbers or take advantage of some adventitious criminal opportunity that earns extra money. So far, she has avoided any engagement with the criminal justice system. Introduce smokable cocaine or crack in 1984, however, and she is on the street, as smartly dressed as progressive involvement with the drug will allow her, busily begging men in pass-

---

*The following 20 paragraphs have been adapted with permission from A. Hamid, Drugs and Opportunity in Inner City, in A. Harrell and G. Peterson (eds.), *Drugs, Crime & Social Isolation*, pp. 209–238, © 1992, Urban Institute Press.

ing cars for a couple of dollars, or however else she "vics" (victimizes) others, abruptly assaulting and robbing a victim, busily running to the crack spot, exchanging dollars for crack, consuming crack and "beaming up," robbing family and neighbors, then returning to the street to begin the cycle again—over and over again for several days until she collapses. The street vocabulary, which portrays the female crack misuser as "vic-ing" innocent passersby, was often ironic. In most cases, it was she who was compelled to sell sexual services for survival, and was more likely to be victimized, both sexually and economically. But she generated dollars in 1984 that she had not generated previously, and that nothing but crack would have induced her to generate.

Or consider the young man who had, pre-crack, a successful routine at Macy's and other department stores on Flatbush Avenue in Brooklyn, he and his accomplices returning from daily forays with arms full of expensive leather jackets and dozens of designer watches. After initiating crack use, they disbanded and discontinued this successful criminal enterprise, adopted desperate low-level crack distribution roles, or put a gun to a shopkeeper's head in a hastily contrived robbery attempt. Again, dollars were generated at a rate, a pace, and a volume not seen before. Smokable cocaine's most critical effect in low-income, inner-city neighborhoods was to reshape the local labor market. Loss of employment, afflicting mostly middle-aged, middle-income persons was another salient feature of the period. While distributors ranged from grandmother to adolescent, interview after interview at places where crack was used confirmed that middle-aged, middle-income men and women were indeed the predominant users.

Although the "War on Drugs" had been engaged to "save America's youth," their elders were actually the victims of the smokable cocaine epidemic. Mature workers are an asset to any community. They are the backbone of local-level home ownership and improvement of the physical plant, sports, politics, religion, tenant patrols, and parent-teachers associations. Often an "old head" or mature worker may cultivate an entourage of younger persons, to whom he teaches the values of work and responsibility and whom he places eventually in actual employment (Anderson, 1990). Mature workers are also a medium by which class and ethnic integration can be accomplished. The decline of American inner cities could not have proceeded so rapidly if a substantial class of middle-aged, middle-income workers had been active.

What happened to the many Caribbean Africans, Latinos, and African Americans who remained resident in the inner cities after they had gained jobs as professionals, entertainment and media personnel, corrections officers, policemen, junior executives, bank tellers, supervisory staff, small businessmen and contractors, skilled or unionized workers, clerks, and secretaries during the early 1970s and after the 1982–1983 recession? Many made rendezvous with smokable cocaine. Heartbroken by divorce, plagued by disease, tossed by unruly appetites, restless in their jobs, confused by the arrival at long last of affluence, the drug charmed and ensnared them. By the end of the decade, they had lost jobs, savings, homes, family, reputation, and self-worth (Hamid, 1992a, 1997b).

The aftermaths of their stories affirmed that a rigorous, common labor-market logic was at work in them, rather than merely contingent crises or the accidents of an individual tragedy. Having lost well-paid jobs and commanding positions in their families and community, middle-aged, formerly middle-income crack misusers were often satisfied with low-paid, intermittent work in the immediate neighborhood. The shape of the local labor market, therefore, had been altered. The bottom tier of "non-competing" laborers (Doeringer & Piore, 1968) had expanded, while retrenchment (the redundancy of both persons and positions, as well as minimal job creation) had shrunk the ranks in primary and secondary tiers of better-paid workers in more secure employment.

For example, Bert, a 31-year-old Trinidadian-African study participant and former electronics technician, was adept at discovering or creating bottom-tier work. Within a small radius of his mother's home in Flatbush, he trimmed hedges, stacked garbage, carried loads, assisted neighbors in home repairs, swept and cleaned driveways and sidewalks, and washed cars. By working close by, he was able to smoke crack at home during the day when his mother was at work. Another advantage was that he stayed close to the crack distributors he knew best, and to his circle of co-users.

In Central Harlem, another study participant, Reggie, had lost his job as a senior hospital employee. Soon after a bitter divorce, he had become a cocaine smoker. Following a few months of homelessness, he was taken in by his friend Chuck, who managed some city-owned low-rent apartment buildings. Chuck, who smoked cocaine, had allowed his basement home in one of these buildings to convert into a "freakhouse." In 1990, Reggie was involved in a staggering number of exchanges almost every day. Chuck, who had soon promoted him to second in command at his apartment, or freakhouse (see Chapter 8), explained that he had given Reggie the post because "he is a hustler. If you need something for the apartment and you tell him about it, it is here [tapping the table for emphasis]. Look, right now he's with Sandy at the church [close by] hustling for some food. And he'll always look out for me" (Hamid, 1992a, p. 232). Chuck pointed an interviewer to a discarded washing machine that Reggie had hauled back to the apartment and repaired. He was hoping to sell it for at least $50.

Reggie himself stated his belief that "New York is paved with gold: people throw away fantastic things, sometimes brand new, which you can scavenge and re-sell." He described himself as a "jack of all trades": fixing cars, doing carpentry, performing construction jobs. He had been seen in the neighborhood selling big, black plastic bags, probably "scammed" at (stolen from) a construction site. On another occasion he was selling gallon cans of paint. In several of these undertakings, labor was contributed by Chuck or other co-residents and fellow crack misusers of the freakhouse (Hamid, 1992a).

"Scrapping," or retrieving and selling scrap metal, was a growth industry during the decade of cocaine smoking. Scrap-metal yards (where metal was weighed, bought and sold) in Brooklyn thrived, and several new yards sprang up, near which crack distributors immediately set up shop. Although it was hard work, scrapping nevertheless brought in a guaranteed daily income. Scrappers were regularly seen around the neighborhood pushing shopping carts filled with odd pieces of metal. They were good at spotting the valuable types (copper and aluminum, for example) and could wring profit out of sites (abandoned buildings or heaps of garbage) that appeared valueless. Scrappers in Bushwick had mapped out trajectories so that each had her or his own route and storage places across the section, which others did not molest.

A specialized variant of scrapping was the retrieval of beverage cans and bottles. The decision to refund a nickel for empty beverage cans and bottles coincided nicely with the period of widest diffusion of crack use. Subsequently, a good place to find crack misusers and polydrug misusers was in the vicinity of depots that exchanged the retrieved items for cash.

Some labor entrepreneurs learned that shelters for the homeless, where many crack misusers slept and ate, formed pools of readily exploitable labor. They were to be seen in the morning at some of the bigger shelters in Brooklyn, recruiting day laborers for such work as "picking" (sorting through and selecting valuables from discarded clothes or garbage), selling watches or other merchandise on sidewalks (under pain of arrest, a day in custody and forfeiture of merchandise), and demolition (removing debris, stairways, and fire escapes from abandoned buildings). The investigation of the murder in the 1980s of a New York City couple at one of several upstate resorts for the elderly revealed that during the summer season, homeless persons were brought in by contractors from New York City to work as kitchen help or in maintenance. Detectives and journalists interviewed many who claimed to be crack misusers, and a news photograph showed one laborer smoking crack.

Many crack misusers managed to secure regular, if low-paid, employment after they had lost better jobs. Typically, however, their employment was both minimum-wage and transient. After one study participant had lost his $50,000-per-annum job as a captain in the Corrections Department, he held a series of jobs that never paid more than $19,000. He was dismissed from each in turn for theft or fraud. In between jobs, he spent several months in treatment (residential, outpatient, frequent attendance at meetings of Alcoholics Anonymous). Unemployed at the time of his last interview in 1991, he was negotiating to spend the next 2 years in upstate New York in a therapeutic community. (A person who helped considerably in several research projects on smokable cocaine or crack, he has been clean and sober since 1994, has reunited with his family, is partner in an auto-repair business, and recently bought a home.)

When middle-aged, middle-income men gathered to smoke cocaine, they attracted bevies of female peers or slightly younger women in their neighborhoods to the practice. Like the young woman considered above, their lives as workers were also dramatically transformed after becoming cocaine smokers. The burden of maintaining an increasingly expensive crack habit forced them onto the street, where straitened conditions obliged them to engage in multiple episodes of prostitution and other criminality (Hamid, 1992a, 1997b; Maher, 1996). Coming very rapidly under the surveillance of several state agencies of social control, and after losing homes, children, and public support as a result of suspected child abuse or neglect, many of these women were forced to depend entirely on "hustling" and sex-for-crack exchanges to survive.

However, women's "hustles" were strikingly different from those of male crack misusers. The "mission" was the street word that summarized the multiple, unique tasks that both male and female crack misusers performed in order to procure crack or cash. But it was sharply gender differentiated. Some women exchanged sexual and other services for money or the drug on missions that lasted several days nonstop. Earning little for these work marathons, they reaped mainly public opprobrium and jail sentences.

These two types of cocaine smoker prodded yet a third segment of the population into unusual labor, namely the younger men of the neighborhood, often their sons, nephews, and junior brothers, who shunned cocaine smoking themselves, but hastened to sell it. As arrests piled up, they too found themselves eligible only for the lowliest work, if they were not excluded from the work force entirely. Often they had to supplement their meager earnings from crack distribution with the proceeds from other crime.

Thus, in succumbing to cocaine smoking, middle-aged, middle-income, seasoned workers not only withdrew substantial wealth, brawn, and intelligence from the upkeep of families and neighborhoods, but also permitted the bottom-tier labor market to expand. In the bottom-tier labor market, laborers received subsistence wages, or payment in kind (drugs, food, shelter) in exchange for long hours of work, with virtually no protection and at high risk of arrest, incarceration, violent injury, or health problems. First the middle-aged workers themselves were recruited to this unique category of labor; next came the coeval men and women whom they had introduced to the drug, followed by the successive waves of young distributors who sold it to them (Hamid, 1992a, 1997b).

Crack revenues were reckoned in several billion dollars and were rapidly removed from inner-city neighborhoods and put to use in the corporate, mainstream economy, either through Southern Florida banks (which launder drug money) or through the reinvestments of the cocaine cartels and their associates throughout the Americas. Thus, crack misusers constituted one of many "noncompeting" working forces, which are indispensable to the global corporate economy.

THE INFORMAL ECONOMIC SECTOR

If drug users and distributors are to be viewed as a laboring population that performs indispensable functions in the composite economic life of the community, it is in the informal economic sector, or the underground economy, that they contribute their labor.

In the 1960s, researchers in Latin America, Asia, and Africa reported sectors of urban economic enterprise that participated in the overall economy, but were at the same time distinct from it. For example, in Trinidad and Tobago and Rio de Janeiro, a small army of workers is mobilized, for at least 6 months in the year, to produce their world-famous carnivals. Indeed, the Trinidad carnival has been integrated with fledgling ones on the other islands and in Caribbean-African communities throughout North America and Europe, and provides year-round employment (Hamid, 1983a). Independently of banks and other official institutions, the carnival personnel provide the financial and fiduciary services, researchers, a clerkdom, and the many types of artisans, costumers, and musicians to produce the event, which may last from a single day to a week. In other Catholic capitals in Latin America, year-long employment is provided for food vendors, manufacturers of religious relics, and ritual specialists who cater to the feast days of several saints. Hindu India employs a similar labor force to celebrate a bursting calendar of national and regional holidays. In Southeast Asia, the kitchens and kitchen gardens of city homeowners are factories where bean curd, condiments, pickles, or other foodstuffs are prepared for local and international markets.

Sidewalks along streets in major Third-World cities are thronged with unlicensed vendors selling goods of every description, and the trend extends to New York City, where more than 10,000 sidewalk vendors operate throughout the year. They congregate especially in midtown, Chinatown, and at Africa Square (125th Street and Lenox Avenue) in Harlem. On Labor Day, or Caribbean-American Day, thousands more line Eastern Parkway in Brooklyn. More recently, Mexicans and Central Americans have installed curbside *taquerias* in midtown Manhattan and in the city's Latino communities. In the cities of the Third World, very many necessities of life—food, shelter, clothing, medical care, spiritual and mental therapy, education, entertainment—are completely satisfied by self-made tinkers, tailors, cooks, builders, artists, "quacks," or other service providers.

Some theorists, relying on a broad definition of informal-sector activity, include the "criminal" or underground economy as part of this sector (e.g., Gaughan & Ferman, 1987; Mattera, 1985), while others reserve the term to apply properly only to "income-generating activities that take place outside the framework of public regulation, where similar activities are regulated" (Sassen-Koob, 1991, p. 89). For example, very many enterprises in the informal economic sector are illegal, and carry the disability for its proprietors of being unceremoniously removed from the place of business, goods and all, by the police. Technically, the sale of goods offered by street vendors and the services provided by doctors or dentists who practice without licenses, or the religious services rendered by ritual specialists whom the state has not recognized, could be undertaken in the formal economy. Criminal activities (including the distribution of drugs), however, are differentiated by their exclusion from other economic sectors. This study adopts the first, more inclusive definition of informal sector activity: especially in regard to the features described below, there is little to choose between selling drugs or selling peanuts at a street corner in Harlem or Flatbush.

Thus, several features of this sector distinguish it from the formal or corporate capitalist, economic sector. Enterprises in the informal sector tend to be small and locally based, usually employing fewer than 15 workers. Several economic indices distinguish such businesses from similarly sized, small-scale capitalist enterprises. They are modestly capitalized. Wages are adjusted to provide bare self-sufficiency for workers. Many exchanges are by barter rather than by cash. Access to labor is furnished by appeal to folk culture or by kinship and ethnic ideologies. Redistribution of wealth, or capital redeployment, is regulated by the same informal contracts that bind labor.

Some enterprises, however, bring affluence and political clout to their proprietors. In Ghana and Nigeria, market women are sources of substantial credit, and sponsor youth groups or other voluntary associations that sometimes assume overt political functions. In South Africa and Angola, "shebeens," or "yards" where women brew and sell beer, and where the beer is consumed nightly by crowds of males, have also been the centers of political activism in the two countries. In Jamaica, "higglers," or itinerant female vendors who link kitchen gardens in the remote countryside with urban households, also transfer politically sensitive information and serve as creditors in a mixed portfolio of rural and urban business undertakings (Katzin, 1959).

In Italy, where estimates suggest that the informal economy represents about 30% of the gross national product (Mattera, 1985), Sicily hosts an informal economic sector sufficiently large to support a "development elite," which controls large voting blocs, agricultural holdings, and entrepreneurial concerns. The "development elite" is opposed to the "modernization elite," which recruits from urban professionals and administrators. While the former approves economic programs for Sicily that emphasize indigenous wealth, talents, and skills, the latter believe that economic growth means greater reliance upon foreign capital and management (Schneider, Schneider, & Hansen, 1972).

In Bolivia, where 80% of the entire economy is based on the production and export of coca, the informal economy has surpassed the formal economy and dominates economic and political life (Craig, 1990). Coca cultivation and cocaine production have penetrated and bolstered existing informal economic sector activities to the point where the size of illegal transactions is equivalent to the balance of trade (Jimenez, 1989).

In the United States, estimates of the size of the informal economy vary from $42 billion to $369 billion (Feige, 1979; Mattera, 1985; McCrohan & Smith, 1986). A recent survey of the cash-exchange component of the informal economy (which ignored drug distribution and sales and other criminal activities) estimated informal expenditures at $42 billion, suggesting that the informal economy accounts for approximately 11.5% of all domestic transactions (McCrohan & Smith, 1986). While these estimates are generally regarded as unreliable (Portes & Sassen-Koob, 1987), a growing body of research indicates that informal-sector activities in major cities in the United States have expanded considerably over the last decade (Sassen-Koob, 1989). Although illegal or the object of various forms of official suppression, the informal economic sector abides in a symbiotic relation with the formal sector (Henry, 1988). Poorly paid workers in the formal sector survive from day to day, and are deterred from labor unrest, because the informal economic sector provides them with cheap or affordable goods and services. Retired workers are heavily reliant on them to make ends meet. And meantime, in the preparation of goods and services, manpower is trained and developed, without costing government training programs or educational resources, and capital is accumulated that eventually may be incorporated into the formal sector.

On the other side of the coin, the availability of capital through sources other than the legally recognized ones and of labor earning less than the minimum legal wage (if necessary) are important prerequisites, when the entrepreneur is uncouth, without creditworthiness and lacking in accredited business and managerial skills for that thrust into the mainstream world. An immigrant especially must first turn to cousins, co-religionists, or his ethnic ties in order to become later an employer who uses employees (Ianni & Ianni, 1972; Light, 1972).

RELATIONSHIP OF INFORMAL ECONOMY TO FORMAL ECONOMY

The coexistence of capitalist enterprise with other forms of economic activity originates in the 13th and 14th centuries, when the former was being established. When capitalist entrepreneurs were initiating such capitalist forms of enterprise as cattle herding and the urban economies in Western Europe, Eastern Europe experienced its "second feudalism." To supply Western Europe with grain and other foodstuffs made scarce by the capitalist novelties in land use, feudal arrangements in Eastern Europe were doubly enforced (and with unprecedented cruelty) in a drive to increase agricultural production (Malowist, 1972).

The reciprocal relationship has continued between the formal corporate sector of the economy and informal economies as capitalist forms of enterprise took root throughout the world (Long, 1984; Meillassoux, 1981). In the Americas, the informal economic system has had a special significance for the African population, among whom it originated in the plot of land planters ceded to slaves four centuries ago. Although the planters intended to reduce their operating costs by prodding slaves to feed themselves, the latter cherished the land as a free space, where African traditions could be revived. They also built a complex internal marketing system by exchanging their agricultural produce. This backbone still supports local trade and rural-urban exchanges in contemporary Haiti and Jamaica.

In the United States, the shift to informalization has necessitated a restructuring of relationships between core and periphery workers. Much agricultural production now utilizes the mix of labor provided by illegal immigrants, homeless populations, and drug users. Recently in New York, a famous fashion designer was arrested for maintaining a sweatshop of Latino seamstresses in the Bronx who were undocumented aliens. To produce her prize-winning fashions, therefore, this designer depended upon the labor of her distributors, such as Bloomingdale's, and upon unionized garment workers and truckers. But the profit margins of the whole enterprise rested upon "unfree," "noncompeting" labor in the informal sector. Much of agricultural production in the United States also utilizes this mix of labor. Indeed, two candidates for high governmental offices in the Clinton administration were disqualified because their housekeepers belonged to this category of workers.

Today, both the formal and informal economic sectors are integrated internationally and respond to global cycles of expansion and depression (Wallerstein, 1974). Corporate, capitalist enterprise is an international entity in which multinational corporations perform crucial functions. The bloc of nations in which it is represented will soon include the republics of former Soviet Russia and the Eastern European nations. In these latter countries, conditions are ripe for the growth of local segments of the informal economy, which has also become an international entity. One of its main pillars, the drug trade, which orchestrates the efforts of growers in rural parts of the world, those of processors and importers in several countries, and finally those of distributors in capital cities, exemplifies its transnational, multicultural character.

On a global level, the trend toward informalization has been accelerated by economic recession and the transition to a postindustrial service economy (Sassen-Koob, 1989). Global multinational corporations utilize workers in the Third World to produce their products at subsistence wages while workers in the West are forced into low-paying service jobs and the informal economy (Portes & Sassen-Koob, 1987). While many different kinds of activities are suited to informalization, however, it is the boundaries of state regulation that determine informalization rather than the characteristics of particular activities: the informal economy "is a highly opportunistic process with changing boundaries" that can only be understood by reference to "the basic dynamics that induce informalization" (Sassen-Koob, 1991, p. 89).

DRUG SWITCHING

Ethnographic experience of the complete developmental cycle of the cocaine smoking epidemic has enabled researchers to differentiate and describe six stages through which it progressed. Successive contexts for cocaine use, and especially the six-stage cycle for cocaine smoking, permitted the diffusion of the practice from one social segment to another, erasing social distinctions, creating new ones, and allowing cocaine to acquire new meanings and effects (Hamid, 1992b).

The developmental cycles of successive drug epidemics cannot be viewed independently of the broader political economy in which they are situated. The modus operandi, income generation, and spending behavior of both distributors and users were transformed from stage to stage (see Chapter 9).

Moreover, ethnographic research has identified a distinctive pattern that characterizes the relationship between the informal and the corporate sectors of the economy. The pattern alternates between coexistence and absorption (Hamid, 1991a, 1991b). In the first stage, both sectors thrive, or the informal sector actually overtakes the mainstream economy in productivity and prosperity (especially in developing countries and underdeveloped or used-up sections of the developed nations, such as the decaying inner cities). For instance, in the 1940s and 1950s, capitalist developers in many Third-World countries experienced labor shortages, as they were unable to detach labor from its traditional pursuits in indigenous, pre-capitalist production (Myrdal, 1944).

In the later stage, however, the accumulated wealth, skills, talented labor, and the political and cultural values of the informal sector are absorbed wholesale by the corporate economy, stripping it bare (Hamid, 1983a, 1983b). The absorption or commoditization of indigenous lines of production through the modernization and development plans of the late 1950s and 1960s, described in Chapter 2, is an example. The relationship then reverts to the first stage. This pattern explains drug switching, or at least the replacement of marijuana in the 1970s by cocaine in the 1980s. In the earlier decade, marijuana had restored and "built up" the structure, functions, and values of the informal economic sector in the Caribbean and Brooklyn, and its principal distributors, the Rastafari, supplied the hearts and minds that accomplished the task (see above). But after significant capital accumulation in the 1970s, the later stage was repeated, and it was again emptied out by smokable cocaine in the 1980s,* especially when the drug had assumed a commodity form as crack.** In 1997, the informal economy appears to be completing the pattern by returning again to the first stage. Marijuana is regaining popularity after smokable cocaine has wrought its worst ravages. Now mainly a domestic product, it is "building up" communities in Kentucky and Illinois (Weishert, 1992), as it had done formerly in the Caribbean, Colombia, Mexico, Hawaii, Southeast Asia, and elsewhere abroad.

The burgeoning marijuana traffic of the 1990s (Hamid et al., 1997) is perhaps only one arena of a recovery of the whole informal economic sector (Sassen-Koob, 1989). Also unresearched, its health may be gauged nevertheless in a cursory glance around the city. For example, street vendors have taken possession of sidewalks in many sections of the five boroughs, and comprise a multicultural, transnational labor force of immigrants with global linkages who have arrived only since the 1990s. Those from Mexico operate sidewalk *taquerias*, Andeans exhibit hand-woven woolens, Arabs and Bangladeshis sell books and fruit, Chinese specialize in children's toys and candy, and Francophone West Africans offer all manners of goods (watches, scarves, T-shirts, leather goods, souvenirs, and ornaments of carved wood and brass). Some enterprising Senegalese women stroll along 125th Street, where the jammed sidewalks already exhibit many previous, successive waves of vendors, with baskets full of platters of West African food (vegetable purées, stews, and fried meats over *jolloffe* [red] rice), which they sell exclusively to the polyglot sidewalk vendors. Legitimate store owners on 125th Street recently halted traffic in a demonstration to protest the presence of so many

---

*Thus marijuana built up neighborhoods in the late 1960s and in the 1970s, and was experienced as benign, when social policy and the corporate economy generally enabled local neighborhood revival. By contrast, smokable cocaine "emptied out" communities during the 1980s, and was experienced as a disaster, when a shift had taken place in the global economy to permit the vast and rapid accumulation of capital in very few hands (Mandel, 1980; Phillips, 1990). The same shift had also prompted the internal migration of millions of peasants in the Eastern Andes, bumper harvests of coca leaves, the overproduction of cocaine hydrochloride powder, and the cartelization of its distributors in Colombia—factors that made the drug available to inner cities in America in the first place (Craig, 1990; Morales, 1989). In the latter, minority users and distributors of smokable cocaine then became an additional labor force, which accomplished critical tasks in the same global process of concentrating and consolidating wealth.

**Cocaine markets, as well as those for smokable cocaine, assumed a commodity form as crack when cultivation, production, and export were cartelized in Colombia, triggering a trend toward hierarchical, tightly organized distribution that was expressed at street level in American cities by posses, gangs, or other crack-distributing businesses (see Chapter 5). Simultaneously, use was separated from sales.

sidewalk vendors in the city. They complained that they were suffering business losses as a result.

As the international corporate sector is linked more tightly through cooperative understandings like the General Agreement on Tariffs and Trade (GATT) and the North American Free Trade Agreement (NAFTA), bringing increased trade and more prosperity to capitalists and workers throughout the world in the high-technology fields favored by governments and the various elites in every participating nation, the remaining hope of employment and survival for growing numbers of displaced, underqualified, or excluded workers will be the informal economy. If the example of the Rastafari in the 1970s were followed and elaborated, marijuana could be a tremendous resource for them. The compound tragedy of the "crackhead" or street-level crack distributor in the South Bronx was that, although he labored extraordinarily long hours for little personal pleasure or compensation, his efforts did not improve the social and environmental stock around him either. Instead, the money he generated at such great personal cost was invested far away from him and the South Bronx, and strengthened the mainstream world in the same process by which his, and the South Bronx's, status and tenure in it grow slighter. The female crack misuser (and very minor distributor) was exploited and alienated even more.

This view of drug users and distributors is a reminder that everybody works in a capitalist world, and especially in America. All Americans do indispensable work in the present order of the economy. There is no other way to exist. The indissoluble bond of the dollar yokes us to it. If a man is homeless or lives in a city shelter and is addicted to drugs, it is to enable him better to do the work of a bottle retriever, who is refunded 5 cents for each bottle or can retrieved. If this worker next buys coffee and a roll, he not only maintains coffee growers and importers or a bakery, but more important he upholds the principle of consumerism upon which business depends. The money he spends on cocaine is a flying buttress, thrust upward by the informal economy, which supports the same principle. An anthropologist at a Queens, New York, shelter for homeless, psychiatric, drug-misusing men noted a well-educated young African-American resident who spent each day collecting about $23 worth of bottles and cans. Before returning to the shelter in the evening, he would go to the liquor store and exchange all the money for a bottle of Taittinger's champagne!

Discussion Questions

1. Read the references on the topic, pursue others, and discuss the origins and development of capitalism as a set of social relations and as an economic system. Pay close attention to its coexistence with other types of economic activity in the same social formation.

2. Discuss types of labor and hierarchical systems of labor in various social systems.
3. Discuss conceptions/conditions of work and the relation of drug use to them in different periods of American history.
4. Discuss the conditions of work in rural Jamaica, and their relation to marijuana use, as described in *Ganja in Jamaica*. Consult other ethnographies that depict laboring lives in other cultures, and note the roles played by drugs.
5. What substances or activities are recommended to boost energy in the reader's community? Do they work? If work could be enhanced by a chemical, should workers consume it for that reason, especially if there are no side effects? Should athletes use drugs to enhance performance? Should drugs be designed to improve memory or other abilities?
6. Comment on the differential roles of marijuana and cocaine in Caribbean immigrant communities in New York City. What forms of drug distribution exist in the reader's community? How do they perform in terms of providing work, generating income, and the reinvestment of revenues?
7. Give a picture of economic life in the reader's community. Differentiate, describe, and estimate the sizes of informal and formal economic sectors.
8. Illegal drug use was nearly nonexistent in America as the country mobilized for the righteous World War II and was fully employed in wartime industry. Would full employment and high national consensus discourage drug use today?

REFERENCES

Anderson, E. (1990). *Streetwise*. Chicago: University of Chicago Press.

Chein, I.D., Gerald, R.L., & Rosenfeld, E. (1964). *The road to H: Narcotics, delinquency, and social policy*. New York: Basic Books.

Cloward, R.D., & Ohlin, L.E. (1960). *Delinquency and opportunity: A theory of delinquent gangs*. Glencoe, IL: Free Press.

Craig, R.B. (1990). South American drug traffic: Domestic impacts and foreign policy implications. In J.A. Inciardi (Ed.), *Handbook of drug control in the United States* (pp. 207–227). Westport, CT: Greenwood Press.

Doeringer, P.B., & Piore, M. (1968). *Internal labor markets and manpower analysis*. Lexington, MA: D.C. Heath.

Feige, E.L. (1979). *The irregular economy: Its size and macro-economic implications*. Madison, WI: University of Wisconsin Press.

Gaughan, J.P., & Ferman, L.A. (1987). Towards an understanding of the informal economy. *Annals of the American Academy of Political and Social Sciences, 493*, 15–25.

Hamid, A. (1980). *A precapitalist mode of production: Ganja and the Rastafarians in San Fernando, Trinidad*. Ph.D. dissertation, Teachers College, Columbia University/Ann Arbor, MI: University Microfilms.

Hamid, A. (1983a). Brooklyn carnival: From periphery to core, use value to commodity. Paper presented at the Colloquium in Applied Anthropology, Teachers College, Columbia University, New York.

Hamid, A. (1983b). The Grenadian invasion. Paper presented at the Colloquium in Applied Anthropology, Teachers College, Columbia University, New York.

Hamid, A. (1991a). From ganja to crack: Caribbean participation in the underground economy in Brooklyn, 1976–1986, Pt. 1. *International Journal of the Addictions, 26*, 735–744.

Hamid, A. (1991b). From ganja to crack: Caribbean participation in the underground economy in Brooklyn, 1976–1986, Pt. 2. *International Journal of the Addictions, 26*, 615–628.

Hamid, A. (1992a). Drugs and patterns of opportunity in the inner city: The case of middle-age, middle-income cocaine smokers. In A. Harrell & G. Peterson (Eds.), *Drugs, crime and social isolation: Barriers to urban opportunity* (pp. 209–239). Washington, DC: Urban Institute Press.

Hamid, A. (1992b). The developmental cycle of a drug epidemic: The cocaine smoking epidemic of 1981–1991 [Special issue, J.A. Inciardi, Ed.]. *Journal of Psychoactive Drugs, 24*, 337–349.

Hamid, A. (1997a). *The political economy of drugs, Pt. I: Ganja and Rastafarians in Trinidad and New York.* Unpublished manuscript.

Hamid, A. (1997b). *The political economy of drugs, Pt. II: The cocaine smoking epidemic in New York City's low income minority neighborhoods, 1981 to 1991.* Unpublished manuscript.

Hamid, A., Curtis, R., McCoy, K., McGuire, J., Conde, A., Bushell, W., Lindenmayer, R., Brimberg, K., Maia, S., Abdur-Rashid, S., & Settembrino, J. (1997). The heroin epidemic in New York City: Current status and prognoses. *Journal of Psychoactive Drugs, 29*, 375–391.

Henry, S. (1988). Can the hidden economy be revolutionary? Towards a dialectical analysis of the relations between formal and informal economies. *Social Justice, 15* (3–4), 29–59.

Ianni, F.A.J., & Ianni, E.R. (1972). *A family business.* London: Routledge & Kegan Paul.

Jimenez, J.B. (1989). Cocaine, informality, and the urban economy in La Paz, Bolivia. In A. Portes, M. Castells, & L. Benton (Eds.), *The informal economy: Studies in advanced and less developed countries.* Baltimore: Johns Hopkins University Press.

Kaplan, J. (Ed.). (1969). *Marijuana: Report of the Indian Hemp Drugs Commission, 1893–1894.* Silver Spring, MD: Thomas Jefferson Publishing Co.

Katzin, M.F. (1959). The Jamaican country higgler. *Social and Economic Studies 8* (5). Mona, Jamaica: Institute of Social and Economic Research.

Light, I.H. (1972). *Ethnic enterprise in America: Business and welfare among Chinese, Japanese and Blacks.* Berkeley, CA: University of California Press.

Long, N. (1984). *Miners, peasants and entrepreneurs: Regional development in the central highlands of Peru.* Manchester, UK: Institute for African Studies, University of Zambia/University of Manchester Press.

Maher, L. (1997). *Sexed work: Gender, race, and resistance in a Brooklyn drug market.* New York: Oxford University Press.

Malowist, M. (1972). *Croissance et regression en Europe, XIVe–XVIIe siécles: Récueil d'articles.* Paris: A. Colin.

Mandel, E. (1980). *Late capitalism* (rev. ed.). Atlantic Highlands, NJ: Humanities Press.

Mattera, P. (1985). *Off the books: The rise of the underground economy.* London: Pluto Press.

McCrohan, K.F., & Smith, J.D. (1986). A consumer expenditure approach to estimating the size of the underground economy. *Journal of Marketing, 50*: 48–60.

Meillassoux, C. (1981). *Maidens, meals and money: Capitalism and the domestic community.* Cambridge, U.K.: Cambridge University Press.

Morales, E. (1989). *Cocaine: White gold rush in Peru.* Tucson, AZ: University of Arizona Press.

Myrdal, G. (1944). *An American dilemma: The Negro problem and modern democracy.* New York: Harper & Brothers.

Phillips, K.P. (1990). *The politics of rich and poor: Wealth and the American electorate in the Reagan aftermath.* New York: Random House.

Portes, A., & Sassen-Koob, S. (1987). Making it underground: Comparative material on the informal sector in western market economics. *American Journal of Sociology, 9*(3), 30–61.

Preble, E., & Casey, J. (1969). Taking care of business: The heroin user's life on the street. *International Journal of the Addictions, 4,* 1–24.

Rubin, V., & Comitas, L. (1975). *Ganja in Jamaica: A medical anthropological study of chronic marijuana use.* Paris: Mouton.

Sassen-Koob, S. (1989). NYC's informal economy. In A. Portes, M. Castells, & L.A. Benton (Eds.). *The informal economy: Studies in advanced and less developed countries.* Baltimore, MD: Johns Hopkins University Press.

Sassen-Koob, S. (1991). The informal economy. In J. H. Mollenkopf & M. Castells (Eds.), *Dual city: Restructuring New York.* New York: Russell Sage Foundation.

Schneider, J., Schneider, P., & Hansen, E. (1972). Modernization and development: The role of the regional elites. *Comparative Studies in Society and History, 4,* 328–350.

Wallerstein, I.M., (1974). *The modern world system: Capitalists, agriculture and the origins of the European world economy in the sixteenth century* (Vols. 1–2). New York: Academic Press.

Weishert, R. (1992). *Domestic marijuana: A neglected industry.* Westport, CT: Greenwood Press.

CHAPTER 4

Policing Drugs

Chapter Objectives

The police were not formed to combat drug use, but to maintain law and order as the privileged classes defined them. As waves of immigration augmented European and North American societies, the police functioned as an increasingly numerous and powerful acculturation agency, which sometimes welcomed foreigners brutally. Drug laws were handy instruments in this task, and drug laws and policing evolved apace. Through policing drugs, the United States is establishing an international enforcement regime. But the attempt to police a popular activity for which some persons have convincing justifications is inherently criminogenic.

The great revolutionary movements of the 20th century have been based in part on a vision of a future society that would not require central control and instruments of coercion. For example, Lenin (1932) predicted that in a Communist Russia there would be no need for police:

> Finally, only Communism renders the state absolutely unnecessary, for there is no one to be suppressed—"no one" in the sense of a class, in the sense of a systematic struggle with a definite section of the population. We are not Utopians, and we do not in the least deny the possibility and inevitability of excesses on the part of individual persons, nor the need to suppress such excesses. But, in the first place, no special machinery, no special apparatus of repression is needed for this; this will be done by the armed people itself, as simply and as readily as any crowd of civilised people, even in the modern society, parts a pair of combatants or does not allow a woman to be outraged. (p. 26)

Furthermore, criminal offending would vanish because the bleak conditions of life that marked pre-Communist Russia—the repression, economic deprivation, and general lack of hope experienced by ordinary people and the poverty-stricken "masses"—would be eliminated.

Of course, only a very few people in the world today live in communist societies, and in most modern-day societies, where crime and violence coexist with remarkable and continuing improvements in the standard of living for many, the police endure as the principal (and increasingly powerful) agency of "law enforcement."

Drug use or misuse is one of those individual excesses that Lenin might have found it necessary to curb. Drug prohibition raises fundamental questions about the relation between society and its members: can (or should) the appetites of individuals be policed? Can persons be forced to give up powerful gratifications from drugs or certain forms of sexual, artistic, or religious expression because they offend or cause (putative) harm to others? A further complication is that societies routinely agree to allow some of these drugs and behaviors while proscribing others. For example, Americans approve of alcohol and tobacco consumption, although they are no less potentially destructive than the substances they have outlawed. Male genital mutilation, or circumcision, is a universal practice in American hospitals, while female genital mutilation among some African immigrants has been criminalized recently.

The inquiry on this topic plumbs the modern psyche, especially in America, uncovering dilemmas and contradictory impulses. The ideals (or constitutional guarantees, when they exist) of unfettered immigration, equality of opportunity, multiculturalism, individualism, and hedonism are compromised by restrictive policies, unequal competition, the exploitation of labor, class struggles over wealth and power, interethnic conflict, the tension between the corporate economy and other economic activity, and a tendency to moral righteousness and social conformity. These quandaries are to be decided on the most explosive (and definitively American) political battlefields, such as negotiating the most comfortable balance between the rights of individuals versus their obligation to the social whole.

Adding to the complexity of these issues is the unlimited heterogeneity of the American population, which continues to absorb immigrants upon whose widely divergent moral codes it has been difficult to impose a standard order. And of course, America's drug policy has also been shaped by ignorance, hysteria, corrupt demagogues, and lawmakers intent on advancing their political careers.

Thus, although the idea of infringing on individual liberties is usually repugnant to Americans, drug prohibition has been upheld because it furthered agendas and responded to fears that actually had little to do with drugs. The latter furnished a stage, for example, for acting out xenophobic fears against many ethnic groups in succession, such as Mexicans, Chinese, Haitians, Dominicans, or African Americans. The alleged alcohol abuse of Irish immigrants justified their repression as an unruly labor force. The condemnation of the bejeweled drug dealer of newspaper lore dramatized the antagonisms between formal and informal economies, or the storekeeper's rage, stoked by steadily rising overhead costs, against the sidewalk vendor. Drugs, rather than the contingencies of an everyday life shaped by social conditions and policy (Sharff, 1997), explained the monstrous fertility of low-income women and why they abused their children. The pleasures of drugs could not be denied, or maybe there was no intention to restrict them, but the "dangerous other" could and should be.

Unsurprisingly, because the prohibition of widely desired goods and services thus frequently masks diffuse aggression against substantial segments of national populations it aborts:

> . . . in many cases the attempt to use the criminal law to prohibit the supply of goods and services which are constantly demanded . . . is one of the most criminogenic forces in our society. By enabling criminals to make vast profits from such sources as gambling and narcotics; by maximising opportunities for bribery and corruption; by attempting to enforce standards which do not command either the respect or compliance of citizens in general; by these and in a variety of other ways, we both encourage disrespect for the law and stimulate the expansion of both individual and organized crime. . . . (Morris & Hawkins, 1970, p. 27)

The policing of prostitution, gambling, drink, and other drugs has particular criminogenic and iatrogenic costs (Dixon, 1995; Parliamentary Joint Committee, 1989).

This chapter aims to guide the reader through these complex issues. It describes the evolution of the modern system of drug policing in America. The symbiotic relationship between the growth of law enforcement agencies and the ever-expanding "crisis" of drug use is explored. It analyzes what policemen actually do in their daily intercourse with drug users and distributors, and how all parties are affected by the encounter. It discusses the discretionary powers that policemen routinely and legally use.

POLICING LABOR AND MAINTAINING ORDER

"Let us say that discipline is the unitary technique by which the body is reduced as a 'political' force at the least cost and maximized as a useful force" (Foucault, 1979, p. 6). The police were not brought into being to discourage or eliminate drug use. Instead, their oldest and most constant functions have been to discipline un-

ruly laborers on behalf of their employers and to ensure that the look and utiliza-
tion of public spaces conformed to the latter's ideal of them. In applying the much
more recent drug laws, policemen keep faith with this tradition.

These functions have existed since antiquity. The earliest records of law enforcement as a tool to achieve social control antedate the ancient Romans and
Greeks, reaching even further back, to the rulers of the ancient civilization of
Sumer. The system of policing that is entrenched throughout the West today, however, is based on the structure developed in England in the first part of the 19th
century.

At that time, the influx of impoverished farm workers to England's urban centers led to extremely dense concentrations of people in towns and cities. This period was marked by egregious working conditions for child and adult laborers
alike. The almost unbearable quality of life at home and at work for the mass of the
population instilled in the governing elite a desperate fear of mass unrest. This
possibility was only exacerbated by the new industrial form of labor, which had
alienated the worker from the product of his work. This fear was certainly not
unfounded. For example, in the city of Leicester, Luddites (workers led by Ned
Lud, who had rallied them to oppose the technological changes that had devastated their livelihoods) smashed labor-saving machinery (Cole & Postgate, 1972).
The advent of the industrial revolution, coupled with economic problems associated with the Napoleonic wars, such as the soaring price of corn, aggravated national crime rates. The easy availability of cheap alcohol (as had been the case
since the gin era of 1720–1750) contributed to this rising crime rate, and the laboring classes as a whole were stigmatized for alcohol abuse (Miller, 1977).

In light of these developments, English leaders recognized the need for sizable
urban police forces to enforce the peace, quell social unrest, and disperse strikes
and unruly gatherings of alcohol-affected laborers. In 1829, Robert Peele (considered the father of modern policing) proposed that London's municipal government employ a corps of civilians to maintain law and order. Each member of the
corps was given a salary, provided with a uniform, and armed with a truncheon. In
the same year, the British Parliament passed the Metropolitan Police Act, which
established a blueprint for the basic structure and organization of this new police
force. This proved to be of long-lasting influence, and the modern-day police
forces of the United States are still based on the original system established by
Robert Peele (Richardson, 1970).

In America, the colonial experience influenced the evolution of policing. Public
order and security in the original 13 states against internal as well as external
threats were maintained by appointed officials and burgher militias. The militias
could be called upon for night watch duties, to light street lamps, to anticipate or
repel attacks by Native Americans, and to control rowdy sailors, prostitutes, and
drunkards. Policing was also undertaken by the British Army, and after Indepen-

dence, alternately by paid forces and citizen levies. By 1800 in New York City, a force of 72 men, known as "leatherheads," since their only uniform consisted of leather helmets, was serving under two captains and two deputies. Workers by day, they slept during their nighttime police duties, when they were supposed to be protecting citizens against disorder, fires, and graveyard-robbing medical students. Finally, inspired by Sir Robert Peele in England, Mayor William F. Havermeyer established a "day and night police" of some 800 men in 1845. Nicknamed the "star police" because of the star-shaped badge they wore, they constituted the first modern American police force (Fogelson, 1977; Richardson, 1970).

THE EFFECTIVENESS OF POLICING

As the majority of current drug offenses have turned out to be street crimes (see below), it is useful to review the success of the police in maintaining public order generally. How effectively did uniformed men on the street discourage drunkards, sex workers, pickpockets, thieves, or other pedestrian criminals? How many men were needed before a positive effect was achieved? What was the ratio between such a reduction in crime and the cost of the policemen? The pertinent question in relation to drugs would be: Did any number of street arrests lessen the quantities of drugs entering the country, their internal distribution, or the number of persons willing to experiment with or use them?

Studies have given mixed answers to these questions. In an East Harlem precinct, where police strength had been doubled during a 4-month experiment to test whether more uniformed men deterred more crimes, the more public episodes of mugging, car theft, and breaking and entering were drastically reduced, but murders and assaults were unaffected. A study of subway crime—robberies of passengers and token booths—showed that the presence of police officers on trains did prevent the occurrence of many crimes. The studies had no way of determining, however, whether the averted criminal acts were then performed elsewhere.

Nonetheless, when policing is compared with social programs and other preventive measures for successes in reducing crime, it emerges as a costly, particularly ineffective method. Policing puts criminals in prison. But victimization surveys have shown that only half of all serious crimes are reported. Only about one fifth of those result in an arrest, and less than two thirds of those result in convictions, of which only a tiny proportion end in incarceration. Half a million incarcerations is therefore the response of policing to more than 20 million crimes. Even if each incarcerated criminal committed multiple crimes, policing and prison, which absorb 33% of the budget for law enforcement, hardly alter rates of crime (Fagan, 1992).

Other studies locate this intransigence in the neighborhood dynamics, which have been shown to generate and maintain specific levels of crime and drugs. The latter are lowered or raised by the informal controls in a neighborhood, and the strength of these depends on a number of factors, such as the degree of homeownership or even the physical layout (see Chapter 5). Social programs affect these, not policing or jails (see Chapter 10).

ENFORCING DRUG LAWS—A BRIEF HISTORY

While they have not been the province of police departments until the modern age, efforts to regulate, deter, and punish drug taking are certainly not new. In traditional societies, drug use was heavily circumscribed by custom, ritual, and religion. Since then, governments have sought to enforce prohibitions against particular classes of drugs—whether those drugs were taken for medicinal or religious purposes, or merely for relaxation and pleasure.

In 1652, the government of Bavaria (in what is today southern Germany) enacted a law strictly forbidding tobacco smoking by peasants, "and other common people" (quoted in Ray & Ksir, 1996, p. 268). Members of Bavaria's social and economic elite could still purchase tobacco from a licensed druggist, but they were required first to obtain a doctor's prescription.

The caffeine in coffee and other beverages is recognized today to be a habit-forming substance, but caffeine still does not require any special medical warning or government regulation (let alone prohibition). In the mid-17th century, however, a movement emerged in England, led primarily by women, to curb coffee drinking. In 1674 a pamphlet entitled "The Women's Petition Against Coffee" asserted that men drank excessive amounts of coffee, causing them to waste their money and pursue prostitutes, among other vices.

Coffee was also prohibited in Muslim societies, apparently because its aficionados spent too much time in coffeehouses (Ray & Ksir, 1996). Since the Middle Ages, the Islamic system of religious law that governs behavior in societies throughout Asia and the Middle East had outlawed the ingestion of any substance that might impair judgment and action. Outright prohibitions against alcohol, for example, were strictly enforced, although those against other substances were often relaxed.

The British had been using opium (in the form of laudanum and in various alcoholic tinctures) since well before the beginning of the 19th century. It was only toward the end of the 19th century that the medical profession investigated the potentially addictive qualities of opium use. Even then, drugs did not become a matter for the police in Britain until 1920, when the British Parliament passed the Dangerous Drugs Act.

Antidrug sentiment and drug prohibition in the United States have been intimately linked since the late 19th century with revivalist religion, the temperance movement, and the professionalization of medical services. Medicine is "a world of power where some are more likely to receive the rewards of reason than are others" (Starr, 1982, p. 4). While scientific research plays a role in societal decisions concerning the classification of various drugs as therapeutic or not, bargainings among economically and politically powerful pharmaceutical companies, insurers, hospitals, the American Medical Association (AMA), and government agencies are ultimately far more important. The struggle in 1997 over the classification of tobacco has outgrown the scientific investigation of nicotine and centers on negotiations among the government, tobacco companies, insurers, and renegade factions of each.

From its inception, the AMA was opposed to the manufacturers of so-called "patent" medicines:

> The status of legislative control of dangerous drugs during the nineteenth century may be summed up as follows: the United States had no practical control over the health professions, no representative national health organization to aid the government in drafting regulations, and no controls on the labeling, composition or advertising of compounds that might contain opiates or cocaine. The United States not only proclaimed a free marketplace, it practised this philosophy with regard to narcotics in a manner unrestrained at every level of preparation and consumption. (Musto, 1973, p. 40)

The AMA classified drugs either as "ethical" or "patent" medicine. Arguing that only the former were of known composition, it officially endorsed them and conducted a long campaign to convince government officials and the general public that "patent" medicines, sold directly by the companies that manufactured them, should be made illegal.

The AMA was aided in this effort in the early part of the 20th century by the "muckrakers"—journalists who filed horrific features about the damage done by some of the less scrupulous makers of "patent" drugs. In a trend that accelerated around 1903, popular and influential magazines such as the *Ladies' Home Journal* warned women in particular about the dangers of taking drugs without consulting a doctor. Often, the emphasis of such stories was on the special dangers posed by "patent" medicines containing opium, cocaine, and alcohol. In 1905, *Collier's Weekly* ran a series of exposés on "patent" medicines and on medical "quacks." The message of that series was the same: only the medical establishment could be trusted when it came to matters of drugs and medication.

A subsequent focus on the abuse of opiates tapped explosively into a bedrock of American nativism, which still erupts in the militias of the late 20th century. During the latter half of the 19th century, the medical establishment had sounded the alarm about the possible addictive qualities of opiates. By 1900, America already had a relatively large population of habitual drug users, estimated to be about 250,000 (Musto, 1973).

In the same period, however, Chinese laborers had been invited to America in large numbers to construct extensive rail networks on the West Coast. Many smoked opium. Opium use had been a common practice among the upper echelon of Chinese society since well before the Middle Ages. Opium smoking, however, only became rampant among Chinese peasants when the British began illegally smuggling opium into China in the early 18th century to exchange with Chinese traders for tea. The Chinese government objected to this trade, but to no avail. The Opium Wars broke out in 1839, after the killing of a Chinese citizen by American and British sailors. The British Navy defeated the Chinese and meted out harsh reparations, which included trading rights and also the Island of Hong Kong.

Anti-Chinese sentiment in America mounted after a severe economic recession had reduced the railroads' demand for manual labor. Civil unrest led to the repeal of the Burlingame Treaty (1868), which had permitted unlimited Chinese immigration to the United States. A new treaty of 1880 empowered the United States to "regulate, limit or suspend" the immigration of Chinese laborers. Two years later, the Exclusion Act prohibited it entirely for a 10-year period. The specter of opium overshadowed the debate. Those arguing against admitting the laborers to the United States feared that malicious Chinese would propagate the evil affliction of opium smoking, peculiar to their race, among Americans.

In 1906, the United States Congress passed the Pure Food and Drug Act to monitor drug purity. The act forbade the manufacture, transportation, or sale of adulterated and fraudulently labeled food and drugs that were sold through interstate commerce. As long as they were clearly and accurately labeled on their packages, drugs such as morphine, cocaine, heroin, and opium could be legally sold. The most signal achievement of the act, however, was to bring the sale and distribution of drugs under federal control.

Federal agencies were soon using the new authority to continue the campaign against narcotics and minorities, first the Chinese and then African Americans and Mexicans. The Opium Exclusion Act of 1909 betrayed its anti-Chinese intent by forbidding the importation of smokable opium into the United States. The other drugs, which the Chinese did not use, remained widely available.

The African-American population and cocaine were next. The incidence of violent crime by African Americans was linked to their rising levels of cocaine use. Even if both increases were fictional, the anticipation of black rebellion had inspired white alarm. Cocaine-crazed African Americans were expected to commit uncontrollable acts of violence, including rapes of European-American women, and police reported that ordinary bullets could not pierce or stop them (Latimer & Goldberg, 1981).

In the Shanghai Commission Report of 1910, Dr. Hamilton Wright, who was retained at the State Department as President Taft's "drug adviser," outlined steps to control both the use of opium by Chinese immigrants and cocaine by African Americans, and to prevent their spread among the wider European-American population. He recommended that the states should make the possession of drugs illegal, unless they served medicinal purposes (Musto, 1973).

Mexicans and their use of marijuana were scapegoated during the Depression, when populist feelings against immigrant workers had turned into a campaign to send them home. The Mexican agricultural laborers were suspected of being driven to crime and violence by marijuana, and were reported to have given the drug to European-American school children (Musto, 1973).

The Harrison Act

Government control of narcotics did not actually begin until 1914, with the passage of the Harrison Act. In 1905, the Chinese government had protested the racism against Chinese living in the United States by imposing an embargo on American goods. American merchants and traders, anxious to maintain their lucrative markets in China, opposed it vigorously.

At an international conference convened in 1911 at The Hague to resolve the dispute, the Chinese representatives were determined to control the importation of opium into China. The U.S. delegates were interested in resurrecting, maintaining, and expanding trade links. An agreement was finally reached among the participating nations to control the international trade and domestic sale of opium, morphine, heroin, and cocaine. The Harrison Bill, sponsored by Senator Harrison of New York in 1914, codified American compliance at home.

The Harrison Act was primarily a tax law. It required dealers and suppliers of opiates and cocaine to register annually with the Internal Revenue Service and to pay a small fee. It named lawyers, physicians, and veterinary surgeons as possible suppliers. Although subsequently it would authorize all the police actions against the several categories of them described below in this chapter, the Harrison Act contained no actual reference to drug users at all. Disallowing neither use nor distribution of narcotics, it was concerned more with the authority of medical personnel than with public health. Indeed, Francis Harrison, the bill's sponsor, was "a notorious congressional drunkard" and his supporters strenuously opposed alcohol prohibition (Latimer & Goldberg, 1981, p. 230).

Contemporary critics of the bill argued that it was not strict enough, and an unintended consequence of the bill did hurt medical practitioners. Zealous police officers, lacking the power under the bill to stop drug use by arresting users and dispensers, targeted physicians instead and investigated them for violations of prescribing practices. For example, they could be arrested and convicted for maintaining "curable" addicts on opiates and were also required to reduce the prescribed dosage over time so as to eliminate the addiction (Musto, 1987). By 1929, a third of the 75,000 persons arrested for violations of the Harrison Act were physicians (Latimer & Goldberg, 1981). Seeking to shield themselves and their patients from scrutiny, many physicians contributed to the establishment of the illegal, unregulated underground drug market, which has persisted to the present day. Others, deterred by law enforcement from treating addicts at all, inadvertently directed them toward these markets. Today, fear of the Drug Enforcement Agency likewise prevents doctors from prescribing "too much" narcotics to persons, such as terminally ill cancer patients, who desperately need the relief (Trebach, 1987).

Prohibition

Six years later, the sale and consumption of alcohol were completely prohibited in the United States. The social-political movement that had accomplished this result represents an instructive example of the tendency in Western societies toward moral righteousness and social conformity. In the early 19th century, the Women's Christian Temperance Union and the Anti-Saloon League leaped from exhorting individuals to stop drinking to aggressive advocacy of a national ban on the production, sale, or consumption of alcohol. Simultaneously, the medical and scientific establishments revised the prevailing view that moderate alcohol consumption was beneficial, declaring instead that its effects were only and wholly negative.

Soon the prohibitionist coalition had embraced most of organized religion. In a few years the Anti-Saloon League had joined the elite group of the most effective political-interest groups and lobbying organizations in America. At its "Jubilee Convention" in November 1913, the League endorsed a national prohibition amendment to the U.S. Constitution. The required two-thirds majority in both the House and the Senate pledged to support it in the 1916 congressional elections. The First World War benefited the platform, allowing appeals to the spirit of sacrifice to be combined with the very real need to avoid diversion of grain from food production. It also stoked the widespread hostility toward predominantly German-American beer companies.

On December 18, 1917, the Congress passed the Eighteenth Amendment and sent it to the states:

> When the Eighteenth Amendment came before the Senate in 1917, it was passed by a one-sided vote after only thirteen hours of debate, part of which was conducted under the ten-minute rule. When the House of Representatives accepted it a few months later, the debate on the Amendment as a whole occupied only a single day. The state legislatures ratified it in short order; by January 1919, some two months after the Armistice, the necessary three-quarters of the state had fallen into line and the Amendment was part of the constitution. (Allen, 1931/ 1964, p. 205)

The unintended consequences of the legislation, however, particularly the unprecedented growth of organized crime, soon provoked a reaction. Prohibition had occasioned

> rum-ships rolling in the sea outside the 12-mile limit and transferring their cargos of whisky by night to fast cabin cruisers, beer-running trucks being hijacked on the interurban boulevards by bandits with Thompson sub-machine guns, illicit stills turning out alcohol by the carload, the fashionable dinner party beginning with contraband cocktails as a matter of course, ladies and gentlemen undergoing scrutiny from behind the curtained grill of the speakeasy, and Alphonse Capone, multi-millionaire master of the Chicago bootleggers, driving through the streets in an armor-plated car with bullet-proof windows. . . . (Allen, 1931/1964, p. 204)

Unsettled by these outcomes, other American elites eventually defeated the experiment.

As is true of the criminalization of heroin, cocaine, and marijuana today, prohibition deregulated alcohol production and entrusted it to organized crime. Gangsters quickly understood that they could earn enormous amounts of money by smuggling alcohol over the Canadian border and marketing it in the "speakeasies" of U.S. cities. Probably the most notorious beneficiary of prohibition was Chicago mobster Al Capone, who in the late 1920s survived the attempts of FBI agent Eliot Ness to destroy his bootlegging operation.

In 1922, Congress passed the Jones-Miller Act, which criminalized the possession of any illegally obtained narcotic. Furthermore, penalties for dealing illegally imported narcotics were increased. Congress in the same year also restricted the import of opium and coca leaves to medicinal purposes through the Narcotic Drugs Import and Export Act. Two years later, The Heroin Act limited the manufacture and possession of heroin to research sponsored and controlled by government. In 1937, the Marijuana Tax Act classified that drug in the same category as opiates and cocaine: dealers were required to register annually with the Internal Revenue Service and pay a fee.

Antidrug legislation has been sustained to the present day by the declaration of three successive "wars on drugs." In 1956, the Congress passed the Narcotic Drug Control Act, easily the most punitive in the short history of U.S. drug-control laws. The sale of heroin to a minor was outlawed on pain of the death penalty. Judges were required to give jail sentences for second or more offenses. Although mitigated somewhat by the Comprehensive Drug Abuse Prevention and Control Act of 1970, these penalties were stiffened further in New York State by the Rockefeller laws, enacted in 1973. The Comprehensive Crime Control Act of 1984 greatly expanded law-enforcement approaches to the regulation of drug use and distribution. The Anti-Drug Abuse Act of 1986 worsened the penalties and set mandatory minimums for certain offenses. Under the Anti-Drug Abuse Act of 1988, the first "drug czar" of the United States, William Bennett, was appointed to coordinate federal agencies and oversee the "war on drugs."

Just as the American Medical Association opposed the patent medicine manufacturers over the consumption of drugs, in the modern day a battle has been joined between those who favor the current system of criminalization and stigmatization of illicit drug use and those who see in the status quo the failure of that approach and who therefore favor returning to a more libertarian system. The Lindesmith Center sits squarely in the latter camp, and is an increasingly prominent voice in the current debate over legalization of marijuana and other drugs. Founded in 1994 by the celebrated investor and philanthropist George Soros, the Center sponsors research on the interface between individual freedoms and social obligation. Its guiding principle is that society's focus should not be on detection and prosecution of drug users, but rather on reducing the harm caused to users both as a result of their habit and as a result of the response of society to the fact of their drug use. The Center seeks to develop an alternative approach to the current system of drug policy and treatment—one that would minimize the adverse effects of drug use as well as of the prohibition and stigmatization of drug use.

In the forefront of those opposed to the Lindesmith Center is William Bennett, the drug czar under President Ronald Reagan, and a traditionalist who has made his name by espousing a socially conservative movement that criticizes sexual permissiveness and promiscuity, a societal decline in "family values," and attacks anyone who is willing to consider legalization of illicit drugs. For Bennett, and for other like-minded voices, the lack of success of drug enforcement efforts does not signal the hopelessness of such a strategy; rather, they contend, this failure has been the result of an inadequate investment in the war on drugs.

Thus, although drugs such as opium have been available in America since before the establishment of the Republic, the evolution of U.S. drug-control efforts, as this brief narrative indicates, spanned a very short time period (less than 100 years) and were brought under the control of law-enforcement agencies only in the past 50 years.

GOALS AND STRATEGIES OF DRUG LAW ENFORCEMENT

Of comparative recency, drug laws in the United States have not been applied consistently. Instead, intensified enforcement has alternated with leniency. Rather like the commitment to social welfare, relief for the needy, or the persecution of other vices, such as prostitution and gambling, the furor over drugs waxes and wanes, dependent upon politics, the availability of resources, and media exposure.

This inconsistency by itself worsens this particular illegal behavior. On the one hand, it is somewhat condoned, since there is almost a guarantee that it cannot be expunged completely and that the pressure against it will eventually lift. Indeed, as researchers suggest for Britain, the "question is, given that we cannot totally prevent illegal drug markets . . . , what kind of markets do we least dislike, and how can we adjust the control mix so as to push markets in the least undesired direction?" (Dorn & South, 1992, p. 186). Yet the intermittent threat of zealous law enforcement goads distributors to take extraordinary steps to avoid possible arrest. Coordinated groups therefore replace small-scale operators, and their precautionary strategies outmatch police offensives in sophistication (Maher & Dixon, 1996). They may so arm themselves as to exceed police firepower.

Another critical consequence is that drug regulation then replaces prohibition as the actual, if not the stated, goal of policing. But since regulation had not been the focus of the original legislation, its practice lacks any guidelines. Politicians, media, and the police themselves are thus enabled to choose against whom and with what weapons the war on drugs will be fought. The perverse low-income or underclass female, the sinister drug distributor who sells within 100 yards of schools, and the casual user who, according to some who favor drug regulation, ultimately pull the trigger in drug-related homicides are serial targets that current realpolitik, and not the law, had selected.

Other priorities also preoccupy police planners and patrol officers as they contrive to execute drug laws. They explain some contradictory aspects of their efforts: "At first glance it may seem a contradiction that law enforcement systems whose most clearly articulated aim is to disrupt higher levels of the drug trade should be netting such volumes of comparatively minor figures" (Sutton & James, 1995, p. 119). Indeed, drug use or distribution per se may not have provoked arrest in many of these cases. For example, in their historical struggle against unruly laborers, the police have struggled for the appearance of order and its maintenance and have been judged according to the safety and comfort to be enjoyed confidently in public spaces. These are sullied in multiple ways by drug users and misusers, and not only by their distribution or consumption of the illicit substance: disorderly and violent, they put shared utilities to improper use, instilling fears and anxieties among others in the community, and are emblematic of immorality and social disutility. Drugs, therefore, have to be located in a long history of public-order policing, which has focused at seasons on a variety of economic, cultural, and recreational practices in public space (Cohen, 1979; Dixon, 1991; Maher & Dixon, 1996; Reiner, 1992).

It must be emphasized that public-order policing has ideological as well as instrumental dimensions: "drug police, like priests are more important for what they symbolize and stand for than for what they do" (Manning, 1980, p. 256; cited in Maher & Dixon, 1996):

> The drug problem should be seen in the same way as the various other sources of fear, threat and disorder: witches, heretics, communists, subversives, hippies, and the like. These figures dance along the edges of our society, telling us we are not them and are therefore something else and symbolizing the edges of the moral order. . . . Policing is shaped by and celebrates fundamental values and beliefs and is thus a ritual of affirmation . . . which is designed to assure more than to accomplish, to celebrate rather than to solve, to remark upon rather than to realize. (Manning, 1980, p. 256)

Their (often erroneous) homegrown ideas of the motivations of drug users and distributors and of how drug markets operate also inform police initiatives. Most, for example, aim to drive up the street price of drugs in order to reduce demand. But many researchers find that "the rate of arrest for heroin use and/or possession exerts no effect on the street-level price of heroin or on the rate at which heroin users seek methadone treatment" (Weatherburn & Lind, 1995).

Law-enforcement agencies have developed a variety of goals and pursued a number of different strategies in seeking to control drug users, as well to expose and prosecute distributors. These have not remained fixed and stagnant but have evolved over time. Kelling and Moore (1988) have related the different types to their sociohistorical contexts and have separated three eras: the political, the reform, and the community problem-solving era.

The political era, characterized by a close relationship between the police and local politicians, lasted from the establishment of the police in the municipalities in the 1840s to the early 1900s. Since cars and helicopters were few or nonexistent, the police relied on foot patrol to control crime. An important function was to cater a range of social services, such as soup kitchens and temporary accommodation for newly arriving immigrants.

The reform era dated from the 1930s to the late 1970s. Reform was in part a reaction to the close relationship between the police and politicians. The latter had abused it by appropriating the services of the police for their own purposes, such as using them to interfere in elections. Gradually, control of the police was moved to other spheres of state government, and tactical decisions were made entirely by the police.

The reorientation was fashioned to emphasize the dual (and complementary) objectives of apprehending criminals and controlling crime. Chiefs of police eliminated the "social" functions, such as the soup kitchens, freeing policemen to focus better on crime. Emergency services were transferred to medical and firefighting units and to private charitable organizations. All calls for police assistance were rerouted from the local precinct to a centralized communications facility (the 911 system). Members of the public were discouraged from calling their local police station for help, and in cases where this message was not heard, some police departments even took the step of changing telephone numbers or disconnecting certain lines altogether. Foot patrol (the venerable tradition of the cop "walking his beat") was replaced by the less neighborly patrol car, which was dispatched only when a complaint was received. "Special units" were created to combat drugs, gangs, gambling, prostitution, or other specific problems.

The reform era in New York City culminated in the Knapp Commission, appointed to investigate charges of rampant corruption in the police force. Presenting its results to Mayor John V. Lindsay in December 1972 after 2½ years of inquiry, in which undercover police officers or "moles" observed and participated in acts of corruption and graft to show how widespread they were among fellow officers, the Knapp Commission documented extensively how narcotics detectives had systematically robbed drug dealers, suppressed and subsequently personally profited from evidence seized in drug busts, and received tens of thousands of dollars from dealers in bribes.

The Knapp Commission expressly recognized special, inherent temptations facing police officers engaged in antinarcotics efforts. Accordingly, it recommended that police officers be restrained from making street arrests for drugs. Without going so far as to argue for the legalization of drugs, or for substituting prosecution and imprisonment with prevention, education, and treatment, the Commission favored replacing the criminal sanctions by more enlightened methods for managing drug addicts (New York Knapp Commission, 1972). It noted that the laws against the use and sale of marijuana "are particularly controversial because of their growing unenforceability and the conviction of many people that they are undesirable" (Knapp Commission, 1972).

In the present day, a new era emphasizes "community problem solving" (Kelling & Moore, 1988), a program that recognizes the importance of community involvement and support in helping to achieve police objectives. Citizens are invited to "contribute more to definition of problems and identification of solutions" (Kelling & Moore, 1988).

The rationale of community policing was to heighten the anxiety and insecurity of prospective offenders by enhancing the feeling of security as well as the general morale of neighborhoods. In New York City, it inspired former Mayor David Dinkins's "Safe Streets, Safe City" project, in which the New York Police Department (NYPD) held regular meetings with neighborhood residents and community group leaders to elicit residents' specific concerns about crime and criminal elements around them, and to enlist their cooperation in identifying, deterring, arresting, and ultimately prosecuting offenders. The program restored the "beat cop" and fostered closer relations between her or him and residents.

The new ethos conforms better to what the police actually do and to the choices they do make. In the narrowly legalistic view, policemen do not implement policy or pursue societal agendas: their sworn duty to enforce the law prevents such latitude. By contrast, "crime fighting has never been, is not, and could not be the prime activity of the police. . . . The core mandate of policing, historically and in terms of concrete demands placed upon the police, the more diffuse one of order maintenance. Only if this is recognised can the problems of police powers and accountability really be confronted in all their complexity, and perhaps intractability" (Reiner, 1992, p. 212). In carrying out such work, police officers are able to draw upon law as a powerful resource that provides powers, definitions, resolutions (Bittner, 1990; Chatterton, 1976; Ericson, 1982; Wilson, 1968). The discretionary powers the police have in reality negates "the conventional idea that laws are things to be enforced and (think) of them instead as resources to be used to achieve the ends of those who are entitled or able to use them" (Chatterton, 1976, p. 114). Drug laws constitute such a resource, "providing uniform officers both with authority to intervene to disrupt or harass drug administration, and with opportunities to make self-initiated arrests" (Maher & Dixon, 1996).

Discretion is essential to the everyday conduct of officers:

> . . . the exercise of discretion lies at the heart of the policing function. . . . Successful policing depends on the exercise of discretion in how the law is enforced. The good reputation of the police as a force depends upon the skill and judgement which policemen display in the particular circumstances of the cases and incidents which they are required to handle. Discretion is the art of suiting action to particular circumstances. It is the policeman's daily task. (Scarman, 1981, p. 63)

Academic critique of the legalistic conception of policing contributed significantly to the development of the new conceptions of policing, such as community policing and problem-oriented policing (Goldstein, 1990; Moore, 1992). In strategies based on such conceptions, law is displaced from its central place: policing is reconceived and redeployed as a flexible means of achieving a variety of public purposes (Maher & Dixon, 1996).

Moore and Kleiman (1989) have summarized six actual goals that the police have pursued in enforcing drug laws. These are, (1) to control drug-related street crime, (2) to control drug-related gang violence, (3) to improve the health and well-being of users, (4) to end street-level dealing and in doing so improve the quality of life in large urban communities, (5) to prevent children from experimenting with drugs, and (6) and to minimize the incidence of corruption by the employees of criminal justice agencies.

Strategies they routinely employ include those listed below.

Buy and Busts, Reverse Stings, and Observation Arrests

In a buy-and-bust operation, an undercover police officer purchases drugs from a "pitcher," or dealer; other officers then close in to arrest the dealer. Alternatively, the officer might leave to return with a warrant for the dealer's arrest. In a reverse sting, the police officer poses as a drug dealer; she or he will then arrest the customers. During an observation arrest, a surveillance officer, watching drug transactions from a hidden spot, summons colleagues by radio to make arrests.

Defense attorneys easily prove that police have entrapped their clients by these methods. They have also encouraged corruption and perjury among police officers: "'Buy and bust' operations, observation arrests . . . create pressures to perform that produce a disproportionate risk of faking, entrapment or perjury" (Bouza, 1988).

Additionally, these operations are labor intensive, and therefore expensive. Police officers are diverted from detecting other types of crime.

Informant Buys

In an informant buy, the informant is provided with marked money and then searched before and after buying drugs to give prosecutors solid evidence for securing a criminal conviction. The informant's background, however, often damages her or his credibility as a witness in court.

Interdiction at the Street Level

Drug couriers are sometimes caught in traffic stops and road blocks. Cars and possessions are searched, and individuals can be tested for drug use through analyses of blood, urine, or hair.

Outstanding Arrest Warrants

Police believe that drug users and dealers are more likely than other members of the population to jump bail or fail to appear in court for traffic offenses. Agencies circulate a "hot list" of such offenders. If officers have insufficient evidence to arrest a suspect, they check whether she or he can be snared on a bail or traffic offense.

Operation Pressure Point

The NYPD designed Operation Pressure Point specifically for Manhattan's Lower East Side. In the early 1980s, consumers commuted from as far away as Westchester and Long Island to buy drugs at blatantly visible street-level drug markets. Puerto Rican drug distributors and their clientele clogged Tompkins Square, the other local parks, and several other spaces noisily and dangerously. The police appeared powerless to stop them.

In the few years preceding Operation Pressure Point, however, the community had been changing. The triumph of capital in regrouping at the expense of emptying out and depleting local neighborhoods during the era of smokable cocaine in the 1980s had created a new moneyed class that needed homes. Originally a Puerto Rican working-class enclave, the Lower East Side now accepted an influx of heterogeneous newcomers: professional and middle-class European Americans intent on buying and restoring property, as well as a youthful, polyethnic, less affluent crowd of musicians, artists, actors, and temporarily employed persons. The latter modestly renovated storefronts, converting them into crafts shops, boutiques, restaurants, and specialty stores. Squatters and park dwellers colonized abandoned buildings and parks. Many new residents patronized drug markets, boosting sales and adding to the lawless, bohemian atmosphere.

The homeowners, however, were particularly alarmed. Citizen groups formed to clamor for action against the steadily worsening street scene. The media reported "an infestation of drugs." And finally, politicians joined the fray (Zimmer, 1990). The battle for Tompkins Square Park in the late 1980s pitted this influential phalanx against remaining neighborhood persons, such as the homeless heroin injectors of the 1960s and the crack users of the 1980s who had joined them in forming colonies of makeshift housing in the park.

The ferocity of the police in this battle has been well documented. Before calling them out, the Commissioner of Parks had declared that it was "irresponsible to allow the homeless to sleep outdoors" in that year's cold winter. Operation Pressure Point, aimed at all elements of the drug trade on the Lower East Side, was the outcome. It would serve in the war on drugs as a model for "saturation policing" nationwide:

> Thanks to Operation Pressure Point, art galleries are replacing shooting galleries. The team was made up primarily of uniformed patrol officers, many just out of the police academy, who swept through the streets, mostly on foot, dispersing the crowds, giving out parking tickets, conducting searches, and making arrests. Extra officers assigned from the Housing Police and the Transit Police used similar tactics on the grounds of the public housing projects and in subway stations within the pressure point area. In the first few weeks, mounted police rode through and cleared the parks, and the canine unit was used to empty out the abandoned buildings which had been turned into drug warehouses and shooting galleries. The Organized Crime Control Bureau (OCCB) conducted hidden surveillance operations and engaged in "buy and bust" arrests. Police helicopters sometimes hovered overhead, watching the rooftops for possible counterattacks against the police. (Zimmer, 1990, p. 52)

Police activity disrupted street drug markets, closed the park, and permitted it to be reopened only after it had been made "homeless-proof."

Operation Pressure Point both improved and worsened the situation it was meant to address. In its initial stages, the police greatly reduced the numbers of drug users and distributors at the most "drug-infested" street corners and in parks. Distributors waited for the repression to subside. But when they learned that Operation Pressure Point was to be continued "indefinitely," they returned to the streets, where they modified markets to reduce the chances of arrest. For example, they relocated them to the poorer, less policed sections of the community. Soon they were flourishing again, magnifying the "drug problem" within narrower boundaries. In contrast, distribution was eradicated in the more prosperous neighborhoods.

Some investigators have identified Operation Pressure Point as one among many strategies by the city administration to encourage the polarization of the Lower East Side into a part undergoing gentrification while the remainder deteriorated (Smith, 1996).

The city helped in other ways to facilitate gentrification. For example, the allocation of in rem properties stimulated intense political maneuvering to decide which properties in what part of the city were to be sold:

> If the real estate cowboys invading LES [Lower East Side] used art to paint their economic quest in romantic hues (see below), they also enlisted the cavalry of city government for more prosaic tasks: reclaiming the land and quelling the natives. In its housing policy, drug crackdowns, and especially its parks strategy, the City devoted its efforts, not towards providing basic services and living opportunities for existing residents but towards routing many of the locals and subsidizing opportunities for real estate developers.

> The city has now given clear signals that it is prepared to aid the return of the middle class by auctioning city-owned properties and sponsoring projects in gentrifying areas to bolster its tax base and aid the revitalization process. (Smith, 1996, p. 86)

Operation TNT

Tactical Narcotics Teams (TNT) were deployed in the late 1980s by the NYPD as the premier method against smokable cocaine or crack, a drug that had then surpassed all others in popularity. In another mode of "saturation policing," several teams of plainclothes narcotic officers bore down simultaneously on "drug-infested" areas of the city for periods of up to 3 months (Sviridoff, Sadd, Curtis, & Grine, 1992). The TNT supplemented the endeavors of the many police officers already at work. The combined police offensive employed the panoply of tactics—buy and bust, reverse stings, observation arrests, informant buys, street-level interdiction, arrests for nondrug offenses, and targeting higher-level distributors.

The TNT approach emphasized systematic interagency cooperation, accelerated enforcement actions, and solicited local patronage. It aimed to disable drug markets long enough for neighborhoods to recover the ability to maintain order and a higher quality of life (Sviridoff et al., 1992). Once the police left a neighborhood, they relied on residents to be vigilant and report any resumption of drug-related activities. Thus, gains would be permanent.

In fact, TNT achieved the same results as Operation Pressure Point:

> Although respondents reported some short-term impacts on visible drug markets on the streets of the target areas, in most locations these effects appeared not to endure. There was little evidence that TNT effected any reduction in other crime in the vicinity of the drugs location targeted, and little evidence that TNT improved perceptions of disorder, reduced fear of crime, increased use of public amenities, or improved attitudes towards the police. (Sviridoff et al., 1992, p. 141)

Quality-of-Life Approach

New York City gained the distinction in the 1990s of leading the nation's major cities in a precipitous drop in crime. Both Mayor Giuliani and ex–Police Commissioner Bratton claimed credit. The essence of their "quality of life" approach was to punish relentlessly even minor infractions of the law, such as jaywalking, "hanging out" (loitering), drinking a beer in public, jumping a subway turnstile or "hustling" as a "squeegee operator" (automobile windshield cleaner) at busy street intersections. The underlying philosophy was that persons breaking minor laws were more likely to commit major crimes and that an uncompromising attitude of zero tolerance deterred criminals more. Arrested at the least provocation, prisoners are met with the full weight of the law. After incarceration, by being shunted continuously between probation and treatment centers, criminals live as though they are perpetually in a minimum security prison, although they are nominally home. Some have even been fitted experimentally with electronic monitoring devices.

Catching "Mr. Big"

It is widely accepted that policing efforts should be focused on the detection and prosecution of large-scale importers, suppliers, and traffickers, rather than users and user/distributors (Green & Purnell, 1995, p. 35). "Catching Mr. Big" was a key national strategy during the 1970s, when it was directed both against the heads of internal distribution and against those abroad who organized production and export. The "Mr. Big" strategy features a number of drawbacks, however. For example, it requires law enforcement to employ sophisticated investigatory techniques, which gamble heavy outlays of labor and capital on uncertain returns. Furthermore, as there are as many "Mr. Bigs" as there are street-level distributors, catching just one or a few is likely to have only limited impact on the supply of drugs (Moore & Kleiman, 1989).

There is the problem of definition. Shifting standards are used to discriminate among "high," "middle," and "low" levels of distribution. Going after "Mr. Big," police officers self-importantly convey an impression of mounting a dangerous but vital mission. It mainly results, however, in the usual large number of inconsequential arrests.

Extradition

Through extradition treaties, foreign "Mr. Bigs" can be brought to trial in the United States, where they can be punished more severely. Carlos Lehder Rivas, once a leader of the Medellín cartel in Colombia, is now serving a life sentence in a federal penitentiary in Texas. Manuel Noriega, former President of Panama, was abducted from his presidential headquarters in a military operation by U.S. personnel, brought to the United States for trial, and was convicted to life imprisonment. A Brooklyn federal court has issued a bench warrant for the arrest of Khun Sa, leader of the Shan Chinese in Myanmar and the world's largest heroin manufacturer.

U.S. efforts to abduct and extradite foreign nationals have sometimes violated both international and U.S. law.

Asset Forfeiture

Law enforcement agencies were given expanded powers under the Comprehensive Crime Control Act of 1984 and the Anti-Drug Abuse Act of 1986 to seize the assets of drug users and distributors. In seizures, the burden of proof lies with the accused: for property to be returned, its owner must prove that it had not been acquired with drug proceeds. Since the sale of assets were credited to the budgets of precincts, local officers aggressively pursued both, sometimes seizing the cars of distributors and taking delight in seeing them buy them a second time from the pound. Asset forfeiture is meant to deter both the casual drug user, who is thereby punished mightily for the possession of small amounts of drugs, and "Mr. Big," who risks the loss of substantial business profits.

Drug Testing

A much-contested method of detecting drug users and finding the evidence to prosecute them is testing for drugs through analyses of blood, urine, or hair. Drug testing is most often carried out in the workplace, where drug use is held accountable for huge losses in productivity. Although these are reckoned to total between $60 billion and $85 billion, there are few hard data to support the estimate. A monograph prepared by the National Institute on Drug Abuse (NIDA), while recommending drug testing in the workplace, is diffident to assert that drug abuse actually occurs there. Indeed, it castigates the legal drugs—alcohol and cigarettes—for most drug-related absenteeism and health complaints (Gust & Walsh, 1989).

Drug tests are sometimes inaccurate, specimens are contaminated, and false negatives and positives are given (Hansen, Caudill, & Boone, 1985). Many workers' unions have refused to allow their workers to be tested.

Targeting Gangs

Police planners find difficulty in believing that unemployed young persons would undertake drug distribution by themselves. Put them in a gang, however, and membership alone apparently supplies the missing motivation. Gangs allegedly engaged in drug distribution are held responsible for the majority of "drug-related" homicides, especially on the West Coast. In January 1997, the NYPD and Mayor Giuliani announced that their top priority for the new year would be to target gangs.

Gang intelligence and interception pose special conceptual challenges. Calling them a "gang," police officers mistakenly endow ordinary groups of neighborhood age-mates with sinister characteristics ("ice-cold killers" or a "criminal group mind") and treat arrestees accordingly. When dealing with genuine gangs, police experts are needed to understand their cohesion, rules of conduct, modus operandi, and future behavior.

Global Drug Enforcement Policy

After three decades, the U.S. war on drugs has long overleaped national boundaries and today entangles virtually every country in the world. By using flexible measures to identify them, the United States rewards allies and punishes enemies in the war by giving or withholding aid. It invites foreign police to the United States for training, while U.S. personnel are everywhere abroad, funding or staffing antidrug programs.

In 1996, the U.S. Justice and State Departments escalated their efforts to force Central American neighbors, in particular Mexico and Colombia, to enforce strictly laws and international agreements forbidding the harvesting of drug crops, and the export of cocaine, heroin and other drugs for sale in the U.S. market. Testifying in February 1997 before the House Subcommittee on National Security, International Affairs and Criminal Justice (the name of the committee holding the hearing reflects the elevated political and policy context in which drug enforcement had been placed), Drug Enforcement Administration (DEA) chief Thomas A. Constantine described the threat posed to U.S. security by Mexican drug cartels:

> I am not exaggerating when I say that these sophisticated drug syndicate groups from Mexico have eclipsed organized crime groups from Colombia as the premier law enforcement threat facing the United States today . . . these crime leaders are far more dangerous, far more influential, and have a great deal more impact on our day to day lives than [the American mafia did in the 1950s and 1960s]. These individuals, from their headquarters [overseas], absolutely influence the choices that too many Americans make about where to live, when to venture out of their homes, or where they send their children to school. The drugs—and the attendant violence which accompanies the drug trade—have reached into every American community and have robbed many Americans of the dreams they once cherished. (Constantine, 1997, p. 3)

In prosecuting the war against these Mexicans, the United States sought permission in May 1997 for DEA officers to carry arms and make arrests in Mexico. Dismissing the request, Premier Zedillo condemned it as an outrageous assault on Mexican sovereignty.

Nadelmann (1993) has argued that an "international enforcement regime" has now been established globally. In 1992, President Bush allocated $1.2 billion to the Pentagon to assist in the drug war, and U.S. military now operates in several countries for that purpose. Joint operations of U.S. and local military eradicate crops, intercept smugglers, and destroy laboratories and warehouses.

Combining foreign policy and drug-war objectives sometimes involves the United States in contradictions. The United States certifies foreign countries as "allies" or "enemies" in the drug war, and withholds aid and other benefits from the latter. Recently the government certified Mexico, which was preparing to join the North American Free Trade Agreement (NAFTA), as an ally, despite evidence of major drug trafficking condoned at the highest levels of government. Meanwhile, Colombia and Peru, which had been brought to the brink of civil war by prosecuting U.S.-directed campaigns against their cocaine-manufacturing cartels, were classified as enemies.

Crop Eradication

One aspect of global law enforcement that the United States has long dominated is the eradication of poppy, coca, and marijuana cultivation and its substitution by other crops. The United States has operated programs against marijuana in Jamaica, Mexico, and Latin America (Cooper, 1990; del Olmo, 1987). The domestic marijuana crop in California and other states was similarly attacked (Boyle, 1984; Weishert, 1992). Efforts to eradicate coca plants in the Andes were discontinued because of resistance by armed guerrillas.

Some crop eradication methods have endangered the environment. Many pesticides, including the infamous paraquat, pose serious dangers to other vegetation, fish, animals, and humans. One bizarre plan, to release millions of malumbia moths, whose caterpillars eat coca plants, in the coca plantations of Peru and Bolivia, was squelched by environmentalists (Isikoff, 1990).

DRUG ENFORCEMENT HAS INFLUENCED POLICING

Campaigns to interdict and arrest drug distributors have caused a concomitant expansion in the size of urban police forces. In 1988 TNT employed 110 new officers. In the early 1990s, the Safe Streets, Safe City program in New York City added 5,000 more. Agency managers are obviously eager to extend their authority and augment their budgets. Stoking public anxiety about drugs and crime, they can force elected officials to divert scarce resources from social service and welfare programs (which might actually prevent social problems) toward policing and incarceration. Thus, although programs such as Headstart and basic welfare programs are being eliminated, President Clinton pledged in the 1992 presidential campaign to fund 100,000 police officers nationwide. It came as no surprise, therefore, when the Fraternal Order of Police, the nation's largest police union, decided to endorse him.

THE EFFECTS OF POLICING DRUGS ON THE CRIMINAL JUSTICE SYSTEM

For more than two decades, the U.S. criminal justice system has grown alarmingly. Between 1984 and 1994, the number of convicts admitted to the nation's state and federal prisons in a year rose 120%, from 246,260 to 541,434, bringing the total prison population from 419,346 to 904,647 (or an increase of 116%). The taxpayers' overall bill for criminal justice—police, courts, and corrections—also nearly doubled in the period, from $45.6 billion in 1985 to $93.8 billion in 1992, with corrections' share of the total increasing from 28.6% to 33.6%, or $31.5 billion. In just the 5 years from 1984 to 1988, the population of people on probation increased by 35.4%, and the population of people on parole increased by 52.8% (see Bureau of Justice Statistics, 1992).

The preoccupation with arresting, prosecuting and incarcerating persons for minor drug offenses removes officers and other resources from other categories of crime-fighting. These cases so obstruct the courts that some judges have refused to hear them. Overcrowding in prisons, leading to violence, rioting, and gang formation, is another costly consequence.

The worst disservice is that these arrests penalize mostly users of marijuana and do little to stop the flow of drugs into the country or drug misuse.

THE DIFFERENTIAL TREATMENT OF OFFENDERS ACCORDING TO ETHNICITY

As noted above, specific actions taken in the policing of drugs were meant not only to further the careers of government officials and the consolidation of professional bodies but also reflected fears about minorities and immigrants. Bitter feelings toward Irish, Chinese, African Americans, and Mexicans could be justified and relieved partially or symbolically by punishing them for "abusing" alcohol, opium, cocaine, and marijuana. African Americans have suffered most from this ostensive purpose of drug-law enforcement.

In the 1990s, under guidelines issued to federal judges by the U.S. Sentencing Commission, mandatory minimums were set for persons convicted of distributing or selling smokable cocaine or crack that were 10 times more severe than those for prisoners convicted of distributing a similar amount of powder cocaine. Because cocaine markets had evolved in such a way that cocaine in its smokable form was more readily available in minority neighborhoods than powder, African Americans and Latinos bore the brunt of the strategy. The stiffer penalties were justified by the greater extremity and frequency of violence allegedly associated with the sale and consumption of crack cocaine.

Thus, while widely accepted estimates of the national population of habitual cocaine users suggest that approximately 80% of them are European American, the majority of people who are in prison for drug-related offenses are African American or Latino. According to an analysis by the Washington, DC-based Sentencing Project organization, one in four black men in their 20s in the United States is in prison, on parole, or on probation. By contrast, only about 6% of white men in their 20s fell into those categories. Nor is the phenomenon any longer exclusively male. The inequitable differences in the treatment of powder versus smokable cocaine, and more broadly, the ferocity of the war on drugs since the mid-1980s, have remanded more women to jail than formerly.

Transplanting the U.S. example in the United Kingdom, the Home Secretary's new crime bill has recommended mandatory minimum sentencing for drug dealers and for persistent burglars (whose criminality is thought to be largely drug related). But so far British courts have resisted furiously fettering their judicial discretion.

THE IMPACT OF POLICING ON DRUG DISTRIBUTORS

In the minority communities where the police make most of their arrests for drug offenses, distributors and their customers exchange money for product in different types of street-level drug markets. While each neighborhood usually contains an example of every possible kind, only one may predominate in particular neighborhoods. Characteristic patterns and rates of crime and violence attended these markets.

For example, in the heyday of the cocaine smoking epidemic of the 1980s, three main types of street-level markets were identified in New York City, where "nickel" vials of crack (the standard retail unit) could be bought. These three types had culminated 6 years in the evolution of markets for smokable cocaine in New York City.

Free-Lance Nickels Markets

In many neighborhoods very little regulation occurred, and a reputation for crack-related violence, crime, and incivility was won instead. In free-lance nickels markets, two dramatis personae in particular created the high-risk, high-energy, fast-burnout atmosphere. One was the street-level, daily compulsive user/free-lance distributor. Typically a young minority male in his mid-20s, he had surrendered to two fantasies: to become a millionaire through selling crack and simultaneously to "smoke lovely" (smoke crack unrestrainedly). The war between the contrary pulls of these two fantasies accounted for his behavior on the street. This type of distributor was on the one hand very much a businessman who was always in an urgent rush to sell crack. On the other hand, the urgency also arose from his being a user who needed to sell the product before he consumed it himself. Ending each day as penniless as the day before, he had to resort to petty criminality or rely on friends and family to have $50 the following morning to make the minimum bulk purchase (half of a gram) from higher-level distributors. On the street he competed aggressively for customers and ensnared some by offering free samples (of which he would contrive to consume the greater share).

Complementing the style of the domineering free-lance distributor was the daily compulsive user. Negotiating crack use among such distributors, he or she was, in William Burroughs's phrase, like the ball in a pinball machine. Although some of them—at the beginning of their crack-smoking careers, when they had money and jobs—could afford to buy bulk quantities from higher-level distributors and thus minimize risk and ensure quality, they preferred nevertheless to buy nickels from the street-level free-lancer. They preferred to use the drug in the exposed curbside setting, perhaps desiring a sense of danger along with crack, or perhaps with the readily available crack-using sexual partners.

Nearly every night in neighborhoods where free-lance nickels markets dominated, there were fights, gunshots, woundings, robberies, unchecked sex work, and visits by police, firefighters, and ambulances. "Zoomers" sold bogus crack. Arrests, hospitalizations, and interventions by state agencies of social control (e.g., Bureau of Child Welfare) were frequent. The highest proportion of crack abusers suffering adverse psychosocial outcomes from use—loss of jobs, family, shelter, other entitlements, respect, and status—was to be found in free-lance nickels markets.

Crack Sellers Coops

Where circumstances permitted, abstinent street-level free-lance distributors made oases of regulation, where both use and distribution were more restrained than in the free-lance market described above. They were especially successful where the physical terrain encouraged monopoly. One Brooklyn housing project was entirely fenced around four city blocks, with one gate per block to admit residents. Free-lancers sold crack on lawns in the middle of the compound, and could escape from there into the residential buildings before police could run up from the gates to apprehend them. A group of 10 young men (mostly sons of residents, ranging in age from 18 to 29) monopolized sales in the complex. As they enjoyed the confidence of resident users, who were mostly working people, they raised the price of vials to $10, but offered in them "jumbo" quantities of crack.

Business Nickels Market

In several neighborhoods, the other extreme of regulation was achieved. The elements of the situation described in the story of Etham and One-Eye (see Chapter 6) had been elaborated, and a few "owners" dominated all distribution in the neighborhood and confined it to well-demarcated areas. Each owner marketed his product under a trademark (usually the color of the plunger of a vial, hence "white tops," "black tops," etc). They employed "runners" to discourage fresh competition and to oversee the conduct of customers and street sellers. The latter were recruited from a pool of neighborhood crack and heroin misusers. As crack use during work shifts was forbidden, however, many sellers used alcohol or heroin instead and sold crack in a relaxed daze. The contrast between these street-level distributors and those of the free-lance nickels market was therefore profound. Female street sellers were frequently prostitutes as well, who worked nearby "strolls." They distinguished themselves from crack misusers who provided sexual services for crack.

In the Bushwick neighborhood four owners tightly controlled distribution from the higher-level of bulk purchases to the street level of retail sales in vials. One owner, Reuben (aged 18) had been selling "white tops" (vials with white caps) here for the past 2 years, from 1987 to 1989. He employed two runners per 12-hour shift to oversee as many street-level daily compulsive user/business distributors (see below) as could be attracted to the job. Runners made $100 cash per shift, while the street-level distributor was given a "bundle" (10 vials at $5 each: a "package" equals 10 bundles), a vial of which will belong to the distributor when he or she has sold the rest. After 2 years of business, Reuben was able to buy himself a brand-new Cherokee and had recently opened up a video game parlor near the location where white tops were usually sold.

The key to Reuben's successful enterprise was top-to-bottom control. Street-level distributors who "messed up" their bundles are harshly treated by "runners." Another owner, who lived on the lower east side of Manhattan but who operated crack and heroin selling locations in the Bushwick and Williamsburg neighborhoods, recently showed newspaper reporters a jar of teeth he kept at home. They were the teeth of street-level distributors who had "messed up." While researchers were tape-recording interviews in November 1989 they were informed that a young Puerto Rican and his friend, an African American, had tried selling crack at the white tops location. The young African American was shot in the crotch. Free-lance distributors of any variety were not tolerated in Bushwick and Williamsburg.

While enforcement was harsh, all personnel in tightly organized crack-distributing businesses knew the rules and the job responsibilities each had. A significant proportion of customers in Reuben's business nickels market in Bushwick were weekend "bingers," who used drugs and bought sex from Friday night through Sunday, but returned to work, family, and suburban homes on Monday morning. Business nickels markets have been attended by a more systematic kind of violence than was experienced in free-lance nickels markets. Usurpers, would-be free-lancers or "zoomers" (sellers of bogus crack) were routinely gunned down, while severe pain was inflicted on street sellers or customers who broke rules laid down by owners. Owners in the Williamsburg neighborhood ordered the slaying of an antidrug crusader, and when gunmen sprayed her home with bullets, they killed not only the woman, but her infant daughter. In 1989, another owner commissioned the murder of a rookie policeman in Queens.

As noted, policing had differential effects on these variously organized markets. On the whole, however, very few (minority) drug distributors escape arrest and imprisonment for long. Even the best protected, the most sophisticated, and the wealthiest, such as Young Boys Inc. or the Chambers Brothers in the Midwest, rapidly fall. Research shows that most seldom earn more than a minimum wage, that most have short, ignominious careers, and that many are murdered at a young age (Hamid, 1992, 1997).

Nevertheless, enhanced or intensive drug policing continuously challenges distributors to finesse their criminality in fabricating more effective methods to avoid detection. The latter may even include homicide. More prosaically, distributors avoid drawing attention to themselves, or reduce some of the costs and inconvenience of arrest, by seducing adolescents, women, and families of single mothers and young children into assuming high-risk, low-paid roles in their businesses, as couriers, "mules," keepers of money or drugs, lessors of apartments, or street sellers.

Of late, distributors have countered the escalating war on drugs in New York City by relying on updated technology. Instead of risking street or apartment sales, many marijuana and cocaine distributors wait for customers to communicate with them by beeper or e-mail before dispatching a messenger to fill their orders. Heroin distributors are following this lead.

Police pressure, the early retirement of distributors through arrest and incarceration, and the technical requirements of distribution demanded by improved technology have transformed distribution by facilitating new organizational forms among distributors. Delivery services, such as those described above, range from large businesses, which employ many bicycle messengers, to the free-lance operation of a single young man or woman on foot.

A grim consequence of transforming distribution affects heroin users chiefly. Inexperienced persons in the retail traffic have used additives to "cut" heroin, which have their own pronounced effects. While powdered morphine and quinine, the usual cuts, have effects to which users have grown accustomed over several generations, scopolamine has caused some deaths.

THE IMPACT OF POLICING ON DRUG USERS

Because of the policing of drugs, the lives of many drug users are infused with risk, and they daily face the dreaded possibility of being arrested. Arrest may lead to fines or imprisonment, which in turn has adverse social and economic consequences. The greater the police presence on the streets, the greater the resort to risky behaviors on the part of users.

By using their discretionary powers, policemen can harass those suspected of being drug users limitlessly. European-American persons in a minority neighborhood, or vice versa, are immediately suspect. In minority neighborhoods, officers on the beat use their truncheons to prod awake vagrants on sidewalks. Pedestrians are charged for jaywalking or loitering. Bicyclists, suspected of being drug couriers, are stopped for traffic violations or nonpossession of licenses. Since it is an axiom that local residents cannot have acquired wealth honestly, motorists in luxury cars are natural quarry. Police systematically search the persons they detain, examining cars, bicycles, clothing, and bags for evidence of drug use.

A reporter for the *Los Angeles Times*, introduced by researchers to a shooting gallery in an abandoned building in Bushwick, New York, described a morning on which police hurled bricks into it to flush out users. As the users escaped, the police whipped them with lengths of electrical cable before searching them (Curtis & Hamid, 1997). The climate of zero tolerance for crime fostered by recent city administrations has resulted arguably in police excess and the deaths by police shootings of several civilians.

In Washington Heights, the editor of the neighborhood paper, *The Bridge Leader*, replaced a boxed advertisement instructing residents how to report drug offenses with one advising them how to register complaints against abusive policemen. Initially supportive of attempts to disperse street-level drug distributors and their clientele from busy intersections and other public spaces, the community balked after two young men were killed by police bullets. Employed persons, including a clergyman, had been harassed and beaten, entire blocks had been "frozen," and residents at leisure on their own stoops were bullied indoors (Gonzales, 1990).

Resisting a perceived intensification of police offensives against them, drug users in New York City in the late 1990s made many adaptations in their lifestyles, both positive and negative. For example, a possible improvement may have been the greater esprit de corps they manifest. A spontaneous fellow-feeling bonds one user to another at copping locations. Strangers exchange notes about the quality of heroin and direct one another to favored distributors or name brands. They give advice on avoidance of arrest (Conde & Hamid, 1998). Both distributors and users are safeguarded when the latter pool together money and entrust bulk purchases to one person, sharply reducing thereby the number and length of transactions. Important shared information among Manhattanites is the location of luxurious or merely serviceable bathrooms from Washington Heights to the Bowery.

Needle exchanges have greatly facilitated the process by which users have learned the topological as well as symbolic boundaries of urban heroin universes. Existing in more than 40 cities in the United States, they are a forum where young and old heroin users, drawn from different socioeconomic backgrounds, meet. They receive free of charge not only needles and other medical supplies, but also counseling, dental and optical consultations, acupuncture, referrals, books, movie shows, conversation, and coffee. Some illicit activity, such as exchanging drugs, also takes place.

Yet another positive change is the preference for sniffing rather than injecting. While the factors determining passages between modes of administration are more than simply economic or pharmacological, new users have either started as sniffers and have remained so throughout their careers or they have switched from injecting to sniffing. The latter requires no paraphernalia, preparation or special space for a use episode, and the user instantly disposes of the only evidence, the bag in which the heroin had been packaged. The risk of acquired immunodeficiency syndrome or transmission of blood-borne disease is avoided, as well as the other complications of injecting. At the same time, sniffers say that the "habit" that results from this method of administration is more insidious than the one earned through injecting, and that "kicking" is correspondingly more painful.

For injecting drug users (IDUs) police pressure translates into high-risk behavior. Users who inject in public or semipublic settings are anxious to "get on" and "get out." Users are also less likely to have a taste first —or to measure their dose. Because they are fearful of interruption and anxious to get rid of the evidence, they typically administer the drug in one dose, increasing the risk of overdose (especially if they have been using benzodiazepines or drinking alcohol). During these episodes, people sometimes get paranoid and start arguing (Maher & Dixon, 1996).

Collective injecting episodes are more likely to occur in public settings. Most of these locations are well known to IDUs, local residents, and the police and provide little, if any, privacy. Conditions tend to be less than hygienic and are typically poorly lit and poorly ventilated. With the exception of public toilets, few have access to running water, and the majority are littered with injecting paraphernalia, including discarded syringes (Maher & Dixon, 1996). Many of these settings can be characterized as "free" shooting galleries in the sense that they provide a "space where IDUs regularly gather to inject drugs but where there is no admission fee" (Ouellet, Jimenez, Johnson, & Wiebel, 1991).

While in one sense the establishment of more commercial galleries may be desirable (i.e., the presence of gatekeepers, the potential for safe using norms and safe disposal), this is highly contingent on the type or nature of galleries that emerge. For example, research in the United States indicates that, in the North American context, certain types of shooting galleries can serve as vectors for the transmission of human immunodeficiency virus and other blood-borne viruses (Des Jarlais & Friedman, 1990; Des Jarlais, Friedman, & Strug, 1986; Marmor, Des Jarlais, & Cohen, 1987; Ouellet et al., 1991).

Police pressure also means that the promising routines of some drug users are interrupted. For example, if a person is undergoing treatment, an arrest is likely to compromise or terminate an often-fragile commitment.

At the community level, dispersing drug users from their usual haunts simply "infects" other areas. When Operation Pressure Point expelled heroin users and distributors from New York City's Lower East Side from 1981 to 1985, they relocated in Williamsburg, Bushwick, and Washington Heights. Shooting galleries, queues of anxious customers awaiting the distributor, groups monopolizing park benches, and the litter of discarded needles, crack vials, heroin bags, and beer cans soon completed the transfer.

Vigorous street-level law enforcement may ultimately lead to more organized, professional, and enduring forms of criminality (Dorn & South, 1992). It has furthered role differentiation and specialization among distributors. In New York City, the latter relied on aging neighborhood misusers to advertise heroin and to identify undercover officers. These arrangements were eventually replaced by delivery services, which reduced risk by further professionalizing distribution.

The police presence may also inadvertently serve to entrench or reinforce the market position of some dealers by solidifying previously ephemeral relationships between them and their clients (Curtis & Sviridoff, 1994). Finally, a complex set of unintended negative effects relates to police misconduct and the ways in which the current system of drug-law enforcement encourages opportunities for police corruption (Manning, 1980; Manning & Redlinger, 1977; Mollen Commission, 1994).

For example, the resurgence of gangs in New York City, after they had been absent from communal life for some 10 years, may be directly related to the large numbers of young Puerto Ricans whom the police had arrested and imprisoned during the drug and crack wars of the 1980s. Incarcerated for the first time, many formed gangs for safety and companionship and carried their loyalty back to the neighborhoods on their release. Finding there the continuing, oppressive, violent police presence, they rallied the gangs as a countervailing force. But gangs differed in their management of violence (Curtis & Hamid, in press).

In fact, gang membership may have been the better of discouraging alternatives. The attitude of "blame the victim" enabled other local youths sometimes to take the law into their own hands. Police violence created a "jungle" atmosphere that prompted them to emulate the officers. Inviting the community to participate in police efforts sometimes attracted opportunists and the more sinister elements in the community. Civil life is militarized, as citizens shoulder the war on drugs. A false polarization causes nonusers to blame drug misusers for the neighborhood deterioration that economic and political processes had caused.

These consequences were differentiated by age, gender, and ethnicity. For young women, gender issues in relation to police treatment may also condition their reluctance to carry syringes.

The police persist in counterproductive and alienating practices, hazardous to themselves and the public, even though they are not specifically demanded by the law. The uncharted gray area in which police discretion applies is ultimately the source of most action against drugs on the street, and can be recognized and renegotiated, even within existing laws, to bring about greater benefits for police, drug users, and the community (see Chapter 10).

Discussion Questions

1. Discuss policing and its functions in modern societies. How were these performed in traditional societies (Gibbs, 1988; Harris, 1977; Hoebel, 1954/1974)? Research the organization of policing in various countries, including the People's Republic of China (Bracey, 1985).
2. Make a list of forbidden, immoral, or illegal activities in the reader's community. How are most persons prevented from committing them?
3. What do different kinds of policemen in the reader's community do on a typical day?
4. What is the history of drug law enforcement in the reader's community? What forms does it assume? Has it been effective? How much does it cost? Has it resulted in greater or less polarization of the local population? Has it intensified or decreased tensions between individuals, age groups or generations, genders, classes, or ethnicities? What are relations between the police and the community?
5. Who gets arrested for drugs in the various neighborhoods?

REFERENCES

Allen, F.A. (1931/1964). *Only yesterday: An informal history of the 1920's* (Perennial Library edition). New York: Harper & Row.

Bittner, E. (1990). *Aspects of police work.* Boston: Northeastern University Press.

Bouza, A.V. (1988). Evaluating street level drug enforcement. In M. R. Chaiken (Ed.), *Enforcement examining the issues: NIJ issues and practices.* Washington, DC: National Institute of Justice.

Boyle, T.C. (1984). *Budding prospects: A pastoral.* New York: Viking/Penguin.

Bracey, D. (1985, March) The system of justice and the concept of human nature in the People's Republic of China. *Justice Quarterly, 2,* 139–144.

Bureau of Justice Statistics. (1992). *Drugs, crime and the justice system. A national report.* Washington, DC: U.S. Government Printing Office.

Chatterton, M. (1976). Police in social control. In J.F.S. King (Ed.), *Control without custody?* Cambridge, England: Institute of Criminology.

Cohen, P. (1979). Policing the working-class city. In B. Fine, J. Lea, S. Picciotto, & J. Young (Eds.), *Capitalism and the rule of law* (pp. 118–136). London: Hutchison.

Cole, G., & Postgate, D. (1972). *The common people: 1746–1946.* London: Routledge.

Conde, A., & Hamid, A. (1998). Police, war on drugs and Haitian heroin injectors in Brooklyn. In preparation.

Constantine, T. (1997). *Testimony before House Subcommittee on National Security, International Affairs and Criminal Justice.* Washington, DC: U.S. Government Printing Office.

Cooper, M.H. (1990). *The business of drugs.* Washington, DC: Congressional Quarterly.

Curtis, R., & Hamid, A. (in press). *State sponsored violence in N.Y.C. and indigenous attempts to contain it: The mediating role of the third crown (Sergeant at Arms) of the Latin Kings* [Monograph]. Rockville, MD: National Institute on Drug Abuse.

Curtis, R., & Sviridoff, M. (1994). The social organization of street-level drug markets and its impact on the displacement effect. In R. P. McNamara (Ed.), *Crime displacement: The other side of prevention* (pp. 155–177). New York: Cummings and Hathaway.

del Olmo, R. (1987). Aerobiology and the war on drugs: A transnational crime. *Crime and Social Justice, 30*, 28–44.

Des Jarlais, D.C., & Friedman, S. (1990). Continuity and change within an HIV epidemic: Injecting drug users in New York City 1984–1992. *Journal of the American Medical Association, 271*, 121–127.

Des Jarlais, D.C., Friedman, S., & Strug, D. (1986). AIDS and needle sharing within the IV drug use subculture. In D. Feldman & T. Johnson (Eds.), *The social dimension of AIDS: Methods and theory*. New York: Praeger.

Dixon, D. (1991). *From prohibition to regulation: Bookmaking, anti-gambling and the law*. Oxford, England: Clarendon Press.

Dixon, D. (1995). *Issues in the legal regulation of policing*. Report prepared for the Royal Commission onto the New South Wales Police Service, Sydney, Australia.

Dorn, N, & South, N. (1992). *Traffickers*. London: Routledge.

Ericson, R. (1982). *Reproducing order: A study of police patrol work*. Toronto: University of Toronto Press.

Fagan, J. A. (1992). *Introduction: The ecology of crime and drug use in inner cities*. New York: Social Science Research Council. Unpublished manuscript.

Fogelson, R. M. (1977). *Big city police*. Cambridge, MA: Harvard University Press.

Foucault, M. (1979). *Discipline and punish: The birth of the prison*. New York: Vintage Books.

Gibbs, J.L., Jr. (1988). The Kpelle moot: A therapeutic model for the informal settlement of disputes. In J.B. Cole (Ed.), *Anthropology for the nineties* (pp. 347–359). New York: Free Press.

Goldstein, P.J. (1990). Female substance abusers and violence. In B. Forster & J. Colman Salloway (Eds.), *The socio-cultural matrix of alcohol and drug use: A sourcebook of patterns and factors* (pp. 81–84). Lewiston, NY: Edwin Meller Press.

Gonzales, D. (1990, May 15). When the survivors are seen as sinners. *The New York Times*, Section 13, p. 1.

Green, P., & Purnell, I. (1995). *Measuring the success of law enforcement agencies in Australia in targeting major drug offenders relative to minor drug offenders*. Payneham, Australia: National Police Research Unit.

Gust, S.W., & Walsh, J.M. (1989). Research on the prevalence, impact and treatment of drug abuse in the workplace. In S. W. Gust, & J. M. Walsh (Eds.), *Drugs in the workplace: Research and evaluation data* (pp. 13–22). Washington, DC: National Institute on Drug Abuse.

Hamid, A. (1992). Drugs and patterns of opportunity in the inner city: The case of middle-age, middle-income cocaine smokers. In A. Harrell & G. Peterson, *Drugs, crime and social isolation: Barriers to urban opportunity* (pp. 209–238). Washington, DC: Urban Institute Press.

Hamid, A. (1997). *The political economy of drugs, part II: The cocaine smoking epidemic in New York City's low income minority neighborhoods, 1981 to 1991*. Unpublished manuscript.

Hansen, H.J., Caudill, S.P., & Boone, D.J. (1985). Crisis in drug testing: Results of CDC blind study. *Journal of the American Medical Association, 253*, 2382–2387.

Harris, M. (1977). *Cannibals and kings: The origins of cultures*. New York: Random House.

Hoebel, E.A. (1954/1974). *The law of primitive man*. New York: Atheneum.

Isikoff, M. (1990, February 20). US drafts insects for drug war. *The Hartford Courant*, pp. A1, A5.

Kelling, G., & Moore, M. (1988). *Fixing broken windows*. Glencoe, IL: Free Press.

Latimer, D., & Goldberg, J. (1981). *Flowers in the blood*. New York: Franklin Watts.

Lenin, V.I. (1932). *The development of capitalism in Russia*. Moscow: Progress Publications.

Maher, L., & Dixon, D. (1996, November 19–23). Policing and public health in a street-level drug market. Paper presented for the Annual meeting of the American Society of Criminology, Chicago.

Manning, P. (1980). *The narcs game: Organizational and informational limits on drug law enforcement*. Cambridge, MA: MIT Press.

Manning, P., & Redlinger, L.J. (1977). Invitational edges of corruption: Some consequences of narcotic law enforcement. In P.E. Rock, (Ed.), *Politics and drugs*. Garden City, NJ: E. P. Dutton Books.

Marmor, M., Des Jarlais, D.C., & Cohen, H. (1987). Risk factors for infection with the human immunodeficiency among IV drug abusers in NYC. *AIDS, 1*, 39–44.

Miller, W.R. (1977). *Cops and bobbies: Police authority in New York and London, 1830–1870*. Chicago: University of Chicago Press.

Mollen Commission. (1994). *Report of commission to investigate allegations of police corruption and the anti-corruption procedures of the police department*. New York: Author.

Moore, D. (1992). Deconstructing dependence: An ethnographic critique of an influential concept. *Contemporary Drug Problems, 19*, 459–499.

Moore, D., & Kleiman, M. (1989). *State and local drug law enforcement: Issues and practice*. Washington, DC: National Institute of Justice.

Morris, N., & Hawkins, G. (1970). *The honest politician's guide to crime control*. Chicago: University of Chicago Press.

Musto, D. (1973). *The American disease: Origins of narcotic control*. New Haven, CT: Yale University Press.

Musto, D. (1987). *The American disease: Origins of narcotic control*. (expanded ed.) New York: Oxford University Press.

Nadelmann, E. (1993). *Cops across borders*. University Park, PA: Pennsylvania State University Press.

New York Knapp Commission. (1972). *Knapp Commission report on police corruption*. New York: G. Brazilier.

Ouellet, L., Jimenez, A., Johnson, W., & Wiebel, W. (1991). Shooting galleries and HIV disease: Variations in places for injecting illicit drugs. *Crime and Delinquency, 37* (1), 64–85.

Parliamentary Joint Committee on the National Crime Authority. (1989). *Drugs, crime and society*. Canberra: Australian Government Publishing Service.

Ray, O., & Ksir, C. (1996). *Drugs, society and human behavior*. St. Louis, MO: Mosby/Times-Mirror.

Reiner, R. (1992). *The politics of the police*. Hemel Hempsted, NJ: Harvester Wheatsheaf.

Richardson, J.F. (1970). *The New York police: Colonial times to 1901*. New York: Oxford University Press.

Scarman, L. (1981). *The Brixton disorders: 10–12 April 1981*. Report of an Inquiry by the Rt. Hon. the Lord Scarman OBE Cmnd. 8427. London: HMSO.

Sharff, J. W. (1997). *King Kong on 4th Street: Families and the violence of poverty on the Lower East Side*. Boulder, CO: Westview Press.

Smith, N. (1996). *The new urban frontier: Gentrification and the revanchist city*. New York: Routledge.

Starr, P. (1982). Health care for the poor: The past twenty years. In E. Danziger & D. Weinberg (Eds.), *Fighting poverty: What works and what doesn't* (pp. 161–193). Cambridge, MA: Harvard University Press.

Sutton, A., & James, S. (1995). *Evaluation of Australian drug anti-trafficking law enforcement.* Payneham, Australia: National Police Research Unit.

Sviridoff, M., Sadd, M., Curtis, R. & Grine, R. (1992). *The neighborhood effects of New York City's tactical narcotics team in three Brooklyn precincts.* New York: Vera Institute of Justice.

Trebach, A. (1987). *The great drug war.* New York: Macmillan.

Weatherburn, D. & Lind, B. (1995). *Drug law enforcement policy and its impact on the heroin market.* Sydney, Australia: NSW Bureau of Crime Statistics and Research.

Weishert, R. (1992). *Domestic marijuana: A neglected industry.* Westport, CT: Greenwood Press.

Wilson, J.Q. (1968). *Varieties of police behavior.* Cambridge, MA: Harvard University Press.

Zimmer, L. (1990). Operation pressure point: The disruption of the street level drug trade on New York's Lower East Side. *American Journal of Police, 9,* (1): 43–74.

CHAPTER 5

Drugs and Crime

Chapter Objectives

Criminals define noncriminal society, and criminal motivation antedates drug use. Because drugs can only be acquired through money, poor persons who want them desperately enough are suspected of committing crimes to get them. In fact, most poor persons rely on many sources other than crime to gain scarce drugs or dollars.

Transgressions, taboos, the forbidden, atonement, purification, crime, punishment—these are archetypal narratives, the great human dramas that sustain the religious, literary, and artistic production of every civilization, and it may trivialize them somewhat to restrict their investigation primarily to two minority teenaged mischief-makers on a crumbling inner-city sidewalk, one selling marijuana, the other smoking it. Yet the mantra, "drugs cause crime," has been sounded, sometimes stridently, sometimes less vocally, throughout the short history of drug prohibition in the United States. Adopted as a contemporary media wisdom, it has justified the war on drugs for policymakers and the general public.

The axiom serves a peculiarly American motive. While Americans, like all other civilized humans, can barely conceal their wide-eyed fascination and complicity with crime, we have an extraordinary need, rooted in colonial and national history, to appear innocent of it. Americans can be criminal only if they are seduced by some mysterious or *external* agency such as drugs, gang or cult membership, peer pressure, or another person's evil charisma. In film noir, "the city" is alien (as it actually is to most Americans, who are from small towns) and criminogenic (Christopher, 1997). Another version is that essentially *external* agents such as minorities or new immigrants, "them" not "us," are the so-called Americans whose drug use (abuse) impels them toward crime.

In this way, we manifestly avoid the truth that human nature has proved corruptible, that civilization itself may imply repression and promote discontent (Freud, 1930/1974) and that, as the last chapter argues, specifically American situations, such as drug prohibition or types of social inequality, are criminogenic. The heterogeneity of Americans translates into a multiplicity of moral outlooks, some explosively at odds with others, while coexisting extremes of wealth and poverty also breed crime.

This denial persists only because segments of the population and areas of major cities have formed a visible "other" in the past three decades. It would not have survived if there were no inner city or underclass. Their presence has "sanitized" the remainder of Americans. Thus, to understand fully the unitary simplicity and acceptability of this common sense, the observer must explain not only the sociological and psychological underpinnings of creating and maintaining the group boundaries, but equally how the scapegoating of minorities and immigrants is tied to uneven urban development.

CRIME IS UNIVERSAL AND INDEPENDENT OF DRUG USE

At a time when the media attach the qualifier "drug-related" to horrendous crimes—homicides, infanticides, drive-by shootings, rapes—with the barest evidence, it helps to be reminded that crime is primordial, unavoidable, and, in some views, constitutive of society. Wrestling with the abiding enigma of human evil and wicked deeds, thinkers have suggested religious, functionalist, fascist/racist, and social scientific explanations of them.

Religious explanations have predominated wherever state and religion are identical or mutually reinforce each other. Humans trespass against their fellows because the Devil, or negative external forces, plants envy, greed, anger, and other vices in their hearts. Fidelity to religious teachings in thought and practice safeguards believers from these seditious intrusions. When misdemeanors are committed, the wrongdoer can atone for them by making an equitable compensation for material damages and through confession or other purificatory rituals. High crimes of treason or blasphemy could be punished by excommunication, exile, or death.

Racist explanations of crime have been comforting: the "other race" always commits the crimes! The ancient Greeks associated bad speech, bad manners, and criminal conduct with non-Greeks, or "barbarians." European colonizers and their apologists justified slavery by an appeal to climate: inclement weather compelled Europeans to be creative and hard-working, while the bountiful tropics permitted laziness and vice. In the fascist interregnum, Nazis who had adopted Lombroso's theories were sure that cranial measurements would prove that the criminal was a throwback to the ape (Lombroso, 1911).

The classical social scientific accounts of the function of crime in society did not refer to drugs. Durkheim, the founder of sociology, reasoned that crime was an integral part of every healthy society and a factor in public health (Durkheim, 1915/1952). Crime was normal and useful, as it reminded honest citizens who they were, and thus bred group solidarity: the catharsis of punishment heightened the thrill of belonging. It also played an important role in the normal evolution of morality and of law (Lukes, 1972). Crime solidified community support for non-criminal behavior. The apprehension and punishment of the criminal provided social lessons regarding the consequences of transgressing societal norms. Presumably, if angels formed a society, they could only be aware of it if the same group process defined infringements and produced angel-criminals. Lévi-Strauss, the founder of structuralist anthropology, ultimately incarnated Durkheim's idea of social oppositions by locating them in the binary operations of the brain (Lévi-Strauss, 1949/1969). For him, therefore, crime was biologically inevitable. A person could not even "think" good without someone else "doing" bad.

Some psychological explanations locate crime in thrill seeking: "For many adolescents, shoplifting and vandalism offer the attractions of a thrilling melodrama about the self as seen from within and from without. Quite apart from what is taken, they may regard 'getting away with it' as a thrilling demonstration of a personal competence, especially if it is accomplished under the eyes of adults" (Katz, 1988, p. 9).

In this perspective, property crimes may appeal to young people, "independent of material gain, or esteem from peers" (Katz, 1988, p. 10). Vandalism does not satisfy a desire for acquisition, nor does petty theft serve that purpose for upper middle-class adolescents. Once stolen, items are forgotten. Rather, they commit petty crimes in order to achieve "sneaky thrills."

For other psychologists, crime originates in childhood fantasies of "somatic" freedom of movement, motivated principally by the wish to run away from "dad" and parental authority. Punishment (jail or confinement) represents a complementary infantile yearning to curl up in "mommy's" restorative lap (Duncan, 1997).

Some criminologists have argued that high rates of divorce, resulting in female-headed households and an absence of fathers, have nurtured ungovernable young Americans who are irked by or ignorant of the conventions of family, work, community, and religion. They always break the rules. Not having ever been habilitated, "rehabilitation" is remote. Instead, prison is a satisfying place where the anxiety of making choices is replaced by the certitude of being told what to do (Fleischer, 1994).

Anthropological investigations have eschewed global explanations, preferring instead to illuminate the influence of contingent factors. Ethnographies emphasize how neighborhoods, although similarly deprived, vary in the type and rate of criminal offending. A more complex picture of crime is afforded as being conditioned by a multitude of processes, including ethnicity and interethnic conflict, the local labor market and structure of opportunity, the prevalence of the informal economy, demographic change, housing, and cultural institutions.

For example, in a comparative study of youth, crime, and employment in three low-income communities in New York City, researchers found that pattern type and rates of criminal offending varied noticeably. Despite similar rates of dropping out of school, high unemployment, or deterioration of the physical plant, neighborhoods differed in the degree of homeownership, the type of household, kin and domestic organization, the extent of the informal economy, and in cultural orientations such as the comparative value placed on education or work as means to upward mobility (Sullivan, 1989). These diacritics were impressed upon the informal social controls that regulated the behaviors of local residents, making different patterns, levels and types of offending more or less tolerable. Just like criminal offending, drug distribution and use, centered around the types of drug markets discussed in Chapter 4, also varied by neighborhood.

CRIME IN AMERICA

Crime in America rises and falls according to a pattern that still eludes precise definition or interpretation. It is clearly affected, however, in ways that need more accurate rendering, by the changing economy, immigration, demography, urbanization, class and ethnic conflict, the widening distance between wealth and poverty, and transformations of household and neighborhood composition.

Crime did not much trouble the early settlers. There were 23 convictions for theft in New England in each of the 4 years preceding the Revolutionary War and 24 in each of the 4 years following it (Greenberg, 1976). Living in small rural communities dominated by religious elders, Americans managed their wrongdoing within the bosom of home, community, and church.

In the mid-1700s, as eastern cities such as New York expanded into cosmopolitan centers, overcrowding and economic uncertainties resulted in an escalation of thefts and assaults. Seaports were notorious for sex work, drunkenness, and violent brawls. Political riots were also commonplace. But the peace was kept in the rest of America.

The first national crime wave occurred in the period of urbanization during the 1830s and 1840s. Unruly and riotous behavior, as well as drunkenness, disrupted civic life in the smallest villages and largest cities (Lane, 1979). The same ill wind swept Europe (Gurr, 1989). The adaptation of rural migrants to city life and a modern industrial work regimen, as well as ethnic and class tensions, had traumatized them. As the temperance movement gained momentum, Irish laborers were singled out by nativist gangs. Pitched battles were waged in the streets between the latter and Irish publicans and the gangs they had formed for self-protection (Gurr, 1989; Silberman, 1978).

Crime continued to rise after Emancipation and the exodus of African Americans from the South. In Philadelphia, as in other northern cities, "the fundamental reason was open racism" (Lane, 1992, p. 35). While rural migrants such as Italians, Irish, and African Americans had all flocked to the rapidly industrializing city to capture the attractive jobs being offered, the latter were systematically excluded from employment, often despite better qualifications than their competitors. Except when they instigated racial assaults on African Americans, levels of crime and violence plunged in the European groups. They rose, however, among African Americans, although their use of alcohol was less extensive (Lane, 1979). They were maintained at that high level as city politicians converted African-American neighborhoods into red-light districts (Lane, 1991). Weapons which African Americans had acquired for self-defense in racial attacks were also used in domestic disputes or within the community. The worst riots of the period in New York City were the Draft Riots of 1863, which began as a protest against union conscription policies but rapidly degenerated into a race riot.

But then crime abated. Barring episodic strikes, labor disputes and riots, gambling and sex work (often protected by politicians), and, later, the rise of organized crime during Prohibition, there was suddenly far less disorderly public behavior, drunkenness, murder, suicide, and petty crime throughout America. By 1935, Philadelphia was a much safer place in which to live than it had been in 1835 (Lane, 1991), especially beyond the African-American neighborhoods. National populations had grown older because of a falling birth rate, police departments were being professionalized, and immigrants were better assimilated. Gradually citizens had submitted more to the disciplines of workplace and school, while Victorian values and the striving to be middle class—disseminated through a myriad religious, civic, and voluntary associations, and later by radio, television, and advertising—regulated and homogenized individual behavior at every rung of the social ladder. These advances might have stifled criminal urges in both America and Europe. In 1945, there were fewer than 300 murders in New York City and 435 in 1960 (Silberman, 1978).

CRIME AND THE INNER CITY

The moratorium lasted until the 1960s, when rates of criminal offending and violence again soared. In 1969, the number of murders in New York City had reached 1,116. Although European Americans certainly contributed, attention was focused on the rise in low-income, minority (African-American and Latino) neighborhoods. Analysts and lawmakers were confounded because it had occurred despite the antipoverty programs and welfare provisions of that decade. Many argued that these programs and policies had not failed but that they had been too few and insufficiently funded. Enhancements such as Operation Headstart were a substantial success, but they had reached only a tiny fraction of the infants badly in need of them. Conservatives, however, felt that the government spending itself was at fault: it had made its recipients dependent and irresponsible (Murray, 1984).

Governmental support notwithstanding, however, the physical plant and infrastructure of these neighborhoods had been deteriorating rapidly. As the original European-American residents migrated to the suburbs, buildings were abandoned or torched. Storefronts that had housed small commercial and manufacturing enterprises were gutted. In short order, therefore, these sections were converted into "inner cities." Arriving to occupy them, new waves of immigrants from the American South and the Caribbean were confronted by a shortage of affordable housing, reduced services, and a ruptured social fabric. Removed from the mainstream of decent living standards, jobs, cultural institutions, and political influence, a small but enlarging proportion dropped from a working-class status into an underclass hobbled by multiple family and community dysfunctions. Both inner city and underclass, as well as their association with crime and violence, were soon viewed as beyond remedies (see Chapter 8).

Rising crime tore the fabric of urban American life. The ordinary pleasures of providing after-school care and supervision for children, of adolescents freely exploring their city, of utilizing parks and play areas, riding the subway, or owning a car were converted into an enemy host of new stresses. Apprehensive forethought, arduous routines, expensive nannies, closed-circuit surveillance television, burglar-proofing, barbed wire, alarms, and private security forces were required to cope with them.

Recent analyses have found that, if white-collar offending (for example, the insider trading, savings-and-loans scandals, tax or computer fraud, and other corrupt practices that humbled Wall Street and many financial and corporate notables nationwide during the 1980s) is excluded, the majority of recorded crimes in New York City are committed by a small number of hard core felons hailing from a few notorious, low-income census tracts. Scholars have labeled them "disaster zones" and their residents "ticking bombs." Citing statistics showing that, from 1985 to 1994, juvenile arrests for homicide had climbed by 150% and had doubled for aggravated assault and for weapons possession, they warned that a new criminal species of "super-predators" was evolving: "radically impulsive, brutally remorseless youngsters, including ever more pre-teenage boys, who murder, assault, rape, rob, burglarize, deal deadly drugs, join gun-toting gangs, and create serious communal disorders. They do not fear the stigma of arrest, the pains of imprisonment, or the pangs of conscience" (DiIulio, 1994, p. 3).

These scholars have emphasized the "moral poverty" of super-predators, and the "criminogenic environment" in which they had been raised: "the poverty of being without loving, capable responsible adults who teach you right from wrong . . . In the extreme, it is the poverty of growing up surrounded by deviant, delinquent, and criminal adults in chaotic, dysfunctional, fatherless, Godless, and jobless settings where drug abuse and child abuse are twins, and self-respecting young men literally aspire to get away with murder" (DiIulio, 1994, p. 4).

By using Census Bureau projections of population growth and of the changing age distribution of the population, they estimate that in 2010 there will be 150,000–200,000 super-predators in jail or prison—or nearly three times as many juveniles as are currently in custody (DiIulio, Bennett, & Walters, 1995).

THE DRUGS-CRIME LINK

Many volumes devoted to the exploration of the link between drugs and crime in fact barely address the connection itself. The omission indicates the unclarity, ambiguity, and obliqueness of thinking on the topic. Drug use is after all a different activity from committing a crime (*pace* the drug laws), springs from incongruous motivations, and aims for a separate gratification. Whereas a possible connection between the two has been suspected, and while the threat of criminal consequences had been invoked to discourage the use of many substances (including chocolate and coffee) drug users in the main were not viewed as criminals or capable of criminality other than their infringements of the drug laws. Indeed, the first American drug misusers of the 20th century were European-American housewives to whom physicians had prescribed opiates in overly liberal quantities. But as the campaign against drugs was prodded forward by ambitious officials such as Anslinger, the crusader against marijuana (see Chapter 2), the picture of the addict as a sex-starved, violent carrier of an awful contagion gained currency.

As noted in Chapter 4, drug use and deviance have been consistently lumped together whenever minority groups, such as Chinese, Mexicans, and African Americans, have attempted integration into society. The link between drugs and crime, however, was truly cemented only in the crime wave of the 1960s. Called upon to explain and curb it, policymakers sought empirical evidence that "addicts," rather than disaffected or marginalized Americans, were responsible for the sudden upsurge in robberies, murders, property and street crime, and race riots.

In fact, at the same time that the inner city and the underclass were forming as permanent elements of the urban landscape, drug use in America was rising. From 3% of the 18- to 25-year age cohort in 1960, marijuana users numbered 50% in

1968. Agitated by political ferment over the Vietnam War and the Civil Rights Movement, young Americans of every background and ethnicity experimented extensively with many other drugs, including the hallucinogens, lysergic acid diethylamide (LSD), barbiturates, and cocaine. For servicemen, Vietnam and southeast Asia were a cornucopia of cheap, powerful drugs—principally heroin and exotic marijuana varietals—some of which eventually reached the U.S. mainland. Heroin injecting was widespread among servicemen abroad and among young African Americans and Puerto Ricans at home from 1964 to 1972. When the epidemic peaked in 1970, some 20% of the latter in the 18- to 25-year age grade were injectors.

Although both drug use and crime in the 1960s had risen most among young European Americans, prompting an expansion of treatment services, the drugs-crime-violence-minorities equation preoccupied national media and made a consolidated target for policymakers and law enforcement initiatives.

That combination has cohered more in the succeeding decades. By the 1970s, the violent, unemployed minority male had replaced the genteel European-American matron as the representative American drug addict. In the 1980s, he was joined by the amoral minority female "crackhead." The pair have generated a "biounderclass" in the 1990s, completing the family portrait with the adolescent super-predator. The biounderclass is disadvantaged like the underclass but additionally suffers the adverse outcomes of parental drug misuse. Its problems, because they are "biological," are irreversible.

POLICE DISCRETION AND THE DRUGS-CRIME LINK

In Chapter 4, specific actions against drug users and distributors were seen to issue not from the drug laws themselves, but from the exercise of police discretion. The latter has focused repeatedly on minorities. The Shanghai Commission and the Treaty of 1909 were among the first documents to hammer together the putative connection among drugs, crime, and minorities. First, Chinese were suspected of using opium to ensnare and enslave European-American women. Next, African Americans affected by cocaine were accused not only of wanting to seduce European-American women but of rebellion. Since then, hidden agendas have targeted Mexicans and other latter-day minorities, among them unwed mothers supported by public transfer payments, and "teenaged drug millionaires" who had "never worked a stroke in their lives."

In the 1960s, rapid, global, political and economic change (see Chapter 8) had created a "legitimation crisis" in Western democracies (Habermas, 1963). In many nations, such as the United States, it was exacerbated by class struggle and conflict over the incorporation of immigrants and racial minorities. Dislike of the latter was channeled into mobilizing the police against "drugs and crime." Thus, although neither may have been greater in low-income communities than in more affluent ones, they were certainly less detected. If Operation Pressure Point or the Tactical Narcotics Teams (see Chapter 4) had been unleashed on middle-class neighborhoods, putting officers in their lobbies and hallways in place of discreet and indulgent doormen, quite extensive criminality (such as drug distribution and use, child neglect and abuse, wife battering, larceny, fraud, or shoplifting) might have been uncovered. A columnist for the *New York Times*, commenting on the murder of a 40-year-old European male by two 15-year-old European-American drinking companions, wrote:

> It is difficult to entirely shake off racial considerations in all this. You would have to be far more colorblind than most Americans not to notice that the police-orchestrated "perp walks" seen on television habitually involve mostly black and Hispanic suspects. But here we have Mr. Schneiderman, a white man [suspected of killing a policeman while attempting to rob his father's apartment]. In the McMorrow killing [a real estate agent murdered in Central Park], the face staring out from the front pages is of a baby-faced white girl right off a box of cornflakes. We have also just witnessed Marv Albert, the sports announcer, being charged with a sex crime—a white counterpoint to the black Dallas Cowboys football players who were falsely accused of rape a few months ago. And there was recently the spectacle of a Danish woman being pilloried for having left her baby outside an East Village restaurant while she was inside having a drink (a routine practice in her native land). That story might not have received so much attention had it not come against the backdrop of a well-publicized parade of black and Hispanic mothers said to have committed unspeakable horrors against their children. While none of these cases is related, they collectively leave behind a necessary reminder that people can do bad things, regardless of whether they are black or white, rich or poor, old or shockingly young. (Marriott, 1997, p. 1)

This truth notwithstanding, minority persons who have been arrested for drug offenses and other crimes far outnumber European Americans. The penalties they receive are frequently (and mandatorily) greater than those European Americans receive. Released from prison, they return to neighborhoods that can offer them little employment. Even in crime, they cannot rely on traditional structures, such as organized crime or the Mafia, to which European Americans have access in some of their neighborhoods.

Crime and violence form powerful rhetorics in mobilizing public approval for restrictive police initiatives against minority populations. While the connection among drugs, crime, and violence has always been a reliable tool in the demagogue's arsenal, it was brought to greater prominence in the last two decades, in step with the heightened awareness of drug issues generally. In these two decades, the position of minorities also worsened appreciably, causing a national crisis.

Thus, what is known about the relationship between drugs and crime is really about that relationship among economically depressed and socially marginalized populations. The findings of social science are only being added recently to the information to be gathered from their novels, memoirs, and biographies about whether, how, and why upper middle-class and middle-class European-American drug users engage in crime (Hamid, et al., 1997).

Samples are further biased for being drawn from captive populations. In most studies addressing this topic, respondents are, in addition to being minority, usually male, and well known to the authorities because of arrests, incarcerations, hospitalizations, or enrollment in treatment programs. "These captive drugs/crime samples cannot be used to generalize findings to all criminally involved drug users. Equally clear, it testifies to the importance of using multiple controls for active/captive comparisons. . . . It seems of particular significance in the context of this collection of studies that the most consistent area of difference is that of the drugs/crime nexus" (Pottieger, 1981, pp. 232–233). (Pottieger reviewed the Baltimore, Miami, San Antonio, and Philadelphia studies discussed in this chapter.)

DO DRUG MISUSERS COMMIT CRIMES?

The majority of drug users, or casual users of alcohol and the illegal drugs, escape notice because their communities are not targeted by the police. Drug misusers from well-to-do homes are shielded and then rapidly admitted to private treatment facilities before criminal or violent engagements occur (Waldorf, Reinarman, & Murphy, 1993). Even in low-income, inner-city neighborhoods where the police are most aggressive, they have a chance of being overlooked because they are usually hard-working citizens who do not commit violent or property crimes. When an unfortunate few are arrested for drug possession (or, in the case of a New York attorney, for cultivating a single marijuana plant for personal use at his upstate home), exemplary lives, distinguished by voluntary community service, exacting careers, and dedicated parenting are often revealed. The penalty for disclosure among this class of drug users is total upheaval of a respectable lifestyle: the attorney not only was sentenced to a long term of imprisonment, but after his home and other property had been seized under the asset forfeiture laws against drug offenders, his family was rendered penniless and homeless.

Studies of mostly captive samples drawn from minority populations offer empirical evidence of a strong correlation between drug use and the commission of violent crime. Correlation, however, does not imply causation; rather, it only indicates probability. For example, young male drinkers were more likely to commit crimes than nondrinkers (O'Donnell, Voss, Clayton, Slatin, & Room, 1976). Similarly, the extent of drug use was correlated with criminality. In a study of the pretreatment behavior of a large sample of opioid and cocaine users, proceeds that had been obtained as a result of criminal activity grew with the frequency and quantity of drug use (Collins, Hubbard, & Rachal, 1985). In Scotland, the more teenagers used licit and illicit drugs, the more frequently they committed crimes (Hammersley, Cassidy, & Oliver, 1995).

Opportunities in crime are of course gendered and determined by age (Datesman, 1981; O'Donnell, 1969; Suffet & Brotman, 1976; Williams & Bates, 1970). For example, pregnant women face more severe penalties than men because their drug use can be punished not only under the drug laws, but for endangering the unborn infant, causing it malicious damage, or even for distributing drugs to a minor via the uterus or breast milk. They also come more frequently in conflict with state agencies for neglecting or abusing older children and adolescents (Maher, 1996).

On the streets, women are discouraged from many kinds of crime, and are restricted in the end to nonviolent income-generating offenses, such as sex work or low-level drug distribution roles. Men are more likely to commit violent crimes, more serious crimes against property (such as burglary) and nonviolent crimes involving a victim, and are more often involved in drug distribution; but women may also turn to crime to raise money for drug purchases.

Thus, studies showed that 40% of all female narcotics addicts partially support their drug habit through sex work (Chambers & Chambers, 1970), with some estimates as high as 70% (Ratner, 1993). A significant association between race and prostitution was also reported (File, McCahill, & Savitz, 1974; Inciardi, Pottieger, Forney, Chotwood, & McBride, 1982). In one study of 380 female arrestees who were clinically diagnosed as narcotics addicts at the time of arrest, 20% of European-American female addicts and 20% of Latinas had ever been arrested for sex work, while almost 50% of the African-American females had been (Weissman & File, 1976). In another study of the 227 female addicts, 49% of the African Americans were sex workers, but only 20% of the European-American women were (File et al., 1974). The researchers offered no explanation for the difference, although it is likely that European Americans had better support networks and Latinas had more extensive roles in drug distribution.

Women also supported their habits by distributing drugs (De Leon, 1986; File et al., 1974; Inciardi & Chambers, 1972; Ratner, 1993; Waldorf, 1973). In a study of 328 female addicts, European-American females spent 44% and Chicanas 50% of their nonincarcerated time distributing drugs (Anglin, Hser, & McGlothin, 1987).

Although less engaged in violent and property crimes, female drug misusers nevertheless committed a significant number of robberies, burglaries, forgeries, and other theft. In a study of 286 active women narcotics users in Miami, participants avoided car theft and burglaries but specialized in shoplifting, pickpocketing, handling stolen goods, and forgeries (Inciardi & Pottieger, 1986).

Another perspective on the relationship between drugs and crime comes from an examination of offenders' postaddiction careers. If they had been committing crimes while active drug users, do they stop when in remission? In the study of 243 Baltimore opiate addicts, it was found that criminality decreased by the staggering amount of 84% during the months or years that these addicts were not dependent on heroin or other opiates. In their periods of heavy use, however, the 109 European-American and 134 African-American males offended repeatedly (Ball, Rosen, Flueck, & Nurco, 1981). These results corroborated those of the study of 239 active male heroin users in Miami, whose offenses over a 12-month numbered 80,644 (Inciardi & Chambers, 1972, p. 9).

THE DIFFERENT DRUGS AND CRIME

Different histories and patterns of criminal offending have been associated with the various drugs.

Alcohol

In the United States, alcohol has been legal for purchase by those over 21 years of age since the end of Prohibition. Its legal status may thus connote relative safety, legitimacy, or social acceptance, which are denied such other "recreational" drugs as cocaine, marijuana, and heroin. Yet the dangers of alcohol consumption—both short-term, such as those associated with drinking and driving or with alcohol poisoning, and long-term, such as liver disease, heart attack, and stroke—had been the subject of scientific study and public debate long before Prohibition.

Numerous studies over many years have amassed compelling evidence of the correlation between alcohol consumption and violent and criminal behavior. They demonstrate that alcohol lowers inhibitions, impairs judgment and motor coordination, and heightens aggression in certain situations. Recent studies have strongly linked alcohol and homicide; in Baltimore, for example, 36% of those convicted of the crime had consumed alcohol before committing it. In societies with high rates of alcoholism, this pattern is even much more pronounced. For example, in Sweden, an estimated 70% of murderers had consumed alcohol prior to the act (Ray & Ksir, 1996, p. 247).

The impact of alcohol use on criminal behavior is not limited to homicide, however. Investigations of persons convicted of committing assault, spousal abuse, and child abuse demonstrate a similar connection. The higher the consumption of alcohol, the greater the incidence of these crimes.

In Australia, the Institute of Criminology at Canberra convened a conference in 1993 to present the latest research into the causes, deterrence, and prevention of violence (Chappell & Egger, 1995). One of the studies presented at the conference examined the situational factors that most accurately predict whether conflict between patrons in bars would result in violence. In each case, the patrons in question were drunk, and in some of those cases they were ultimately asked to leave by the bartender. The patrons' responses to this request varied from compliance, to shouting but eventually complying, to acting out their aggression physically in a manner that required calling the police. Of the 102 incidents of aggression studied, 29 (28.4%) involved violence. The factor that best predicted violent behavior was intervention by the bartender, in particular if the bartender refused to serve more alcohol to the patron.

In 1994, the U.S. Bureau of Justice Statistics released a report summarizing the data obtained in the U.S. National Crime Victimization Study's survey on violence against women (which covered the period from 1987 to 1991). This survey was of a nationally representative sample of approximately 400,000 women who were asked whether they had been the victim of violent crime; if they had been, information about their attacker and about the nature of the incident was recorded (Bachman, 1994). The report revealed that nearly 50% of all rape victims believed that the man who raped them was under the influence of drugs or alcohol at the time the incident occurred. Alcohol has long been regarded as a major contributing influence (if not an outright cause) in cases of domestic abuse.

Cocaine

Since the late 19th century, American lawmakers and drug experts have feared that cocaine impelled African Americans to crime and rebellion. The fear was revived during the cocaine smoking epidemic of the 1980s and early 1990s. While both did increase, most researchers explained it by the larger numbers of persons attracted to use or distribution of the drug, rather than by a rise in the rate of offending.

None has convincingly blamed the pharmacological effects of cocaine for this outcome, although the phenomena of excitation and withdrawal, succeeding each other rapidly in the case of this drug, have been held accountable for it. In this view, the user feels so omnipotent and free of moral restraints soon after she or he administers the drug that violent or criminal acts swiftly follow. Alternatively, the user commits the acts because of the utter dejection and craving for readministration, which rapidly follow excitation. A physiological explanation is offered for these effects. During excitation, lawless behavior results from the elevated levels of dopamine in the brain; during withdrawal, reuptake of dopamine across synapses is prevented, causing a possibly criminogenic depression. Ethnographers, observing use in its naturalistic settings, report that the drug typically prompts users to become somewhat reclusive and to avoid contact with others. Crack misusers—often distinguishable from nonusers because they exhibit physical symptoms, such as abnormally bright or shining eyes, a tongue that appears to be "glued" to the roof of the mouth, as well as trembling limbs—are likely to present themselves as panhandlers or perpetrators of petty property theft (such as shoplifting, kiting checks, and so on), rather than as ruthless predators (Hamid, 1992a).

Marijuana

Before World War II, the most commonly cited argument employed by opponents of marijuana (including law enforcement officials, prosecutors, and many public health advocates) was that prolonged, extensive use of the drug tended to lead to aggressive, senseless, and even violent criminal behavior. Writers used pejorative labels such as the "killer weed," and "the weed of madness" to indicate the undesirable effects of marijuana smoking (Goode, 1993, p. 128).

During the 1930s and the 1940s, the Federal Bureau of Narcotics published a series of reports and articles for widespread distribution that described in lurid detail and purple prose the violent acts committed by persons under the spell of marijuana. In this period, state legislatures and the U.S. Congress were enacting laws dictating stiff sentences for the sale and possession of marijuana.

The classic antidrug film, *Reefer Madness* (1937) also disseminated the message. In it, marijuana was called "the real Public Enemy Number One." Its "soul-destroying" effects included: "emotional disturbances, the total inability to direct thought, the loss of all power to resist physical emotions, leading finally to acts of shocking violence . . . ending often in incurable insanity" (quoted in Ray & Ksir, 1996, pp. 31–32).

The Comprehensive Drug Abuse Prevention and Control Act (1970) established an impressive-sounding official body called the National Commission on Marijuana and Drug Abuse. The Commission was charged with investigating all aspects of marijuana use and addiction, and reporting on its findings to the Congress. For 3 years, it gathered and analyzed massive quantities of data; in 1972 and 1973 the Commission published six volumes of findings.

Among the dozens of studies carried out for this Commission on the health and behavioral effects of marijuana use was one conducted in Philadelphia in which 559 males, aged 15 to 34, were interviewed about their marijuana use and criminal activity. The results of this particular study directly contradicted the assumptions and preconceived biases of the Congress and the Commission. As Erich Goode, the sociologist who conducted the Philadelphia study, has reported, 96% of the people interviewed said that they "never" or "almost never" felt an urge to hurt someone while under the influence of marijuana. Nearly as high a proportion (88%) said that they never, or almost never, felt angrier while under the drug's influence than they did normally. Furthermore, the effects on the interviewees' moods and actions were found to be exactly the opposite of what critics of the drug had alleged. Indeed, rather than encouraging users to engage in violent, aggressive, or otherwise senseless activities, marijuana made an overwhelming majority of respondents feel more peaceful and passive than before use.

On the other hand, the Philadelphia study, and other similar studies, did find that people who smoked marijuana were significantly more likely than nonusers to have committed criminal offenses; they were also significantly more likely than nonusers to have committed multiple offenses. However, the extent to which these offenses were acquisitive is not clear. The study also found that over a third of the users interviewed had committed none of the specified offenses. Although these findings cannot be considered definitive (a cautionary qualification that probably applies to all such studies), they suggest that people who used other, "harder" drugs in addition to marijuana were more likely to commit criminal offenses (Goode, 1972). From this result, it appears that marijuana use on its own does not lead to criminal activity for the majority of users. Yet while marijuana use may not cause crime per se, it may still be part of the lifestyle of people who commit crime.

In Canada, Hartnagel and Krahn (1989) studied the work history and employment status of school dropouts who were users of alcohol and other drugs. They found a relationship between employment and crime among users. This study produced no evidence that marijuana use caused, or led to, violent crime. What appeared to be most predictive of criminal activity, in fact, was not drug use, but rather a subject's employment status and financial record.

In the United Kingdom, in the late 1960s, the government responded to mounting public concern about the perceived effects of marijuana smoking (particularly among young people) in a fashion similar to that of the U.S. government. With increased awareness of the ever-growing population of marijuana users, the government established a Standing Interdepartmental Advisory Committee on Drug Dependence to study the problem and formulate possible public policy responses. In 1968 this Committee issued a report that reviewed what was known at that time concerning the health effects of marijuana smoking, as well the provisions in the existing Dangerous Drugs Act that might be employed to control and prosecute marijuana use. The Committee concurred that more teenagers and young adults— across all social classes—were experimenting with marijuana use, but emphasized that there was no evidence to suggest that it was causing violent crime or aggressive behavior.

Heroin

"Of all the drugs in the vast pharmacopeia of mind-altering and addictive drugs, there is only one which is responsible for significant amounts of street crime—heroin" (American Bar Association [ABA], 1972, p. 9). The ABA goes on to say that its opinion is based on "informal estimates" since there "are no precise statistics that demonstrate exactly what proportion of urban crime is committed by addicts." For decades, experts who conducted research on heroin users have found an association between being habituated to heroin and engaging in other forms of criminal activity. In this simplified model, young people first begin to experiment with drug use by taking "soft" drugs, which serve in turn as a stepping stone to "harder" drugs such as cocaine and heroin. The cost of using these relatively expensive drugs then may lead users to commit crimes in order to finance their habits. The obvious policy conclusion was that young people should be discouraged from ever experimenting with drugs, and that strenuous efforts should be made to combat heroin use. If using heroin leads to aggressive or violent behavior, then reducing or eliminating heroin use should, in and of itself, significantly reduce violence.

In the past couple of decades, however, the scholarly consensus regarding the impact of hard-drug use on other criminal behavior has been challenged and largely deflated. It now seems clear to most researchers that the link between heroin use and predatory behavior is far more complex than was formerly believed. Nevertheless, the data continue to indicate a strong *association* between heroin use and predatory crime. Two prominent studies demonstrate such an association. First, in a study of prison inmates in California, Michigan, and Texas (Chaiken & Chaiken, 1982), heroin addicts were found to have committed a range of criminal acts on significantly more days than convicts who used heroin without being addicted to it; and the nonaddicted users in their sample committed crime more often than convicts who did not use the drug at all. Second (Inciardi, 1979), crimes committed by hard-drug users in Miami were compared with those committed by users of soft drugs (nonnarcotic drugs). The study found that while both the hard-drug users and the soft-drug users committed a great deal of crime, the users of narcotics committed, on average, 375 crimes per year—whereas the nonnarcotics users committed "only" 320 crimes per year. Crimes committed by narcotics users were also more serious, such as robbery and burglary.

In their exhaustive review of the research literature on the association or correlation between drug use and predatory (acquisitive) crime, Chaiken and Chaiken (1990) found that the latter tends to occur before drug abuse—not, as is commonly assumed, the other way around. People who commit criminal offenses and are habitual users of "softer" drugs such as alcohol or marijuana may eventually drift over the drug threshold to become addicted to heroin. As this pattern progresses, the rate of criminal offending is likely to increase commensurately. Interestingly, if these frequent offenders then reduce the frequency and amount of their drug taking, their rate of criminal activity is likely to drop by approximately the same proportion.

There is considerable evidence to suggest that heroin use is associated with acquisitive (predatory) crime. Respondents in a study of heroin users in East Harlem were, on average, raising $7,597 per year from crime (Johnson et al., 1985). In England, Parker, Newcombe, and Bakx (1988) found that the annual rate of convictions in their sample of London-based heroin users almost doubled following the onset of heroin use, and this use was mostly financed through acquisitive crime. Furthermore, Parker (1996), in his study of heroin users in northwest England also found that acquisitive crime (particularly domestic burglary) and heroin use were strongly associated.

HOW DRUG USERS ACTUALLY EARN MONEY FOR DRUGS (TAKING CARE OF BUSINESS)

Usually purchases of marijuana and alcohol are not a heavy financial burden for users, unless, in the case of alcohol, they become compulsive users or alcoholics who pursue it through losses of job, savings, family, and social standing. Marijuana users typically spend no more than $5 a day on a "nickel bag," occasionally improving it with "dime bags," worth $10, of sinsemilla (a more carefully cultivated, potent marijuana) or an exotic variety (marijuanas grown hydroponically or using special hybrids). Compared with what a consumer might spend on alcoholic beverages or other drugs, marijuana purchases are modest indeed. The savings are best appreciated in Third-World marijuana-growing countries, where the $5 nickel bag translates into about U.S. $1 by many rates of exchange, and is to be compared with the price of imported liquors, which sell for more than U.S. $50 for a 26-oz. bottle.

Because of the costliness of heroin and cocaine, it is assumed that users must resort to robbery, burglary, car theft, shoplifting, or selling drugs to pay for their habit. Especially if they are unemployed or employed at low wages, they are unable to do so solely out of their legal earnings. A conservative estimate, formulated in the late 1980s and widely cited in the media, was that $1 million in cash, goods, and property was stolen every day by heroin users in New York City alone. If that figure is multiplied by the number of cities nationwide where large populations of heroin users may reside, a very significant societal cost is reached.

Ethnographers, who observe users in the daily round of drug seeking and consumption, are unconvinced that drug habits are largely dependent on the proceeds of criminal undertakings. Certainly all drug users do not commit crime in order to finance their drug use, even in the most depressed economic conditions. Many male and female cocaine or heroin users do not ever have to rely on either crime or employment to support their habits. Their spouses or lovers supply all the drugs they need (Eldred & Washington, 1976; File 1976; File, McCahill & Savitz, 1974; Johnson et al., 1985). Some male cocaine smokers, especially freebasers, or those who prepare the smokable precipitate themselves rather than the ready-made crack, have the means to buy bulk quantities of cocaine, to rent rooms in luxury hotels for several days, and to invite several low-income women to "party" with them. Apparently, a craving for company rather than sex motivates them (Hamid, 1992b, 1997). Some female sex workers support their boyfriends. In one study, heroin users in East Harlem were found to have obtained as much as 42% of their heroin through in-kind arrangements with dealers and distributors (Johnson et al., 1985).

Researchers are frequently impressed by the amount of other community support drug users can mobilize. Often portrayed as estranged from kin and neighbors or a danger to them, they in fact rely heavily on gifts or money lent by family and friends. Food and lodgings are routinely provided by these sources. Public transfer payments, or welfare entitlements, have been known to travel directly from the Treasury Department to the drug distributor, via the misuser.

Drug distribution roles account for much of the criminality of drug users and is perhaps the principal means by which they earn money or drugs. In return for heroin, some users engage in such tasks as dividing larger quantities of heroin into street-salable bags, referring customers to their dealer, and selling the drug on the street. Other jobs exist for holders, touts, cop men, resource providers, and testers (Goldstein & Duchaine, 1980). In a study of the economics of drug dealing in the nation's capital, researchers focused on the role played by drug sales in the survival strategies of the long-term poor in Washington, D.C. Their data were based on the pretrial records of more than 11,000 District residents who had been charged with selling drugs, as well as on interviews conducted with nearly 200 people serving probationary sentences. The total earnings from street drug sales were estimated to be approximately $350 million in 1988, a figure that was more than twice the estimated income earned in the District from property-related crimes such as burglary, robbery, mugging, and shoplifting (Reuter, MacCoun, & Murphy, 1990).

Drug users sometimes show considerable ingenuity in creating legitimate employment in their neighborhood. In a study of New York City's minority neighborhoods, middle-class cocaine smokers had eventually lost their middle-income jobs because of various misadventures related to their illegal drug use. Bounding back energetically to find money to buy drugs, they for the most part shunned crime but trimmed hedges; carried groceries; unloaded trucks; washed cars; salvaged and repaired discarded appliances; stripped abandoned buildings of scrap metals; retrieved bottles and cans from garbage; or sought piecemeal, intermittent labor (Hamid, 1992a).

Those who do commit nondrug crimes in order to "take care of business" generally do not offend on a grand scale. The majority of acquisitive offenders committed acts of petty theft and shoplifting, not sophisticated fraud. In a sample of drug users in Glasgow, the majority of offenders were shoplifters or burglars (Hammersley et al., 1995). In a recent study of crack cocaine users in the northwest of England, most acquisitive offenders in the sample had committed shoplifting, mugging, or petty theft (Parker, 1996).

It should be noted that supraindividual factors, quite independent of the perpetrator's drug or other personal problems, also motivate crime. Acquisitive crime can also aid local capital accumulation. For instance, drug users may steal in neighborhoods other than their own, where they are less likely to be recognized and will also be far from neighbors and friends. When they fence (sell) what they have stolen, however, they may turn to local networks at home. The profits that they and the buyer return from the transaction may be spent locally, leading over time to modest indigenous capital accumulation (Hamid, 1997). Even when crime is directed against relatives or neighbors, wealth is not lost but redistributed within the local community.

THEORIES OF THE DRUGS-CRIME RELATIONSHIP

The idea that drug use and criminality are causally connected forms the basis of many of the laws regulating or prohibiting drug use and emerged only recently. Causal interpretations of the drugs-crime relationship can be divided into four camps, as follows:

1. *Drug use causes crime.* Chemical substances, by impairing judgment, lowering inhibitions, and reducing self control, lead to criminal activity. Or drug users may commit acquisitive crime in order to raise money to obtain more drugs. In both explanations, the causal relationship is "unidirectional."
2. *Crime causes drug use.* In this view, persons who are criminally predisposed also take drugs. Drug use is seen as integral or normative to a "criminal lifestyle." Drugs may be used before the offending to bolster courage, or afterward to celebrate success. This unidirectional causal relationship between the two variables flows in the direction opposite the first.
3. *Drug use involves a third variable.* In this explanation, the relationship between drugs and crime is said to exist only in relation to one or more additional variables. They both result from a common cause, such as "social disaffection," or legal-political factors. Otherwise, there is no connection between the two variables.

4. *There is a reciprocal relationship between drugs and crime.* In this model, drug use and offending are seen as "interrelated lifestyles" and the relationship between drugs and crime lies in the "overlap" between the two lifestyles.

Few studies have proved or disproved these hypothetical causal relationships (Ball et al., 1981; Elliot, Huizinga, & Ageton, 1985; Speckart & Anglin 1986). Some researchers reported that few addicts engaged in property crime while under the influence of narcotics (Barton, 1976), while others found that few crimes were committed by them when they were not intoxicated (Ball et al., 1981; McGlothlin, Anglin, & Wilson, 1978).

In this chapter and the last, additional views of the relationship between drugs and crime have been proffered. First, the drug laws are themselves criminogenic. Prohibition causes crime because it enormously inflates the actual cost of producing and distributing drugs, leaves drug markets without regulation, fosters rivalries between distributors, corrupts police, and artificially enlarges demand. Second, the "drugs cause crime" platform was a self-fulfilling prophecy that the police made as they targeted unruly minorities and immigrants.

Possibly because of prohibition and actual policing, addicts are prepared to do whatever is necessary to "get over," and will commit crimes, borrow, beg, sell treasured possessions, work, deceive others, or distribute drugs to do so (Goldstein, 1981). Several distinct styles may maintain addiction, and some may emphasize crime more than others (Nurco, Cisin, & Balter, 1981; Nurco & Shaffer, 1982).

THE DECLINE OF CRIME IN THE LATE 1990s

The late 1990s have posed fresh challenges for theorists of crime and the drugs-crime relationship, and for the Cassandras prophesying super-predators. Serious crimes—property crime and violent crime—have declined by 3% in 1996, the fifth annual decrease in a row. These improvements have occurred in every major American city, and New York, once the most dangerous city in the world, leads the national trend.

The plunge in homicides, the largest since the modern crime wave engulfed the nation in the late 1960s and early 1970s, has been the most heartening news. Homicides dropped 11%; in New York City, there were 986 in 1996, compared with 1,117 in 1995. Although the homicide rate remains far greater than it is in Japan or Western Europe, where it is less than 0.1% per 100,000 of population, the drop from 8–10 to 7.3 per 100,000 of population in the United States represents a major breakthrough (Halbfinger, 1998).

Police and politicians have eagerly claimed the credit for these glad tidings. In New York City, Mayor Giuliani and ex-Police Commissioner Bratton have claimed that their "quality of life" and "zero-tolerance" approaches (see Chapter 4) have thrown all the criminals in jail and have deterred others who wished to emulate them. Demographers have argued that the "baby boomers" have aged beyond their peak years for criminal offending.

Yet numerous informal, grassroots efforts to rebuild neighborhoods and to rebuild the quality of civic life in neglected neighborhoods must also be given their due. In many low-income sections of New York City, the abandoned buildings that had harbored drug misusers and distributors in the 1980s have been renovated, and now shelter workers and their families instead. Following the start former Mayor Dinkins had made in the 1980s, the sponsors of this renewal include not only governmental agencies but, more significantly, ministers and their churches, minority business partnerships, and voluntary organizations. Even gang members in the dawning 21st century seem dedicated to community uplift.

Older persons are also modeling less criminal or deviant behaviors and attitudes for their younger mentors. Harlem and Brooklyn are full of baby boomers who had spent the 1960s as career criminals, Black Panthers, or other revolutionaries but who, in their 50s today, are as vocal in their opposition to drugs and crime and as activist in their promotion of spiritual renewal, educational programs, cultural events and sports. They also seek better relations with the police and to end their excessive use of force.

Finally, employment is an important factor. More persons are employed in 1998, as unemployment rates plunge to their lowest in three decades. Upward mobility has not only put more spending capital at the disposal of more persons previously disadvantaged, but has buoyed hopes and expectations. Personal behavior has adjusted correspondingly. Citizens dress better, eat wisely, have a higher regard for themselves, and expect more responsible behavior from their children.

Thus a process of learning has been underway. Exposed to the excesses of heroin and cocaine use in preceding generations and existing in an altered ideological milieu, younger persons in minority neighborhoods have settled for marijuana, which they smoke communally in blunts, thereby regulating and reducing its consumption. While some young Puerto Ricans have recently started sniffing heroin, young African Americans and Caribbean Africans remain implacably opposed to it. In the United Kingdom and Europe, where their mates have elevated heroin to the level of "Trainspotting" trendiness, young persons of African and Caribbean ancestry repudiate it.

The reversal of widely held expectations forces a reexamination of policy and the premises underlying it. As this chapter has shown, the "drugs-crime connection" rests on little empirical evidence, but has been responsive to changing ideological currents. For policy to be effective, these have to be laid bare for examination and changed.

Discussion Questions

1. How do persons in the reader's community account for wrongdoing, evil, misfortune, and crime?
2. What are rates of criminal offending for different offenses in the reader's community? How reliable are these records? Have they fluctuated over time? What accounted for changes? How is drug use related to these crimes?
3. The list of films, novels, plays, and other art in which crime is the major theme begins in antiquity and is immense. Oedipus, Macbeth, and Raskolnikov are famous fictional criminals; Cain and Judas are at the head of real ones. The American film noir genre, distinguished by actors like Humphrey Bogart and Lauren Bacall, is entirely dedicated to portrayals of crime. Another genre of films, such as *Scarface*, focus on drug criminals. Develop a list, review works, and discuss themes, assumptions, and explanations and how they change over time.
4. Review reasons for the association of criminal offending with the different drugs.
5. Enumerate the ways in which drug prohibition promotes crime. Would legalization prevent these crimes, or would they be replaced by new ones?
6. How can the present decline in crime occurring in American and European cities be sustained? Have U.S. deportation policies helped, by returning convicted criminal immigrants to their home countries? What are the likely consequences in the latter, and do they serve long-term American security?
7. Interview different types of drug users (wealthy, low-income, male, female, young, old). Focus on income generation and criminal ideation, and discuss findings. Discuss and observe rules governing confidentiality and protection of human subjects from research risks before beginning.

REFERENCES

American Bar Association (1972). *Annual report.* Washington, DC: Author.

Anglin, M., Hser, Y., & McGlothin, W. (1987). Sex differences in addict careers: Becoming addicted. *American Journal of Drug and Alcohol Abuse, 13,* 253–280.

Bachman, C. (1994). Report of US National Crime Victimization Study. Washington, DC: National Institute of Justice.

Ball, J., Rosen, L., Flueck, J., & Nurco, D. (1981). Lifetime criminality of heroin addicts in the United States. *Journal of Drug Issues, 12,* 225–239.

Barton, W. (1976). Heroin use and criminality: Survey of inmates of state correctional facilities, January, 1974. In Research Triangle Institute, *Drug use and crime* (pp. 419–440). Springfield, VA: National Technical Information Service (PB-259 167).

Chaiken, J., & Chaiken, M. (1982). *Varieties of criminal behavior*. Santa Monica, CA: Rand.

Chaiken, J., & Chaiken, M. (1990). *Multijurisdictional drug law enforcement strategies: Reducing supply and demand*. U.S. Department of Justice, Office of Justice Programs, National Institute of Justice.

Chambers, J., & Chambers, C. (1970). *The epidemiology of opiate addiction in the United States*. Springfield, IL: Charles C Thomas.

Chappell, D., & Egger, S. (Eds.). (1995). *Australian violence: Contemporary perspectives, 11*. (Proceedings of the 2nd National Conference on Violence, 1993). Canberra: Australian Institute of Criminology.

Christopher, N. (1997). *Somewhere in the night: Film noir and the American city*. New York: Henry Holt.

Collins, J., Jr., Hubbard, R., & Rachal, J. (1985). Expensive drug use and illegal income: A test of explanatory hypotheses. *Criminology, 23*, 74–64.

Datesman, S. (1981). Women, crime, and drugs. In J. A. Inciardi, (Ed.), *The drugs-crime connection*. (pp. 85–104). Beverly Hills, CA: Sage.

De Leon, G. (1986). Legal pressure in therapeutic communities. In G. De Leon (Ed.), *Compulsory treatment of drug use: Research and clinical practice*. NIDA Research Monograph 118 (pp. 160–177). Rockville, MD: National Institute on Drug Abuse.

DiIulio, J. (1994). *The truly deviant: Crime, punishment and the disadvantaged*. New York: Simon & Schuster.

DiIulio, J.J., Jr., Bennett, W., & Walters, J.P. (1995). *Body count*. New York: Simon & Schuster.

Duncan, M.G. (1997). *Romantic outlaws, beloved prisons: The unconscious meanings of crime and punishment*. New York: New York University Press.

Durkheim, E. (1915/1952). *Suicide*. London: Tavistock Press.

Eldred, C.A., & Washington, M.M. (1976). Interpersonal relationships in heroin use by women and their role in treatment outcome. *International Journal of the Addictions, 11*:117–130.

Elliot, D., Huizinga, D., & Ageton, S. (1985). *Explaining delinquency and drug abuse*. Beverly Hills, CA: Sage.

File, K. (1976). Sex roles and street roles. *International Journal of the Addictions, 11*, 263–268.

File, K., McCahill, T., & Savitz, L. (1974). Narcotics involvement and female criminality. *Addictive Diseases: An International Journal, 1*, 177–188.

Fleischer, M. (1994). *Warehousing violence*. Santa Barbara, CA: University of California Press.

Freud, S. (1930/1974). In R. Wallheim (Ed.), *Civilization and its discontents*. New York: Anchor Books.

Goldstein, P. (1981). Getting over: Economic alternatives to predatory crime among street drug users. In J. A. Inciardi, (Ed.), *The drugs-crime connection* (pp. 67–85). Beverly Hills, CA: Sage.

Goldstein, P., & Duchaine, N. (1980). Daily criminal activities of street drug users. Paper presented at the annual meeting of The American Society of Criminology.

Goode, E. (1972). *Drugs in American society*. New York: McGraw-Hill.

Goode, E. (1993). *Drugs, society, and behavior*. New York: Dushkin.

Greenberg, D. (1976). *Crime and law enforcement in the colony of New York*. Ithaca, NY: Cornell University Press.

Gurr, T.R. (1989). *Violence in America, Vol. I: The history of crime*. Newbury Park, CA: Sage.

Habermas, J. (1963). *Legitimation crisis*. London: Tavistock.

Halbfinger, D. (1998, May 18). A neighborhood gives peace a wary look. *The New York Times,* pp. A1, B6.

Hamid, A. (1992a). Drugs and patterns of opportunity in the inner city: The case of middle-age, middle-income cocaine smokers. In A. Harrell & G. Peterson (Eds.), *Drugs, crime and social isolation: Barriers to urban opportunity* (pp. 209–238). Washington, DC: Urban Institute Press.

Hamid, A. (1992b). The developmental cycle of a drug epidemic: The cocaine smoking epidemic of 1981-1991. [Special issue, J. A. Inciardi (Ed.)] *Journal of Psychoactive Drugs, 24,* 337–349.

Hamid, A. (1997). *The political economy of drugs, Pt. II: The cocaine smoking epidemic in New York City's low income minority neighborhoods, 1981 to 1991.* Unpublished manuscript.

Hamid, A., Curtis, McCoy, K., McGuire, J., Conde, A., Bushell, W., Lindenmayer, R., Brimberg, K., Maia, S., Abdur-Rashid, S., & Settembrino, J. (1997). The heroin epidemic in New York City: Current status and prognoses. *Journal of Psychoactive Drugs, 29,* 375–391.

Hammersley, M., & Atkinson, P. (1983). *Ethnography: Principles in practice.* London: Tavistock.

Hammersley, R., Cassidy, M.T., & Oliver, J. (1995). Drugs associated with drug-related deaths in Edinburgh and Glasgow, November 1990–October 1992. *Addiction, 9,* 959–965.

Hartnagel, T.F., & Krahn, H. (1989). High school dropouts, labor market success, and criminal behavior. *Youth and Society, 20,* 416–444.

Inciardi, J. (1979). Heroin use and street crime. *Crime and Delinquency, 25,* 335–346.

Inciardi, J., & Chambers, C.D. (1972, Spring). Unreported criminal involvement of narcotic addicts. *Journal of Drug Issues, 2,* 57–64.

Inciardi, J., & Pottieger, A. (1986). Drug use and crime among two cohorts of women narcotic users: An empirical assessment. *Journal of Drug Issues, 16,* 91–106.

Inciardi, J., Pottieger, A., Forney, M., Chotwood, D., & McBride, D. (1982). Prostitution, IV drug use, sex for crack exchanges among serious delinquents: Risks for HIV infection. *Criminology, 29,* 221–235.

Johnson, B., Goldstein, P., Preble, E., Schmeidler, J., Lipton, D., Spunt, B., & Miller, T. (1985). *Taking care of business: The economics of crime by heroin abusers.* Lexington, MA: Heath.

Katz, J. (1988). *Seductions of crime.* New York: Basic Books.

Lane, R. (1979). *Violent death in the city: Suicide, accident, and murder in nineteenth century Philadelphia.* Cambridge, MA: Harvard University Press.

Lane, R. (1991). *William Dorsey's Philadelphia and ours: On the history and future of the black city in America.* New York: Oxford University Press.

Lane, R. (1992). Black Philadelphia then and now: The underclass of the late 20th century compared with African Americans of the late 19th century. In A. Harrell & G. Peterson (Eds.), *Drugs, crime and social isolation: Barriers to urban opportunity* (pp. 27–44). Washington, DC: Urban Institute Press.

Lévi-Strauss, C. (1949/1969). *The elementary structures of kinship.* Boston, MA: Beacon Press.

Lombroso, C. (1911). *Crime: Its causes and remedies.* Boston: Little, Brown.

Lukes, S. (1972). Capitalism and social theory: An analysis of the writings of Marx, Durkheim, Weber and Giddens. *British Journal of Sociology, 6,* 466–467.

Maher, L. (1997). *Sexed work: Gender, race, and resistance in a Brooklyn drug market.* New York: Oxford University Press.

Marriott, M. (1997, May 27) Race and crime in New York—a reappraisal. *The New York Times,* B1, p. 1.

McGlothlin, W., Anglin, M., & Wilson, B. (1978). Narcotic addiction and crime. *Criminology, 16*, 293–315.

Murray, C. (1984). *Losing ground: American social policy, 1950–1980.* New York: Basic Books.

Nurco, D., Cisin, I., & Balter, M. (1981). Addict careers, I: A new typology. *International Journal of the Addictions, 16*, 1305–1325.

Nurco, D., & Shaffer, J. (1982). Types and characteristics of addicts in the community. *Drug and Alcohol Dependence, 9*, 43–78.

O'Donnell, J. (1969). *Narcotic addicts in Kentucky.* Washington, DC: U.S. Government Printing Office.

O'Donnell, J., Voss, H., Clayton R., Slatin, G., & Room, R. (1976). *Young men and drugs: A nationwide survey.* Rockville, MD: National Institute on Drug Abuse.

Parker, H.J. (1996). *Methadone maintenance and crime reduction in the Merseyside.* London: Home Office Police Research Group.

Parker, H., Newcombe, R., & Bakx, K. (1988). *Living with heroin.* Philadelphia: Open University Press.

Pottieger, A. (1981). Sample bias in drugs/crime research: An empirical study. In J. A. Inciardi (Ed.), *The drugs crime connection* (pp. 207–257). Beverly Hills, CA: Sage.

Ratner, M. (Ed.). (1993). *Crack pipe as pimp: An ethnographic investigation of sex-for-crack exchanges.* New York: Lexington Books.

Ray, O., & Ksir, C. (1996). *Drugs, society and human behavior.* St. Louis: Mosby.

Reuter, P., MacCoun, R., & Murphy, P. (1990). *Money from crime: A study of the economics of drug dealing in Washington, D.C.* Santa Monica, CA: Rand Corporation.

Silberman, C. (1978). *Criminal violence, criminal justice.* New York: Random House.

Speckart, G., & Anglin, M. (1986). Narcotics and crime: A causal modeling approach. *Journal of Quantitative Criminology, 2*, 3–28.

Suffet, F., & Brotman, R. (1976). Female drug use: Some observations. *International Journal of the Addictions, 11*, 19–33.

Sullivan, M. (1989). *Getting paid: Youth, crime, and work in the inner-city.* Ithaca, NY: Cornell University Press.

Waldorf, D.O. (1973). *Careers in dope.* Englewood Cliffs, NJ: Prentice-Hall.

Waldorf, D., Reinarman, C., & Murphy, S. (1993). *Cocaine changes: The experience of using and quitting.* Philadelphia: Temple University Press.

Weissman, J.C., & File, K. (1976). Criminal behavior patterns of female addicts: A comparison of findings in two cities. *International Journal of the Addictions, 11*, 1063–1077.

Williams, J., & Bates, W. (1970). Some characteristics of female narcotic addicts. *International Journal of the Addictions, 5*, 245–256.

CHAPTER 6

Drugs and Violence

Chapter Objectives

The phenomenal world is inherently terrifying and violent and a hope of human evolution is to outgrow or vanquish this limitation. Drugs have been used to justify and motivate both violence and pacifism. Societies use different drugs to "excuse" either. But for the most part, drug users are as violent as the next person. "Sure, all sorts of thugs, thieves, crooks and murderers get drawn into it. But the largest amount of users are just ordinary folks trying to get high." (Tim, European-American male heroin injector in New York City, 1997)

DOES INTOXICATION CAUSE VIOLENCE AND AGGRESSIVE BEHAVIOR?

The fear that drug abuse causes crime led to the establishment of the Special Action Office for Drug Abuse Prevention (SAODAP) in 1971 and the National Institute on Drug Abuse in 1974. The budget of the latter is much larger than that of the National Institute on Alcohol Abuse (NIAA), although it addresses the problems of a population that is only 10% of that of the NIAA. The inordinate fear that "drugs cause crime" justifies this disparity.

There is pervasive evidence of a relationship between substance abuse and aggressive behavior. Drug abuse has been found to be a critical factor in homicide (Goldstein, Brownstein, Ryan, & Bellucci, 1989); robbery, and other "predatory" crime (Chaiken & Chaiken, 1982; Johnson et al., 1985; Petersilia, 1980); school violence (Gold & Moles, 1978); and violence among adolescents (Elliott, Huizinga, & Ageton, 1985; Fagan, 1989; Fagan, Piper, & Moore, 1986; Hartstone

139

& Hansen, 1984; Johnson, Schmeidler, Wish, & Huizinga, 1986; Tinklenberg et al., 1981; White, Pandina, & La Grange, 1987). Goldstein (1985) found that drug use and drug trafficking were etiological factors in violence, while McBride (1981) and Goldstein et al. (1989) found that systemic factors in drug dealing were causal factors in homicides.

Adolescent drug use has been cited as a predictor of violent adult crime and criminal careers. Among the general youth population, both official and self-reported crime rates are highest for heroin or cocaine users. Criminality among heroin users is quite high, especially during periods of addiction (Fagan, 1990).

Intoxication does not consistently lead to aggression. How it does when it does is not well understood. The link between the two is complex, mediated by personality, expectancy, and situational and sociocultural factors that channel the arousal excited by drugs into behavior patterns that may or may not include interpersonal aggression. The effects of intoxicants also differ according to the amounts consumed per unit of body weight, tolerances, and genetic or biological predispositions (Akers, 1984).

Many studies have linked drug use to nonviolent property crime. Finestone (1967) found that heroin users primarily engaged in nonviolent property crimes. Furthermore, he claimed that as rates of heroin addiction increased in a given area, crimes against the person decreased and property crimes increased. In Finestone's perspective, heroin addicts concentrated their activities on behaviors that would result in the most monetary gain to enable them to buy heroin. Noneconomically productive activities such as assault were avoided. Inciardi and Chambers (1972) also found that heroin addicts were more likely to commit property crimes than crimes against the person. Jacoby et al. (1973) and Johnson et al. (1976) found that all kinds of illicit-drug users are more likely to commit property crimes than other types of crime. A consensus has been reached, therefore, that users of illicit drugs are less violent than nonusers. Indeed, many of the commonly abused drugs are central nervous system depressants. The pharmacological action of these drugs sedates and induces less aggressive or violent behavior (Fagan, 1990).

A trend toward greater violence among narcotics users, or among users of heroin, cocaine, phenylcyclohexepiperidine (PCP), and inhalants has been noted. In studying New York City samples of heroin users, Zahn and Bencivengo (1974) and Stephens and Ellis (1975) have argued that the criminal behavior patterns of heroin users are changing. These researchers suggest that, while older cohorts of heroin users, who initiated use in 1955–1970, may have been relatively nonviolent, new, initiating cohorts are increasingly engaging in crimes against persons. Yet higher rates were reported among cocaine smokers and distributors a decade later. The greater interstate traffic in guns and the intensified battle between the police and outlaws have aggravated the risk of violent confrontations.

Does aggression precede substance use or vice versa? Longitudinal research has provided answers. Robbins (1979) studied the natural histories of addiction and adolescent substance abuse. McCord (1983, 1988) followed informants in the Cambridge-Somerville Youth Study (Powers & Witmer, 1951), begun in 1936, for four decades and examined antisocial behaviors such as alcohol abuse and criminal activity. Children were classified as aggressive or nonaggressive by teacher evaluations in seventh and eighth grades, well before initiation to substance use. Half of the alcoholics and nearly as many nonalcoholics had been aggressive youngsters. There was no conclusive evidence that aggression preceded alcoholism, but early childhood aggressiveness and alcoholism as an adult resulted in the highest levels of interpersonal violence. The study, however, did not identify the personality variables that might influence aggression as a child. Greenberg (1977) found that delinquency preceded amphetamine use. Collins, Hubbard, and Rachal (1985) suggested that violence preceded certain types of substance abuse among adults (Fagan, 1990).

Meanwhile, most drug users, and even most persons who use alcohol, report that intoxication eventually isolates them. Staying out of trouble, keeping the peace with others, or out of their reach, remaining at home or returning safely, are major goals.

VIOLENCE AND THE HUMAN CONDITION

From times beyond reckoning, images of fearsome violence in animal, human, and physical worlds have overwhelmed consciousness. Storms, tornadoes, floods, earthquakes, and volcanoes still underscore the fragility of most life forms. Deprived of sexually available females, young male seals rape and murder untended babies of either sex. Every species defends territory and family with tooth and claw. Ordinarily vegan apes and monkeys plan cannibalistic outings, when they stealthily and singlemindedly hunt and devour members of other simian bands.

Few persons have not despaired of the bloodiness of human history. From the "senseless" killings that may occur in any neighborhood to the grand orchestrations of slaughter during wars, humans have reveled in assaulting one another. As readers complete this chapter, Bosnians and Irish in Europe, Rwandans in Africa, and Cambodians in Southeast Asia are being felled in plenty by their countrymen.

Traditionally, men have monopolized the bloodletting in human societies. The few exceptions include the fabled Amazons of yore and salaried servicewomen in modern armed forces. Biological determinists have argued that human males are preserving a behavior trait that they inherited from a primate past. A "territorial imperative" to defend what is most familiar and dearest is embedded in their brains (Ardrey, 1956/1997; Lorenz, 1951/1974). Human perception is thought to depend upon oppositions that separate "them," who must be excluded and resisted, from "us," whom we embrace and protect.

Social anthropologists have focused on the web of meanings that invest human actions with purposiveness to investigate what a "man" is, in order to understand why he intimidates, terrorizes, maims, tortures, scarifies, burns, brands, cuts, hurts, and kills so readily and ubiquitously (Leiris, 1962). They have concluded that the crux of the puzzle is that no one really wants to be a man. Being one is a willful enterprise.

In the preface to an influential article, Gilmore (1990) quotes Norman Mailer: "Masculinity is not something given to you, something you're born with, but something you gain. . . . And you gain it by winning small battles with honor" (p. 250). Gilmore is puzzled by the stress and drama of manhood, the trials and tribulations, and the persistent indoctrination required in becoming and being one:

> In East Africa, young boys from cattleherding tribes, including the Masai, Rendille, Jie and Samburu, are taken from their mothers and subjected to painful circumcision rites by which they become men. If the Samburu boy cries out as his flesh is being cut, if he so much as blinks an eye, he is shamed for life as being unworthy of manhood. The Amhara, an Ethiopian tribe, have a passionate belief in masculinity called *wand-nat*. To show their *wand-nat*, Amhara youth are forced to engage in bloody whipping contests known as *buhe*. (Gilmore, 1990, p. 253)

Trials of manhood for other tribes include killing an animal large enough to feed the entire tribe, fathering children, facing a charging lion, and surviving alone in the jungle.

Gilmore finds the clue to the paradox in the inherent weaknesses of human nature and the plasticity of gender roles. Humans, both male and female, prefer to run from danger, to shy away from trouble and exertion, and to cling to the safety of hearth and home. Thus, manhood can be seen as a "moral instigation for performance—the moral force that culture erects against the eternal child in men, that makes retreat impossible by creating a cultural sanction literally worse than death: the theft of one's sexual identity" (Gilmore, 1990, p. 254).

Conflict, violence, and warfare have served important functions in tribal societies. Among horticulturalists who practice swidden agriculture, the continuous rotation of fields (and sometimes domestic settlements) within a limited space ensures that the paths of groups will cross and that they will compete. Groups form frangible alliances with one another to oppose yet others. The scrupulously sequenced destruction of forests, animals, and humans prevents any of these populations from growing so large that the existence of the others is threatened. In the territory of the Dani of New Guinea and the Yanomamo of the Amazonian rain forest, forests are cut and regenerated, pigs are slaughtered ritually, and a few humans (of all ages) die in raids and warfare. In the Pacific Northwest, groups such as the Kwakiutl, Haida, and Tsimshian had established a centuries-old pattern in which the residents of localities with few resources raided those who controlled major salmon rivers and other prime fishing ground. Access to lands for grazing, the size of herds of cattle, and human numbers were also regulated by formalized raids and warfare among East African tribes. Rights of passage and trading relations with producers of cereals and vegetables were occasions in other corners of the globe for limited violence among herders of sheep, goats, camels, and reindeer. The deaths of a few humans and the slaughter of herds through raids and pruning resulted in population sizes of all living creatures—including viruses and pests—best adapted to a particular environment.

These configurations of violence were transformed in the modern age. Although European explorers and colonialists often justified their aggressions against and enslavement of other peoples as the necessary methods for imposing peace among warlike savages, it was the arrival of European lusts, rivalries, goods, and Europeans themselves that introduced tribal societies to levels of violence they had never known hitherto (Thomas, 1997).

In North America, the Kwakiutl, Haida, and Tsimshian of the Northwest consumed one another in the rush to exchange furs for liquor and firearms with European trappers. In the Southwest and Southeast, in response to the European demand for slaves, the Cherokee raided tribes to their west, the Fima raided the Yavapai, and yet other groups raided the Navajo. The introduction of horses, firearms, and liquor entirely transformed the way of life of these peoples, reorienting them toward greater violence (Ferguson & Whitehead, 1992; Hill, 1970).

In South America, the Amazonian Mundurucu allied themselves to the invading Portuguese, who paid them to attack less friendly tribes and to bring back heads as trophies. Their ferocious long-distance raiding soon gained them the reputation of being the most warlike tribe of the region. In European imaginations, they vied for the status with the Andean Jivaros, famous for the "shrunken heads" of their enemies. But the traffic in these gruesome relics had actually been stimulated by Europeans, who paid a rifle per head.

A European hand can be detected in many similar tribal wars throughout the world. Muslims, Hindus, and Sikhs in India; Turks and Greeks in Asia Minor; North and South Koreans in Indochina; Muslims and Jews in the Middle East; and Hausa, Ibo, and other groups in sub-Saharan Africa have been locked in struggle because of the purposes and agendas of powerbrokers in European and American capitals.

In Europe itself, where European nations competed for mastery of the emerging world economic system, warfare has been the mother of powerful and fearsome technologies. Destruction on a scale unknown in prior human history was accomplished in Europe in the brief 100 years that culminated in World War II. The aftermath of that war, or the Cold War, produced terrible carnage throughout the world, including major conflicts in Korea, Vietnam, Cambodia, the Dominican Republic, Haiti, Panama, and the Congo.

In the contemporary world, following the demise of the Soviet Union as a competing world power, the United States has emerged as the unchallenged world leader and the European-American male as the dominant animal in the world. Yet conflicts continuously erupt, such as those in Bosnia, the Middle East, Somalia, and Northern Ireland. As the undisputed world superpower, the United States must lead in resolving them. The drug war sends American troops to Panama, while at home it pits one half of the community against the other. Instead of the "peace dividend," which the collapse of the Soviet Union was expected to yield, increasing expenditure on the armed forces and arms sales to foreign countries are featured in the national budget.

Thus, aggression and violence are unavoidable. Its sanctioned use upholds the social order in societies divided by race, ethnicity, gender, or class. Political theorists had long foreseen that the logical outcome is a life that is "nasty, brutish, and short" (Hobbes, 1632/1996).

The premium on aggressive masculinity has formed subcultures of war in every society. In Germany, they reached their greatest elaboration in the deadly regime of Nazism under Hitler. Informing the latter were several subcultural trends: repudiation of one's own body and of femininity to build masculinity on self-denial, hardness, and destruction (Theweleit, 1989); an "opposing landscape of myth" that fascists inhabited and a "repudiation of the quotidian" (Bataille, 1962); or the "dreamt-of metalization of the body" and the maintenance of capitalism (Benjamin, 1970).

In America, subcultures of war and masculinity have been constructed around the Puritan subjection of the unconscious to repression. They are fostered in the homoerotic and homophobic bonding among adolescent males. They have as outcomes an image of the warrior as the "individual gunman who acts on his own (or in loose concert with other men)" . . . or as the "good soldier who belongs to an official military or police unit and serves as representative defender of national honor" (Gibson, 1994, p. 4).

American masculinity suffered some reverses after the Vietnam War. Despite superior matériel and manpower, the Americans sustained heavy losses, were repeatedly outwitted by the enemies, betrayed by their allies, and defeated; they finally withdrew from Indochina in disgrace. Some American males passionately believe that American masculinity had been compromised by the indecision and cowardice of policymakers and protesters against the war at home. Meanwhile, another image of masculinity, "the peace-loving hippie" had indeed been constructed in America. Returning home, many of them as heroin addicts, Vietnam veterans were denied the heroic status that soldiers returning from earlier wars had been awarded. Since the war, American presidents have resisted rushing into battle. To compensate for the perceived loss of soldierly honor, militias have flourished in several states, and semimilitary organizations such as the Ku Klux Klan have been revived.

Wife-beating and child abuse are common consequences of the culture of male domination in hierarchical societies. While men also mutilate themselves in their trials of strength and endurance, they are especially zealous when cutting off women's genital labia; sewing them up; altering their breasts or facial features; composing their posture by breaking and rearranging bones; regulating fat distribution and body mass to conform with prevailing standards of male sexual arousal; and prescribing drugs, surgery, diet, exercise, or plain, hard, domestic labor. Among the Yanomamo,

> Women must respond quickly to the demands of their husbands. When a man returns from a hunting trip, the woman, no matter what she is doing, hurries home and quietly but rapidly prepares a meal for her husband. Should the wife be slow in doing this, the husband is within his rights to beat her. Most reprimands . . . take the form of blows with the hand or with a piece of firewood. . . . Some of them chop their wives with the sharp edge of a machete or axe, . . . burn them with a glowing brand . . . or shoot them with a barbed arrow in some nonvital area such as the buttocks or leg. (Chagnon, 1983, p. 112)

In analyzing the torture and rape of their mentally retarded neighborhood playmate by 13 teen-aged boys in affluent Glen Ridge, New Jersey, in 1992, a researcher emphasizes: "These Glen Ridge kids, they were pure gold, every mother's dream, every father's pride. They were not only Glen Ridge's finest, but in their perfection they belonged to all of us. They were Our Guys" (Lefkowitz, 1997, p. 10). The boys, all popular high school athletes, had taken the handicapped girl, a needy person craving their approval whom most had known from infancy, to the basement playroom of two brothers among them; there, they stripped, sexually humiliated, and orally sodomized the girl. Finally, they raped her with a baseball bat and a broom handle. Although six boys left when they realized what was happening, the next day they returned with more friends to persuade the girl to repeat the events of the day before. They brought along a classmate with a movie camera with the idea of making a pornographic film as they proceeded. The observer concluded that in Glen Ridge, as in similar wealthy communities across the nation, European Americans raise their young sons to abuse their young daughters by devaluing humanistic education and promoting instead "masculine" qualities, such as winning in material and sexual competitions, athleticism, and the belief that privileged European-American males can make their own rules and set themselves above the law (Lefkowitz, 1997).

Feminist theorists have concluded that aiming to be a man on these terms is wrongheaded (De Beauvoir, 1952/1973; Firestone, 1970; Hooks, 1990).

Running counter to male aggressiveness and confrontational social organization is an altruistic imperative that has proven adaptive and indispensable in human evolution (De Waal, 1996). Mutual benefits are gained when individuals can be persuaded to keep their hands off one another's throats. Then families can raise children to maturity, populations grow, the depth of lineages is extended, differentiation and specialization result, and the store of material and cultural riches is preserved and enlarged. In every society, to be *only* the man who faces charging beasts or other challenges is to be scorned as a weakling. Men are also expected to be nurturing:

> Yet real men do nurture. They do this by shedding their blood, their sweat, their semen; by bringing home food, producing children or dying if necessary in far away places to provide security for their families. But this masculine nurturing is paradoxical. To be supporting, a man must first be tough in order to ward off enemies; to be generous, he must first be selfish in order to amass goods; to be tender, he must first be aggressive enough to court, seduce, "win" a wife. (Gilmore, 1990, p. 254)

Women have contributed mightily to the creation of a more moral social universe. Bonobo society has been offered by feminists as a model for conflict-free communal life. Dominated by elder females, these pygmy chimpanzees enjoy freedom of sexual expression, plentiful sexual gratifications, an absence of jealousy, sharing of resources, many shared sessions of grooming and merrymaking, and no strife. Exploiting their advantages as mothers, sisters, daughters, and desirable sexual partners, women have introjected into human affairs their own special concerns to care for the young, old, infirm, and incapacitated members of the community. They have forced men to mind their manners and to be more nurturing.

WHY INTOXICATION?

Since men's nurturing side has to prevail for civilization at all to be possible, they must dissemble about their belligerent motives and find "excuses" for them. The noblest motives lead to the deadliest conflicts. At the more local level, the use of intoxication to intensify and excuse the aggressivity of males can be verified cross-culturally. Each culture selects a particular method to do this work. Although it most often means the administration of a drug, warriors have also arrived at altered states of consciousness conducive to ferocity in war through chastity, sensory deprivation, fasting, or prayer. American troops (during World War II and the Vietnam War, especially) were fêted on the eve of battle not only with special rations, cigarettes, and alcohol, but with comedy shows, concerts, and erotic displays of naked female American flesh, perhaps the better to remind them of the bounty they were preparing to secure with their lives. Both Americans and Japanese regarded Southeast Asian countries as "comfort stations" where they turned local women into sex workers to refresh and reinvigorate their troops.

Abundant cross-cultural evidence shows that individuals "plan to be aggressive" and use drinking or other drugs as an excuse (Brisset, 1978). Mexican gang members use PCP and alcohol to attain *locura*, a state in which aggressive acts are permitted (Vigil, 1988). By contrast, young African-American Los Angelenos, preferring to be "cool," smoked marijuana (Feldman, Mandel, & Fields, 1985).

Intoxication, or "drunken comportment," may also offer time out from cultural norms and expectations. It justifies breaking the rules. Conflicts and tensions that normally are suppressed can be vented. And since the occasion, place, time, and intensity, as well as the targets, of these special moments of license are precisely specified, the net effect may be to reduce violence by eliminating random, uncontrolled episodes (Levinson, 1983).

Among the Yanomamo, who sometimes need to intimidate neighboring Amazonian tribes and one another, ayahausca was prepared by pulverizing the roots of the *baniopteris caapi* vine to make a fine powder, which was then blown into the user's nostrils through a hollow bamboo tube several feet long. Hostile displays by the men, such as banging their chests, assuming threatening postures, and screaming insults, soon followed.

While marijuana is usually praised for its pacific effects (see below), it is said to have emboldened Turkish dissidents to become assassins (literally, "high on hashish"). Turks in the 16th century had also used opium to become warlike. Muslim and Arab expansionism and colonialism introduced the plant, or dagga, to Central and Southern Africa, where distinct dagga "use-complexes" emerged among herders, hunters, and warriors (Du Toit, 1975). When mixed with indigenous herbs into powders and pastes for eating, inhaling, and smoking, the drug bred aggressivity during battle and efficiency at work. In Rwanda, the Twa, a vassal lineage of the erstwhile ruling minority caste, the Tutsi, constructed a reputation for extraordinary strength, rowdiness, bestiality, unflinching loyalty to their lords, and unbridled vengefulness around their consumption of the drug (Codere, 1975).

During World War II, Japanese kamikaze pilots were given large dosages of amphetamine before their raids. Indeed, the drug was popular with the entire Japanese military.

Among European peoples, alcohol was "liquid courage" and remains so. In Greece and Rome of antiquity, their conquering armies survived on wine and cereals. Alcohol was also the only anesthetic that army doctors had available. Among the Lapps of Finland, drunken binges invariably ended in fights, woundings, and homicides (Ahlstrom, 1981). Wherever drinking alcohol was diffused by Europeans, its reputation for causing and excusing violent acts was firmly wedded to it. It thereby destroyed many indigenous cultures, such as the Native Americans and West Africans mentioned above.

Drugs were also given by aggressors to their victims so that they would succumb to attack more easily. While readying themselves with amphetamine, the Japanese flooded China and Manchuria with opium, to addict and demoralize the population it was preparing to invade. Datura, or jimson weed, was given to householders by the burglars of ancient India, causing them to toss between sleep and hallucination while their treasures were being carted away.

ALCOHOL AND AGGRESSION IN AMERICA

Alcohol intoxication is often cited by American scientists as contributing to violence and aggression. Affected by alcohol, study populations (mostly young males) assault family members, commit sex-related crimes, and perpetrate homicides or other violent acts in a pattern that persists into adulthood. In many altercations, both aggressor and victim may be drunk.

In fact, the drug selected most frequently by American males to ratchet up and excuse their aggressivity is alcohol. The majority of Americans accepts as an eternal verity the thesis that alcohol causes aggression. Personal memoirs, novels, and films describe soldiers drinking it before combat and bathing their wounds in it afterward. There is an easily discernible circularity, therefore, in studies of the relationship between alcohol consumption and aggression. When young European-American males of low-income backgrounds want to assault someone, they drink alcohol and say afterward that "alcohol made me do it; I was drunk."

As in other societies, young males are in fact the most likely to act aggressively when intoxicated (Blane & Hewitt, 1977; Cahalan & Cisin, 1976; Gandossy, Williams, Cohen, & Hardwood, 1980). In inner-city neighborhoods, although the majority of substance users were nonviolent, the most violent youths were more likely to be of their number (Fagan, Weis, Cheng, & Watters, 1987). These violent offenders shared a common background of early delinquency and drug use, fractured families, inconsistent socialization, truancy and unsatisfactory school performance, low self-esteem, poor interpersonal coping skills, strong feelings of resentment, dropping out of school, and absenteeism (Huba & Bentler, 1984; Kaplan, Martin, & Johnson, 1986; Newcomb & Bentler, 1988). The maintenance of masculine power is by itself sufficient to cause violence, without the help of external factors (Bourgois, 1996; Bowker, 1983; Dobash & Dobash, 1979).

Young males are strongly influenced by the peer associations they form. Friends dictate what is normative conduct or whether or not to participate in deviant behavior. In particular, they decide whether violence and drug use will escalate or diminish as they grow older, rewarding the preferred behavior with approval and punishing the opposite with ostracism (Akers, Krohn, Lanza-Kaduce, & Radosevich, 1979; Elliott et al., 1985; Fagan et al., 1987; Giordano, Cernkovich, & Pugh, 1985; Jessor & Jessor, 1977; Kandel, 1980, 1985; Kandel, Simcha-Fagan, & Davies, 1986; Kaplan, Martin, & Johnson, 1986; White et al., 1987).

Accompanied by an ethnographer during an evening of drinking, four young European-American males from a working-class neighborhood in Boston were brought closer by their displays of aggression. While they had been deferential at local bars to elder drinkers, they ran amok in the "adult entertainment" sections of the city. Their aggressive behavior included "loud conversation, good-natured wrestling, piling into a car, speeding, verbal boasting, verbal threatening, raucous comments, verbal disparagement, being rowdy, yelling, screaming, arguing, putting a fist through a store window, fighting, bottle crashing, threatening with a gun, and sexual aggressiveness." The more beers the boys consumed, the more aggressive they were (Burns, 1980).

Since colonial times, domestic violence, such as wife beating and child abuse, has commonly been regarded as a consequence of drunkenness. Literature, popular song, and the media have perpetuated the view. In many homicides, the victims had been drunk. Some researchers have found that the greater the spousal abuse, the more alcohol the assailant had consumed (Fagan, Hansen, & Stewart, 1983). But other studies reported only weak associations between the two variables (Bard & Zacker, 1976; Kantor & Straus, 1987). In some families in which child abuse occurred, there was a wide range of involvement with alcohol (Mayer & Black, 1981), but in others, there was none (Hotaling & Sugarman, 1986; Steele & Pollack, 1968). Studies of a nationally representative sample of families established a strong correlation between heavy alcohol use and intrafamily violence, but, although co-inhabitants turned violent after heavy drinking, 80% of respondents had been nonviolent, including two thirds of blue-collar workers (Gottheil, Druley, Skoloda, & Waxman, 1983).

Other studies have shown striking similarities between persons violent toward family members and alcohol misusers. Such persons, needing power and control, have periods of extreme jealousy, external blame, sexual dysfunction, and bizarre mood shifts (Star, 1980). Both perpetrators and victims blamed alcohol for the violent episodes, thereby preserving their social standing and self-image (Gottheil et al., 1983).

Class plays a significant role in drug-induced violence. Working-class men, who are most embedded in "male subcultures," are likewise the most violent toward spouses. They are encouraged by the modeling of behaviors during intoxication, social learning experiences, and societal approval for the use of force within families to assert and maintain supremacy (Kantor & Straus, 1987). Middle-class men by contrast may commit violence during a time-out blamed on intoxication.

Despite a vast literature spanning many disciplines, there is little empirical evidence to support any of the explanations that purport to show why alcohol intoxication causes aggression. The most influential evidence shows that a person's belief that he or she is drunk affects behavior in much the same way as does actually drinking. The effects of alcohol are learned, and believing that one is intoxicated could lead to aggressive or sexual displays (Briddell et al., 1978).

For example, the difference between male and female aggressivity has been researched in widely varying ways, such as in hormonal and socialization studies. Among nonhuman primates, aggressive males are identified at an early age and their condition is related to the concentration of testosterone (Maccoby & Jacklin, 1974). Violent parents produce violent children (Eron, Walder, & Lefkowitz, 1971). But, although there may be a genetic predisposition for drinking alcohol or using opioids, there is none for drug- or alcohol-induced aggression.

The disproportionate involvement of young males in alcohol- or drug-induced violence is sometimes explained by the sociopsychological dynamics of the transition from adolescence to adulthood (Collins, 1981). One dynamic is the struggle for personal dominance, or the power to gain victories in confrontation with personal adversaries (McClelland, 1975; McClelland & Davis, 1972; McClelland, Davis, Kalin, & Wanner, 1972). It is often the motive for intrafamily violence (Kantor & Straus, 1987).

Another dynamic is the uncertainty young males experience as they are in transition from roles as adolescents to those of worker and marital partner. They often exhibit a "hypermasculinity" that results in problem behaviors (Jessor & Jessor, 1977; Kandel et al., 1986). These behaviors may decide whether or not a young man becomes a controlled or problem drug user capable of aggressive acts (Fagan, 1990).

Finally, male sex role socialization, by suppressing some feelings and cognitions and promoting others, is stressful. The limited social and personality development of the young males obliges them to be excessively dependent on external norms for defining expected and appropriate behaviors. In this context, substance use may enhance personal power, which is maintained through force.

Experimental studies have been conducted on young males to determine the effects of intoxication on them. In one project, male college students, given alcohol in varying doses but less than is necessary for drunkenness, are cast as aggressors in controlled and manipulated interactions with a potential victim. In teacher-learner simulations, the teacher administers an electric shock when the learner makes a mistake. In the competition model, the subject commits aggressive acts against an opponent during competition in a reaction time test (Fagan, 1990).

In the competition format, intoxicated subjects behaved more aggressively than those who had received a placebo or no drink at all (Shuntich & Taylor, 1972; Taylor & Gammon, 1975). The teacher-learner paradigm had quite different results. There were no aggressive acts. Since the teacher-pupil game was inherently nonthreatening, in that the pupil could not retaliate, the subjects were immobilized. Without a threat, they would not respond violently. Alcohol probably also influences the perception of threat (Taylor, Gammon, & Capasso, 1976) and may affect the same physiological processes stimulated during a violent encounter, thus decreasing the threshold of provocation or stimulation to violence (Moyer, 1983; Vogel, 1983).

Other studies suggest that alcohol either intensifies or diminishes perceptions of the social contexts of drinking situations. The intoxication-aggression link is mediated by emotional and cognitive states. For example, alcohol may reduce the ability to perceive the negative consequences of aggressive acts or increased risk taking (Russell & Mherabian, 1974). According to another set of explanations, underlying pathologies of the individual cause both drug use and violence. These may be activated by the drug use, leading to anxiety, paranoia, and hostility, which culminate in violence. Sometimes prolonged drug use may create the pathology (Wilson & Abrams, 1977).

Some experts claim that substance use disorganizes cognitive functions. It interferes with the ability to process the cues of communication, to cope in confusing or threatening situations, and narrows the perceptual field (Pernanen, 1981). Instead of behaving cautiously, the substance user reacts rashly (Pihl, Peterson, & Lau, 1993). Disinhibition theory posits that the central nervous system is altered by substance use, freeing individuals of the social and cultural norms that usually constrain behavior (Room & Collins, 1983). Alcohol also has stimulant effects that may aggravate feelings of being provoked (Lau, Pihl, & Peterson, 1995).

Attempts to resolve these competing explanations by resort to biological and physiological processes have not been successful. Although neural mechanisms, endocrine and other glandular responses to substances, comparative ethological processes, brain response, testosterone levels, and catecholamine measures have been examined, there is no clear understanding about how alcohol intoxication causes drunkenness, or what specific parts of the brain are affected. The study samples usually comprise normal college students, under conditions of mild intoxication and simulated stress, so that only a narrow range of behavior is studied (Fagan, 1990). The bases of aggression have been sought in the electrical or chemical stimulation of brain pathways and in lesions (Moyer, 1983;

Muehlenkamp, Lucion, & Vogel, 1995). For example, researchers showed that aggression in monkeys was triggered by electrical stimulation of the anterior hypothalamus (Robinson, Alexander, & Bowne, 1969). Manipulating norepinephrine levels in rats produced the same result (Haller, 1995). In a study of 1,800 cases of tumors in three areas of the brain (the septal region, the temporal lobe, and the frontal lobe), lesions provoked irritability (Sano, 1962). Destructive behavior and bursts of anger were also reported among psychomotor epileptic patients (Schwab, Sweet, Mark, Kjelberg, & Ervin, 1965). Aggression has been related to testosterone levels (Bradford, 1988), the premenstrual week, and hypoglycemia (Bolton, 1973). Although basic brain and glandular functions are altered in these ways, it is not known how they are linked to violence. All approaches converge on a critical observation. Intoxication affects cognitive processes that shape and interpret perceptions of one's own physiology (e.g., expectancy) and the associated behavioral response. The cognitive processes themselves are influenced by cultural and situational events that determine the norms, beliefs, and sanctions regarding behaviors following intoxification (Chermack & Taylor, 1995; Fagan, 1990).

In developing a general model of the influence of alcohol on aggression, researchers have suggested two major independent variables that increase the probability of violence during social interactions following alcohol use: psychological proclivity toward the exercise of personal power in an overt manner and beliefs that alcohol causes aggression. Each of these factors in turn influences cognitive processes that interpret both the situation and the appropriate behavioral response (Gottheil et al., 1983). One effect of alcohol on cognitive processes is a reduction in the behavioral repertoire, and the use of violence results either from personal proclivity or cultural beliefs, forces that further proscribe responses to social interactions during drinking situations. Culture, therefore, has both direct effects through expectancy and indirect effects through its influence on mediating cognitive processes. Moreover, cultural beliefs are likely to produce "accounts" that allow him or her to shift blame to alcohol and therefore perceive fewer social rules against aggressive behaviors (Fagan, 1990).

Research proves that alcohol does not invariably cause violence. Alcohol use accompanies aggression in some cultures and not in others, in some situations rather than others (MacAndrew & Edgerton, 1969). In a probability sample of 60 folk societies, men got drunk in nearly all, but were subsequently involved in brawls in only 27 (Schaefer, 1973). Where aggression is normative, alcohol increases it. In traditional societies, however, alcoholic beverages often pacify drinkers. For example, Camba subsistence farmers of Bolivia binge regularly on 178-proof rum. Their drinking parties are famous for their conviviality, during which there is no aggressive display of any kind (Heath, 1983). The Lapps, however, who are peaceful when sober, stab and kill one another (Ahlstrom, 1981). A pattern of "belligerent drinking" in the American South has bequeathed the region with the highest manslaughter and homicide rates in the nation (Levinson, 1983).

Among the Navajo, fights during intoxication occur only within the kin group (Heath, 1983). Expected behavior changes in relation to age, gender, social class, or ethnicity. When intoxicated, Plains Indians are hell-raisers as youths, but are gentle as mature adults. Rowdy young marijuana smokers in Jamaica grow up to be discreet old men who drink marijuana teas or tonics. An American blue-collar worker gets in more fights after a few beers than an American businessman after several martinis. Cocaine enhances sociability in the indigenous cultures of the Andes, but creates danger in inner-city America. The cultural patterns of drunken comportment actually reveal and communicate the shared values and norms of a culture or social group (Heath, 1983). For example, aggressive drinkers among Naskapi men in northern Canada were unsuccessful miners in a mining community (Robbins, 1979). When Dominicans migrated to the United States and experienced upward mobility, they removed their drinking from male-only bars and confined it at home, where the principles of discipline, sacrifice, and the common good prevailed, thereby reducing the level of associated violence (Gordon, 1978). By contrast, Guatemalan males, who migrated without families, were plunged more steeply into the culture of male bars, where machismo and violent displays were the norm (Bowker, 1986a, 1986b; Gordon, 1982).

Levinson (1983) hypothesizes that in cohesive cultures, where there is economic integration among members and intoxication is integrated into their social rituals, there is little difference between intoxicated and nonintoxicated behavior. The behavior of Africans and Indians on the Caribbean island of Trinidad is illustrative. Among Africans, social drinking is acceptable and adolescents are cheerfully inducted into the practice at frequent celebrations throughout the year. Among their Indian neighbors, however, the activity is overshadowed by deep uncertainty and guilt, adult males indulge it privately, and young persons are prevented from joining them. When the latter do eventually drink, they do so problematically (Angrosino, 1972; Yawney, 1969).

The causes of aggression have also been sought in comorbidity studies. Domestic abuse, spouse abuse, sex abuse, and battering have many features in common with problem drinking or drug misuse and often coexist with them. In both types of disorder, the sufferer loses control, persists in the behavior despite adverse consequences, and becomes obsessed with it. She or he grows tolerant, requiring more drugs and to inflict more pain, and suffers withdrawal if either is denied. For a patient to recover from either condition, separate treatments for both must be offered (Irons & Schneider, 1997).

AGGRESSION IN AMERICA AND OTHER DRUGS

While alcohol was firewater for European Americans, they feared that the pro-scribed drugs—marijuana, heroin, cocaine—would arouse violence in persons belonging to opposed classes or to racial and ethnic minorities. Thus, Chinese, Mexicans, African Americans, Colombians, Jamaicans, Central Americans, and Russians and the drugs they used have all been stigmatized in turn (see Chapter 3). On the whole, however, central nervous system depressants such as the opioids and marijuana are specifically used to produce a tranquilized, euphoric effect. In drug-free periods, opiate users showed profound anxiety, which sometimes re-sulted in violence (Woody, Perskey, McLellan, O'Brian, & Arndt, 1983). The hallucinogenic drugs, such as LSD, have produced bizarre effects, but very few persons use them regularly.

Other American masculine poses, however, are elaborated through additional drug use. Anabolic steroids, for example, are valued by athletes and their coaches for enhancing performance and stimulating muscle growth. Prolonged use of ana-bolic steroids caused some weight lifters to self-report feelings of aggression. The steroids reduce testosterone production and produce instead hormones resembling estrogen (Schuckitt, 1988).

A relationship between amphetamine and PCP use and violence has been sought. Researchers claim that they probably affect perceptions or the chemistry of the brain so that bizarre, aggressive, or violent behavior may occur (Ellinswood, 1971; Feldman, Agar, & Beschner, 1979; McBride & Russe, 1979; Tinklenberg & Woodrow, 1974). The violence is to a large extent unpredictable and random. One researcher, in a study of 13 individuals, reported that amphet-amine use had led directly to the commission of murders. He argued that the am-phetamine had produced paranoid thought patterns and delusions and conse-quently led to violent behavior directed at supposed persecutors. Accordingly, a subculture of violence had developed among amphetamine users (Ellinswood, 1971). In a study of three murderers, delusional paranoia and social isolation had resulted in extreme violence (Asnis & Smith, 1978). While researchers have noted that drug-related violent behavior is mediated routinely by personality characteris-tics and situational context, in the case of amphetamine, they emphasized its direct role in causing violence (Carey & Mandel, 1968; Griffith, 1966; Grinspoon & Hedblom, 1975; Rawlings, 1968). While many extremely violent crimes are com-mitted under the influence of stimulants, methylphenidate (Ritalin) reduces ag-gression in children with attention deficit disorder (Casat, Pearson, van Davelaar, & Cherek, 1995). Benzodiazepines, such as Valium, Librium, and Ativan, in-creased aggressiveness at very high dosages (Bond & Silveira, 1993; Pagano, 1981). These results, however, which were based on studies of a few individuals only, have been questioned (Fagan, 1990).

Studies of laboratory animals have supported some of these conclusions, although the relevance of animal studies for an understanding of human drug use, which is so much mediated by culture, has not been established (Morgan & Zimmer, 1996). In certain species, amphetamine, PCP, and ethanol increase attack and threat behaviors (e.g.,s bites, gestures, and vocalizations), while tetrahydrocannabinol (THC) and opioids quell them. The results held whether the animals were attacking or defending themselves, during raids and break-ins, or under brain stimulation. Low doses of alcohol enraged mice and monkeys, but their defensive biting and postures lessened at higher dosages. Alcohol had the same effect on dominant rats confronting their subordinates. While opioids generally suppressed aggressivity, animals suddenly withdrawn from a regular supply of morphine postured and bit randomly (Miczek & Thompson, 1983).

Cocaine has been adopted by some American males as a performance enhancer. It has been popular, therefore, among businessmen on Wall Street, entertainers, and other elite professionals. Frequent and high levels of cocaine use have been associated with a variety of personality disorders, such as paranoid delusions and depression (Spotts & Shontz, 1980; Washton, Gold, & Pottash, 1984). These findings, however, were based on observations of a self-selected sample of upperclass persons seeking treatment. Their experience was likely to diverge from the majority of cocaine users, who did not seek treatment or belonged to different social classes (Chitwood & Morningstar, 1985; Erickson et al., 1987). Low-dose users reported having "mellow" positive experiences with the drug (Goldstein et al., 1989). The route of administration (inhaling, smoking, or injecting) may also affect outcomes (Siegel, 1980, 1982). An economic-compulsive model of drug-related violence (Goldstein, 1985) may account for the violence of heavy cocaine smokers reported by Washton and Gold (1987) and Bourgois (1989).

Most drug users, however, control both their drug use and attendant behaviors (Ball, Rosen, Flueck, & Nurco, 1982; Biernacki, 1986; Waldorf, 1973). Waldorf, Reinarman, and Murphy (1993) studied cocaine users whose personalities had changed as a result of heavy use but who avoided interpersonal violence. Different behaviors may result from acute, rather than chronic, effects.

THE ROLE OF PROHIBITION

As in the case of other crime (see Chapter 4), most drug-related violence is actually caused by prohibition. Because drugs are illegal, policemen become corrupt and shoot one another and drug users and dealers. If drugs were legal, marijuana would be grown on every window ledge, cocaine would cost $200 a kilo, and heroin $400 a kilo. If users and dealers murder one another to possess them, or the money to buy them, it is because prohibition has artificially inflated these prices. If drugs were subjected to the same customs, regulations, and laws that govern the exchange of other commodities, rival distributors would no more gun down one another than pharmacists on opposite sides of a street.

The stories of Eliot Ness versus Al Capone or modern-day police chiefs versus Colombian, Jamaican, Nigerian, or other marijuana, cocaine, or heroin distributors are a peculiarly American script that prohibition has written. Nowhere else in the world, including South Africa during apartheid and the former Soviet Union, have policemen waged such a ferocious battle against the civilian population. The images of policemen, adrenalin running high, invading private homes with battering rams, guns drawn, hurling suspects to the ground, and screaming ethnic slurs while trying to find some marijuana are solely American. Frequently, a police dispatcher misreads an address, the wrong home is raided, and innocent persons are terrorized.

The American prohibitionist attitude has particularly pernicious results abroad. Panama was invaded in 1992 to extradite its president, Colonel Manuel Noriega, on drug trafficking charges. Sustained by cocaine revenues, Haitian armed forces loyal to the deposed dictator François Duvalier continued a reign of terror long after Haitians had democratically elected his successor, Reverend Jean Bertrand Aristide. In many countries, police chiefs, trained by the Drug Enforcement Administration (DEA) in the United States, have returned home with new equipment and weapons. They use them to gun down a wide range of undesirables, who are labeled "drug dealers" or "drug producers" no matter what their actual business is (Hamid, 1997; Nadelmann, 1989).

A consequence of prohibition is to confine the violence among the disenfranchised. Colombians, Cubans, and Jamaicans in Miami fought a bitter three-way battle in the early 1980s to control domestic distribution of cocaine. On the streets where the drugs are bought and used, rivals may sometimes eliminate one another. In the interests of good business and self-preservation, however, they devote considerable energy to avoiding the cues for violence inherent in their illegal, unregulated enterprise.

Violence occurs most often in the context of the drug deal. The illegal activity nourishes suspicion and paranoia and permits questionable actions: "being burned," getting "ripped off," selling worthless or bogus dope, "ripping off" dealers or others are standard experiences. The single largest cause of death among heroin users in several studies was homicide.

When analyzing crack-related violence, for example, it is necessary to distinguish between crack users and the (often nonusing) distributors of crack. While there may be some overlap between these two categories, most of those who attempted to operate as "user-distributors" did not last long in that role. Instead, a majority of the crack users derived their income from varying combinations of both legal sources and petty property crimes; comparatively few engaged in violent crime (Hamid, 1992; Maher, 1996; Mieczkowski, 1992; Williams, 1989).

Nonetheless, one can discern and readily account for historical fluctuations in the levels of violence involving crack distributors (Hamid, 1990, 1992). Most of these violent episodes were attributable to territorial conflicts (turf battles) between rival distributors. For this reason, the levels of violence tended to vary considerably according to how a given local street-level drug market was organized (whether it was freelance or highly structured, for example) during different phases in the epidemic's development cycle. It is important to bear in mind, however, that most of the distributors who remained successful in the business for any length of time were careful to "keep the money straight" by abstaining from, or strictly controlling, their own cocaine habits.

Violence among rival distributors, then, stemmed from disputes over money and power in a lucrative marketplace, and was often exacerbated when intensified law-enforcement activity disrupted relatively stable distribution arrangements. The nature of this violence is best understood as being similar to the violence that erupted during Prohibition in the 1920s, or even among those attempting to exert control of such nondrug-related illicit enterprises as gambling, extortion rackets, loan-sharking, and prostitution. For that matter, nation states have sometimes escalated conflicts among each other to war when they were unable to resolve disputes peacefully over scarce but sought-after resources. That is, the causes of violence among crack distributors have no direct relationship whatsoever to any peculiar properties of the drug, but to the drive for material self-aggrandizement.

Drug transactions may involve large sums of cash, and drug traffickers, who must hide every aspect of their business from the legal authorities, have no recourse to official channels for resolving disputes or obtaining justice (in the event of theft or other victimization). For this reason, they make tempting targets for thieves. These include—as New York City's Mollen Commission revealed—more than a few corrupt police officers.

Various sanctions apply in different lines of business, and within the informal (or underground) economy, there is a crucial distinction among market sectors. On the other hand, in an otherwise legitimate area of business, if one or more competitors boost profits by evading the costs of taxes and regulations (e.g., clothing manufacturers who operate clandestine sweatshops), their law-abiding competitors can appeal to the authorities to enforce the well-established rules against those who gain unfair advantage through unethical means. On the other hand, when an entire sector of economic activity is driven underground, the only means of protection is self-protection (often violent).

Ultimately, drug prohibition may foment violence at all levels, even where two destitute persons get together to use drugs.

DRUG USE AS SELF-INFLICTED VIOLENCE

Drug use is sometimes viewed as a suicidal activity in which users seek to inflict harm or violence upon themselves. Especially when intravenous drug use is considered, when users repeatedly inject themselves, or permit sores and abscesses to fester and compromise their health, a deliberate urge to mutilate the body may be identified.

Many body mutilators use drugs. Punk rockers, who tattoo body surfaces and pierce ears, eyelids, nose, mouth, nipples, navel, and genitals in order to insert rings or other jewelry, were among the first to initiate heroin use in the 1980s. The same persons are often fond of sadomasochistic sexual play, which can be life-threatening. Indeed, the sexual pleasure is heightened by giddily surrendering one's life to a partner. A little more pressure can make an unbearably exciting choke-hold lethal!

Among the nonviolent !Kung of the Kalahari, men make incisions in their scalps, into which they rub a psychoactive powder prepared from the roots of a local plant, thus delivering the drug subcutaneously.

Several kinds of relations among personality factors, substance abuse, and aggression have been proposed. The latter may function as a substitute for sexual pleasure, or as a fixation at the oral or anal or phallic stages. All addicted persons show a polymorphous, diverse need for love, repressed but sometimes blatant homosexuality, mild neuroticism hiding anger and low self-esteem, a counterphobic tendency, expression of unmet dependency needs, ambivalent feelings toward parents, self-destructive drives, hysteria, obsessive-compulsive neuroses, sexual disorder, suicide, and psychoses. But these studies are seriously flawed and base results on the observation of sample populations drawn from treatment facilities; no controls were used (Fagan, 1990; Gottheil et al., 1983).

VIOLENCE AGAINST DRUG USERS AND DISTRIBUTORS

In a suggestive (but probably unethical and unnecessary) laboratory experiment, unlucky monkeys drugged with PCP behaved so inappropriately that their peers threatened and attacked them (Miller, Levine, & Mirsky, 1973). The reaction evidently has an analogue among humans. No public issue divides Americans more, or sets one half against the other with greater vitriol, than drugs. From the days of the temperance movement, crusaders against drugs have waxed exceedingly warm about the kinds of punishments they would like to mete out to drug users and drug dealers. In the 19th century, saloons were burned to the ground and pitched battles fought between their proprietors, patrons, and the arsonists. Today, groups influenced by the prohibitionist ideology threaten cocaine and heroin users and distributors with capital punishment, exile, attack by the military, and incarceration. It is no mistake that America has labeled its attempts to deal with the problems of its drug users as a "war" on drugs.

A principal outcome of the war on drugs has been the removal of many young men and women from their families and neighborhoods to prison. The greatest number of prisoners come from low-income minority populations, so that the least advantaged neighborhoods are robbed of their only asset, young human males and females. In jail, young persons who have been guilty of no other offenses than drug possession or sales are exposed to situations in which force is frequently the only medium of negotiation.

An unfortunate but predictable outcome of the war on drugs imagery has been vigilantism. Imitating the brutal tactics of police officers (see below), adolescents in low-income sections of New York City have set fire to homeless persons and slashed or murdered female sex workers, two well-known categories of drug misusers (Curtis & Maher, 1992).

THE INFORMAL ECONOMY AND VIOLENCE: THE CONTRAST BETWEEN MARIJUANA AND COCAINE*

Beliefs and expectations about the psychopharmacological effects of a substance help shape the rules governing use and the actual experience of using it. Normative processes develop and operate among peers to regulate use and to control effects (Zinberg, 1984), but they change over time. Forms of social organization and social rituals of drug use grow, but then are dismantled and reconstituted in novel ways when one substance replaces another. As new networks of users and distribution appear, so, too, do new forms of social control. The latter also evolve in response to other social, economic, cultural, and political influences.

The supplanting of marijuana by cocaine in Caribbean-African communities illustrated these processes. Marijuana, dominant in the 1960s when substantial local-level capital accumulation was occurring, encouraged nonviolence by building up persons and neighborhood. By contrast, when the global economy had shifted in the 1980s into a phase of concentration of capital in a few hands (Mandel, 1975; Phillips, 1990), smokable cocaine "emptied out" communities and swept hitherto hidden values rapidly upward and out of them. As the rug was pulled from under them, literally, low-income minority or immigrant communities "imploded" violently.

Marijuana smoking had been introduced in the 1960s to the neighborhoods of young urban, unemployed Caribbean-African males, both in the Caribbean and in Caribbean immigrant communities abroad, during a period of great psychosocial distress. Modernization and development plans, engineered by American businessmen and social scientists, had commoditized many lines of production in the thriving informal economy, shrinking it and the neighborhood-based associations through which it had mobilized indigenous labor and capital. The food vendors on the sidewalk were replaced by the glittering franchises of U.S. fast-food chains,

---

*The following two sections were adapted with permission from A. Hamid, Political Economy of Crack Violence, *Contemporary Drug Problems*, Vol. 17, No. 1, pp. 31–78, © 1990 Federal Legal Publications.

while designer or ready-to-wear clothes in the new department stores closed the busy "parlors" and shops of neighborhood tailors and seamstresses. Modernization thus brought in its wake high rates of unemployment, inflation, and migration. Young persons resorted to petty crime, bitter squabbling over the little legal or illegal income available, and finally political protest.

As discontent climbed in the late 1960s, the young men, certainly influenced by the press reports and popular music from abroad that approved and encouraged marijuana use (and, of course, by returning students, workers, and migrants), started to experiment with it in abandoned buildings or other secluded settings. They reported before long that marijuana brought "peace" and "togetherness" and made them "brothers." It helped them to set aside their violent rivalries.

At first, initiates on most of the islands were dependent upon irregular imported supplies (from Colombia, Panama, and Jamaica), which they bartered or shared among themselves without thinking of profit. They moved next, however, to encourage local production on islands that hid remote or forested areas, such as Trinidad, Grenada, Dominica, and St. Lucia; and, responding to a growing city demand, they experimented with partnerships that could distribute marijuana around the clock. Marijuana now made men "think constructive."

Finally, some 10–15 years after the onset of marijuana use (i.e., in 1973–1978), when cultivation to meet domestic and export demand was firmly in place, and a loose-knit international network of marijuana-distributing "blocks" or "gates" (selling locations) linked the islands with immigrant communities in North American cities, the United Kingdom, and Europe, marijuana made men "see the light" (Hamid, 1980).

In this stage of marijuana-induced revelation, and especially as blocks or gates emerged as distinct social-organizational forms capable of distributing marijuana effectively at international and local levels, a majority of distributors and a core of their low-income clientele became converted to Rastafari, an ideology of self-sufficiency and "African" self-reliance (Barrett, 1977; Boot & Thomas, 1977; Hamid, 1980; Owen, 1976).

A central feature of Rastafari and the subsequent Rastafari-dominated development of Caribbean marijuana distribution was "control": disciplined—and therefore peaceful and thoughtful—action in every area of cultivation, distribution, and use. The Rastafari felt that they had received a biblical "calling" to these occupations. Through restrained and quasi-ritual use of marijuana, they had stopped being petty criminals and had become wealthy men able to make their uniquely subversive voices heard. They felt obligated, therefore, to make marijuana revered by everyone. They expanded and improved marijuana cultivation; and in America, they secured suppliers of sinsemilla from northern California and Oregon. Extensive and relaxed credit arrangements linked growers, middlemen or importers, and street-level distributors internationally. This international network was acephalous and favored expansion rather than monopoly. In New York, it enabled a sizable corner of the marijuana market to be "Caribbeanized" completely. Finally, Rastafari musicians invented reggae music, which promoted marijuana worldwide (Hamid, 1980).

At the interpersonal level, the belief in "Jah Rastafari" included a surrender to Him of judgmental and punitive functions, and gave Rastafari a common moral framework derived from the Old Testament. Belief in it allowed many peccadilloes on the part of individuals to be ignored. Several reggae songs, based on the psalms of David, encouraged this attitude. For example, different versions of "Fret Not Thyself of Evildoers" (Psalm 37) have been written by nearly every major reggae recording artist. Also popular were the many versions of "Jah is my Savior/ Whom Shall I Fear?" Although the Rastafari ideology directed scathing polemics against mainstream society, or "Babylon," it contained no call to arms—except for the upcoming spiritual battle, or Armageddon.

At the neighborhood or community level, Rastafari were admired by the general public, whether buyers or nonbuyers of marijuana (and in Brooklyn, even among African Americans, Hispanics, and European Americans, who only grudgingly respected Caribbean immigrants), not only as generous shopkeepers selling a superior, reliable product, but also as reggae musicians, artists, sponsors of learning and learned discussion, and spokesmen for the most recent "African" rejection of white civilization ("Babylon") and its bases in organized violence (Boot & Thomas, 1977; Nettleford, 1972). They spearheaded the health food movement in minority urban communities by opening the first health food stores and organizing seminars, food coops, and related programs. They set an example as strict vegetarians themselves, who excluded processed foods, alcohol, and most other psychoactive substances except marijuana from their diets. The community appreciated them best, however, for reinvesting marijuana revenues to revive a variety of cottage industries (leathercraft, clothes making, arts and crafts, music, child care) and to explore new ones such as vegetarian food production. On the islands, they bought farmland to cultivate fruits and vegetables. Many owed them employment.

Rastafari took pains to be recognized as a peaceful, lawful presence, despite the illegality of marijuana (which they have challenged, and are challenging, in several law courts, both in the United States and abroad). In San Fernando, Trinidad, when an alleged Rasta was being sought for child molestation, a coalition of Rastafari blocks was formed to aid the police in their investigations. It helped prove that the assailant was not a co-religionist.

Another loose federation of blocks in the same town had been supplying marijuana to the smaller Eastern Caribbean islands, where they stimulated indigenous block formation and Rastafarianism. In Trinidad, they operated produce stalls at local markets, at which mountains of fresh vegetables and ground provisions were offered at below-market prices. On Saturdays and Sundays, crowds of shoppers gathered to listen to the reggae music at their stalls, making a party atmosphere.

Flyers they distributed proclaimed that the low prices were a Rastafari aid to low-income, Trinidadian consumers as they struggled with inflated prices for food.

In Jamaica, reggae musicians, whose songs advertised the beneficial effects of marijuana use and distribution, helped organize a peace rally to bring together rival politicians whose followers had been turning electoral campaigns into armed conflicts. In Grenada, Rastafari marijuana growers and distributors were in the vanguard of Maurice Bishop's socialist revolution in 1983—a wholly bloodless revolution in which not a single shot was fired.

Rastafari did feel that they needed to protect themselves against thieves, who knew that marijuana distributors dealt in large sums of cash. Therefore they armed themselves with weapons, perhaps like every other shopkeeper, and supported a minor traffic in firearms. (Blocks often operated out of candy stores, boutiques, record stores, and grocery stores that were indistinguishable from legitimate businesses.)

Greater protection for Rastafari, however, was simply the good will the public bore them. A very prosperous distributor owned a cluster of three blocks in New York, and he would donate a box of Pampers to needy housewives who were regular customers. The same distributor also displayed in his store windows the quilts and other handicrafts that women co-religionists had made for sale. Children in the neighborhood received gifts of imported Haitian mangoes from him when they were in season. Some customers received marijuana on credit.

Thus the marijuana economy helped restore vitality, prosperity, and cooperation in disintegrating neighborhoods. Embittered relationships among young persons were healed, and a new religion enfolded them. In many cases, their relationship with their parents improved when marijuana revenues bought mom and pop stores and other property for their families.

Abroad, marijuana use and distribution also served an integrative function at the level of interethnic relations. Rastafari conformed well with, and provided influential symbols for, the thrust that Caribbean politicians, powerbrokers, and entrepreneurs ("Babylon!") were mounting to develop a Caribbean constituency or market in America or Europe. Rastafari, those of its roots in marijuana cultivation, distribution, and use barely concealed, was a rallying point in the search for a distinctive Caribbean identity in the multiethnic, cosmopolitan New York milieu.

In 1981 the plentiful supplies of marijuana flowing from every corner of the world to America were interrupted by DEA-inspired campaigns. At the street level, distributors faced stepped-up police surveillance and harassment. In that year too, however, vast stands of *Erythroxylon coca* that had been planted in 1975–1978 in Colombia, Ecuador, and Peru and in new areas of Bolivia (formerly the sole cultivator of *E. coca* in the world) had grown to maturity (Morales, 1989). Colombian distributors came into possession of an estimated 70 metric tons of cocaine hydrochloride powder, where formerly annual production had been below

14 metric tons (Eddy, Sabogal, & Walden, 1989). Seeking new markets, the Colombian distributors looked to the Caribbean islands and to the United States. Entrepreneurs arrived in Caribbean capitals, offering attractive deals to islanders and diffusing also the practice of preparing freebase (for smoking) from "basuca" paste (a less refined product than cocaine hydrochloride powder) (Hamid, 1991).

At the same time, in Brooklyn, Caribbean marijuana distributors, searching for a new medium of exchange to supplement the declining marijuana market, very reluctantly put aside their strong ideological (Rastafari) resistance against all psychoactive substances other than marijuana to respond to a growing consumer demand for cocaine hydrochloride powder for intranasal use. At the time, there were very few distributors of cocaine hydrochloride powder in the community to supply them, and the Rastafari marijuana distributors were greatly enriching them (Hamid, 1991).

Rastafari were delighted by the energy and "peachiness" with which snorting cocaine rewarded them. One very wealthy distributor, enjoying a few minutes' respite from a busy schedule, explained that he had been exhausted through searching the night long for marijuana. Producing a foil wrapper containing cocaine hydrochloride powder, he snorted a few lines and declared that this powder provided him with the energy to endure the tiring searches.

During this time, users and distributors took the time to go to nightclubs to listen to concerts by reggae musicians and calypsonians. These musicians were frequently the house guests of wealthy distributors. Here the singers affirmed, like 19th century Italian singers, that cocaine strengthened their vocal muscles.

Thus Rastafari enjoyed cocaine hydrochloride powder as a tonic and, strengthened by it, redoubled their efforts in Rastafari and drug distribution and in making themselves agreeable in the neighborhood. Although cocaine hydrochloride powder was sold then at $1,800–$2,800 an ounce, they appeared not to mind the heavy expense. At the same time, they were embarrassed by the fact that they had no ideological justification for its use or distribution. It was enjoyed as a sinful pleasure, and there were many who shunned it. All continued to choose marijuana when they wished for "I-ditation" (or to "get high"). Only later was a biblical justification found for cocaine (see below).

In 1982, as word of the practice reached them in New York, Rastafari sought to convert cocaine hydrochloride powder to freebase for smoking. They needed more, and as the few distributors available could not supply it, they themselves undertook its import and distribution. For them, the changeover was rather like one from selling food in a grocery store to becoming a restaurateur (who, moreover, sits down to eat with his guests): the logistics are different, as well as the relationship to the clientele. Rastafari retreated from their street-level blocks or gates and moved to private apartments to teach a growing clientele how to transform cocaine hydrochloride powder into freebase and to nurture the new market.

Learning that they could buy an ounce of high-grade cocaine for $900 or less on the islands (still for retail in New York at $1,800–$2,800, or more, if the substance was adulterated or "cut"), they sent couriers with U.S. currency to the islands on buying expeditions.

The cases of four extremely wealthy Rastafari (Musa, Rafi, Icob, and Blackheart) who initiated the distribution of cocaine hydrochloride powder (for conversion to freebase) are described in considerable detail in Hamid (1991). In the initial stage, they combined marijuana distribution with cocaine distribution and realized enormous profits in the combined market. Worried by their continuing religious strictures against other drug use, one of them unearthed a passage in Revelations (Chapter 2, verses 17–29) in which the chosen were rewarded with a "white stone." This biblical justification for use allayed their fears.

In all such groups of freebase initiates, a universally reported effect of freebase smoking was escalation to compulsive or "binge" use. Rastafari found themselves in difficult straits when they moved from the street-level marijuana distribution settings (which separated client from distributor by bulletproof glass partitions or heavily barred doors) and invited their clientele into apartments. Driven by their own craving for readministrations and by the importunings of their clients/guests, they began preparing indiscriminate amounts of freebase to be consumed on the spot. Selling locations now acquired the air of nonstop binges financed by the distributor and attended by a polyethnic clientele. Within months, distributors had completely depleted marijuana fortunes that they had accumulated over a period of 15 years.

It took from 1982 to 1984 for the four distributors, Musa, Icob, Rafi, and Blackheart, to deplete their sizable fortunes (Hamid, 1991). For the first time, they quarreled. Smarting as status and wealth dwindled, needing cash desperately and immediately to obtain cocaine for their personal use—let alone to sell—they turned violently short-tempered with subdistributors who owed them money. They threatened and assaulted the latter. They fought with clients who employed offers of sex or friendship to get cocaine free of charge. In their turn, clients grumbled about distributors who adulterated their product or sold short quantities. In late 1983, one of them, Rafi, returned abruptly to Trinidad, very much impoverished.

The other three soon fell further into disarray and violence. At length, Musa and Blackheart retired from drug distribution and left the United States to join another Rastafari in Africa. Only one—Icob—remained a viable distributor. He was soon joined by Rafi again. For a while, the two lived together at one of Icob's apartments, near his cluster of selling locations. Rafi helped Icob oversee the combined cocaine and marijuana business. But they were soon quarreling again because of personal cocaine smoking; on one memorable occasion, Icob, himself "beamed up," chased Rafi around the neighborhood several times with a machete. After another furlough in Trinidad, Rafi returned in 1988 as a wholesale seller of marijuana. He had reduced his cocaine consumption to occasional "wulla" joints (marijuana joints to which finely powdered freebase was added).

For a while, Icob remained a leading distributor of both cocaine and marijuana, but at last he was undone by his personal use, and, before losing them, was to be seen prowling in his empty selling locations with an Uzi automatic rifle and his freebase pipes. In late 1986, apparently homeless and peddling crack curbside at a very busy intersection, he was badly beaten by competitors. An informant reported that he died after remaining brain-dead for several days.

The death of Icob presaged the doom that would overtake all subsequent phenomena of crack use and distribution in New York. Toward 1984, as Rastafari lost further viability and sank toward the status of "pusher/junky," newcomers succeeded them. The cases of One-Eye and Etham exemplified the new corner turned in distribution. They were from a predominantly African-American neighborhood in East Harlem, where marijuana and cocaine hydrochloride powder distribution had remained in Caribbean hands.

One-Eye was a 56-year-old migrant from South Carolina who came to New York City in his early teens with his mother. He has always lived in Harlem. It was as a workman in the 1940s that he first became acquainted with cocaine. He and co-workers in the construction business would buy and snort several hundred dollars' worth of cocaine on weekends. One-Eye said that he snorted cocaine for several years until the 1970s, when a Jamaican and a white friend taught him how to prepare cocaine powder with ammonia to produce "small-base," as it was called then. The "small-base" was packed into cigarettes and gave a "cheeto" high.

One-Eye said that he preferred cocaine smoking right away, because snorting had destroyed the membranes in his nose. Then around 1973, other cocaine-using friends taught him how to prepare smokable cocaine with baking soda for smoking in pipes, or freebasing. One-Eye completely stopped snorting, and freebasing became his only method of daily cocaine consumption.

One-Eye was primarily a user from 1973 to 1984. Sometimes, to offset some of his expenses on cocaine, he would distribute it among his circle of friends and fellow users, who bought it for snorting, "small-base," and freebase. One-Eye purchased it from three or four bulk retailers he knew and derived useful profits from his distribution efforts.

But his fortune changed in 1984. Demand for freebase was rising, and Rastafari were the principal suppliers. After making connections with a couple of them in Brooklyn, One-Eye decided to sell cocaine full time.

From 1984 to 1985, One-Eye could be observed fully in charge of his apartment/selling location (or "freebase parlor," as such locations were called). He had a large desk that dominated the room into which one entered from the street door, and at this desk, he had all his cooking and smoking paraphernalia. Customers would come in great numbers, sit down, and wait while One-Eye prepared batches of freebase for them from cocaine hydrochloride powder. He made over $10,000 weekly and traveled often to visit his Rastafari suppliers in Brooklyn. By 1985, however, One-Eye had run out of funds. His personal use consumed much of the profits; then indiscriminate binges with women users also proved a great strain. In addition, One-Eye's conscience regularly troubled him over the amounts of money he was making from drug sales. He felt obliged to give the money away to whoever in need asked for it. He said he felt relieved without all the cash that came from the pockets of customers who were clearly suffering tremendous difficulties on account of freebase.

A young Puerto Rican nonuser named Etham, 20 years of age, now entered the story. A high school dropout who used to "hang out" with Rastafari and other Caribbean and African-American users in the neighborhood, he told One-Eye that he wanted to sell freebase. One-Eye showed him how to prepare it and recommended the new technique of packaging it in vials and offering it ready to use ("crack") as the best marketing strategy. Thus, One-Eye started buying cocaine from his Rastafari suppliers and selling it for Etham, again from his apartment.

Etham was soon making formidable profits. He found Cuban and Dominican suppliers uptown, to whom he paid $600 an ounce for pure, uncut cocaine hydrochloride powder. His average daily purchase was 10–12 ounces. Next he started getting product directly from Florida. By 1987, he had four other outlets in Manhattan and the Bronx like One-Eye's. They were known as "crack houses."

Etham was the sole boss of his business. He made purchases and prepared and packaged the crack. When called on his beeper, he drove to the location in his Cherokee and parked a few blocks away. His runner delivered the fresh supplies and picked up cash. Relations with his workers were good; he never dismissed anyone and accepted the few resignations he had without demur.

But then Etham retired suddenly from business. Eight other selling locations in the neighborhood (freebase parlors and crack houses) also disbanded. Newer, younger distributors sold the drug curbside. One-Eye was evicted from his apartment and rendered homeless. He lived for a time in hallways in the neighborhood, seeking crack. He died in a hospital in 1989.

Aided by the tremendous demand and steadily falling wholesale and retail prices for the drug, the violence that had been gathering since the introduction of smokable cocaine in 1981–1982 now exploded.

First, increased demand meant that there was a very large ready-made market. Unlike marijuana distributors, therefore, who had to develop a clientele in the 1960s, and who began to handle substantial fortunes only in middle age (1974–1981), their successors like Etham, who were extremely young men, were able to make instant fortunes. The immaturity of such youthful nouveaux riche distributors, and especially their reinvestment preferences (which in the main involved conspicuous consumption of such luxury goods as gold, clothes, and imported motor vehicles), would leave their mark on subsequent crack-related developments. Ages continued to fall, until many distributing groups were primarily groups of teenagers. Similarly, while marijuana distributors had formerly been exclusively Caribbean, the ethnicities of crack-distributing groups included Hispanics and African Americans. Polyethnicity, extreme youth, immaturity, and high revenues brought strains that erupted in violence.

Second, among distributors, the centralizing tendency that Etham represented was accelerated by his successors. His relaxed approach to business was abandoned. Centralized crack distribution "businesses," popularly known as "posses" or "crews," replaced him, and they were pressured to monopolize distribution and to operate cross-nationally. To do business at all, it seemed, it was necessary for single organizations to control tightly small urban markets per street distributor and, at the same time, several such operations in many cities. Thus in Detroit, the Chambers Brothers emerged as an organization structured like a corporate firm, which handled millions of dollars weekly. In Los Angeles, the Bloods and Crips achieved notoriety as suppliers of crack to the entire western United States. In New York, some 20 Jamaican posses controlled a large corner of the cocaine market. In order to maintain tight control, violence within organizations, among organizations, and against such outsiders as thieves, informers, and the police was instrumental (Bourgois, 1989).

Competition among distributing organizations—an increase beyond the level reported for pioneers such as Etham—rested upon peculiarities of the evolving crack market. For example, the crack market depended heavily upon repeat sales from relatively small numbers of users per seller or selling location in a given locality. Thus, rival distributing groups were drawn into violent confrontation to monopolize access to clientele (Hamid, 1991).

Another peculiarity of crack distribution that certainly contributed to the likelihood of violent confrontation was the move to curbside operations. Where marijuana distribution had moved from the streets to candy stores and similar fixed locations, crack distributors reversed that trend. When crack houses such as Etham's and One-Eye's proved unreliable (distributors like Etham retired; or "employees" like One-Eye became unreliable, sometimes "tapping" the vials, sometimes "coming up short" with money), they were replaced briefly by another sort of selling operation, also known as a crack house. In this sort of crack house (Bourgois, 1989; Williams, 1989), which somewhat resembled the opium dens of China or turn-of-the-century ones in New York, users were frisked for weapons by guards, then admitted into a space with tables and chairs. Here they purchased crack, rented paraphernalia, and used up their purchases. This sort of crack house had a short life; the brusque manner of proprietors, the threat of being surprised by the police in a locked space that had only one exit, and the approaches made by other customers (often female users offering prostitution, or their "vics" [victims] offering retaliatory violence) made consumers paranoid.

In 1990, crack distribution was predominantly curbside, and crack markets had differentiated. Neighborhoods hosted one type or contained examples of different types of market. A different level of violence attached to each (see Chapter 4).

Using conventions adapted to these developments, the many paraphernalia were replaced by merely a "stem" (a length of heat-proof glass with a screen or scrap of metal netting inserted into it) and a Bic lighter. When a vial of crack is added, one uses curbside too—in parks, stairwells, subway stations, doorways, roofs, and basements. Curbside use, exposed to the general public, also promotes violence.

Third, inside distributing groups, in addition to the stresses of polyethnicity and extreme youth, members were poised tensely around the issue of control of use among founding members (for without control, kilos of the substance would be consumed, leaving nothing to sell). They needed to replace pushers/junkies (such as One-Eye in Etham's operation) as street-level employees with more reliable, controlled-use, or nonusing personnel. Extremely young distributors appeared to adapt better than their elders to this requirement of the control of crack use. Evidence of the degree of a person's control was also his efficient use of force: to differentiate himself from the hapless user and to register his arrival among the significant contestants—the police, the robber, and the rival. One also had to control one's feelings about crack-using females, even to the point of leading them into prostitution; otherwise they could lead a distributor into uncontrolled use wrapped in uncontrolled sexuality (Bourgois, 1989).

These themes of control, power, violence, sex, and misogyny were repeatedly explored in rap music, which was to crack what reggae was to marijuana. For example, in the California rapper Ice-T's hit record of the time, "Posse Crew," all were given ample coverage. The first "jam" on this record, which began with one "homeboy" shooting another in a dispute over an Ice-T tape, served well as the young crack distributor's anthem.

Fourth, many crack distributors also used users outrageously. Since they did not regularly maintain fixed selling locations themselves, a common tactic was to take over a client's apartment as a selling location by offering free supplies of crack. Distributors would then sell to the client's using companions or neighbors—and move on after this clientele was completely depleted: jobs terminated and bank accounts emptied, public transfer payments interrupted or under investigation, on the verge of eviction because of nonpayment of rent or homeless, overwhelmed by child neglect charges, saddled with suspicious deaths or homicides to explain to authorities, sought after by the police for robberies or other criminality, and sought after too by public health authorities because of the risk of acquired immunodeficiency syndrome (AIDS) or other infectious diseases. Examples of several such takeovers abounded in ethnographies. In one Brooklyn case, a housewife received advances of crack against the subsequent lease of her apartment. When her husband refused the deal, the housewife was shot to death.

Fifth, users utterly rearranged the households to which they had returned in ways that increased friction and promoted violence. They alienated themselves from their kin networks and from their association with nonusing neighbors and friends on account of repeated stealing, assaults, and quarreling and because of their indifference to their children. Accordingly, they placed onerous child care responsibilities and security precautions upon other household members. Grandmothers, for example, emerged as the resentful caretakers of yet another generation. Having brought up a generation that crack wasted, they were forced to raise their grandchildren; and if teenaged child-bearing grandchildren stumbled, great-grandchildren. When whole kin circles or friendship and neighborhood associations succumbed together to crack use, quarrels and fights over crack dispersed members into more heterogeneous companies of users, where unfamiliarity led to greater suspicion.

Users, bound together in the quest for crack ("the mission"), quarreled incessantly and violently among themselves. For example, ethnographers have witnessed many scenes in crack houses or in private apartments among gatherings of users where users hid crack in their fingernails, then carefully searched rugs or carpets for scraps of the substance, and invariably fought when none was discovered. Sometimes these frangible groups of users embarked on the suicidal path of robbing distributors.

For Rastafari users, an additional embittering pain was the erosion of beliefs by which they had lived faithfully for at least 10 years. For example, crack use, which is nearly always polydrug use, always implied at least use of alcohol, a substance particularly avoided by Rastafari. Meat-eating too, for Rastafari the most abominable of practices—something straight from Sodom and Gomorrah, considered by them to be the symbol and chief nourishment of violence, warmongering, self-aggrandizement, and vanity—became acceptable when meat was the only food available upon recovery from many mealless days of "bingeing." Thus use diluted cherished beliefs, and the violation of central taboos encouraged a more general recklessness.

And finally, a marked male-female differentiation in crack use also promoted violence (Hamid, 1991; Williams, 1989). Recent reports by the Justice Department and by the New York State Division of Substance Abuse Services (Goldstein et al., 1987) confirm that as many women as men have become addicted to crack, a circumstance not observed in earlier drug epidemics. To maintain their addiction, female crack users routinely "vic-ed" (victimized) both using and nonusing males, who in turn victimized them on account of their vulnerability (or their willingness to do anything for more crack). These conditions were powerful prompts to violence.

Violence modeled after these circumstances of crack use and distribution infected a whole generation. The lifestyle of the many crack distributors in low-income minority communities was highly visible. Apparently anticipating a short life, they appeared to be fonder of "conspicuous consumption" than of solid reinvestments of crack revenues. Central to this lifestyle, this "presentation of self," were a repudiation of the ordinary world (of low wages, low status, and ceaseless petty frustrations) and the violence that was both instrumental in crack distribution and expressive of that repudiation. Adults of the parent generation, who should have been apologists of the mainstream, were compromised because they were buying crack from these youngsters—oftentimes, their actual sons—and it undermined their worldview. Even if parents were not dependent on them for drugs, some gladly accepted money for rent, food, and other expenses.

Thus, even among youth who were not crack users or distributors, the regime of crack stimulated violence. The model it so vividly presented—extreme youth in control; adults "out of control"; women exploited; the short, violent life glorified—absorbed whole communities faster than crack itself could addict.

WHY WAS MARIJUANA A FORCE FOR PEACE, AND SMOKABLE COCAINE ONE FOR DESTRUCTION?

The differences between the marijuana and cocaine eras show that drug use and distribution are not the work of the alienated, the deviant, the anomie, or the diseased, nor yet the pastime of "reserve pools of labor." The activities of drug users and distributors may be seen to be in perfect accord with transformations in the physical appearance of the study neighborhoods, in local housing conditions, in household composition, in relations between members of households, and in the social integration of neighborhoods that occurred over the past three decades. They accelerated or facilitated these transformations and expressed them at the ideological level.

Thus, the use and distribution of marijuana, especially in its heyday from 1974 to 1981, was a symbol and exemplary working model of control, capital accumulation, restrained and orderly interpersonal relations, reconciled families, and neighborhood integration and upliftment at a time when a class of Caribbean (and minority) migrants (intellectuals, politicians, businessmen, the comfortably employed) was consolidating itself politically, economically, socially, and culturally both in New York and in the Caribbean or abroad (Hamid, 1997; Kasinitz, 1992; Sassen, 1981). Migrants who had gained a good foothold were quitting their first homes for more exclusive, better-serviced neighborhoods.

As more of these wealthier and better-assimilated migrants moved out, the evacuated sections began to accept a more heterogeneous, polyethnic influx of tenants coming from nearby decaying neighborhoods. In Brooklyn, therefore, East Flatbush had been receiving refugees from derelict neighborhoods in Brownsville, East New York, and Bedford-Stuyvesant since the mid-1970s. The pattern of forced interborough migration since the 1970s—tenants fleeing decaying housing to more recently evacuated buildings nearby, causing overcrowding in the latter and greater susceptibility to eventual decay in their turn—has been well documented for Brooklyn, Harlem, and the Bronx (Hopper, Susser, & Conover, 1985; Wallace, 1985). The role that a smaller budget for fire, sanitation, and municipal services played in converting overcrowded buildings into abandoned ones has also been measured (Wallace & Wallace, 1989).

Overcrowding obviously affects household composition (Hopper et al., 1985), and it also alters relationships within households in ways that presage intrahousehold vandalism, breakdown in authority relations, decrease in maintenance services, and eventual abandonment of buildings by landlords. In East Flatbush, for example, a mother (a refugee from Brownsville) had reportedly locked herself in her bedroom after repeatedly trying to lock her crack-addicted children out. During the late 1970s, when the mother's common-law husband supported it, parental authority had occupied the whole space of the apartment. Toward 1980, however, that authority was fragmented when other families arrived to double up, and the male breadwinner left. The present situation, therefore, in which parental authority is restricted to the mother's bedroom, is the end of a sequence that closely parallels the one described for housing stock in general (Hopper et al., 1985; Wallace, 1985).

At the level of neighborhood social integration, forced migration continuously throws strangers together and prevents stable associations from developing. This type of social destabilization is linked to individual failure and violent or pathological outcomes.

Thus the shiftless crowds of victimizing and victimized "crackheads," as well as the ruthless, violent, crack-distributing adolescent—neighborhood emblems of crack—are the actual foot soldiers in a contemporary housing crisis that political decisions and economic processes have launched.

Underlying neighborhood destabilization are the flight of capital from local-level communities and the role of crack users and distributors in this particular drama. Crack performed as a super-efficient "vacuum cleaner" that went over the physical and social rubble of the study sites to detect and draw in overlooked wealth. These dollars were not reinvested at the local level. In Harlem and Brooklyn, crack dollars did not contribute a single vegetarian cookshop, nor is there evidence of other local-level secondary economic activity that it stimulated. Instead, as youthful crack distributors spent on "gold cables" and luxury motorcars, more apartments were being abandoned and more buildings being rendered derelict (and others being gentrified). Crack dollars for the most part traveled abroad to the supplier countries, leaving significant deposits in the United States only in the hands of the corporate institutions that launder drug money or facilitate distribution. The ethos of reinvestment that characterized marijuana distribution has taken the opposite, extreme form of capital depletion in the era of crack. In this transfer of capital upward and out of local communities, the agencies of crack-using females and of those others who initiated drug use with crack (a surprising number of older persons, for example) were not negligible. They empowered the crack vacuum cleaner by contributing additional labor to its mission and through the proceeds of their crack-specific criminality and expenditure.

Thus, feeding into the violence described as circumstantial to crack use and distribution (and that may indeed be psychopharmacological, economic-compulsive, and systemic, to follow Goldstein's [1985] classification) is the violence of persons reacting violently to conditions that violate. The latter were produced by economic processes and political decisions (which transformed neighborhoods, households, and the most intimate behaviors within them) and can be repaired only by measures that match them in complexity and influence.

MARIJUANA AND AGGRESSION

Male aggression has bedeviled human history from its inception, and its utility diminishes with every passing year. As an evolving species, humans are attempting to reduce its prevalence. Just as men in many cultures have chosen alcohol to stimulate and excuse bellicose ideation, there is much cross-cultural evidence indicating that, when desiring to champion peace, they select marijuana. In nearly every study, researchers found that marijuana and the opiates reduce aggression. High doses of THC did not produce aggressive responses but suppressed them (Taylor et al., 1976).

In 1997, voters in Arizona and California approved the medical use of marijuana, thus sanctioning the everyday practice of thousands of physicians who have been (illegally) recommending marijuana to their patients for the relief of pain, stress, and the discomfort caused by chemotherapy or AIDS treatment. Chronically ill patients who have used marijuana have witnessed dramatic improvements in their appetites, rest, and general well-being.

In the example of Rastafari, marijuana was the drug "selected" to represent the "positive vibrations" among unemployed, desperate Caribbean-African youths that impelled them to repair destroyed forms of social organizations and revive an informal economy in shambles.

In the late 1990s, inner-city minority youths, whose older siblings and even parents had grim encounters with smokable cocaine in the previous decade, have learned from the latter's example and diligently avoid both heroin and cocaine. Even beer, which had been heavily marketed in their neighborhoods, is in disfavor. The turnabout is also registered in low rates of criminal and violent offending. The young people seem more eager to complete their education or training and to find jobs. The drug they use as they busy themselves in these mainstream pursuits is marijuana.

GANGS, MARIJUANA, AND REDUCING VIOLENCE

The pacific effects users claim for marijuana may be appreciated even more if the history and present disposition of gangs in New York City is considered.

The American imagination is obsessed with images of the violent gang (fighting over turf, employment, girlfriends, and criminal opportunities), which it has poured into a flood of films, novels, plays, journalistic reports, commentaries, and tabloid features. A procession that began with the showdowns of Jesse James and his peers, and into which the autos-da-fé of the likes of Bonnie and Clyde had also wandered, was continued by the switchblade choreographies of *West Side Story*, drive-by shootings between the Bloods and Crips, and (some say) law enforcement retaliatory tactics by the Los Angeles Police Department (LAPD).

The same preoccupation marks the scholarly literature and researchers, who make the implicit (or explicit) assumption that gang allegiance automatically leads to greater violence. They have advanced many reasons to explain their relationship. The canonical typology includes forms of violence, such as *instrumental or corporate* (Skolnick, Blumenthal, Correl, Navarro, & Babb, 1989; Taylor, 1993), *territorial* (Moore, Vigil, & Garcia, 1983), *defense of honor and respect* (Horowitz, 1983), *expressive or symbolic* (Conquergood, 1994; Erlanger, 1979), *race/ethnic* (Brotherton, 1994), *internally ritualistic* (Vigil, 1996), and *sociopathic* (Yablonsky, 1962). A peripheral type also occurs when the victim is not a gang member and is hurt as a result of predatory crimes or stray gunfire (Klein & Maxson, 1989). Another important area of gang violence to come under scrutiny from criminal justice agencies is the proliferation of weapons among members (Spergel, 1990). It has been associated with gangs whose structures and boundaries are atrophying or whose sole purpose is the conquest of market competitors. Prison, in which many inmates suffer at the hands of peers and custodians, is another catalyst.

Violence is even constructed as essential to the gang experience. Researchers have recently likened the "beatdown," in which initiates run the gauntlet of established members to gain admission to the gang, to a "street baptism" and to male initiation rites in preindustrial tribal societies. They argue that the inaugural ordeal is in fact outward violence, or the "gang bang," turned inward, and that both dramatize the need for protection and escape from fear, as well as "pent-up aggression born of trauma and rage." While addressing problems of youths' gender and age-role identity resolution, they also test the fighting skills and combative courage of newcomers. Accordingly, these West Coast (Chicano) gangs are defined as "a territorially affiliated group of youths (typically organized into age-graded cliques) dedicated at least in part to fighting other similar groups" (Vigil, 1996).

Of course, there is no doubt that gangs have sometimes been guilty of heinous acts, and they are rightly accused of being involved in a wide variety of crimes, including drug distribution and major crimes of every type, and in violence against one another (Cloward & Ohlin, 1960; Cohen, 1955; Fagan, 1989; Hagedorn & Macon, 1988; Jankowski, 1991; Moore, 1979; Padilla, 1992; Thrasher, 1936; Vigil, 1988; Yablonsky, 1962). In recent years, gangs have diffused across the United States, and some officials believe that a centrally organized, evil intelligence, or master criminal bent on propagating drugs, crime, and mayhem nationwide was responsible.

Youth gangs form a specific arena of violence. They are, however, diverse, complex, and shifting organizations whose members participate variably in crime and drug use (Hagedorn & Macon, 1988; Klein & Maxson, 1989; Spergel, 1990).

Recent studies suggest that gang members become more involved in drug distribution than other youths, thus involving them in "systemic" violence related to drug distribution (Goldstein et al., 1989). Mieczkowski (1986) reported on youngsters in Detroit who sold heroin, and Cooper (1987) described other Detroit youngsters who sold crack cocaine. In several Chicago neighborhoods, gangs control drug sales. Crack cocaine lured many gang members into drug sales. In drug distribution, violence is the means by which discipline and retribution for wrongs are accomplished.

Other prompts for violence for gangs include territoriality, the control of resources, the control of female movement and fertility, and as a token of affiliation (as in "beatdowns" or initiations). Self-inflicted wounds and the shedding and blending of blood express loyalty. Feldman et al. (1985) found three styles of Latino gangs in San Francisco: the "fighting" style prompted members to compete for territory with rivals, the "entrepreneurial" style discouraged it as bad for business (except when necessary to maintain authority and discipline), while "recreational" gangs completely avoided it. More recent gangs have repulsed these kinds of violence and act as a pacifying presence in neighborhoods torn by drug wars (Curtis & Hamid, 1997).

Gangs sometimes used force to prevent members from using drugs. Chinese gangs forbade drug use, although involved in heroin trafficking (Chin, 1986). Adolescent crack sellers forbade it in their ranks (Cooper, 1987). In

Mieczkowski's Detroit gangs (1986), members were forbidden the use of heroin but used marijuana and cocaine recreationally in off-hours.

Contemporary resurgent Puerto Rican gangs in New York City, such as the Latin Kings and Netas, stand in sharp rebuke of these representations. In ongoing research, three variants of the Latin Kings gang have been identified, none of which is a fighting gang. Some chapters are of the *youth movement* variety and interpret "uplift of the community" as the promotion of education, health, and peaceful political action. Others, or *criminal* chapters, seek advancement "by any means necessary," and engage heavily in drug distribution and other criminal activity. Most, however, are *fence-sitters*, unable to decide between these two ideologies (Curtis & Hamid, 1997).

Indeed, it appears that a wish to pacify "war-torn" neighborhoods had generated the formation of these gangs. The gangs/violence nexus originates in the multiple levels of oppression and contradiction that many third-generation Nuyoricans face as involuntary immigrants. Socialized without a significant male presence, they are gender-confused and homophobic; partially assimilated, they are more American than Puerto Rican, more English-speaking than Spanish; experiencing high rates of imprisonment and unemployment and low rates of high school completion, they lack mainstream adult role models; climbing demeaning rungs from foster care into the orbit of the police, they resent social control; forced to compete with first-generation, upwardly mobile peers (such as Dominicans), their self-esteem is battered; struggling to maintain a fractured, hybrid, mutable identity in the "imagined community" of the gang, they are assailed within by self-doubt and by criminalization in the wider society. Teaching youths a relatively safe passage through this mine field, the Latin Kings may well lower the level of violence that might have existed in their absence. In this form of grassroots sociocultural and political organizing, lower class/underclass youths adapt progressively and more or less composedly to pressures of adolescent development and alterations of family structure, and in legal/illegal labor markets.

Instead of contributing to communal strife, each type appears to be an indigenous attempt to grasp and aggregate a runaway, out-of-control violence that had antedated their formation. By monopolizing and channeling it, they have had a calming effect in their neighborhoods.

Police and media deny this view. Prosecutors describe the Latin Kings as "one of the best organized and most violent gangs in New York," while the United States Attorney declared that "the Latin Kings were a rigid hierarchical organization that beheaded, burned and beat up wayward members, and maimed and killed outsiders as well."

Certainly the symbols of violence were everywhere. The young men who participated in research often had tremendous musculatures. Some weighed more than 350 lb and rippled with huge biceps, shoulders, torsos, and thighs. And their discourse was frequently corrosive: full of threats, graphic descriptions of beatings administered or planned, and ingenious refinements of torture.

But a close examination revealed that in the past two decades, levels of violence had risen in their neighborhoods independently of the young men. Three reasons were foremost: (1) the destruction of the infrastructure; (2) the rise of drug supermarkets; and (3) the war on drugs.

Destruction of the Infrastructure

If incivilities or "quality of life" offenses can lead to greater and more serious offending (Kelling, 1989; Reiss & Tonry, 1986), the physical transformation of neighborhoods, which reminded many observers of "Dresden after the war" (Hamid, 1990; Wallace & Wallace, 1989), have had multiple negative effects. In Bushwick, the South Bronx, and other neighborhoods, block after block of apartment buildings had been abandoned; or homeowners, seeking to collect insurance monies when they could not sell their houses, torched them. By 1977, more than 1,000 lots in Bushwick, or fully one fifth of available space, were empty (Curtis & Hamid, 1997). The section had become an urban wasteland whose charred, derelict landscape was matched by a frontier mentality where confrontation and violence were commonly used to impose order and resolve disputes.

The intimate contexts in which human beings are socialized and discover their self-worth were dealt the greatest blow. Because of the shortage of affordable housing, families were forced to "double up" and "treble up," and authority relations were undermined within households (Maher, Hamid, Dunlop, & Johnson, 1996). Instead of cohesive units, the latter were fractured, setting genders and generations on a collision course with one another. While grandmothers barricaded themselves and their meager valuables behind locks within their single bedrooms, their sons and daughters, mostly 30-year-olds, roamed the rest of the apartment during crack and alcohol binges. Their children, ranging in age from newborn to 16 to 17 years old, had their own outlooks which, in addition to teen-aged parenthood and dropping out of school, included avoidance of hard drugs (and gang membership).

The high turnover of tenants and homeowners weakened voluntary associations, if they were not completely discontinued. The disinvestment in schools and community had emptied PTAs, clubs, church groups, and grassroots political groupings. The informal controls that define and protect neighborhoods were thus slackened (Curtis & Maher, 1992).

Drug Supermarkets

The conversion of drug markets to a few supermarkets also precipitated greater tumult. Drug distributors have long commanded attention (Fagan, 1989;

Goldstein, 1985; Hamid, 1990; Skolnick et al., 1989) for their unprecedented levels of and novel approaches to violence, including the infamous "Colombian necktie," the use of boxcutters to slash faces, and their promotion of the 9-mm pistol to the status of cultural icon. Ethnographic research in the past decade, however, has shown that there is a wide variety of distribution styles and that the role and incidence of force varies greatly among them (Bourgois, 1989; Curtis & Hamid, 1997; Hamid, 1997; Maher & Curtis, 1994; Williams, 1989). Some markets earned reputations for controlling it (e.g., Hamid's marijuana distributors, Williams' crack dealers) while others employed it regularly and systematically (Curtis & Maher, 1992; Taylor, 1993).

A quantum leap separated these usual markets from the drug supermarkets described earlier. In them, large corporate-like organizations directed street-level drug sales, and since institutional and neighborhood-level restraints had already vanished, they completely disregarded the sensibilities of residents in doing so. They also undermined the prosperity of the communities that hosted them, just as corporate giants were doing simultaneously in the formal economy. Returning nothing but dangerous, low-level, dead-end jobs for youths, the damages included plummeting property values, a greater incidence of drug misuse, and high rates of incarceration. But the most crippling legacy was violence.

By 1992, one Puerto Rican and three Dominican "owners" ruled over crack distribution at the northern end of the Bushwick area in New York. Each had a trademark, or the color of the tops of the crack vials they sold: white, blue, brown, and pink. Dominican families monitored the day-to-day operations of the largest three. Younger family members and close nonkin "associates" managed street sales, while older family members, entirely removed from the street scene, were the "executives." When there were not enough family members for these managerial roles, "owners" employed other Dominicans. The practice angered the street-level workers, especially the Puerto Ricans. "Owners" had been Puerto Rican throughout the 1970s and early 1980s but had been toppled by the Dominicans in the late 1980s. The rivalry that had long existed between Puerto Ricans and Dominicans in New York City was thus intensified in the drug business.

As the war on drugs daily depleted the supply of Latinos/Latinas who could work as street-level employees, African Americans, European Americans, and heavy drug users replaced them. The gulf separating management from labor widened, and their already contentious and adversarial relationships turned even more distrustful and violence prone. Resenting their harsh and hazardous conditions of labor and the disrespect of Dominican managers, they took every opportunity to abscond with the drugs. They fully expected physical punishment for transgressions.

In effect, while brute force or the threat of it is the ultimate means distributors have to enforce rules, a business is ruined when it invites police attention too frequently. Accordingly, sensible or successful distributors avoided or minimized its use. But Bushwick's corporate owners were reckless. Violent acts were more common in their markets because of the divisions and animosities that rigidly separated different levels of the organizations, because the owners did not live in the neighborhood and did not have to witness or confront the aftermath of their deeds, and because they could easily relocate supplies to outlets they maintained in other neighborhoods. Indeed, owners encouraged their managers to use public displays of force regularly as a way of intimidating untrustworthy employees and to send the message that they should not be crossed. For example, one owner hired an enforcer who strolled around the neighborhood with a baseball bat on which he wrote the names of his targets. After punishing them, he rubbed off their names.

In the Bushwick of the early 1990s, "face to face" or "man to man" confrontations between individuals were replaced by humiliating group beatings, or "gang bangs." Their unrestrained brutality affected local adolescents, who were its daily witnesses. Sometimes they too participated gratuitously in "beatdowns" and other bloody episodes in which they had no stake: they simply saw someone being chased and, with malicious smiles on their faces, picked up their baseball bats or bicycle chains and joined the chase. For them, "fun" was no longer spraying graffiti, playing ball, or dancing: it was the number and severity of "beatdowns" they administered daily. Drug supermarkets made these atrocities an unremarkable commonplace feature of everyday life.

The War on Drugs

As described in Chapter 4, the Tactical Narcotics Teams (TNT) were adopted by the New York Police Department (NYPD) in 1988 as its premier method against street-level drug markets, and they were replicated in four of the city's five boroughs. Although any police operation that targets street-level drug markets may prompt the use of force, perhaps as people resist being arrested or during their attempts to flee, the TNT were innovative, and conceived many unusual applications that deeply alienated neighborhood residents. For example, when "sweeping" the main drug selling areas, they would cordon off both ends of a street and require everyone in between to lie down on the asphalt, regardless of who they were. While this tactic nearly always yielded a handsome body count of arrests, it also obliged elderly grandmothers and young children to grovel on the ground while being roughly searched, and it enraged many residents. As for the TNT, they seemed to regard everybody as a potential "bad guy."

When the TNT could not find drug distributors to arrest, they raided well-known shooting galleries. These were often in abandoned buildings, into which officers loathed to go. They believed that too many hiding places lurked in their dark and sometimes labyrinthine interiors and that they were an obstacle course of discarded human immunodeficiency virus (HIV)-infected syringes. To flush the drug users out instead, some officers, in plain view of honest citizens, used to throw large rocks through the windows. They were caught in the act by a prize-winning reporter for the *Los Angeles Times*, who had been interviewing heroin injectors in a shooting gallery when the police avalanche thudded around him. Drug users showed the reporter large welts across their torsos. Officers had whipped them with sections of thick television cable as they fled the galleries in previous campaigns (Bearak, 1992).

In the summer, local police officers mercilessly and systematically harassed drug users who loitered near the major drug-selling locales. Early in the morning when they had fallen asleep on the sidewalk, foot patrol officers would routinely rouse them with kicks and order them to move. Sometimes the kick simply nudged the unfortunate person awake; at other times it was meant to cause pain. So habituated were they to the pastime that the police officers continued it even when video cameras were brought to photograph them. They also responded with an overwhelming show of force at almost any infraction, be it a drug user's, dealer's, or passerby's.

By late summer 1992, the populace was close to insurrection, and television and newspaper crews came to interview unruly crowds who were protesting the indiscriminate police shootings and beatings of youths. Police had responded in full riot gear, and residents had pelted them from rooftops with bottles, debris, and hateful epithets. Apparently thinking that beleaguered drug distributors were fomenting the neighborhood's growing hostility toward them, the police mounted yet another major offensive against street-level drug markets in September 1992. They stationed a mobile trailer in a nearby park to serve as the base of operations for more than 300 additional uniformed officers. These were positioned around the park and on each corner of drug "hot spots." Mounted police trotted by to discourage trafficking or "loitering." Officers stopped and questioned all pedestrians and asked for their identification and destination. Nonresidents were told to stay out. Streets with the heaviest drug trafficking were sealed with wooden barricades and police vans, and traffic was diverted to other streets. When evening came, they drove in large flat-bed trucks with gas-powered generators and klieg lights, which, parked at strategic corners, illuminated entire blocks. Police painted the street numbers of buildings on rooftops to enable helicopters to give additional support to officers pursuing suspects on foot. For the next 18 months, Bushwick was virtually occupied by the small army of police.

In 1994, a household survey of 18- to 21-year-olds in Bushwick measured instances and perceptions of local violence. Thirty-two percent (47% of males) of the young people reported that they had been beaten up, 25% (40% of males) said they had been threatened or stabbed with a knife, 20% (23% of males) that they had been caught in a random shoot-out, 19% (27% of males) that they had been threatened or shot at with a gun, and 35% (37% of males) had been mugged or robbed with a threat of bodily harm.

Youths responded to living in a war zone in two ways. Some stayed at home. In focus groups and interviews the researchers conducted during winter 1993–1994, many said that they were so fearful of random and/or police violence that they no longer spent much time in parks, playgrounds, stoops, or the other places where youths had traditionally "hung out." Indeed, the question, "Where do you hang out?" seemed to offend them.

But others formed gangs. By early 1993, following the massive police initiative of September 1992 in which hundreds of neighborhood youth were jailed, sizable chapters of the Latin Kings and Netas formed and asserted their control over some blocks, especially those where there had been large street-level drug markets and unchecked violence. Predominantly of Puerto Rican descent, they reported that they had experienced a genuine rebirth, and in leaving behind the past, their new goal was to "uplift the Latino community." As former street-level drug workers who had suffered at the hands of their Dominican bosses and the police, they were disillusioned. Although they had long realized their limitations in American society, the sweeping arrests had also taught them the shallowness of the drug distribution organizations that had employed them. The Dominican owners did not bail them out of jail, hire lawyers, look after family, or compensate them for the time in prison. They remained indifferent to Puerto Rican sensibilities, although mainly Puerto Ricans suffered the brunt of the war on drugs.

In the war zone that public policy had created in Bushwick, pacific functions of gangs included the following:

- They brought social organization among youths. The Latin Kings imposed organization, government, and order on atomized, marginalized individuals. For example, Salsa, the "primero" of the Bushwick chapter of the Netas, has more than 100 youths from the neighborhood in an antidrug, proeducation program, "jovenes para el progresso."
- They brought peace in prison. The Latin Kings solved many of the difficulties of young Puerto Rican men and women locked up in the war on drugs. The most pressing need was protection from other inmates. For a first-time arrestee, membership in an organization that applied blanket protection throughout the prison system was a blessing. It bestowed status and prestige, prevented victimization, and allowed disputes with other members to be arbitrated peacefully.
- They brought domestic peace. Gang membership was also advantageous on return to civilian life. Where many members' households were chaotic, the gang functioned as an alternative family that prescribed rules and justifications for behavior, thereby bringing order and structure into potentially unmanageable social and emotional situations.

- They forestalled intergang violence. Despite the literature and the usual perceptions of gangs, the Latin Kings in New York City, who generally enjoy cordial relations with other gangs such as the Netas and the (mainly African-American) Zulu Nation, are significantly different from the gangs that researchers have characterized as "fighting gangs" (Jankowski, 1991; Vigil, 1996). They have been involved in only a few incidents of group or intergang strife. Instead, all the gangs are collaborating to build a positive image in Latino neighborhoods by performing charitable and civic-minded work such as sweeping and mopping hospital lobbies, supporting Latino political candidates, caring for people living with AIDS, and feeding the homeless.

In interviews with the Third Crown of a Latin Kings chapter in Bushwick, researchers found that in the majority of cases that were brought before him, he was quelling violence, not promoting it. The Third Crown—the sergeant at arms—authorizes the use of violence.

In two cases, interborough feuding was avoided. In one case, a Latin Queen—her husband was also a Latin King—was having an affair with a trigger-happy young man. On edge about the infidelity, the latter had pulled a gun on a Latin King, the husband's friend. The specter of a Bushwick-wide war between Latin Kings and the lover's faction loomed. Instead, the Third Crown arranged to disarm the young man and discipline him rather than risk an indiscriminate shootout.

In another case, the Third Crown prevented a young Latin Queen from creating a war between Netas and Kings. She had been fighting on the train with another girl, and, in the melee, had slashed the latter's boyfriend, a Neta. The wounded young man and the Latin Queen were ready for blows, but the Third Crown communicated with his counterparts in the Netas and quashed the dispute.

A truly impressive achievement was this Third Crown's control over guns. In a neighborhood where gun ownership and use had become rampant, he had 100 weapons locked up in a stash apartment, he alone had the keys, and he alone decided who would use them, when, where, and why.

By investing in the two decades of drug wars in Bushwick, the city has diverted resources from other priorities. Local populations have recognized that official efforts to deal with AIDS, drug abuse, and violence have not been very effective. The gangs are evidence that they have begun to do the work themselves. Female members of the Latin Kings have a leverage that previous female gang members never had, and they are able to determine the ethos of gang chapters. They bring their own agendas, drawn from such areas of primary concern as child care, religion, and the welfare of seniors and the disabled, into the gang's overall program. Latin Kings help those with AIDS, sweep hospital floors voluntarily, and rally in support of politicians in favor of spending on relevant social services.

Over the past 3 years, crime in New York City (and other major U.S. cities) has plunged to a surprisingly low level. Mayor Rudolph Giuliani and his police commissioners hastened to take credit. They claimed that their unrelenting prosecution of "quality of life" misdemeanors such as panhandling on the subway or drinking a beer in public have deterred more serious offending. But gangs may have helped more than the police to produce this outcome.

The only drug gangs permit their members to use is marijuana! Indeed, some top leaders had been "crackheads" and marijuana had helped them to quit. Other heroin and cocaine misusers report the same experience.

WOMEN, AGGRESSION, AND DRUGS

As Chapter 7 will show, women's relationship to drugs is highly contested. Those who believe that, by an invariable pharmacological or chemical logic, drugs cause violent crime and that the current preference for "stronger" drugs (including more potent strains of marijuana) bespeaks a population whose deviance and lawlessness are worsening are convinced that the greater popularity of drug use among women has led to greater transgressions by them. Those who recognize the critical mediation of the human-drug interaction by social, economic, political, and cultural factors find the status of women in male-dominated societies little affected by their drug use.

Several drug researchers have noted that women drug users—particularly heroin users—were likely to commit violent crimes when they experienced withdrawal symptoms (Goldstein, 1979, 1990; Inciardi, 1986; Rosenbaum, 1981). However, more recent research on cocaine use (Goldstein, 1990) found that while greater use by men led them to become more violent, greater use by women was associated with their being more often the victim rather than the perpetrator of violence.

Between 1967 and 1984, the number of women involved in criminal activity increased at a faster rate than the number of men. Women are using drugs (cocaine) in greater numbers than ever. Few studies have investigated the types of crime committed by female drug users, although many authors cite shoplifting, drug sales, and sex work as the most commonly committed offenses.

In a study of 175 female inmates at Rikers Island, researchers found that women who used marijuana, depressants, stimulants, or illegal methadone/look-a-likes reported low crime rates compared with heroin and/or cocaine users. They found that heroin users exhibited high crime rates (many of these users also abuse cocaine). Sanchez and Johnson (1987) found the following:

> The crime rates of nonusers (i.e., neither cocaine nor heroin) and irregular (1 to 20 times in the past 60 days) cocaine/heroin users were considerably lower than the rates of near-daily and daily cocaine/heroin users. Nevertheless, the association of crime rates and cocaine/heroin use was

not linear. That is, multiple-daily users of cocaine/heroin exhibited somewhat lower crime rates than once-daily cocaine/heroin users. . . . (p. 211)

The mean rate of criminal violence, however, was low among all levels of cocaine/heroin users and among nonusers. This is consistent with the low rate of violent crime found by most studies of female offenders and drug users. (p. 211)

Female violence "expresses inner rage as opposed to male violence which is instrumental toward dominating others" (Campbell, 1993, p. 50). Gang girls do not like to fight, but if they must, they explode. Hagedorn and Devitt (1996), the authors of a longitudinal study of Milwaukee girl gangs, discovered the opposite phenomenon. They found that their sample of girl gangs actually "loved to fight." They also found that lethal violence was far less common than with male gangs. Gang girls used weapons and gunfire less. They noted, however, that female gang violence was

less about power and domination than about the thrill of fighting, or observing norms of solidarity with their home girls. . . . (p. 21)

The conception of fighting as "power" is predominantly a masculine notion, and helps explain the aversion to the use of weapons by women. (p. 21)

The joy of fighting expressed by our Milwaukee respondents represents an active rebellion from stereotyped female gender roles, as well as from the threat of a bleak future. (p. 29)

There is a higher rate of "maturing out" among female gang members in Milwaukee than among males. But in resurgent New York City, in gangs such as the Latin Kings/Queens or Netas, Latinas are permitted into the highest decision-making circles, are long-term members, and advance feminist agendas.

In the past two decades, the women drug users whom ethnographers have interviewed and observed have suffered such economic reverses that many were forced into sex work, petty crime, and low-level drug distribution in order to survive. Violence often accompanies these professions.

Discussion Questions

1. Debate whether aggression is a basic, ineradicable primate and human instinct that at best can only be sublimated. Are men more violent, or have women caught up? Is death an aggression?

2. How does the human mind cope with violence in the natural world, or as witness or survivor of human slaughter, as in wars, riots, or other mass killings?

3. Review the kinds of violence that occur among hunters and gatherers, nomads, and horticulturalists; in the great agrarian civilizations; in modern industrial societies; and in totalitarian states. Identify and explain any differences.

4. Research examples of pacifism (Gandhi, Martin Luther King, Jr., communes, conscientious objectors). How did they achieve political goals without using force?

5. Research the rising availability of guns, the diffusion of rural America's "guns and weapons culture" to minorities in the inner cities, and the consequences.

6. Give other examples of the use of drugs as "excuses" for particular behaviors.

7. Review the history of gangs in America, and comment on their reputation for violence. Give reasons why more recent gangs, like the Latin Kings or Netas, may have less violent agendas.

8. Why did marijuana have pacific effects in the 1960s and presently, while cocaine in the 1980s was associated with high levels of violence?

9. The reader should record instances of violence, interview and observe participants, and examine possible causes. How many cases involved drugs? How were the drugs implicated?

10. Review the literature on the relation of particular drugs, such as alcohol, marijuana, cocaine, heroin, amphetamine, anabolic steroids, Ecstasy, or ketamine, to violence.

REFERENCES

Ahlstrom, S. (1981). *Finnish drinking habits: A review of research and trends in acute effects of heavy drinking*. Report no. 150. Helsinki: Social Research Institute of Alcohol Studies.

Akers, R.L. (1984). Delinquent behavior, drugs and alcohol: What is the relationship? *Today's Delinquent*, *3*, 19–48.

Akers, R.L., Krohn, M., Lanza-Kaduce, L., & Radosevich, M. (1979). Social learning and deviant behavior: A specific test of a general theory. *American Sociological Review*, *44*, 636–655.

Angrosino, M. (1972). *Outside is death: Alcoholism among East Indians in Trinidad and Tobago*. Ph.D. Dissertation. Teachers College, Columbia University/Ann Arbor, MI: University Microfilms.

Ardrey, R. (1956/1997). *Territorial imperative: A personal enquiry into the animal origins of property and nations*. New York: Kodansha.

Asnis, S., & Smith, R. (1978). Amphetamine abuse and violence. *Journal of Psychedelic Drugs*, *10*, 317–377.

Ball, J., Rosen, L., Flueck, J., & Nurco, D. (1982). Lifetime criminality of heroin addicts in the United States. *Journal of Drug Issues, 12*, 225–239.

Bard, M., & Zacker, J. (1976). The police and interpersonal conflict: Third-party intervention approaches. Washington, DC: Police Foundation.

Barrett, L. (1977). *The Rastafarians*. Boston: Beacon Press.

Bataille, G. (1962). *Death and sensuality: A study of eroticism and the taboo*. London: Routledge.

Bearak, B. (1992, September 27). A room for heroin and HIV. *Los Angeles Times*, p. A1.

Benjamin, W. (1970). Illuminations, In H. Arent (Ed.), *On Violence*. London: Jonathan Cape.

Biernacki, P. (1986). *Pathways from heroin addiction: Recovery without treatment*. Philadelphia: Temple University Press.

Blane, H., & Hewitt, L. (1977). Alcohol and youth: An analysis of the literature, 1960–1975. Final report prepared for the National Institute on Alcohol Abuse and Alcoholism, Contract no. ADM281-75-0026. Rockville, MD: U.S. Public Health Service.

Bolton, R. (1973). Aggression and hypoglycemia among the Quolla: A study in psychobiological anthropology. *Ethnology, 12*, 227–257.

Bond, A., & Silveira, J. (1993). The combination of alprazolam and alcohol on behavioral aggression. *Journal of Studies on Alcohol, 11* (Suppl), 30–39.

Boot, A., & Thomas, M. (1977). *Jamaica: Babylon on a thin wire*. New York: Schocken.

Bourgois, P. (1989). In search of Horatio Alger: Culture and ideology in the crack economy. *Contemporary Drug Problems, 16,* 619–649.

Bourgois, P. (1996). *In search of respect: Selling crack in el barrio*. New York: Cambridge University Press.

Bowker, L. (1983). *Wife-beating*. Lexington, MA: Heath.

Bowker, L. (1986a). *Ending the violence: A guidebook based on 1,000 battered wives*. Holmes Beach, FL: Learning Publications, Inc.

Bowker, L. (1986b). The meaning of wife beating. *Currents, 2*, 39–43.

Bradford, J.M.W. (1988). Organic treatment for the male sexual offender. *Annals of the New York Academy of Sciences, 528*, 193–222.

Briddell, D.W., Rimm, D.C., Caddy, G.R., Dorawitz, G., Sholis, D., & Wunderlin, R.J. (1978). Effects of alcohol and cognitive set on sexual arousal to deviant stimuli. *Journal of Abnormal Psychology, 87*, 418–430.

Brisset, D. (1978). Toward an interactionist understanding of heavy drinking. *Pacific Sociological Review, 21*, 3–20.

Brotherton, D. (1994). Who do you claim: Gang formation and rivalry in an inner city high school. In J. Holstein & G. Miller (Eds.), *Perspectives on Social Problems, 5*, 141–171.

Burns, T.F. (1980). Getting rowdy with the boys. *Journal of Drug Issues, 10*, 273–286.

Cahalan, D., & Cisin, I. (1976). Drinking behavior and drinking problems in the United States. In B. Kissin & H. Begleiter (Eds.), *The biology of alcoholism* (Vol. 4). New York: Plenum.

Campbell, A. (1993). *Girls in the gang: A report from New York City*. Oxford, UK: B. Blackwell.

Carey, J., & Mandel, J. (1968). The Bay Area speed scene. *Journal of Health and Social Behavior, 9*, 164–174.

Casat, C.D., Pearson, D.A., van Davelaar, M.J., & Cherek, D.R. (1995). Methylphenidate effect on a laboratory aggression measure in children with ADHD. *Psychopharmacology Bulletin, 31*, 353–356.

Chagnon, N. (1983). Yanomamo: The fierce people. Excerpt reprinted in J.P. Spradley & D. McCurdy (Eds.), *Conformity and conflict: Readings in cultural anthropology* (8th ed., pp. 278–286). New York: HarperCollins.

Chaiken, J.M., & Chaiken, M. (1982). *Varieties of criminal behavior*. Santa Monica, CA: Rand.

Chermack, S., & Taylor, S. (1995). Alcohol and human physical aggression: Pharmacological vs. expectancy effects. *Journal of Studies on Alcohol, 56*, 449–456.

Chin, K.L. (1986). *Chinese triad societies, Tongs, organized crime, and street gangs in Asia and the United States*. Ph.D. dissertation, University of Pennsylvania, Department of Sociology.

Chitwood, D.D., & Morningstar, P.J. (1985). Factors which differentiate cocaine users in treatment and non-treatment users. *International Journal of the Addictions, 20*, 449–460.

Cloward, R.D., & Ohlin, L.E. (1960). *Delinquency and opportunity: A theory of delinquent gangs*. Glencoe, IL: Free Press.

Codere, H. (1975). Power in Rwanda. *Anthropolice*, N.S. IV 1, 45–85.

Cohen, A.K. (1955). *Delinquent boys: The culture of gangs*. Glencoe, IL: Free Press.

Collins, J.J., Jr. (1981). Alcohol use and criminal behavior: An empirical, theoretical and methodological overview. In J.J. Collins (Ed.), *Drinking and crime: Perspectives on the relationship between alcohol consumption and criminal behavior*. New York: Guilford.

Collins, J.J., Jr., Hubbard, R.L., & Rachal, J.V. (1985). Expensive drug use and illegal income: A test of explanatory hypotheses. *Criminology, 23*, 743–764.

Conquergood, D. (1994). Homeboys and hoods. In L. Frey (Ed.), *Group communication in context: Studies of natural groups*. Hillsdale, NJ: Lawrence Erlbaum.

Cooper, B. (1987, December 1). Motor city breakdown. *Village Voice*, pp. 23–35.

Curtis, R., & Hamid, A. (1997). State-sponsored violence and indigenous responses to it: The role of the Third Crown (sgt. at arms) of the Latin Kings gang. Rockville, MD: NIDA monograph.

Curtis, R., & Maher, L. (1992). Women on the edge of crime: Crack cocaine and the changing contexts of street-level sex work in New York City. *Crime Law and Social Change, 18*, 221–258.

De Beauvoir, S. (1952/1973). *The second sex*. New York: Vintage.

De Waal, F. (1996). *Good natured: The origins of right and wrong in humans and other animals*. Cambridge, MA: Harvard University Press.

Dobash, R.E., & Dobash, R. (1979). *Violence against wives: A case against the patriarchy*. New York: Free Press.

Du Toit, B. (1975). Dagga: The history and ethnographic setting of cannabis sativa. In V. Rubin (Ed.), *Cannabis and culture* (pp. 81–116). The Hague, Netherlands: Mouton.

Eddy, P., Sabogal, H., & Walden, S. (1989). *Cocaine wars*. New York: Norton.

Ellinswood, E. (1971). Assault and homicide associated with amphetamine abuse. *American Journal of Psychiatry, 127*, 90–95.

Elliott, D.S., Huizinga, D., & Ageton, S. (1985). *Explaining delinquency and drug abuse*. Beverly Hills, CA: Sage.

Erickson, P.G., et al. (1987). *The steel drug: Cocaine in perspective*. Lexington, MA: Heath.

Erlanger, H. (1979). Estrangement, machismo, and gang violence. *Sociological Quarterly, 60*, 235–248.

Eron, L.D., Walder, L.O., & Lefkowitz, M.M. (1971). *Learning of aggression in children*. Boston: Little, Brown.

Fagan, J. (1989). The social organization of drug use and drug dealing among urban gangs. *Criminology, 27*, 633–669.

Fagan, J. (1990). Intoxication and Aggression. In M. Tonry & J. Wilson (Eds.), *Drugs and crime* (Vol. 13). Chicago: University of Chicago Press.

Fagan, J., Hansen, V., & Stewart, D.K. (1983). Violent men or violent husbands? Background factors and situational correlates of violence toward intimates and strangers. In D. Finkelhor, R.J. Gelles, G.T. Hotaling, & M.A. Straus (Eds.), *The dark side of families: Current family violence research.* Beverly Hills, CA: Sage.

Fagan, J., Piper, E.S., & Moore, M. (1986). Violent delinquents and urban youth. *Criminology, 23,* 439–466.

Fagan, J., Weis, J.G., Cheng, Y.T., & Watters, J.K. (1987). Drug use, violent delinquency and social bonding: Implications for theory and intervention. Final Report. Grant No. 85-IJ-CX-0056. Washington, DC: National Institute of Justice.

Feldman, H. W., Agar, M.H., & Beschner, G.M. (Eds.). (1979). *Angel dust: An ethnographic study of PCP users.* Lexington, MA: Lexington Books.

Feldman, H.W., Mandel, J., & Fields, A. (1985). In the neighborhood: A strategy for delivering early intervention services to young drug users in their natural environments. In A.S. Friedman & G.M. Beschner (Eds.), *Treatment services for adolescent substance abusers.* Rockville, MD: National Institute on Drug Abuse.

Ferguson, B., & Whitehead, N. (Eds.). (1992). *War in the tribal zone: Expanding states and indigenous warfare.* Santa Fe, NM: School of American Research Press.

Finestone, H. (1967). Narcotics and criminality. *Law and Contemporary Problems, 22,* 60–85.

Firestone, S. (1970). *The dialectic of sex: The case for feminist revolution.* New York: Morrow.

Gandossy, R.P., Williams, J., Cohen, J., & Hardwood, H. (1980). Drugs and crime: A survey and analysis of the literature. Washington, DC: National Institute of Justice.

Gibson, W. (1994). *Warrior dreams.* New York: Sage.

Gilmore, D. (1990). Manhood. In J.P. Spradley & D. McCurdy (Eds.). (1994). *Conformity and conflict: Readings in cultural anthropology* (8th ed.) (pp. 249–255). New York: HarperCollins.

Giordano, P.C., Cernkovich, S., & Pugh, M.D. (1985). Friendships and delinquency. *American Journal of Sociology, 91,* 1170–1202.

Gold, M., & Moles, O.C. (1978). Delinquency and violence in schools and the community. In J.A. Inciardi & A.E. Pottieger (Eds.), *Violent crime* (pp. 63–88). Beverly Hills, CA: Sage.

Goldstein, P.J. (1979). *Prostitution and drugs.* Lexington, MA: D. C. Heath.

Goldstein, P.J. (1985). The drugs-violence nexus: A tri-partite conceptual framework. *Journal of Drug Issues, 15,* 493–506.

Goldstein, P.J. (1990). Female substance abusers and violence. In B. Forster, J. Colman, & E. Salloway (Eds.), *The socio-cultural matrix of alcohol and drug use: A sourcebook of patterns and factors.* Lewiston, NY: Edwin Meller Press.

Goldstein, P.J., Brownstein, H.H., Ryan, P.J., & Bellucci, P.A. (1989, Winter). Crack and homicide in New York City, 1988: A conceptually-based event analysis. *Contemporary Drug Problems, 17,* 615–670.

Goldstein, P.J., Lipton, D.S., Spunt, B.J., Bellucci, P.A., Miller, T., Cortez, N., Kahn, M., & Kale, A. (1987). Drug related involvement in violent episodes: Final report. Grants DA-03182 and DA-04017, National Institute on Drug Abuse. New York: Narcotic and Drug Research, Inc.

Gordon, A.J. (1978). Hispanic drinking after migration: The case of Dominicans. *Medical Anthropology, 2,* 61–84.

Gordon, A.J. (1982). The cultural context of drinking and indigenous therapy for alcohol problems in three migrant Hispanic cultures. *Journal of Studies on Alcohol, 42,* 217–240.

Gottheil, E., Druley, K.A., Skoloda, T.E., & Waxman, H.M. (Eds.). (1983). *Alcohol, drug abuse and aggression.* Springfield, IL: Charles C Thomas.

Greenberg, S.W. (1977). The relationship between crime and amphetamine abuse: An empirical review of the literature. *Contemporary Drug Problems, 5,* 101–130.

Griffith, J. (1966). A study of illicit amphetamine traffic in Oklahoma City. *American Journal of Psychiatry, 123,* 560–568.

Grinspoon, L., & Hedblom, P. (1975). *The speed culture: Amphetamine use and abuse in America.* Cambridge, MA: Harvard University Press.

Hagedorn, J., & Devitt, M. (1996, June). Fighting female: Variation, violence, and gender roles in female gangs. Paper presented at the 1996 Annual Meeting of the American Sociological Association, New York.

Hagedorn, J., & Macon, P. (1988). *People and folks: Gangs, crime and the underclass in a rustbelt city.* Chicago: Lake View Press.

Haller, J. (1995). Alpha-2 adrenoceptor blockade and the response to intruder aggression in Long-Evans rats. *Physiological Behavior, 58,* 101–106.

Hamid, A. (1980). *A precapitalist mode of production: Ganja and the Rastafarians in San Fernando, Trinidad.* Ph.D. dissertation, Teachers College, Columbia University/Ann Arbor, MI: University Microfilms.

Hamid, A. (1990). The political economy of crack-related violence. *Contemporary Drug Problems, 17,* 31–79.

Hamid, A. (1991). From ganja to crack: Caribbean participation in the underground economy in Brooklyn, 1976–1986, Pt. 2. *International Journal of the Addictions, 26,* 735–744.

Hamid, A. (1992). Drugs and patterns of opportunity in the inner city: The case of middle-age, middle-income cocaine smokers. In A. Harrell and G. Peterson (Eds.), *Drugs, crime and social isolation: Barriers to urban opportunity* (pp. 209–238). Washington, DC: Urban Institute Press.

Hamid, A. (1997). *The political economy of drugs, Pt I: Ganja and Rastafarians in Trinidad and New York.* Unpublished manuscript.

Hartstone, E.C., & Hansen, K.V. (1984). The violent juvenile offender: An empirical portrait. In R.A. Mathais, P. DeMuro, & R.A. Allinson (Eds.), *Violent juvenile offenders: An anthology.* San Francisco: National Council on Crime and Delinquency.

Heath, D.B. (1983). Alcohol and aggression: A "missing link" in worldwide perspective. In E. Gottheil, K.A. Druley, T.E. Skoloda, & H.M. Waxman (Eds.), *Alcohol, drug abuse and aggression.* Springfield, IL: Charles C Thomas.

Hill, W.W. (1970). *Navajo warfare.* New Haven, CT: Human Relations Area Files Press.

Hobbes, T. (1632/1996). *Leviathan.* New York: Oxford University Press.

Hooks, B. (1990). *Yearning: Race, gender and cultural politics.* Boston: South End Press.

Hopper, K., Susser, E., & Conover, S. (1985). Economies of makeshift: Deindustrialization and homelessness in New York City. *Urban Anthropology, 14,* 183–236.

Hotaling, G.T., & Sugarman, D.B. (1986). An analysis of risk markers in husband to wife violence: The current state of knowledge. *Violence and Victims, 1,* 101–124.

Huba, G.J., & Bentler, P.M. (1984). Casual models of personality, peer culture characteristics, drug use, and criminal behaviors over a five-year span. In D.W. Goodwin, K. van Dusen, & S. Mednick (Eds.), *Longitudinal Research in Alcoholism.* Boston: Kluwer-Nijhof.

Inciardi, J.A. (1986). *The war on drugs: Heroin, cocaine and public policy.* Palo Alto, CA: Mayfield.

Inciardi, J.A., & Chambers, C.D. (1972). Unreported criminal involvement of narcotic addicts. *Journal of Drug Issues, 2*, 57–64.

Irons, R., & Schneider, J.P. (1997). When is domestic violence a hidden face of addiction? *Journal of Psychoactive Drugs, 29*, 337–344.

Jacoby, J., et al. (1973). Drug use in a birth cohort. National Commission on Marijuana and Drug Abuse. *Drug Use in America: Problem in Perspective* (pp. 300–343). Washington, DC: U.S. Government Printing Office.

Jankowski, M. (1991). *Islands in the streets: Gangs and American urban society.* Berkeley, CA: University of California Press.

Jessor, R., & Jessor, S.L. (1977). *Problem behavior and psychosocial development: A longitudinal study of youth.* New York: Academic Press.

Johnson, B.D., Goldstein, P.J., Preble, E., Schmeidler, J., Lipton, D., Spunt, B., & Miller, T. (1985). *Taking care of business: The economics of crime by heroin abusers.* Lexington, MA: Heath.

Johnson, B.D., Schmeidler, J., Wish, E., & Huizinga, D. (1986). The concentration of delinquent offending: The contribution of serious drug involvement to high delinquency rates. Unpublished manuscript. New York: Narcotic and Drug Research, Inc.

Johnson, B.D. et al., (1976). Drugs and delinquency: A search for casual connections. In D. Kandel (Ed.) *Longitudinal research on drug use.* New York: Wiley.

Kandel, D.B. (1980). Developmental stages in adolescent drug involvement. In M. Lettieri (Ed.), *Theories on drug abuse: Selected contemporary perspectives.* NIDA Research Monograph No. 30. Washington, DC: Hemisphere-Wiley.

Kandel, D.B., (1985). On processes of peer influence in adolescent drug use: A developmental perspective. *Alcohol and Substance Abuse in Adolescence, 4*, 139–163.

Kandel, D.B., Simcha-Fagan, R., & Davies, M. (1986). Risk factors for delinquency and illicit drug use from adolescence to young adulthood. *Journal of Drug Issues, 16*, 67–90.

Kantor, G.K., & Straus, M.A. (1987). The drunken bum theory of wife beating. *Social Problems, 34*, 213–231.

Kaplan, H.B., Martin, S.S., & Johnson, R.J. (1986). Self-rejection and the explanation of deviance: Specification of the structure among latent constructs. *American Journal of Sociology, 92*, 384–411.

Kasinitz, P. (1992). *Caribbean New York: Black immigrants and the politics of race.* Ithaca, NY: Cornell University Press.

Kelling, G.L. (1989). Neighborhoods and police: The maintenance of civil authority. Washington, DC: U.S. Department of Justice, Office of Justice Programs, National Institute of Justice.

Klein, M.W., & Maxson, C. (1989). Street gang violence. In N.A. Weiner & M.E. Wolfgang (Eds.), *Violent crime, violent criminals.* Newbury Park, CA: Sage.

Lau, M.A., Pihl, R.O., & Peterson, J.B. (1995). Provocation, acute alcohol intoxication, cognitive performance, and aggression. *Journal of Abnormal Psychology, 104*, 150–155.

Lefkowitz, M. (1997). *Our guys: The Glen Ridge rape and the secret life of a perfect suburb.* Berkeley, CA: University of California Press.

Leiris, M. (1962). *Manhood: A journey from childhood to the fierce order of virility.* London: Jonathan Cape.

Levinson, D. (1983). Alcohol use and aggression in American subcultures. In R. Room & G. Collins (Eds.), *Alcohol and disinhibition: Nature and meaning of the link.* Research Monograph No. 12.

Washington, DC: National Institute on Alcohol Abuse and Alcoholism. U.S. Department of Health and Human Services, U.S. Public Health Service.

Lorenz, K. (1951/1974). *On aggression*. San Diego, CA: Harcourt, Brace (Harvest Book).

MacAndrew, C., & Edgerton, R. (1969). *Drunken comportment: A social explanation.* Chicago: Aldine.

Maccoby, E.E., & Jacklin, C.N. (1974). *The psychology of sex differences.* Palo Alto, CA: Stanford University Press.

Maher, L. (1996). Hidden in the light: Occupational norms among crack-using street-level sex workers. *Journal of Drug Issues, 26*, 145–175.

Maher, L., & Curtis, R. (1994). In search of the female gangsta: change, culture and crack cocaine. In B. Raffel-Price & N. Sokoloff (Eds.), *The criminal justice system and women.* New York: Sage.

Maher, L., Hamid, A., Dunlap, E., & Johnson, B. (1996). Gender power and alternative living arrangements in the inner city crack culture. *Journal of Research in Crime and Delinquency, 33*, 181–205.

Mandel, E. (1975). *Late capitalism.* Atlantic Highlands, NJ: Humanities Press.

Mayer, J., & Black, R. (1981). The relationship between alcoholism and child abuse and neglect. In F.A. Sexias (Ed.), *Currents in alcoholism* (Vol. 2). New York: Grune & Stratton.

McBride, D.C. (1981). Drugs and violence. In J.A. Inciardi (Ed.), *The drug-crime connection.* Beverly Hills, CA: Sage.

McBride, D.C., & Russe, B.R. (1979). The social characteristics of PCP users. *Addictive Diseases.*

McClelland, D.C., (1975). *Power: The inner experience.* New York: Irvington.

McClelland, D.C., & Davis, W.N. (1972). The influence of unrestrained power concerns in drinking in working class men. In D.C. McClelland, W.N. Davis, R. Kalin, & E. Wanner (Eds.), *The drinking man.* New York: Free Press.

McClelland, D.C., Davis, W.N., Kalin, R., & Wanner, E. (Eds.). (1972). *The drinking man.* New York: Free Press.

McCord, J. (1983). Alcohol in the service of aggression. In E. Gottheil, K.A. Druley, T.E. Skoloda, & H.M. Waxman (Eds.), *Alcohol, drug abuse and aggression.* Springfield, IL: Charles C Thomas.

McCord, J. (1988). Parental aggressiveness and physical punishment in long-term perspective. In G.T. Hotaling, D. Finkelhor, J.T. Kirtpatrick, & M.A. Straus (Eds.), *Family abuse and its consequences: New directions in research.* Newbury Park, CA: Sage.

Miczek, K.A., & Thompson, M.L. (1983). Drugs of abuse and aggression: An ethnopharmacological analysis. In E. Gottheil, K.A. Druley, T.E. Skoloda, & H.M. Waxman (Eds.), *Alcohol, drug abuse and aggression.* Springfield, IL: Charles C Thomas.

Mieczkowski, T. (1986). Geeking up and throwing down: Heroin street-life in Detroit. *Criminology, 24*, 645–667.

Mieczkowski, T. (1992). The Detroit crack ethnography project. Report to the Bureau of Justice Assistance, Contract OJP-88-M-39J. Washington, DC: National Institute of Justice.

Miller, R.E., Levine, J.M., & Mirsky, I.A. (1973). Effects of psychoactive drugs on nonverbal communication and group social behavior of monkeys. *Journal of Personality and Social Psychology, 28*, 396–405.

Moore, J. (1979). *Homeboys.* Philadelphia: Temple University Press.

Moore, J., Vigil, D., & Garcia, R. (1983). Residence and territoriality in Chicano gangs. *Social Problems, 31*, 182–194.

Morales, E. (1989). *Cocaine: White gold rush in Peru.* Tucson, AZ: University of Arizona Press.

Morgan, J., & Zimmer, L. (1996). *Marijuana myths and realities.* New York: Lindesmith Center.

Moyer, K.E. (1983). A psychobiological model of aggressive behavior: Substance abuse implications. In E. Gottheil, K.A. Druley, T.E. Skoloda, & H.M. Waxman (Eds.), *Alcohol, drug abuse and aggression.* Springfield, IL: Charles C Thomas.

Muehlenkamp, F., Lucion, A., & Vogel, W. (1995). Effects of selective serotonergic agonists on aggressive behavior in rats. *Pharmacology, Biochemistry and Behavior, 50,* 671–674.

Nadelmann, E. (1989). Drug prohibition in the United States: Costs, consequences, and alternatives. *Science, 245,* 939–946.

Nettleford, R. (1972). *Identity, race and protest in Jamaica.* New York: William Morrow Press.

Newcomb, M.D., & Bentler, P.M. (1988). *Consequences of adolescent drug use: Impact on the lives of young adults.* Newbury Park, CA: Sage.

Owen, J. (1976). *Dread.* Kingston, Jamaica: Sangster.

Padilla, F. (1992). *The gang as American enterprise.* New Brunswick, NJ: Rutgers University Press.

Pagano, R. (1981). The effects of diazepam on human physical aggression. Ph.D. dissertation. Kent State University, Department of Psychology.

Pernanen, K. (1981). Theoretical aspects of the relationship between alcohol use and crime. In J.J. Collins (Ed.), *Drinking and crime: Perspectives on the relationship between alcohol consumption and criminal behavior.* New York: Guilford.

Petersilia, J. (1980). Career criminal research: A review of recent evidence. In N. Morris & M. Tonry, (Eds.), *Crime and justice: An annual review of research* (Vol. 2). Chicago: University of Chicago Press.

Phillips, K.P. (1990). *The politics of rich and poor: Wealth and the American electorate in the Reagan aftermath.* New York: Random House.

Pihl, R.O., Peterson, J., & Lau, M. (1993). A biosocial model of the alcohol-aggression relationship. *Journal of Studies on Alcohol, 11* (suppl.), 128–139.

Powers, E., & Witmer, H. (1951). *An experiment in the prevention of delinquency: The Cambridge-Somerville youth study.* New York: Columbia University Press.

Rawlings, J.W. (1968). Street level abuse of amphetamines. In J.R. Russo (Ed.), *Amphetamine abuse.* Springfield, IL: Charles C Thomas.

Reiss, A.J., Jr., & Tonry, M. (1986). *Communities and crime—crime and justice: An annual review of research* (Vol. 8). Chicago: University of Chicago Press.

Robbins, R.H. (1979). Alcohol and the identity struggle: Some effects of economic changes on interpersonal relations. In M. Marshall (Ed.), *Beliefs, behaviors and alcoholic beverages: A cross-cultural survey.* Ann Arbor, MI: University of Michigan.

Robinson, B.W., Alexander, M., & Bowne, G. (1969). Dominance reversal resulting from aggressive responses evoked by brain telestimulation. *Journal of Neurophysiology, 26,* 705–720.

Room, R., & Collins, G. (1983). Introduction. In R. Room & G. Collins (Eds.), *Alcohol and disinhibition: The nature and meaning of the link.* Research Monograph No. 12. National Institute on Alcohol Abuse and Alcoholism. Washington, DC: U.S. Department of Health and Human Services, U.S. Public Health Service.

Rosenbaum, M. (1981). *Women on heroin.* New Brunswick, NJ: Rutgers University Press.

Russell, J.A., & Mherabian, A. (1974). The mediating role of emotions in alcohol use. *Journal of Studies on Alcohol, 36,* 1509–1536.

Sanchez, J.E., and Johnson, B.D. (1987). Women and the drugs-crime connection: Crime rates among drug abusing women at Rikers Island. *Journal of Psychoactive Drugs, 19,* 205–216.

Sano, K. (1962). Sedative neurosurgery: With special reference to postremedial hypothalamotomy. *Neurologia Medico-Chirugica, 4*, 112–142.

Sassen, S. (1981). *Exporting capital and importing labor: The role of the Caribbean migration to New York City.* New York: New York University, Faculty of Arts and Sciences, Center for Latin American and Caribbean Studies.

Schaefer, J.M. (1973). *A hologeistic study of family structure and sentiment, supernatural beliefs, and drunkenness.* Ph.D. dissertation. State University of New York at Buffalo, Department of Anthropology.

Schuckitt, M.A. (1988). Weight lifters folly: The abuse of anabolic steroids. *Drug Use and Alcoholism Newsletter, 17*, 8.

Schwab, R.S., Sweet, W.H., Mark, V.H., Kjelberg, R.N., & Ervin, F.R. (1965). Treatment of intractable temporal lobe epilepsy by stereotactic amygdala lesions. *Transactions of the American Neurological Association, 90*, 12–19.

Shuntich, R., & Taylor, S.P. (1972). The effects of alcohol on human physical aggression. *Journal of Experimental Research in Personality, 6*, 34–38.

Siegel, R.K. (1980). Long term effects of recreational cocaine use: A four year study. In F.R. Jeri (Ed.), *Cocaine 1980.* Lima, Peru: Pacific Press.

Siegel, R.K. (1982). History of cocaine smoking. *Journal of Psychoactive Drugs, 14*, 277–299.

Skolnick, J., Blumenthal, R., Correl, R., Navarro, T., & Babb, E. (1989). *The social structure of street drug dealing.* Sacramento, CA: California Bureau of Community Statistics.

Spergel, I. (1990). Youth gangs: Continuity and change. In M. Tonry & N. Morris (Eds.), *Crime and justice: A review of research* (Vol. 12). Chicago: University of Chicago Press.

Spotts, J.V., & Shontz, F.C. (1980). *Cocaine users: A representative case approach.* New York: Free Press.

Star, B. (1980). Patterns in family violence. *Social Casework, 61*, 339–346.

Steele, B.F., & Pollack, C.A. (1968). A psychiatric study of parents who abuse infants and small children. In R. Helfer & H. Kempe (Eds.), *The battered child.* Chicago: University of Chicago Press.

Stephens, R.C., & Ellis, R.D. (1975). Narcotics addicts and crime: Analysis of recent trends. *Criminology, 12*, 474–488.

Taylor, A. (1993). *Women drug users: An ethnography of a female injecting community.* Oxford, UK: Clarendon Press.

Taylor, S.P., & Gammon, C.B. (1975). Effects of type and dose of alcohol on human physical aggression. *Journal of Personality and Social Psychology, 32*, 169–175.

Taylor, S.P., Gammon, C.B., & Capasso, D.R. (1976). Aggression as a function of alcohol and threat. *Journal of Personality and Social Psychology, 34*, 261–267.

Theweleit, K. (1989). *Male Fantasies* (Vols. 1 and 2). Minneapolis, MN: University of Minnesota Press.

Thomas, H. (1997). *The slave trade.* New York: Simon & Schuster.

Thrasher, F.M. (1936). *The gang: A study of one thousand, three hundred and thirteen gangs in Chicago.* Chicago: University of Chicago Press.

Tinklenberg, J.R., & Woodrow, K. (1974). Drug use among youthful assaultive and sexual offenders. In S.H. Frazier (Ed.), *Aggression: Proceedings of the 1972 annual meeting of the Association for Research in Nervous and Mental Disease.* Baltimore: Williams & Wilkins.

Tinklenberg, J.R., et al. (1981). Drugs and criminal assaults by adolescents: A replication study. *Journal of Psychoactive Drugs, 13*, 277–287.

Vigil, J.D. (1988). *Barrio gangs*. Austin, TX: University of Texas Press.

Vigil, J.D. (1996). Street baptism: Chicano gang initiation. *Human Organization, 55*, 149–153.

Vogel, W.H. (1983). Aggression-stress-alcoholism. In E. Gottheil, K.A. Druley, T.E. Skoloda, & H.M. Waxman (Eds.), *Alcohol, drug abuse and aggression*. Springfield, IL: Charles C Thomas.

Waldorf, D.O. (1973). *Careers in dope*. Englewood Cliffs, NJ: Prentice Hall.

Waldorf, D.O., Reinarman, C., & Murphy, S. (1993). *Cocaine changes: The experience of using and quitting*. Philadelphia: Temple University Press.

Wallace, R. (1985). *Shock waves of community disintegration in New York*. New York: PISCS.

Wallace, R., & Wallace, D. (1989). *Origins of public health collapse in New York City: The dynamics of planned shrinkage, contagious urban decay and social disintegration*. New York: PISCS, Inc.

Washton, A.M., & Gold, M.S. (1987). *Cocaine: A clinician's handbook*. New York: Guilford Press.

Washton, A.M., Gold, M.S., & Pottash, C. (1984). Upper income cocaine abusers. *Advances in Alcohol and Substance Abuse, 4*, 51–57.

White, H.R., Pandina, R.J., & LaGrange, R.L. (1987). Longitudinal predictors of serious substance abuse and delinquency. *Criminology, 25*, 715–740.

Williams, T. (1989). *Cocaine kids*. Reading, MA: Addison-Wesley.

Wilson, G., & Abrams, D. (1977). Effects of alcohol on social anxiety: Cognitive versus pharmacological processes. *Cognitive Therapy and Research, 1*, 195–210.

Woody, G.E., Persky, A., McLellan, A.T., O'Brian, C.P., & Arndt, I. (1983). Psychoendocrine correlates of hostility and anxiety in addicts. In E. Gottheil, K.A. Druley, T.E. Skoloda, & H.M. Waxman (Eds.), *Alcohol, drug abuse and aggression*. Springfield, IL: Charles C Thomas.

Yablonsky, L. (1962). *The violent gang*. New York: Macmillan.

Yawney, C. (1969). *Drinking patterns and alcoholism in Trinidad*. Caribbean anthropology. Montreal: McGill University Center for Developing Area Studies.

Zahn, M.A., & Bencivengo, M. (1974). Violent death: A comparison between drug users and non-drug users. *Addictive Diseases, 1*, 283.

Zinberg, N.E. (1984). *Drug, set, and setting: The social bases of controlled drug use*. New Haven, CT: Yale University Press.

SUGGESTED READING

Becker, H. (1963). *Outsiders: Studies in the sociology of deviance*. London: Free Press.

Dolan, E., & Finney, S. (1984). *Youth gangs*. New York: J. Messner.

Goldstein, P.J., Spunt, B., Bellucci, P., & Miller, T. (1991). Frequency of cocaine use and violence: A comparison between men and women. In S. Schuber & C. Schade (Eds.), *The epidemiology of cocaine use and abuse* (pp. 113–138). NIDA Research Monograph No. 110. Rockville, MD: National Institute of Drug Abuse.

Hamid, A. (1992). The development cycle of a drug epidemic: The cocaine smoking epidemic of 1981–1991 (Special issue, A. Inciardi, Ed.). *Journal of Psychoactive Drugs, 24*, 337–349.

Hamid, A., Curtis, R., McCoy, K., McGuire, J., Conde, A., Bushell, W., Lindenmayer, R., Brimberg, K., Maia, S., Abdur-Rashid, S., & Settembrino, J. (1997). The heroin epidemic in New York City: Current status and prognoses. *Journal of Psychoactive Drugs, 29*, 375–391.

Kandel, D.B. (1986). Processes of peer influences in adolescence. In R.K. Silberstein, K. Eyferth, & G. Rudinger (Eds.), *Development as action in context: Problem behavior and normal youth development.* Berlin: Springer-Verlag.

Kandel, D.B., Kessler, R., & Marguiles, R. (1978). Antecedents of adolescent initiation into stages of drug use. In D.B. Kandel (Ed.), *Longitudinal research on drug use: Empirical findings and methodological issues.* Washington, DC: Hemisphere.

Portes, A. (1983). The informal sector: Definition, controversy, and relation to national development. *Review, 7,* 151–174.

Smith, G.M., & Fogg, M. (1978). Psychological predictors of early use, late use, and nonuse of marijuana among teenage students. In D. Kandel (Ed.), *Longitudinal research on drug use: Empirical findings and methodological issues.* Washington, DC: Hemisphere.

Waldorf, D.O. (1983). Natural recovery from opiate addiction: Some social psychological processes of untreated recovery. *Journal of Drug Issues, 13,* 237–280.

Wallace, B. (1989). Psychological and environmental determinants of relapse. *Journal of Substance Abuse Treatment, 6,* 95–106.

Wallace, B. (1991). *Crack cocaine: A practical treatment approach for the chemically dependent.* New York: Brunner/Mazel.

CHAPTER 7

Women, Parenting, Sex, and Drugs

Chapter Objectives

Independently of drugs, human societies are transfixed by issues of sexuality, parenting, and the desire of women. The concern has translated into the universal oppression of women and control of female sexuality and fertility. Drug law enforcement against women thus sustains a regrettable feature of human organization. Drug use by women is less tolerated and punishments are greater for them than for men. Despite fears that more have become users and distributors, and that their recruitment signifies worsening female deviance, these activities remain dominated by men.

It is small wonder that a cornerstone of current American drug policy is an affrighted concern for the effects of drugs on women, their sexuality, and their motherhood. Women have been oppressed and their bodies have been objects of exchange between men in every known society (Lévi-Strauss, 1969). In controlling reproduction and the perpetuation of the social order, men have paid close attention to women's bodies and what does or does not go into them (Foucault, 1978, 1985). For example, men have taken great pains to ensure premarital virginity and postmarital fidelity, by methods including clitoridectomies to inhibit women from experiencing sexual pleasure, and sewing the vagina shut to prevent intercourse.

In the modern era, the locus of control over women's bodies has shifted from domestic and familial arenas to oversight by the state. Perhaps the most egregious example of state control was the eugenics movement of the early 20th century, when pseudoscientific notions about the "purity" of "blood" and the superiority of certain "races" over others led to the involuntary sterilization of hundreds of thousands of poor and minority women (Lopez, 1993). Today, despite women's liberation, equal opportunity legislation, and other attempts to achieve greater parity, women are still ruled by men, although in increasingly insidious ways.

The condition of women is contradictory in all societies. Worshipped as the fountainhead of life, women are wives, mothers, and daughters, but they are also devalued, dangerous, "whores," and "rubbish" to be thrown out of a patrilineage. Female infanticide is still commonly practiced (Harris, 1974; Nanda, 1990) in China, where parents are restricted by the state to a single child, and in India, where males are considered an asset, but females are considered a financial burden to families. And although female infants are not taken to the "bush" for extermination in the United States, abortion, cloning, and other technologies may preselect the gender of children.

Since the family, community, and larger society invariably invest more heavily in boys, the fate of girls is often one of unending neglect. When allowed to live, a frail and vulnerable female child is fanatically guarded by male kin against real or imagined threats. Girls who violate the *cordon sanitaire* of male influence are deemed dangerous to themselves, their families, and society in general.

Throughout the ages, revered and reviled, women's bodies have been the stage of epic struggles between good and evil. The idea that women's bodies are unruly, uncontrollable, diseased, hysterical, and immoral and therefore in need of subjugation, regulation, and close monitoring has a lengthy history (Donzelot, 1980; Foucault, 1978, 1985; Mort, 1987; Smart, 1989; Weeks, 1981, 1985). More than anywhere else, the panics that accompany "epidemics" of AIDS, sexually transmitted diseases (STDs), drug abuse, child abuse, and unwanted pregnancy are inscribed in women's demonized bodies. They constitute a primary battleground in which morally upright and civilized persons must quell threats to the social order.

WOMEN AND DRUGS IN MODERN SOCIETIES—A BRIEF HISTORY

The biblical story of the Garden of Eden has been construed as a parable of female drug use. Thus, it was a forbidden psychoactive, not the honest apple, that Eve ate, and the deed made her the first human to gain godlike knowledge. That made God angry. Banished from paradise but with gifts of wisdom, sexuality, and fertility, women have since had a unique and emotionally charged relationship with drugs. Lawbreakers—but healers, witches, oracles, and psychics who know the mysteries of nature, including the pharmacology of plants—they embody contradiction. Exalted as goddesses and burned at the stake as demonic witches, women are all-seeing and powerful, yet they are the "weaker sex" around whom men must draw protective circles.

American stories about drug-using females have been less rich and multilayered than the Bible's, and conform to the society's more puritanical approach to drugs (see Chapter 1). Never entertaining, they are meant to mobilize moral outrage. They portray the women as "polluted" and "despoiled" (Kane, 1882; Murphy, 1992), "hypersexual" female "vampires" (Graham-Mulhall, 1926), and, perhaps worst of all, "unfit" mothers (Maher, 1990, 1992; Maher & Curtis, 1994; Nelson & Milliken, 1988; Roberts, 1991; Zedner, 1991). While stories about male drug users describe moral depravity, crime, and punishment, they have celebrated ecstasy, exultation, discovery, redemption, and enlightenment. These themes are absent in the stories about women drug users, and even in their stories about themselves (Yablonsky, 1997).

Modern society has especially condemned drug use by childbearing women. Indeed, during childbirth, when women could benefit from painkilling drugs, they have been told, even by contemporary medical personnel, to endure "natural" child delivery. Invoking the example of Native American women who secluded themselves in forests to deliver babies, fashionable male gynecologists advise their patients to forgo the "artificiality" of modern painkillers.

Eve's model of lawbreaking has persisted, however, despite the many discouragements. While most women were denied the illicit pleasures and indulgences that men reserved for themselves, a select number repeatedly preempted a few liminal roles that gave them the license to venture into areas such as drug use. Beyond childbearing age or existing outside the domain of family or community, they occupied unique statuses that not only set them apart from other women, but also made them valuable and attractive to male society. Thus, as prostitutes, saloon keepers, shebeen operators (Bujra, 1975; Colson & Scudder, 1988; Malahleha, 1984; Nelson, 1978), fortune-tellers, exotic dancers, and healers they absorb and rediffuse tabooed excess and pleasure. Invested with ambiguous power, they are elected to be confessionals, where men (and sometimes other women) go privately to unburden themselves, to confess their desires, weaknesses, and secrets. Ministering to powerful men, they are elevated as (often tragic) public figures themselves. In the classic American Western films, she is the world-weary, slightly over-the-hill saloon owner in the frontier town. Despised by God-fearing folk but with an easy manner and a heart of gold, she counsels and soothes needy men instinctively. In the end, she is killed to allow the hero to marry the less accessible heroine.

The ultimate slaughter of women who were tolerated in equivocal roles, often explicitly connected with specific drugs, such as alcohol in the saloon, was not confined to the Western genre of American film. Since antiquity, such women were feared for their supernatural powers. They were suspected of concocting magical potions from belladonna, henbane, mandrake root, foxglove, datura, and other psychoactive ingredients. During the witch-hunts of medieval Europe and colonial America, their persecutors alleged that these preparations, rubbed into the sensitive membranes of the vagina, enabled them to mount broomsticks and fly abroad in search of trouble. They threatened individual, morally weak men (and therefore, their women) and the entire social order.

Of course, the fear of witches in the Middle Ages served greater societal ends, as the fear of drugs does today. As Europe transformed from feudalism to a capitalist mode of production, thousands of peasants were uprooted from their homes and farms and disenfranchised from community. Homeless women were forced to wander the countryside in search of food and shelter. Recognizing and fearing them as harbingers of the coming end of their world order, Roman Catholic authorities responded by persecuting and systematically eradicating them. Women who revealed a knowledge of herbs, tonics, elixirs, or drugs were especially denounced as heretics.

Women, on their part, have labored tirelessly to expand their spheres of freedom and agency. Opportunities came with the expansion of consumerism in Europe (see Chapter 1). A great number sought diversion, pleasure, and relief in the wealth of consumer goods that had become available. In the 19th century, they benefited from current advances in pharmacology. Defined as the fairer, weaker sex whose fragile mental and physical health made them susceptible to strange and quirky illnesses, women were prescribed "miracle" drugs such as heroin and cocaine, both by their physicians and by such nontraditional practitioners as psychiatrists and psychoanalysts, to help them cope with the rigors of a society in continuous transformation. Thus, the capitalist drive for profits identified women as the most avid consumers of drugs and medicines: "Women were medicated excessively not only for a wide range of organic complaints but also for a vague set of nonorganic complaints labeled 'neurasthenia' or 'nervous weakness.' In fact, women's addictions were to some degree responsible for the growth of an entire branch of the American pharmaceutical industry at the turn of the century" (Kandall, 1996, p. 3). While the pious adherents of the growing temperance movement targeted alcohol, with its unsavory connection to the lawless western frontier, they inadvertently promoted other drug use. They favored the many new opiate- and/or cocaine-based "patent medicines": "Despite the admonitions of the Woman's Christian Temperance Union, founded in 1874, hypodermic syringes for a time replaced hip flasks and decanters as respectable social paraphernalia" (Kandall, 1996, p. 18).

Their use of opiates, ether, chloroform, and other drugs, however, soon tarnished women's shining image. "Woman the Destroyer" was threatening to burst out of her tightly corseted exterior. After the hypodermic syringe was invented, the use of opiates and other drugs had soared. In the age of Victoria, European women were regarded as the special "guardians of moral purity and social standards" (Kandall, 1996, p. 43), and many middle- and upper-class women aspired to translate the calling into social activism. In the United States, the same motivation resulted in religious fervor and, as many Protestant religions frowned upon frivolous pursuits, turned into a crusade against vice. The enthusiasm for the stark, stripped-down, simple styles of the Shakers in New England or the Amish in Pennsylvania expressed their frame of mind.

Middle- and upper-class European-American female drug users persisted, however, during the decade-long battle in the 1920s, which culminated in the Volstead Act of 1919 and Prohibition. While prohibitionists railed against opiates, the drug that pimps were said to use to seduce and enslave impressionable European-American women, "At the other end of the social spectrum, the 'smart set'—chic and stylish movie stars, artists, and the 'idle rich'—experimented freely with cocaine and marijuana, and even brought opium smoking back into style in their circle during the 1920s and 1930s" (Kandall, 1996, p. 106).

Enactment of the first antidrug laws against opium and cocaine was a direct response to the perception that Chinese immigrants were ruining the lives of respectable European-American women in opium dens and, worse, that southern African Americans were plying them with cocaine to feed their insatiable sexual appetites (Musto, 1973).

The antivice crusaders conceived a special contempt for these fallen, "morally loose" drug-using women who were undermining their messages of temperance and abstinence. According to Graham-Mulhall (1926):

> Only in the final stages of dissipation does opium destroy a woman's looks. Often it improves them, which is one of the most dangerous influences among young girls. . . . They were unusually pretty, young, clever with a sly, half-innocent air which disarmed suspicion. They were all actresses in the great drama of opium. . . . (pp. 56–57)

> A warning against the opium vampire is all that can be done to save the boys, the young men, from her entanglements, except to make the drug unobtainable. She is everywhere, in the flashy restaurant, at the exclusive private dances, in the movie theaters, on the stage, in the studios among those who create the movie plays for millions to applaud them. Opium is among the women who are rich in idleness and money, among the ambitious girls who are well-born but who are trapped by the opium trafficker in the college dormitories, in business colleges, in their hospital training homes for nurses. (p. 58)

The latest in a long line of temptresses who threatened men and decent society, the "opium vampires" targeted by prohibitionists nevertheless posed yet another kind of challenge. Their iniquity had worsened to include drug distribution:

In other cases, women were portrayed not as hapless victims but as drug ring organizers. A San Francisco newspaper reported on Mrs. Rose Mentor, a "woman arrested for dealing in opium." Another story told of a "woman taken in a $1,000,000" Mexican border drug smuggling ring, and still another detailed the arrest of the Bennetts, "self-styled world's greatest dancers," in a "big opium raid in the hotel room of the tango pair." It was apparent, however, that these rings were run by men, and they were easily viewed as further examples of women's ruin in the drug trade. (Kandall, 1996, p. 67)

Accordingly, a new type of worry about women alarmed male policymakers and law enforcement officials at the beginning of the 20th century. For example, the Bureau of Social Morals in progressive era New York identified, among a sample of 311 women, 78 female "entrepreneurs" who had "achieved a management position usually in a vice operation or displayed special business skills such as fencing stolen goods or corrupt bail bonding" (Block, 1977, p. 8). Women were thus doubly threatening: while luring men into overindulgence and self-destruction, they were also slyly applying their feminine wiles to replace them in enterprises that men had always dominated. The fear that women were violating the natural and social order by usurping male prerogatives was fueled during Prohibition when unescorted women frequented "speakeasies" and learned to smoke cigarettes, drink liquor, and gamble.

Despite the fear that cold, calculating women were unbalancing a precarious social order by deserting the family and setting aside the "instincts of moral decency that are none too well taken care of in the modern whirl of sensational, overstrained habits of life" (Graham-Mulhall, 1926, p. 49), few women were actually able to compete in male-dominated arenas. Still, even if they were not well-represented in the business and criminal worlds, they were resented for whatever leverage they had created for themselves inside the Victorian strictures that confined them socially and as individuals.

A strength of the social order of modern capitalism is its capacity to absorb and co-opt threats to itself. The shocking new look of liberated women was soon employed to generate profits, as cigarette and alcohol merchants identified them as a lucrative new market. Advertisers and Hollywood movies such as *The Thin Man* normalized this style of female overindulgence immediately after Prohibition was repealed. They portrayed the "thoroughly modern miss" as an emancipated consumer, who started the day with breakfasts of gin and cigarettes. Another image of the independent woman, counteracting the first, was the emasculating "control fanatic" in charge of her vices, a role played very effectively by actresses like Katherine Hepburn in movies like *African Queen*.

The pharmaceutical industry, which had profited earlier from the idiosyncratic medical needs of women, did not tarry long before reclaiming this lucrative market from the alcohol and tobacco companies. In the post–World War II era, as more women joined the work force, the beleaguered suburban housewife, juggling among family, job, and social obligations, was discovered by psychiatric and psychological counseling services. Dispensing psychotropic medications for ailments that had no obvious organic basis, such as anxiety, mild depression, and lethargy, the pharmaceutical companies prospered mightily. When the use of illicit drugs rose in the 1960s, many women were already experienced consumers of mind-altering substances. If their familiarity with illicit drugs did not equal men's, their substantial consumption of prescription drugs more than offset the deficit.

> Many physicians refused to believe women capable of tolerating minor ailments without the support of drugs. As a result, in 1974, two-thirds of the almost twenty-two million new prescriptions and thirty-eight million refill prescriptions for Valium were written for women, and 71 percent of the over six million new prescriptions and twelve million refill prescriptions for Librium were for women. (Kandall, 1996, p. 193)

The gap between male and female drug use closed somewhat during the 1960s and early 1970s. Women gave the same range of ostensible reasons as men to explain why they initiated illicit drugs: to symbolize opposition to the war in Vietnam, racism, and sexism, as rebellion against parental authority, to expand consciousness, to loosen inhibitions, to boost energy, to seek harmony with nature, and for fun and recreation. But women found drugs attractive for "strictly feminine" reasons too: "Women also used cocaine as an appetite suppressant; it helped them feel thin, young, and energetic. . . . This ultra-slender body image not only became the standard for classical ballet but, aided by the fashion industry, strongly influenced how ordinary women evaluated their own bodies" (Kandall, 1996, p. 189).

In conforming thus to the prevailing dictates of fashion, women were not only the dupes of advertising, the pawns of the pharmaceutical industry, or the appeasers of men's whims. Feminism and women's liberation had formed as potent political forces during the social unrest of the 1960s, and they had spurred women to search for their own standards of self-definition (Deckard, 1975). Drugs were some of many cultural items that women appropriated and adapted for their unique purposes.

By the time of the cocaine smoking epidemic of the 1980s, men and women were competing for illicit drugs. It was hardly surprising, therefore, that the conservative backlash, then rallying against the permissiveness and excesses of the 1960s and 1970s, would freight women's bodies with their rhetorical concerns about crime, violence, morality, disease, the young, neighborhood deterioration, and America's economic competitiveness in global markets in the future. The viability and perpetuation of the male-dominated social order were again endangered, this time by minority female cocaine smokers. The latter were begrudged and resented, and throughout subsequent wars on drugs, bore the brunt of campaigns to reassert male supremacy (see Chapter 6). For example, they were blamed for the decay of American cities, a crisis simultaneously gaining recognition (see Chapter 8).

Meanwhile, women who abused prescription drugs—the suburban housewives—were quietly tolerated as long as they did not call attention to themselves:

> Although the emerging stereotype of the female heroin addict was of a minority urban dweller living in poverty, the social spectrum was much broader . . . addicted women were just as likely to describe their family lives as happy, to come from stable economic environments and intact family networks, and to regard both their fathers and mothers as supportive parents. (Kandall, 1996, p. 183)

RESEARCH ON WOMEN AND DRUG USE: WHY WOMEN USE DRUGS

Even though women were actually a small minority of those who used illicit drugs during the 1960s and 1970s, they nevertheless alarmed policymakers and social scientists, who fretted about how the unruly few would affect other women, families, children, and the stability of the social order. Research explicitly focused on women's drug use was funded in this period (Inciardi, Lockwood, & Pottieger, 1993, p. 18). The researchers concluded that women were growing more deviant and criminal, like their male counterparts who were using more drugs and becoming more violent (Datesman, 1981).

Seeking the causes of worsening deviance, the literature on women's drug use has grown in two opposite directions. In one, women are the hapless and helpless victims of manipulative males who entrap them in addiction, crime, and depravity. In the other, more modern view, they are apotheosized as updated versions of Ma Barker, seeking and taking advantage of every "deviant" or "criminal" opportunity. Unshackled by the women's liberation movement, they employed their sexuality to further their nefarious and criminal agendas (Blom & van den Berg, 1989; Eldred & Washington, 1976; File, 1976; Freeland & Campbell, 1973; Hser, Anglin, & McGlothlin, 1987; Parker, Bakx, & Newcombe, 1988; Rosenbaum, 1981; Steffensmeier, 1983; Waldorf, 1973).

Feminist research breaks with these orientations. Attempting to replace sexist explanations for women's drug use, feminist scholars have focused on changes in women's statuses in the economy and society of the United States, and on factors such as victimization, particularly childhood sexual abuse, as a primary determinant of drug use later in life (Arnold, 1990; Gilfus, 1992; Harrison, 1989; Hurley, 1991; Hussey & Petchers, 1989; Miller, 1986; Miller, Downs, Gondoli, & Keil, 1987; Reed, 1991; Russell & Wilsnack, 1991; Russell, Wilsnack, Klassen, & Dietz, 1988; Young, 1990). Women, however, were still afforded little agency in this formulation, and drug use was interpreted as an involuntary but effective coping mechanism by which they medicated themselves to overcome the psychological hurdles placed by earlier traumatic experiences or to blunt the pain of patriarchal manhandling (Blume, 1990; Ettore, 1992; Greenleaf, 1989; Hamilton, 1993; Hser et al., 1987; Mondanaro, 1989; Reed, 1991; Suffet & Brotman, 1976).

Researchers have estimated that more than 50% of women have been sexually abused by the age of 18 (Russell, 1983; Wyatt, 1985). If they are correct, a national tragedy is being underreported. If women automatically respond to abuse by using drugs, it follows too that a drug epidemic of massive proportions is undetected. Another problem with the belief that women self-medicate to overcome psychological injury is that they do not always choose drugs that classically blunt pain, such as heroin. For example, many women prefer smokable cocaine to other drugs, but it is not expected to dull the senses (Inciardi et al., 1993). Indeed, smokable cocaine is valued for the heightened awareness and greater sociability its users experience.

WOMEN'S INITIATION INTO DRUG USE

The conviction that men are primarily responsible for initiating women into drug use (who would otherwise not use them) has a long history and is reinvented during each successive drug "epidemic" (Blom & van den Berg, 1989; Dai, 1937; Eldred & Washington, 1976; File, 1976; Freeland & Campbell, 1973; Gerstein, Judd, & Rovner, 1979; Kohn, 1992; Lemert, 1951; Moore, 1991; Musto, 1973; Parker et al., 1988; Rosenbaum, 1981; Suffet & Brotman, 1976; Waldorf, 1973; Williams, 1992). From this perspective, women are the innocent and often unsuspecting victims of men's machinations. Like the mythologized, cloaked drug dealer who lurks near school yards offering "candy" to unsuspecting and innocent children, male "pimps" lure women into drug use as a way of increasing sales (Anderson, 1990; Goldstein et al., 1992; Morningstar & Chitwood, 1985). Furthermore, once they have been drawn into drug use, women drug users, especially heroin users, must depend on the guidance of a man or the assistance of a male-dominated drug and criminal subculture to support their consumption (Covington, 1985; Fiddle, 1976; File, 1976; File, McCahill, & Savitz, 1974; Hser et al., 1987; Morningstar & Chitwood, 1985; Pettiway, 1987; Smithberg & Westermeyer, 1985; Sutter, 1966).

These formulations rob women of intelligence and choice, and, at the same time, misrepresent most street-level dealers who, as minor operatives in drug distribution organizations, do not have the means to generate sales in this manner or to afford largesse. More independent female agents may be recalled: "In the upper strata of a society where money is plenty, where gayety and pleasure are the chief aims of life, the opium vampire is also often bred. Until she reaches the financial ruin that all these talented, brilliant spendthrifts do, she is not looked upon as a menace. When that time comes, she uses the drug to ensnare her prey" (Graham-Mulhall, 1926, p. 57).

Recent ethnographic research has supplied a corrective lens for the distorted and unidimensional image of women's initiation into drug use. Several recent studies have found that women are just as likely to be initiated by another woman (Maher, 1996; Taylor, 1993). For example, one female ethnographer found that nearly half of her sample of Chicana ex-gang heroin users on the West Coast first used heroin with other females at a party, while only 38% used first with a boyfriend or husband (Moore, 1990). Another discovered that pathways into drugs were extraordinarily diverse among her ethnically mixed sample of crack users, but that "African American women [were] more likely than other women to initiate drug use with female companions" (Maher, 1996, p. 134). A recent study of heroin users in New York City found that most of the young Puerto Rican women in the sample were initiated in leisure contexts, often by girlfriends (Hamid et al., 1997). Sniffing the drug added to the enjoyment of small cliques of girlfriends "hanging out" while getting dressed for a night out at clubs or parties. Thus, while it may have been true in the past that men introduced them to drugs, they are initiated now in all-girl parties. The same study discovered that upper- and middle-class European-American women heroin users were equally likely to have introduced their boyfriends to the drug as vice versa. The finding suggests that women's drug use is as complex and multidimensional as men's.

In some respects, the focus on who gave what to whom in the literature on female initiation into drug use misses the mark. Drug taking is behavior that both men and women learn to do in specific contexts, and these contexts exert a great influence on their drug-using careers (Faupel, 1991; Hamid et al., 1997). The important observation was not who handed a young woman her first "joint," but rather, the wider social context that allowed the drug exchange to take place at all. Placed in the context of transformations in global society and economy and in the United States since the 1960s, such as the change from a manufacturing to a service economy, the growth of the informal sector, and the roles of women in them, women's induction into drug use is clearly "overdetermined" (see Chapter 2) and not simply reducible to the sway that individuals have over one another.

The problematic issue of drug use in the Latino/Latina community, for example, has been confused by seemingly contradictory evidence on the part of researchers. On one hand, some researchers have pointed out that female drug use is often "enacted within a familial context. It might be seen as a twisted version of the usual Mexican emphasis on family roles for women" (Moore, 1991, p. 109). For these women, "the values that foster [drug] use are deeply embedded in the culture with which the young woman is likely to be surrounded" (Miller, 1986, p. 113). Other researchers, however, have insisted that the extended family functions protectively to keep its members away from drugs. Both perspectives have merit: situated at ground zero of the greatest excesses associated with illicit drugs—the glitz, glamour, money, mayhem, competition, murder, destitution, and disease—the Latino community has had a profoundly ambivalent relationship with them. "Not only did the extended family protect the non-addict, it created a community environment in which the addict did not feel completely rejected" (Miller, 1986, p. 114).

WOMEN, CRACK, AND THE WAR ON DRUGS

The latest drug war coincides with important changes in the composition of the American labor force and global society. When European Americans inhabited the neighborhoods of large metropolitan centers, drug distribution and use was handled discreetly by local authorities and the "beat cop." As second- and third-generation European Americans departed for the suburbs, taking industry and jobs with them, the "inner city" remained. These were low-income, minority neighborhoods where "poorly socialized" males and females, "irrationally hedonistic," strangers to honest work and "prone to unpredictable violent criminality," recklessly produced children for whom they were incapable and unwilling to provide homes and parenting.

Although many believe that the war on drugs has primarily been waged against inner-city males, there is growing evidence that women, who have always been more closely supervised by the state than men, were disproportionately hurt by it. While men had more direct involvement with the criminal justice system, and police departments, courts, jails, prisons, probation, and parole services were expanded because of minority male offenders, women have come under greater scrutiny, control, and punishment from administrative branches of government such as welfare, children's services, and housing authorities (Maher, 1990, 1992). Where men's involvements with drugs typically result in a cycle of arrest, incarceration, and release, women drug users must endure governmental oversight of almost every aspect of their daily lives. Older women have even been punished for the drug-related offenses of their more elusive male relatives. For example, grandmothers have faced eviction proceedings in public housing projects when an errant grandson was arrested for selling drugs, despite long-term tenancies. When women provide a stable and often tolerant home, they have been labeled as "enablers" and "co-dependent" facilitators who perpetuate men's problematic drug taking. The "girlfriend crime," or cases in which women's homes are used by men to store contraband without their permission, regularly puts the innocent in more trouble than the culprits themselves.

Regarded traditionally and in the current era, feminism and women's liberation notwithstanding, as unable to control their lives, women were thought to be powerless to withstand the allure and temptations of crack. It compelled them, more so than men, to engage in lawbreaking and high-risk sexual behaviors (Allen, 1987; Anderson, 1990; Koester & Schwartz, 1993). During the crack era, for example, the rate of arrests of women for drug-law violations doubled that of men (Bureau of Justice Statistics, 1991). The mythology of the "crack whore" included "instant addiction," through which women were converted from caring wives and mothers into conniving predators who "vic-ed" [victimized] men for drugs and cash. Their "mothering instinct" evaporated, causing them to abandon children to friends, relatives, the state, or, if the media are to be trusted, simply to toss them off balconies and rooftops. Plenty of pseudoethnographic, federally funded "research" contributed to these myths:

> While working (prostituting), [a mother and daughter, both crack smokers] were routinely observed arguing, fighting, hitting, and even "cutting" each other over money or crack—but both women actually equated such behaviors as expressions of affection to and from the other. Thus, in their thinking, a "fight" was equal to "loving" the other.

> Persons who routinely engage in illegal sales of heroin, cocaine, and crack are disproportionately recruited from among those who are most violent. Most sellers were raised in household/family systems that were plagued by violence, and these people currently reside in violent households as well.

> Parents and other kin bring these violent and aggressive behavioral patterns into their relationships with children, such that the . . . parents and other relatives provided deviant role models for their children in the context of their drug and alcohol consumption. (Dunlap, Johnson, & Rath, 1997, pp. 4–14 passim)

In Dunlap's crack universe, which is obscurely related to Central Harlem in New York City, not only are women abusive mothers and poor role models, but men too cannot be trusted because they exhibit a "sexual interest in prepubescent girl[s] [which] may result in early intercourse if the man was left alone with her" (Dunlap et al., 1997, p. 16):

> Within this family/kin system, a reasonably accurate prediction of almost any girl's future occupation would include prostitution.

Their normal everyday vocabulary included profanity, reflecting the way they thought. Profanity was a fundamental and normative part of their personality and socialization: it was not merely used for emphasis.

Since violence and aggression languaging were a part of everyday inter- action, individuals were not comfortable interacting with other persons in any other manner.

. . . these aggressive/violent patterns had often worsened among succes- sive generations . . . such that by the 1990s, aggression and violence had become so deeply entrenched within families with adult drug abusers that entire kin networks could not comprehend the existence of non- violent alternatives. (Dunlap et al., 1997, pp. 16–49 passim)

In addition to causing them to reverse or violate the conduct norms of conven- tional society, crack allegedly impelled women to usurp the exclusively male do- mains of gangsterism and gratuitous violence. In the "virtual ethnography" of some research projects, women played flamboyant roles. As femmes fatales, they dressed in flashy clothes and drove expensive cars while fashioning a substantial niche for themselves in drug distribution and deploying a new and terrible female ruthlessness to do it. Thousands of them populated the fertile imaginations of some male criminologists.

It requires, however, a certain "suspension of disbelief" to accept that, although women have been dominated by men throughout human history—at risk of mur- der at birth, starvation and neglect, foot-binding and other quaint practices, assault and rape, as well as the more specifically modern forms of economic and social discrimination—women drug dealers and users have prospered in the inner cities (of all places!), carving up territory for their profit and enjoyment. While their counterparts in corporate and mainstream America still faced formidable ob- stacles, these women outstripped male competition in a terrain where the rule of law bows to brawn and might. Needless to say, these Amazons absented them- selves from the field notes of most anthropologists. Battered, marginalized, unfor- tunate women were the majority they interviewed and observed.

Researchers have attributed the alleged ascendancy of women in crack distribu- tion and crime to the expansion of the drug economy and to putative shifts in the gender composition of street distributing networks. They claimed that, as the war on drugs scored a substantial body count among inner-city males, women replaced them (Baskin, Sommers, & Fagan, 1993; Fagan, 1994; Mieczkowski, 1994; Wil- son, 1993). "Changes in drugs and drug markets [have] made possible new av- enues and contexts for women to participate in drug use and selling" (Fagan, 1994, p. 181).

Another explanation for the presence of women among drug users and distribu- tors was women's emancipation in the wider society (Bourgois, 1989; Bourgois &

Dunlap, 1993). Adler has noted that, "in assuming the mantle of male power [women] have also become vulnerable to the infirmities of male vice (1975, p. 128)." Bourgois surmised that:

> Greater female involvement in crack reflects in a rather straightforward manner the growing emancipation of women throughout all aspects of inner-city life, culture and economy. Women—especially the emerging generation, which is most at risk for crack addiction—are no longer obliged to stay at home and maintain the family as they were a generation ago. They no longer so readily sacrifice public life or forgo independent opportunities to generate personally disposable income. . . . To a certain extent, the emancipation of women has taken place at a faster rate on inner-city streets than it has in middle-class suburbs. (1989, pp. 643–644)

Accounting for the assaults women crack users suffer at the hands of their male counterparts, Bourgois and Dunlap argued that

> One way of interpreting the virulence with which many men abuse vulnerable women in the crack scene is as a frustrated attempt by traditional patriarchally oriented men to stave off the challenge to gender roles posed by the growing public presence of addicted women. In short, men on the street are not accepting the new roles that women are attempting to carve out for themselves in the world of substance abuse. Instead males are lashing out at females, and they are desperately striving to reimpose violently the gender order of the previous generation. According to their repressive patriarchal logic, submitting a woman, or even a teenage girl, to violent sex or a gang rape is justifiable since "she wasn't acting like a lady. (p. 125)

The recent surge in domestic violence indicates, however, that the purported backlash against women is neither unique to the drug world nor an outcome of "unladylike behavior."

As with other drugs and previous generations of female drug involvement, facts have to be separated from the more colorful fictions about women in crack distribution. A well-documented fact was that the number of women arrested for drugs did rise during the 1980s. Another was that the arrests were mostly for possession or very low-level retail dealing. As Maher (1996) notes: "During the 1980s, the number of women arrested for drug law violations increased at twice the rate of men, resulting in a 307 percent increase between 1980 and 1989 for women, compared to a 147 percent increase for men over the same period" (Bureau of Justice Statistics, 1991).

The figures, however, were computed against a very low baseline. Thus, in spite of it, women still accounted for only 7.6% of all "high-level" arrests, and only 17% of all Drug Enforcement Administration (DEA) arrests, according to DEA statistics (Hemphill, 1988). Researchers have argued, therefore, that, far from assuming male roles in street-level drug distribution, women have proved valuable to male drug distributors in supportive roles because of their greater stability (with apartments, phones, and regular incomes) than men (Wilson, 1993). Other researchers explained the absence of women in the upper echelons of the drug business by the belief that women are unable to manage male workers effectively (Waterston, 1993, p. 114). A woman's participation in drug selling is often terminated if she separates from her boyfriend/husband, when he is arrested, or when they cannot control their own use (Koester & Schwartz, 1993, p. 192).

The war of attrition by police against street-level drug markets evacuated men and multiplied opportunities for women, but almost invariably only for the riskiest jobs for which there were few applicants (Dunlap & Johnson, 1992; Inciardi et al., 1993; Maher & Curtis, 1994). Women took jobs men did not want, and since the highly structured drug markets that dominated street sales were governed by tight networks of male kinship, they were denied meaningful participation (Curtis & Maher, 1992; Waterston, 1993). As Maher observed, "occupational hierarchies within the drug economy serve to reproduce the gender, ethnic and class relations that structure social relations at a more general level" (1996, p. 23). She demonstrated that in the crack economy, the traditional gender separation of "workplace" roles was reproduced, or perhaps even reinforced, but certainly never ruptured:

> . . . cultural practices remain firmly anchored in broader relations and structures of gender, race and class. . . . Indeed, it cannot be emphasized enough that the advent of crack cocaine and the concomitant expansion of the drug economy can in no way be read as "emancipatory" for women drug users. Within the drug economy, women have neither been "masculinized" nor have their opportunities for illicit income generation expanded. Men still very much control the streets and the drug economy. . . . (Maher, 1996, p. 24)

Hence, women were relegated predictably to sex work and—except for a few with family ties to higher-level dealers or suppliers—were rarely admitted even into the lowest echelons of drug distribution.

While women have been largely blocked from greater participation in the drug economy by the male kin networks that have traditionally dominated it, a few young women, projecting the persona of a razor-toting, tattoo-laden "gangsta bitch" (Campbell, 1993; Hagedorn & Devitt, 1996), have taken advantage of opportunities in a system that is "looking for people who can demonstrate their capacity for effective violence and terror" (Bourgois, 1989, p. 632). Ironically, however, retail drug dealing is rapidly evolving in the mid-1990s from a dangerous, violence-prone, curbside business to one that is client driven, conducted behind closed doors and reliant on trust, personal relationships, and social networks—the strengths of more traditional women!

Thus, while a few academics and the media have favored the image of the violent female drug dealer and criminal, most research has concluded that she is something of a cultural anomaly (Harris, 1977; Weiner & Wolfgang, 1985). Women drug users—particularly heroin users—were likely to commit violent crimes when they experienced withdrawal symptoms (Goldstein, 1979, 1991; Inciardi, 1986, p. 137; Rosenbaum, 1981, p. 76), but more recent research on cocaine use (Goldstein, 1991) found that while greater use by men led them to become more violent, greater use by women led to their greater victimization. Women's experiences with violence were associated with worsening conditions in the inner city and were "attributable to neither the pharmacology of crack cocaine nor individual pathologies" (Maher & Curtis, 1994):

> Our data appear to contradict the conclusions reached by Sterk-Elifson and Elifson (1990), when they state that "more violent episodes on the prostitution market are related to the prostitutes' drug-using behaviors and increased involvement in the drug trade" (Sterk-Elifson & Elifson, 1990, p. 218). Our research suggests that most prostitutes are marginally involved in drug distribution and that both drug-use on behalf of their "dates" and the deteriorating conditions of street-level sex work are the source of a much larger share of the violent episodes taking place in the street-level sex markets of prostitution "strolls" where the women work. (p. 20)

Finally, many minority crack-using women, even when engaged in sex work or other behavior that only crack had encouraged them to undertake, exhibited the deep conservatism of the working class or of recent immigrants:

> Many female respondents were also deeply ambivalent about traditional female gender roles. While they valued their social freedoms and enjoyed aspects of their fast-paced lives, at times they felt alone and without satisfying relationships. Many held out hope of a future when they would be loving wives and mothers, though they felt powerless to take actual steps toward that future. (Ratner, 1993, p. 18)

DID COCAINE SMOKING MAKE WOMEN "HYPERSEXUAL?"

Nearly all the illegal drugs have been suspected of aphrodisiac properties. Chocolate was once prohibited for the lusts it unleashed, and the idea still lingers in the Saint Valentine's Day gift of them (Weil, 1972; Weil & Rosen, 1983). Opium and marijuana were included in aphrodisiac preparations since ancient India and China. Marijuana's libidinal effects were an underlying premise in *Reefer Madness*, and some users like to boast of enhanced desire and improved performance. Opium was the means by which unscrupulous Chinese enslaved European-American women and turned them into willing prostitutes, while "heroin stimulates the indiscretions of youth" (Graham-Mulhall, 1926, p. 49). Some users believe that cocaine will cure impotence and frigidity and prolong sexual encounters, while others contend that long-term or excessive use increases sexual arousal but impairs sexual performance (Ratner, 1993; Weatherby et al., 1992). Aphrodisiac properties have been claimed for alcohol, amphetamine, and barbiturates.

In addition to catapulting females into the traditionally male domains of drug dealing and violence, the pharmacology of crack was thought to produce a new generation of "sex fiends" whose sexual appetites were insatiable. Before crack, the conviction was that women participated in sex work "only as an expedient means to support their drug habits and do not have a commitment to prostitution as a lifestyle" (Datesman, 1981, p. 100). The advent of crack, however, questioned it. Many researchers have concluded that smokable cocaine is a powerful aphrodisiac and is responsible for the rapid pace and increased risk associated with street-level sex work (Goldstein, Ouellet, & Fendrich, 1992; Koester & Schwartz, 1993).

> A strong association between crack use and apparent "hypersexual behaviors" is evident in the observations and interviews in Miami, as well as in other ethnographic analyses of the crack scene (Inciardi et al., 1993). . . . Many crack-addicted women engage in any manner of sexual activity, under any circumstances, in private or in public, and with multiple partners of either sex (or both sexes simultaneously). Indeed, the tendency of crack users to engage in high-frequency sex with numerous anonymous partners is a feature of crack dependence and crack-house life in a myriad of locales. Sex-for-drugs exchanges, though far from a new phenomenon (Goldstein, 1979), are far more common among female crack addicts than they ever were among female narcotics addicts even at the height of the 1967–1974 heroin epidemics (Bourgois & Dunlap, 1993; Feldman, Espada, Penn, & Byrd, 1993; Inciardi et al., 1993; Ouellet, Wiebel, Jimenez, & Johnson, 1993; Ratner, 1993). Moreover, neither the "strawberries," "skeezers," "head-hunters," or "toss-ups" (the crack "house-girls" who provide oral sex for just a few cents worth of drugs), nor the crack-house "freaks" (the "house-girls" who have public sex with other women for similarly small amounts of drugs), have any parallel in either the heroin subculture or that of the old-style brothels. (Inciardi et al., 1993, pp. 17–18)

Debating whether "the crack-sex association is primarily pharmacological or sociocultural in nature," Inciardi et al. (1993) assert:

> Medical authorities generally concede that because of the disinhibiting effects of cocaine, its use among new users does indeed enhance enjoyment and improve sexual functioning, including more intense orgasms. These same reports maintain, however, that among long-term addicts, cocaine decreases both sexual desire and performance. (p. 18)

If smokable cocaine is regarded as a consumer good (see Chapter 3), the alleged "hypersexuality" of users can be decoded differently. Crack-seeking behavior accelerated the high consumption periodicities that low-income Americans exhibit, as do many poor persons around the world (Douglas & Isherwood, 1981), and reduced already small consumption ranges to the consumption of a few goods, "streamlining" thereby the transfer of values from local communities. The habit 3-year-olds acquire in inner-city neighborhoods of soliciting a quarter from strangers and then racing ecstatically to the corner store to splurge it on "junk foods" (potato chips, artificial drinks, candy) is converted, at an older age, into repeated visits to the drug seller to buy yet another kind of "junk." Unique as income generators, crack users and distributors are thus equally remarkable as spenders. Crack addicts are first noticed at a street corner as "pathological consumers" (on a "mission," or ceaselessly generating income for continuous spending on crack). Thus the sexuality cocaine smokers report is not a result of the pharmacological properties of the drug: rather, it is the product of a confluence of the two evolving commodity markets, cocaine and sex (Maher, 1996, p. 323).

When luxury goods become commoditized, the market may differentiate itself with respect to "authenticity" instead of "exclusivity." Contemporary crack markets may have been constructed historically by following such a tendency. In the luxury stage, smoking cocaine was a very restricted good, requiring several paraphernalia and esoteric knowledge. Researchers were told that half the fun of freebasing during 1982–1984 was "doing chemistry" or finding pleasure and sense in activity that once may have been a boring or confusing classroom chore. In the commodity stage, however, the culture of smoking cocaine is debased. In becoming more the perfect commodity, crack brought other restricted goods, such as sex, into more general circulation, or helped to commodify them too.

The reports of heightened sexuality also reflect the increasing availability of women for sex work as the epidemic proceeded. This was particularly true of low-income inner-city women of limited formal education, who could not avail themselves of the expanded opportunities for advancement in the mainstream economy that had opened for better educated, more affluent age-mates. If smokable cocaine did function as a "vacuum cleaner" to move capital rapidly upward and out of local communities (see Chapter 3), the efforts of additional workers were required. Women were "turned out" by smokable cocaine in (apparently) unprecedented numbers to provide them. In the strictly gendered context of the informal economy, sex work was all that they found available. Entry into this field exacerbated already strained gender relations, and intensified the (sexual) victimization of women locally (Maher, 1996). One outcome of the larger number of women employed in sex work was that the price of sexual services declined. In turn, as sex work generated less income, the roles of managers or pimps were superannuated (Inciardi et al., 1993; Maher, 1996).

Separated from family and friends, adrift in makeshift communities of fellow sufferers, and relegated to the progressively more risky business of street-level sex work, crack-using women were left to prowl the streets alone in search of "vics" (victims of circumstance). Thus, instead of an expression of the worsening criminality of women, "vic"-ing "more accurately reflects women's continued subjugation—not only their marginalization within prostitution, but the impact of recent changes in the sex markets themselves which have exacerbated women's vulnerability to violent victimization and necessitated adaptations in order to survive" (Maher, 1996, p. 283).

While the violent criminality of crack-using women was clearly overstated, crack-using sex workers were dangerous to men in other ways. The threat of "pollution" through exchanging bodily fluids has long aroused fear in men. Menstruation, for example, has often been associated with the threat of contamination and, in many societies, women have been physically separated from men (and sometimes other women) when they were "unclean." In the current period, the threats of AIDS, hepatitis, syphilis, gonorrhea, chlamydia, herpes, and other sexually transmitted diseases have been widely advertised in schools, through the media, and on the street. Like Typhoid Mary, crack-using women were suspected of being the primary vectors for the transmission of these diseases. Despite the alarm, however, sex workers reported that the majority of their male customers paid them more for not using condoms. Social service agencies in the fight against AIDS actually taught sex workers how to conceal condoms in their mouths without the customers detecting the deception.

Some men seem irrationally drawn to dangerous sexual encounters (including the high probability of arrest, since oral sex is often performed in cars parked on the street), but the fear of contagion has spurred the proliferation of pseudosex industries in the 1990s. Novelties such as cybersex, phone sex, lapdancing, S&M (sadism and masochism) clubs, and upscale strip bars and restaurants abound. Since a "hands-off" policy precludes the exchange of dangerous fluids, virtuous men can pay for these services with a credit card without having to hide the bill from their wives.

DO DRUGS DESTROY THE "INSTINCT FOR MOTHERHOOD?"

The idea that drug-using women will harm their children has caused outrage since at least the turn of the century. While fathers have usually enjoyed a free ride with respect to procreation and upbringing, mothers have been "held responsible and accountable in terms of the end product of their child-bearing and rearing" (Maher, 1992, p. 39). For example, one antidrug crusader felt that the damage they inflicted on children was irreparable: "The cells and nerves of the parental drug addicts are so impregnated with the poison of the narcotic—auto intoxication— that it is impossible for them to beget healthy children. Their unfortunate descendants are born with brain and nerve defects, many of them with defective hearts" (Graham-Mulhall, 1926, p. 30).

During the 1920s and 1930s, when female drug users were likely to be European American, the "problem" of drug use was not a criminal justice issue and was resolved mainly through consultations between families and their physicians. Furthermore, drug-using women were not blamed fully for their "mistakes": "She had a good home, but her mother was one of those women of the new generation who allow their daughters too much freedom, so as to be relieved of a too irksome care of them" (Graham-Mulhall, 1926, p. 32).

As the face of drug-using women changed in the 1950s and 1960s, and minority females on welfare replaced the European-American housewife as the chief offender, a moral and political campaign to criminalize pregnancy was part of the growing resentment toward women of the "unruly urban underclass" (Maher, 1990, p. 123). The demonization of women drug users was spearheaded by the media:

> Television and newspaper portrayals of these [drug exposed] infants stigmatized them as "junkie babies" and "babies with a habit." This kind of publicity, coupled with the fact that heroin-exposed babies were born primarily to disadvantaged black women, made it easy for society to regard these infants as "innocent victims" of their mothers' "wanton" drug use. (Kandall, 1991, p. 120)

The popularization of crack in the mid-1980s intensified these deep-seated fears and anxieties about minority women, sexuality, pregnancy, and crime and violence, and crack use justified recriminations against them (Maher, 1990, p. 124). The shocking image of "monstrously debilitated or deformed crack babies" resulted in "more than two hundred criminal prosecutions . . . against women in almost twenty states" (Siegel, 1997, p. 249). Prosecutors and judges attempted, successfully in several cases, to incarcerate pregnant women on the grounds that a positive toxicology amounted to "fetal abuse" that endangered the life of the unborn baby. While clinical evidence that maternal cocaine use harms the developing fetus is far from conclusive (Alexander, 1990; Kandall, 1991; Mayes, 1992; Mayes, Granger, & Zuckerman, 1992; Neuspiel & Hamel, 1991), it is significant to note that no men were ever charged with similar crimes. "In the U.S., one women in twelve is beaten during pregnancy. But violent husbands have not been charged with fetal abuse" (Siegel, 1997, p. 256).

The witch-hunt to ferret out and punish drug-using women focused on publicly financed hospitals located in the inner city, and as a result, "black women were nearly ten times more likely to be reported for substance abuse than their white counterparts" (Siegel, 1997, p. 251). Despite the admonitions by some public health officials that such a draconian approach would drive poor women away from prenatal care, thereby ensuring higher rates of infant mortality and morbidity, the fear that minority women were churning out a crack-induced biounderclass drove the hysteria to unprecedented levels. Predictably, women avoided health care providers for fear that they would be remanded to involuntary treatment facilities:

> Through ethnographic explorations with female drug users, it became clear that "beating the system" was a central theme. The women described their strategies in "escaping" from detection as a drug user at emergency rooms and drug treatment clinics. However, they experienced more difficulty in preventing detection by law enforcement officials. It was because of targeted law enforcement efforts that female drug users were more likely than their male counterparts to be arrested and not because they were more involved in crimes or were less professional in crimes. (Sterk-Elifson, 1996, p. 64)

Pregnant crack-using women were subject to harsh and unwavering scorn by health care professionals, and they were quickly reported to state agencies that tried to impose strict control over them. While the contested legal grounds concerning the rights of mothers versus the rights of fetuses resulted in inconsistent rulings from court to court and state to state, once a baby was born, the issues were more clearly defined, and decisive action to separate mother from child was swift and certain. As Maher (1996) has noted, "smokable cocaine initiates were more likely to feel that they were being judged and punished in their roles as mothers, and not without good reason" (p. 149).

On July, 13, 1989, Jennifer Johnson, of Altamonte, Florida, became the first woman in the United States to be convicted under a drug-trafficking statute for delivery of drugs to her newborn. During her pregnancy, Ms. Johnson informed her obstetrician that she had been using crack cocaine for 3 years and was still using the drug. The hospital notified a state child protection investigator and they, in turn, notified the county sheriff. Since a fetus is not considered a child/human being in the state of Florida, the prosecutor argued that cocaine was "delivered" during the pregnancy. Judge O. H. Eaton commented that the guilty verdict would warn pregnant addicts that they had a responsibility to seek treatment for their addiction prior to giving birth. Otherwise, the state could use criminal prosecution to force future compliance with the law or, in appropriate cases, to punish those who violated it.

Johnson was sentenced to 1 year of house arrest and 14 years of closely supervised probation. In addition, she was also subjected to random urine drug testing and warrantless searches of her home.

In 1989, 18 women in South Carolina were charged with criminal neglect of their fetuses. This protocol was developed jointly by public hospitals, the police, the department of social services, and prosecutors. In Washington, D.C., a woman was convicted of check forgery. When the judge discovered that she was pregnant and a cocaine addict, he gave her "an unusually long sentence" because, as he explained, " . . . I'll be darned if I'm going to have a baby born that way . . ." (Siegel, 1997, p. 251).

More prevalent than the criminal proceedings are the civil suits that are brought against these women. Hundreds of women have lost custody of their children as a result of testing positively for crack and other drugs. Both the criminal and civil proceedings are triggered by the hospital's report of a positive drug screen. Hospitals are bound by law to make such reports, and a hospital's failure to do so could result in criminal prosecution. "Black and poor women have been disproportionately targeted for prosecution under these statutes. . . . In a 1989 study in Florida, 15.4% of white women versus 14.1% of black women tested positive. Although white women outnumbered black women in their results, black women were 10 times more likely to be reported for drug abuse and child neglect" (Siegel, 1997, p. 251).

Indeed, from the moment of birth, minority crack-using mothers were depicted as constituting a grave danger to their babies:

> In *State v. Hall*, No 89 CR 2331 18th Jud. Dist. Ct., Sedgwick Co., Kansas Criminal Department, 1990, a woman was prosecuted for endangering her child by breast-feeding while using cocaine. The court eventually dismissed that charge on the grounds that the state's child endangerment statute was not intended to apply to breast-feeding. In October 1992, a California woman was sentenced to six years in prison for child endangerment. The county coroner had attributed the death of her twenty-four-day-old infant to traces of methamphetamine in the woman's breast milk. The woman pleaded guilty to child endangerment rather than go to trial on a second degree murder charge. (Siegel, 1997, p. 259)

In a more recent case in Arizona, a woman was charged with murdering her 27-day-old infant after the coroner ruled that the baby had died of heroin and methadone intoxication. It had received these via breast milk. Charges were leveled despite evidence that babies born to drug-dependent mothers have often built up a tolerance to the drugs themselves and without scientific support for the notion that the breast can become a fountain of toxic milk.

After their children had been removed from their custody, these mothers were required to surmount formidable obstacles to get their children back. Many were not of their own making but the result of punitive actions by the state:

> [Drug using] women are subject to an array of harsh sanctions imposed by the administrative welfare system: their babies are taken from them at birth and often a positive toxicology on a newborn will subsequently lead to the placement of other older children into foster homes. Their welfare benefits are often reduced, and many lost their eligibility for subsidized housing. Going into treatment to deal with their drug problems can often bring about the same set of disastrous consequences. (Maher, 1992, p. 57)

Many legal experts have declared that the criminalization of poor women who ingest drugs while pregnant is misguided and constitutionally questionable (Siegel, 1997). It is also a major concern of physicians and pediatricians. Because of it, doctors now rely on their female patients to tell the truth about their drug use for fear of criminal prosecution. The secrecy could seriously endanger both the pregnant mother and her child. The head nurse at Greenville Memorial Hospital in North Carolina warned: "I think these prosecutions are dangerous. The mother won't seek medical help. If they don't seek medical help, we're going to have a lot of dead babies." Worrisome legal and ethical issues have been raised: What about doctor-patient confidentiality? What about a patient's right to nondisclosure of private information? Because of the ethical bind between a doctor and his or her patient many doctors are not reporting positive drug test results. But failure to report does constitute a crime. The American Civil Liberties Union (ACLU) and defense attorneys have "vigorously" defended these women. The ACLU successfully appealed the Jennifer Johnson conviction and other such cases.

Dire predictions that an entire generation of children will grow up to be sociopathic "superpredators" have yet to materialize (DiIulio, Bennett, & Walters, 1994), and indeed a growing body of evidence suggests that the current generation of youth is less violent and no less intellectually capable than their predecessors (Curtis & Hamid, in press), and yet the widespread fear persists that crack-affected children are different from their peers and that as they mature they will present some thorny problems for policymakers.

ARE CHILDREN PRENATALLY EXPOSED TO SMOKABLE COCAINE ("CRACK BABIES") MONSTERS?

By some estimates, many more than 100,000 children nationwide had been exposed prenatally to smokable cocaine during the 1980s (Neuspiel & Hamel, 1991). These children and many others now live in the inner city in care-giving environments shaped by parental drug misuse and national drug policy. In addition to deficits arising from poverty (Wetherington, Smeriglio, & Finnegan, 1996), therefore, they may have others that derive from either their prenatal exposure to smokable cocaine or the drug-affected environments in which they are being raised. During the early media hysteria over crack in the mid-1980s, some researchers, clinicians, and educators had prejudged the issue and blamed the teratogenic properties of the drug exclusively for the behavioral, developmental, and educational problems they have encountered.

Several scientific studies of the effects of cocaine on the young have been conducted. In the main, however, these have been neurobehavioral studies of animal and human offspring during pregnancy and as neonates and infants. They reported decreased fetal growth, head circumference, gestational age, and birth weight. Other reported effects have included increased tremulousness, more irritability, greater startle responses, depressed interactive behavior, impaired responses to environmental stimuli, impairment of orientation, autism, poor motor coordination, higher rates of abnormal listlessness, poorly focused play behavior, poor emotional responses, attentional deficits, and language delays (Chasnoff, 1989; Griffith, Azuma, & Chasnoff, 1994). These studies were limited by the scope of their methodologies, and they did not provide a reliable description or explanation of the effects of parental drug misuse (and society's condemnation of it) on offspring. They failed to control for factors such as poverty, substandard housing, general poor health, inadequate nutrition, nicotine use, and little or no prenatal care (Wetherington et al., 1996). Follow-up studies of older children were not conducted, and none of the clinical studies of neonates and infants were replicated in a community-based population (Neuspiel & Hamel, 1991).

It is by now generally acknowledged that the terrifying prospect of thousands of irreparably damaged "crack babies" had been preposterously exaggerated, yet another product of crack-era media sensationalism. As Siegel (1997, p. 257) has remarked, "the 'crack baby' story was based almost entirely on exaggeration and hyperbole." Similarly, Carroll (1995) notes that:

> Early reports indicated that cocaine's effects on the developing fetus and the newborn could be devastating. Such accounts were eventually proved to be flawed . . . most of the symptoms disappear by age 3. Though mothers' cocaine use during pregnancy is only one of many undesirable influences on their own children, in most cases it seems to have caused no serious, lasting brain injury. (p. 212)

Indeed, even at a National Institute on Drug Abuse (NIDA) Technical Review meeting, a consensus had been reached that prenatal effects of the mother's crack use could be quickly reversed, while those of upbringing were cumulative over time (Finnegan, 1993). To date, however, very little is known with certainty about how children grow in drug-affected households and neighborhoods in the inner city, where, in New York City, low-income populations of African Americans, Caribbean Africans, and Latinos reside. A research priority is to find out.

Ethnographers have come to know many cocaine-exposed children in their study sites and have noted the great variation in disposition, competencies, personality, and behavior that they have exhibited. They did not appear to share a common affliction. Rather, what seemed most to differentiate the children was the diverse set of care-giving environments in which they had been placed and their transience in them. Several characteristics defined and differentiated these environments. They had been created by the particular circumstances of parental drug misuse and the response of state and kin to it. In each, a specific adult, who was often not a natural parent, had legal responsibility for the children. The roles and expectations of each unit were legally or socially defined. Its functions were to provide food, shelter, and clothing, and to satisfy emotional needs. The interactions between adults and children in each type of care-giving environment, and the relation between it and the community, were unique. The performances of the children reflected the strengths and liabilities of these care-giving environments. Their behavior was also influenced by the political and economic relationship between the care-giving environments and the larger society.

This researcher has catalogued the diversity of the care-giving environments in which children prenatally exposed to smokable cocaine have been placed. At least six types have been described. In *foster care* and *group homes*, participation by natural parents is minimal, and state rules dictate guidelines for semiprofessional care and for the allocation of resources to care giving. In the *kinship program*, foster care is assumed by kin, who receive a stipend from the state; participation by natural parents is restricted, and can be increased only by informal agreement. *With drug-misusing parent(s)*, a child is given care by natural parents and kin. The state is not penalizing the drug misuse; nevertheless, care givers come under state surveillance at the welfare office, in the courts, in hospitals, and in penal institutions. They are also subjected to informal neighborhood pressures and sanctions. With *drug-free parents and extended families*, the natural parents and care givers are free of state supervision except as the latter applies to the general population (as in school, in regard to public health regulations, or the child abuse and neglect statutes). Freedom from many types of state supervision would presumably apply to *adoptive parents*, but no example of them was encountered.

This researcher also found that the inconsistency of care giving over time was as striking as the diversity of care-giving environments. Children did not remain for long in one care-giving environment, but frequently were shuttled back and forth between them as they grew.

Most of the children prenatally exposed to cocaine who were befriended by this researcher and with whom he has remained in contact have coped admirably. Although lacking the advantages that more privileged children take for granted—good schooling, educated parenting, a rich, material culture, and exposure to diverse stimuli—they have competed equally with their peers who were not exposed prenatally to smokable cocaine. The oldest are more than 20 years of age, have refrained from personal drug use, have avoided early sexual engagements, are active in sports, and gain good grades. The youngest are healthy, full-term, weighty infants who exuberantly rush past developmental milestones. One bright but wayward 6-year-old girl was struck by a car and made an excellent recovery.

WOMEN AND TREATMENT

Seen as the source of all social ills, illicit drug use has been targeted by state agencies with a zeal unmatched since the Red scare of the 1950s. Through blood, urine, hair, sweat, and breath to tests for drugs, users have been sought out in hospitals, clinics, welfare offices, methadone programs, places of employment, cars, and even in the privacy of their own homes. More so than men, drug-using women unfortunate enough to have been detected by these increasingly intrusive methods have had welfare benefits and food stamps terminated, been fired from jobs, been kicked out of schools and training programs, been evicted from their homes, and had their children forcibly, and often traumatically, whisked away. The path to redemption forces these women to traverse an interlocking maze of regulatory agencies whose contradictory rules, arcane regulations, and severe limitations make it virtually impossible for even the most committed woman to succeed. For them, access to drug treatment has been especially restricted; when it has been available, it is often ill-suited to their particular constellation of needs. Siegel (1997, p. 252) has observed that "In New York City, of seventy eight drug treatment programs surveyed in 1989, 54% refused to treat pregnant women on Medicaid, and 87% had no services available for pregnant women on Medicaid who used crack." Despite the concern about the tragedy of maternal drug use, treatment has always been geared toward men:

> Up to [the 1980s] drug treatment programs had focused almost entirely on men and thus based their treatment approach on a confrontational, male-oriented model, one that was soon recognized as counterproductive, and even potentially destructive, for most women. Traditionally, women who used drugs had been regarded as "sicker," more deviant, and more difficult to treat than addicted men, a partial explanation of why treatment options for addicted women were so limited until the mid-1970s. (Kandall, 1996, p. 199)

The situation has only worsened:

> Access to prenatal care and delivery services has diminished in recent years for poor women . . . despite the universal recommendation that such care services are necessary for healthy births. Drug treatment for poor women is even scarcer although surveys indicate that the incidence of maternal substance abuse has tripled since 1981. In NYC, of seventy-eight drug treatment programs surveyed in 1989, 54% refused to treat pregnant women, 67% refused to treat pregnant women on Medicaid, and 87% had no services available for pregnant women on Medicaid who used crack . . . less than half that did accept pregnant women provided or arranged for pre-natal care. (Siegel, 1997, p. 260)

Rehabilitation counselors were also gladiators who honed their skills by psychologically (and sometimes physically) chopping up fresh recruits to the system, separating the "men from the boys," and the "serious from the fainthearted" in order to weed out the few potential successes from the majority of pretenders or abject failures in life. Women who were desperate or bold enough to venture into the arena with this rearguard army of the drug war were often scarred by the experience:

> The findings [about the inadequacy of treatment for women] were basically a series of horror stories about treatment programs: sexual exploitation, humiliation, sexual voyeurism by both male staff and male clients, being used as an aid in the treatment of male addicts (e.g., by role-playing problem situations), or being excluded from aspects of the program deemed unnecessary for women—such as employment training. (Inciardi, 1993, pp. 20–21)

Program development was also slow because many addicted women failed to seek treatment. For many women, this failure was a direct result of their guilt and shame as pregnant drug users. Even within the community of addicts, pregnant addicts occupied the lowest status. Female addicts who were not pregnant at the time agreed on only a single issue: their contempt for pregnant addicts. Many women, therefore, avoided seeking prenatal care because they were unwilling to confront their own self-hatred or to face the negative attitudes of hospital staff (Kandall, 1996; Rosenbaum, 1981).

In the end, the use of drugs by women has served to indicate the contradictions and shortcomings of these users' place in modern societies. Better answers to problems such as educational opportunity, access to quality health care, universal drug treatment upon request, and adequate housing and jobs need to be considered—not prosecution and punishment.

Discussion Questions

1. Review the statuses, rights, and disabilities attached to being female in several societies, both traditional and modern, such as hunters and gatherers, nomads, horticulturalists, the great agrarian civilizations, modern industrial societies, and totalitarian states such as the People's Republic of China. Identify and explain any differences.

2. Discuss feminism and the struggle for equal rights for women in the different countries of the world. Is ours a "rape culture," as many feminists assert? Does pornography promote violence against women? Have sexual harassment laws improved gender relations?

3. Research the history of women's fashion in America, noting periods in which slenderness or corpulence were especially enjoined. Were there matching dietary or drug restrictions?

4. Give some examples of how medical science and practice, mostly dominated by middle-class males, regard and treat women.

5. Comment on the ambiguous attitudes men have toward women, and show how they apply in matters of sexuality, drug use, leisure, or art.

6. Why were many women in low-income, minority neighborhoods in major American cities attracted to smokable cocaine in the 1980s? Why were they sometimes drawn into sex work?

7. Bring up to date the history of the specific fear that "evil foreigners" will "ensnare white women" into sex work or slavery through drugs.

8. Give details of how the fear of minority female crack misusers translated into policy. Discuss the advisability or legality of removing neonates from "drug-addicted" mothers, prosecuting same for drug crimes against their infants, or mandatory minimum sentences. Review the ways in which women were more harshly punished than men for drug misuse.

9. What are the sanctions against drug use or misuse for men and women in the reader's community?

10. How can good ethnographies be distinguished from unprofessional ones? (See Chapter 2.)

REFERENCES

Adler, F. (1975). *Sisters in crime: The rise of the new female criminal*. New York: McGraw-Hill.

Alexander, B.K. (1990). Peaceful measures: Canada's way out of the "war on drugs." Toronto: University of Toronto Press.

Allen, H. (1987). Rendering them harmless: The professional portrayal of women charged with serious violent crimes. In P. Carlen & A. Worrall (Eds.), *Gender, crime and justice*. London: Milton Keynes, Open University Press.

Anderson, E. (1990). *Streetwise: Race, class and change in an urban community*. Chicago: University of Chicago Press.

Arnold, R. (1990). Processes of victimization and criminalization of Black women. *Social Justice, 17*, 153–166.

Baskin, D., Sommers, I., & Fagan, J. (1993). The political economy of violent female street crime. *Fordham Urban Law Journal, 20*, 401–407.

Block, A. (1977). Aw! Your mother's in the mafia: Women criminals in progressive era New York. *Criminology, 17*, 75–99.

Blom, M., & van den Berg, T. (1989). A typology of the life and work styles of "heroin prostitutes": From a male career model to a feminized career model. In M. Cain (Ed.), *Growing up good: Policing the behavior of girls in Europe* (pp. 55–59). Newbury Park, CA: Sage.

Blume, S. (1990). Alcohol and drug problems in women: old attitudes, new knowledge. In L. Sederer (Ed.), *Treatment choices for alcoholism and substance abuse*. Lexington, MA: Lexington Books.

Bourgois, P. (1989). In search of Horatio Alger: Culture and ideology in the crack economy. *Contemporary Drug Problems, 16*, 619–649.

Bourgois, P., & Dunlap, E. (1993). Exorcising sex for crack: An ethnographic perspective from Harlem. In M. Ratner (Ed.), *Crack pipe as pimp: An ethnographic investigation of sex-for-crack exchanges* (pp. 97–132). New York: Lexington Books.

Bujra, J. (1975). Women entrepreneurs of early Nairobi. *Canadian Journal of African Studies, 9*, 213–234.

Bureau of Justice Statistics. (1991, March). *Special report: Women in prison*. Washington, DC: U.S. Department of Justice.

Campbell, A. (1993). *Out of control: Men, women and aggression*. London: Pandora.

Carroll, M.E. (1995). Reducing drug abuse by enriching the environment with alternative drug reinforcement. In L. Green & J.H. Kagal (Eds.), *Advances in behavioral economics* (Vol. 3, pp. 209–221). Norwood, NJ: Ablex.

Chasnoff, J. (1989). Cocaine, pregnancy and the neonate. *Women and Health, 15*, 23–35.

Colson, E., & Scudder, T. (1988). *For prayer and profit: The ritual, economic and social importance of beer in Gwembe District, Zambia*. Stanford, CA: Stanford University Press.

Covington, J. (1985). Crime and heroin: The effects of race and gender. *Journal of Black Studies, 18*, 486–506.

Curtis, R., & Hamid, A. (in press). State-sponsored violence and indigenous responses to it: The role of the Third Crown (sgt. at arms) of the Latin Kings gang. Rockville, MD: NIDA monograph.

Curtis, R., & Maher, L. (1992). Women on the edge of crime: Crack cocaine and the changing contexts of street-level sex work in New York City. *Crime, Law and Social Change, 18*, 221–258.

Dai, B. (1937). *Opium addiction in Chicago*. Montclair, NJ: Patterson Smith.

Datesman, S.K. (1981). Women, crime, and drugs. In J.A. Inciardi (Ed.), *The drugs-crime connection* (pp. 85–104). Beverly Hills, CA: Sage.

Deckard, B.S. (1975). *The women's movement: Political, socioeconomic, and psychological issues*. New York: Harper & Row.

DiIulio, J.J., Jr., Bennett, W., & Walters, J.P. (1994). *Body count*. New York: Simon & Schuster.

Donzelot, J. (1980). *The policing of families*. London: Hutchinson.

Douglas, M., & Isherwood, B. (1981). *The world of goods*. New York: Norton.

Dunlap, E., & Johnson, B. (1992, November). *Who they are and what they do: Female crack dealers in New York City*. Paper presented at the annual meeting of the American Society of Criminology, New Orleans.

Dunlap E., Johnson, B.D., & Rath, J.W. (1997). Intergenerational processes toward aggression and violence in households of crack sellers/abusers. *American Behavioral Science Review.*

Eldred, C., & Washington, M. (1976). Interpersonal relationships in heroin use by men and women and their role in treatment outcome. *International Journal of the Addictions, 11,* 117–130.

Ettore, E. (1992). *Women and substance abuse.* London: Macmillan.

Fagan, J. (1994). Women and drugs revisited: Female participation in the cocaine economy. *Journal of Drug Issues, 24,* 179–225.

Faupel, C. (1991). *Shooting dope: Career patterns of hard core heroin users.* Gainesville, FL: University of Florida Press.

Feldman, H., Espada, F., Penn, S., & Byrd, S. (1993). Street status and the sex-for-crack scene in San Francisco. In M. Ratner (Ed.), *Crack pipe as pimp: An ethnographic investigation of sex-for-crack exchanges* (pp. 133–158). New York: Lexington Books.

Fiddle, S. (1976). *Portraits from a shooting gallery.* New York: Harper & Row.

File, K. (1976). Sex roles and street roles. *International Journal of the Addictions, 11,* 263–268.

File, K., McCahill, T., & Savitz, L. (1974). Narcotics involvement and female criminality. *Addictive Diseases: An International Journal, 1,* 177–188.

Finnegan, L.P. (1993, September). Crack babies: A review. Paper given at the technical review meetings, National Institute on Drug Abuse, Bethesda, MD.

Foucault, M. (1978). *The history of sexuality, Part 1: An introduction.* London: Allen Lane.

Foucault, M. (1985). *The history of sexuality, Part 2: An introduction.* New York: Vintage Books.

Freeland, J., & Campbell, R. (1973). The social context of first marijuana use. *International Journal of the Addictions, 8,* 317–324.

Gerstein, D., Judd, L., & Rovner, S. (1979). Career dynamics of female heroin addicts. *American Journal of Drug and Alcohol Abuse, 6,* 1–23.

Gilfus, M. (1992). From victims to survivors to offenders: Women's routes of entry and immersion into street crime. *Women and Criminal Justice, 4,* 63–88.

Goldstein, P. (1979). *Prostitution and drugs.* Lexington, MA: Lexington Books.

Goldstein, P. (1991). Female substance abusers and violence. In B. Forster & J. Salloway (Eds.), *The socio-cultural matrix of alcohol and drug use: A sourcebook of patterns and factors.* Lewiston, NY: Edwin Meller.

Goldstein, P., Ouellet, L., & Fendrich, M. (1992). From bag brides to skeezers: A historical perspective on sex-for-drugs behavior. *Journal of Psychoactive Drugs, 24,* 349–361.

Graham-Mulhall, S. (1926). *Opium the demon flower.* New York: Harold Vinal.

Greenleaf, V. (1989). *Women and cocaine: Personal stories of addiction and recovery.* Los Angeles: Lowell House.

Griffith, D., Azuma, S.D., & Chasnoff, I.J. (1994). Three-year outcome of children exposed prenatally to drugs (part of special section on cocaine babies). *Journal of the American Academy of Child and Adolescent Psychiatry, 33,* 20–27.

Hagedorn, J., & Devitt, M. (1996). *Fighting female: Variation, violence, and gender roles in female gangs.* Paper presented at the 1996 annual meeting of the American Sociological Association, New York.

Hamid, A., Curtis, R., McCoy, K., McGuire, J., Conde, A., Bushell, W., Lindenmayer, R., Brimberg, K., Maia, S., Abdur-Rashid, S., & Settembrino, J. (1997). The heroin epidemic in New York City: Current status and prognoses. *Journal of Psychoactive Drugs, 29,* 375–391.

Hamilton, M. (1993). Sociology—The poor relation in alcohol and drug research? *Drug and Alcohol Review, 12,* 359–367.

Harris, A.R. (1977). Sex and theories of deviance. *American Sociological Review, 42,* 3–16.

Harris, M. (1974). *Cows, pigs, wars and witches: The riddles of culture.* New York: Random House (Vintage).

Harrison, P. (1989). Women in treatment: Changing over time. *International Journal of the Addictions, 24,* 655–673.

Hemphill, C. (1990). Turning a corner on crack: Statistics show decline in drug's use. *Newsday,* p. 1.

Hser, Y., Anglin, M., & McGlothlin, W. (1987). Sex differences in addict careers, 1: Initiation of use. *American Journal of Drug and Alcohol Abuse, 13,* 33–57.

Hurley, D. (1991). Women, alcohol and incest: An analytical review. *Journal of Studies on Alcohol, 52,* 253–262.

Hussey, M., & Petchers, M. (1989). The relationship between sexual abuse and substance abuse among psychiatrically hospitalized adolescents. *Child Abuse and Neglect, 13,* 319–325.

Inciardi, J.A. (1986). *The war on drugs: Heroin, cocaine and public policy.* Palo Alto, CA: Mayfield.

Inciardi, J.A., Lockwood, D., & Pottieger, A. (1993). *Women and crack-cocaine.* New York: Macmillan.

Kandall, S.R. (1991). Physician dispels myths about drug-exposed infants. *Crack-Cocaine Research Working Group Newsletter, 2,* 7–8.

Kandall, S.R. (1996). *Substance and shadow: Women and addiction in the United States.* Cambridge, MA: Harvard University Press.

Kane, H.H. (1882). *Opium smoking in America and China.* New York: Putnam.

Koester, S., & Schwartz, J. (1993). Crack, gangs, sex and powerlessness: A view from Denver. In M. Ratner (Ed.), *Crack pipe as pimp: An ethnographic investigation of sex-for-crack exchanges* (pp. 187–203). New York: Lexington Books.

Kohn, M. (1992). *Dope girls: The birth of the British drug underground.* London: Lawrence and Wishart.

Lemert, E. (1951). *Social pathology.* New York: McGraw-Hill.

Lévi-Strauss, C. (1969). The elementary structures of kinship. J.H. Bell & J.R. von Sturmer (Trans.) & R. Needham (Ed.). Boston: Beacon Press.

Lopez, I.O. (1993, Fall and Winter). Agency and constraint: Sterilization and reproductive freedom among Puerto Rican women in New York City. *Urban Anthropology and Studies of Cultural Systems and Economic Development, 22,* 299–323.

Maher, L. (1990). Criminalizing pregnancy—The downside of a kinder, gentler nation? *Social Justice, 17,* 111–135.

Maher, L. (1992). Punishment and welfare: Crack cocaine and the regulation of mothering. *Women and Criminal Justice, 3,* 35–70.

Maher, L. (1997). *Sexed work: Gender, race, and resistance in a Brooklyn drug market.* New York: Oxford University Press.

Maher, L., & Curtis, R. (1994). In search of the female gangsta: Change, culture and crack cocaine. In B. Raffel-Price & N. Sokoloff (Eds.), *The criminal justice system and women* (pp. 96–121). New York: Plenum.

Malahleha, G. (1984). An ethnographic study of shebeens in Lesotho. Unpublished Ph.D. thesis, Department of Sociology, University of Surrey.

Mayes, L.C. (1992). Prenatal cocaine exposure and young children's development. *Annals of the American Academy of Political and Social Sciences, 521*, 11–27.

Mayes, L.C., Granger, R., & Zuckerman, B. (1992). The problem of prenatal cocaine exposure: A rush to judgment. *Journal of the American Medical Association, 267*, 406–408.

Mieczkowski, T. (1994). The experiences of women who sell crack: Some descriptive data from the Detroit crack ethnography project. *Journal of Drug Issues, 24*, 227–248.

Miller, E. (1986). *Street woman*. Philadelphia: Temple University Press.

Miller, B., Downs, W., Gondoli, D., & Keil, A. (1987). The role of childhood sexual abuse in the development of alcoholism in women. *Violence and Victims, 2*, 157–172.

Mondanaro, J. (1989). *Chemically dependent women: Assessment and treatment*. Lexington, MA: Lexington Books.

Moore, J.W. (1991). *Going down to the barrio: Homeboys and homegirls in change*. Philadelphia: Temple University Press.

Moore, J. (1990). Institutionalized youth gangs: Why White Fence and El Hoyo Maravilla change so slowly. Paper prepared for working group on the Ecology of Crime and Drug Use in American Cities. *Social Science Research Council*.

Morningstar, P.J., & Chitwood, D.D. (1985). Factors which differentiate cocaine users in treatment and non-treatment users. *International Journal of the Addictions, 20*, 449–460.

Mort, F. (1987). *Dangerous sexualities: Medico-moral panics in England since 1830*. London: Routledge.

Murphy, J. (1992). *In the decade of the child: Addicted mothers, imprisonment and alternatives*. Albany, NY: New York State Coalition for Criminal Justice/Center for Justice Education.

Musto, D. (1973). *The American disease: Origins of narcotic control*. New Haven, CT: Yale University Press.

Nanda, S. (1990). *Neither man nor woman: The Hijras of India*. Belmont, CA: Wadsworth.

Nelson, A., & Milliken, B. (1988). Compelled medical treatment of pregnant women: Life, liberty and law in conflict. *Journal of the American Medical Association, 255*, 1060–1066.

Nelson, N. (1978). Women must help each other: The operation of personal networks among Buzaa beer brewers in Mathare Valley, Kenya. In P. Caplan & J. Bujra (Eds.), *Women united, women divided: Cross cultural perspectives on female solidarity* (pp. 77–98). London: Tavistock.

Neuspiel, D.R., & Hamel, S.C. (1991). Cocaine and infant behavior. *Journal of Developmental Behavior and Pediatrics, 12*, 55–64.

Ouellet, L., Wiebel, W., Jimenez, A., & Johnson, W. (1993). Crack cocaine and the transformation of prostitution in three Chicago neighborhoods. In M. Ratner (Ed.), *Crack pipe as pimp: An ethnographic investigation of sex-for-crack exchanges* (pp. 69–96). New York: Lexington Books.

Parker, H., Bakx, K., & Newcombe, R. (1988). *Living with heroin*. London: Milton Keynes, Open University Press.

Pettiway, L.E. (1987). Participation in crime partnerships by female drug users: The effects of domestic arrangements, drug use and criminal involvement. *Criminology, 25*, 741–766.

Ratner, M. (Ed.). (1993). *Crack pipe as pimp: An ethnographic investigation of sex-for-crack exchanges*. New York: Lexington Books.

Reed, G. (1991). Linkages: Battering, sexual assault, incest, child sexual abuse, teen pregnancy, dropping out of school and the alcohol and drug connection. In P. Roth (Ed.), *Alcohol and drugs are women's issues: Vol. 1. A review of the issues* (pp. 130–149). Metuchen, NJ: Women's Action Alliance and the Scarecrow Press.

Roberts, D. (1991). Punishing drug addicts who have babies: Women of color, equality and the right of privacy. *Harvard Law Review, 104*, 1419–1482.

Rosenbaum, M. (1981). *Women on heroin.* New Brunswick, NJ: Rutgers University Press.

Russell, D. (1983). The incidence and prevalence of intrafamilial and extrafamilial sexual abuse of female children. *Child Abuse and Neglect: The International Journal, 7*, 133–146.

Russell, S., & Wilsnack, S. (1991). Adult survivors of child sexual abuse: Substance abuse and other consequences. In P. Roth (Ed.), *Alcohol and drugs are women's issues: Vol. 1. A review of the issues* (pp. 61–70). Metuchen, NJ: Women's Action Alliance and the Scarecrow Press.

Russell, S., Wilsnack, S., Klassen, A., & Deitz, S. (1988, November). Consequences of childhood sexual abuse among problem drinking and nonproblem drinking women in a U.S. national survey. Paper presented at the annual meeting of the American Society of Criminology, Chicago.

Siegel, L. (1997). The pregnancy police fight the war on drugs. In C. Reinarman & H. Levine (Eds.), *Crack in America: Demon drugs and social justice* (pp. 249–259). Berkeley, CA: University of California Press.

Smart, C. (1989). *Feminism and the power of law.* New York: Routledge.

Smithberg, N., & Westermeyer, J. (1985). White dragon pearl syndrome: A female pattern of drug dependence. *American Journal of Drug and Alcohol Abuse, 11*, 199–207.

Steffensmeier, D. (1983). Organization properties and sex-segregation in the underworld: Building a sociological theory of sex differences in crime. *Social Forces, 61*, 1010–1032.

Sterk-Elifson, C. (1996, Winter) Just for fun?: Cocaine use among middle-class women. *Journal of Drug Issues, 26*, 63–76.

Sterk-Elifson, C., & Elifson, K.W. (1990). Drug-related violence and street prostitution. In M. de la Rosa, E.Y. Lambert, & B. Gropper (Eds.), *Drugs and violence: Causes, correlates, and consequences.* NIDA Research Monograph No. 103. Rockville, MD: National Institute on Drug Abuse.

Suffet, F., & Brotman, R. (1976, February). Female drug use: Some observations. *International Journal of the Addictions, 11*, 19–33.

Sutter, A. (1966). The world of the righteous dope fiend. *Issues in Criminology, 2*, 177–222.

Taylor, A. (1993). *Women drug users: An ethnography of a female injecting community.* Oxford, UK: Clarendon Press.

Waldorf, D. (1973). *Careers in dope.* Englewood Cliffs, NJ: Prentice Hall.

Waterston, A. (1993). *Street addicts in the political economy.* Philadelphia: Temple University Press.

Weatherby, N., Schultz, J., Chitwood, D., McCoy, H., Ludwig, D., & Edlin, B. (1992). Crack cocaine use and sexual activity in Miami, Florida. *Journal of Psychoactive Drugs, 24*, 373–380.

Weeks, J. (1981). *Sex, politics and society: The regulation of modern sexuality since 1800.* London: Longman.

Weeks, J. (1985). *Sexuality and its discontents: Meanings, myths and modern sexuality.* London: Routledge and Kegan Paul.

Weil, A. (1972). *The natural mind: A new way of looking at drugs and the higher consciousness.* Boston: Houghton Mifflin.

Weil, A., & Rosen, W. (1983). *Chocolate to morphine.* Boston: Houghton Mifflin.

Weiner, N.A., & Wolfgang, M.E. (1985). The extent and character of violent crime in America. In L.A. Curtis (Ed.), *American violence and public policy.* New Haven, CT: Yale University Press.

Wetherington, C., Smeriglio, V.L., & Finnegan, L.P. (1996). *Behavioral studies of drug-exposed offspring: Methodological issues in human and animal research.* NIDA Research Monograph No. 164. Rockville, MD: National Institute on Drug Abuse.

Williams, T. (1992). *Crackhouse: Notes from the end of the line.* New York: Addison-Wesley.

Wilson, N. (1993). Stealing and dealing: The drug war and gendered criminal opportunity. In C. Culliver (Ed.), *Female criminality: The state of the art* (pp. 169–194). New York: Gatland Publishing.

Wyatt, G. (1985). The sexual abuse of Afro-American women and white women in childhood. *Child Abuse and Neglect: The International Journal, 9,* 507–519.

Yablonsky, L. (1997). *The story of junk.* New York: Farrar, Strauss & Giroux.

Young, E. (1990). The role of incest issues in relapse. *Journal of Psychoactive Drugs, 22,* 249–258.

Zedner, L. (1991). Women, crime and penal responses: A historical account. In M. Tonry (Ed.), *Crime and justice: A review of research* (pp. 307–362). (Vol. 14). Chicago: University of Chicago Press.

SUGGESTED READING

Chesney-Lind, M. (in press). Rethinking women's imprisonment: A critical examination of trends in female incarceration. In B. Raffel-Price & N. Sokoloff (Eds.), *The Criminal Justice System and Women* (2nd ed.).

Coles, C. (1991, May 15). *Substance abuse in pregnancy: The infant's risk. How great?* Paper presented at symposium on pregnant drug abusers: Clinical and legal controversy, annual meeting of the American Psychiatric Association, New Orleans.

Goldstein, P. (1981). Getting over: Economic alternatives to predatory street crime among street drug users. In J. Inciardi (Ed.), *The drugs/crime connection.* Beverly Hills, CA: Sage.

Goldstein, P. (1984). The marketing of street heroin in New York City. *Journal of Drug Issues, 14,* 553–566.

Inciardi, J.A., & Metsch, L.R. (1995). Women, crack, and crime: A gender comparison of criminal activity among crack cocaine users. *Contemporary Drug Problems, 22,* 435–451.

CHAPTER 8

Drugs and Neighborhood Deterioration

Chapter Objectives

Drugs do not destroy neighborhoods and historically have even enriched them. Neighborhoods are principally destroyed by neglectful economic and political policies. Neighborhood variation in drug use, distribution, supply, demand, and effects militates against exclusively pharmacological and psychological explanations.

The relation between minority populations in American inner cities and the worst drug-related outcomes is not obvious. European Americans, while improving their neighborhoods, have had multiple engagements with drugs for longer periods of time than the rest of the national population (Kandel, 1991). In adolescence and early adulthood, lower lifetime rates of reported use of illicit drugs, particularly cocaine, are generally observed among African Americans than among European Americans, with Latinos in between these two groups (Kandel, 1991). An age difference appears to be critical. Forty to 50% fewer African Americans than European Americans report any lifetime experience with cocaine among those younger than 35, while 20% more African Americans than European Americans report such experiences among those aged 35 and over. An explanation is that African Americans may persist in heavier use later in life (Kandel, 1991; NIDA [National Institute on Drug Abuse], 1990). The lower prevalence of reported use of a variety of drugs by African Americans compared with European Americans has also been reported by most other surveys that have examined ethnic patterns in drug use (Kandel, 1991; Prendergast, Austin, Maton, & Baker, 1989) whether the data are obtained by household surveys (Kandel & Davies, 1991) or in-school self-administered questionnaires (Bachman et al., 1991;

Gillmore et al., 1990; Johnston, O'Malley, & Bachman, 1991; Kandel, Davies, & Davis, 1990; Kandel, Single, & Kessler, 1976; Maddahian, Newcomb, & Bentler, 1986; Trimble, Padilla, & Bell, 1987; Welte & Barnes, 1987; Zabin, Hardy, Smith, & Hirsch, 1985). Lower rates of cases of drug abuse/dependence meeting diagnostic criteria were observed among minorities in the general population from 1980 to 1984 (Anthony & Helzer, 1991; Kandel, 1991).

When the figures for drug arrests are considered, however, minorities are presented again in a more sinister light. According to the National Household Survey on Drug Abuse (NIDA, 1990), 75 million Americans used illicit drugs in 1990, but only 763,340 drug arrests were made. European Americans were 58.1% of arrestees, while African Americans were 41%. A disproportionate number of African Americans were therefore being arrested. In fact, between 1980 and 1990, despite lower reported drug use among African-American juveniles, arrests of European-American juveniles increased by 251%, but arrests of African-American juveniles rose by 2,373% (NIDA, 1990)!

One reason, therefore, for the fusion of inner-city/drug images is the inordinate number of highly publicized arrests that are made there. Why are so many minority persons being arrested for drug offenses when fewer of them, in comparison with European-American age-mates, are involved with drugs at all?

Selective application of drug prohibition laws is a powerful explanation of the higher arrest rates of African Americans. Racial animosity alone mobilizes public opinion, the media, and the law enforcement agencies against "the drug problem in the inner city." In Chapter 4, forms of intensive policing in New York, such as Operation Pressure Point and the Tactical Narcotics Teams (TNT), which have been directed exclusively against minorities and minority neighborhoods, have been discussed.

Despite lower rates of drug use, African Americans and other minorities are also overrepresented when it is a question of morbidity and mortality cases of illicit drug users, and especially of cocaine users who have come to the attention of various medical treatment or criminal institutions, such as drug-related emergency rooms, treatment programs, or medical examiners' offices (Kandel, 1991). The high visibility of African-American users, as well as their lack of access to more discreet and expensive health care, again account for this circumstance.

Inner-city populations are of course overrepresented in research. The main reason is the tremendous willingness of inner-city residents to be interviewed and observed by ethnographers. The skewed results of research when unequal power relations obtain between researcher and study participants has been a major focus of anthropological introspection (Hymes, 1974). It should be recalled that when the European masters of ethnographic methodology (Evans-Pritchard and Radcliffe-Brown) conducted fieldwork, they did so with the blessing, backed by armed might, of colonial administrators, and they often operated out of the latter's homes or other premises. In Samoa and New Guinea, Margaret Mead had been comforted and protected by the assurance that any native who harmed her would be swiftly punished (Baldwin & Mead, 1971).

While the cooperation between inner-city resident and visiting ethnographer may express such an exploitative power relationship, this researcher has found nevertheless that persons who have been chronically unheard and misunderstood, or whose opinions are continuously ignored, are often eager for the chance to express themselves. In this way, anthropological research, which relies on open-ended questioning, free-ranging discussion, and the originality of participants, can be itself a powerful intervention through which personal lives and communities may be improved.

Much of the research reported in the earlier chapters of this book was conducted in low-income, minority neighborhoods in cities across the United States. A conviction that the crack discourse planted deeply in the American consciousness during the 1980s was that these neighborhoods had been destroyed by the drug use of their residents. It exempted the socioeconomic mainstream from responsibility for multiple inner-city crises. Within the social sciences, variations on the "deviant subculture" theme sealed off the inner-city drug economy as if it were in a virtual vacuum, impervious to all forces from the surrounding local, national, and global economies. At its most extreme, this ideology of individual blame revived long-discredited theories of "genetic predisposition" as the cause of criminal activity (Wilson & Herrnstein, 1985). Even drug researchers who make passing reference to the role of larger structural forces in recent urban decline rely uncritically upon the analytically specious idea of a "criminal underclass":

> Although many factors have contributed to the relative decline of American inner cities, or "ghettos," this essay advances the thesis that the expansion of hard drugs, and particularly the sale and distribution of heroin and cocaine, is both a symptom and an important factor in the continued relative decline of inner-city communities and persons who reside in those communities.

> Living in inner-city communities with severe social and economic conditions, however, does not "select" which persons will become most impoverished and experience multiple social problems. As we argue in this essay, involvement with drugs and the criminal underclass is a major factor in creating persons who will experience such multiple social problems, with wide-ranging negative impacts on their families and neighbors.

> The criminal underclass refers to the values, conduct norms, lifestyles and performance of roles in the criminal underclass. The criminal

underclass subculture appears to have several major conduct norms: illegal means are better than legal means to earn money; other people are to be manipulated and their goods or money taken for the offender's benefit; violence and its threat should be used to gain criminal returns and maintain reputation; expenditures of illicit money should support "fast living," even at the cost of necessary items. Thus illegal income is to be spent for luxury items (gold, fancy clothes), illicit drugs and the entertainment of friends, rather than on basic necessities (food, shelter, family obligations, and lifetime savings), and participants should attempt to remain unknown to official institutions, especially police, taxing authorities, and other officials. (Johnson, Williams, Dei, & Sanabria, 1990, p. 23)

The conviction has gained strength over time. For example, Stimmel (1996, p. 16) states that "The results of drug use and sales remain the same: destruction of inner city communities and, all too often, death of innocent people." Chitwood, Rivers, and Inciardi (1996, p. ix) have commented that "the rivalries in crack distribution networks . . . have turned some inner-city communities into urban 'dead zones,' where homicide rates are so high that "police have written them off as anarchic badlands." Throughout the United States, once-thriving centers of industry and commerce are depicted as being overrun and undermined by drugs, such as New York City (Johnson et al., 1990), Philadelphia (Anderson, 1990), Detroit (Mieczkowski, 1990; Taylor, 1990), Miami (Inciardi & McElrath, 1996), Chicago (Padilla, 1992), and Washington, D.C. (Reuter, MacCoun, & Murphy, 1990).

Other researchers have presented the opposing viewpoint that political and economic processes were responsible. Thus, Reaganomics in the 1980s had made Flatbush a "land fit for cocaine smoking": workers idle, low-income families in disarray, skewed marriage and birth rates, buildings abandoned, housing scarce or substandard, services and amenities reduced, the "beat cop" replaced by a speeding patrol car, with fresh immigrants arriving daily to be greeted by these inhospitable conditions (Hamid, 1997b).

These issues are addressed in this chapter.

DRUGS AND THE INNER CITY

The marginalization of the inner city after World War II fatefully altered the history of drug use in America, and drug prohibition was to have its worst outcomes there. It became a litmus paper in subsequent public debate on drugs and was regarded as a test case in arguments for and against legalization or other liberalization of drug policy. Both sides agreed that it was the site of the worst drug-related problems: frequent cases of misuse, flagrant open-air drug markets, high rates of accompanying crime and violence, sex-for-drug exchanges with attendant public health risks, family dysfunction, and child abuse and neglect. The inner city also harbored environments such as freakhouses (Hamid, 1992, 1997b; Ratner, 1993; Williams, 1992) and shooting galleries (Curtis et al., 1995) in which many of the risky or undesirable behaviors were concentrated. Many predicted that these conditions would worsen if prohibition was lifted, and they condemned drug legalization as a genocidal proposal aimed particularly at African Americans, Latinos, or other ethnic minorities who live in the inner city.

Since the 1960s, low-income minority neighborhoods in American cities have been declining steadily. New York City, Philadelphia, Atlanta, Chicago, Detroit, Milwaukee, Los Angeles, and Seattle are some where the common trend, which derived from the restructuring of global, national and regional socioeconomic arrangements in the same period (Mandel, 1980; Phillips, 1990), has proceeded farthest. For example, in such areas as New York City's South Bronx, Central Harlem, the Lower Eastside, and many sections of Brooklyn, European-American migrants had pulled up their roots in settled local communities to relocate in the nascent suburbs. More than 500,000 manufacturing jobs left the city with them. Nearly half of the stock of affordable housing had been torched or destroyed through neglect, and as the city's tax base shrank, expenditure on public services was sharply reduced (Kasarda, 1992). Whole city blocks were thus converted into a bleak landscape of empty, rubble-strewn lots and the cavernous shells of abandoned buildings (Hamid, 1990; Wallace & Wallace, 1989).

As European Americans moved out, their place was taken by immigrants arriving from the American South, Latin America, and the Caribbean basin, and from other parts of the world where U.S.-directed modernization and development programs had transformed indigenous economies, causing malintegration between economic sectors, unemployment, and new waves of migration (Koslofsky, 1981; Sassen-Koob, 1989; Wallerstein, 1974). (See Chapter 3.) On arrival in cities in the United States, a significant proportion was trapped in the steadily deteriorating neighborhoods by unemployment and the lack of alternative, low-income housing. Scholars and policymakers labeled this segment the urban "underclass" (Hughes, 1988; Jencks & Peterson, 1991; Moynihan, 1965; Murray, 1984; Wilson, 1987). They characterized it by its enormous distance from the institutions of mainstream America: members are putative strangers to work, family, home, enduring moral values, or respect for property and legitimate business (Murray, 1984). They were separated by race (Hacker, 1992). They survived on welfare and through criminality, and thrived only in heavily institutionalized settings, such as foster care, homeless shelters, prisons, rehabilitation centers, therapeutic homes, and lodgings for the mentally disturbed. Their latest progeny (for example, "crack babies") was expected to spend its entire life in them. Occasional riots, from Washington to Los Angeles and from 1963 to 1998, have vented their sense of grievance and resentment.

Thus, working simultaneously with drug prohibition to bring about the worst drug-related outcomes were multiple emblematic conditions of the inner city, such as the performance of the local informal economy, altered labor and housing markets, transformed household organization, subcultural (peer) pressure, and gender relations. They fused into a favorable environment for illegal drug distribution and use. Exogenous factors, such as the falling price of cocaine and law-enforcement interventions, completed the crisis.

In the same period of time that crumbling urban neighborhoods and the underclass were being categorized as social and political problems, illegal drug use in America was rising. Nationally, the number of users of illegal drugs climbed from a mere few in the early 1960s to several millions by 1990 (NIDA, 1990). The inner city was by then poised to admit drugs. First, an epidemic of heroin injecting afflicted young African Americans and Latinos in the 1960s (Agar, 1973; Preble & Casey, 1969); then phenylcyclohexylpiperidine (PCP) and lysergic acid diethylamide (LSD) became popular in the 1970s; and in the 1980s, cocaine smoking would attract even larger numbers (Boyle & Brunswick, 1980; Clayton & Voss, 1981; Fagan, 1990; Hamid, 1992). Use of marijuana had also grown incrementally over the 30-year period (Hamid, 1980, 1997a; NIDA, 1990).

Thus, the prohibitionist ideology has insisted on "putting the cart before the horse," as it were, or mistaking a consequence for its cause. Ignoring the changes in the political economy that caused European Americans and jobs to quit the inner city, they persist in blaming drugs for the social and economic deterioration that many cities in the United States have experienced since the 1960s. Many Americans believe that the drug use by residents had destroyed their habitat, as impaired (or endangered) animals destroy theirs. Drugs, they say, devastate housing as swiftly and certainly as a wrecking ball, and, in their wake, entire swaths of cities resemble "Dresden after the war."

In this view, the contagious drug virus erodes the flesh of communities and turns domestic and communal spaces meant for sociability and recreation into danger zones that need to be quarantined from uninfected areas (Crane, 1991; Montgomery, 1991; Peterson & Harrell, 1992, p. 7). Degraded into drug bazaars, parks are rendered unsuitable for children. Mothers fear pushing baby carriages along streets, made by the media to resemble Sarejevo's "sniper alley," where even the police will not go. Local businesses are systematically driven out by mounting losses as goods mysteriously fly off shelves and land on street corners. Others are co-opted by nefarious warlords who callously invert once-legitimate enterprises into thinly disguised shelters for drug profits, personnel, and product. Entrepreneurs who attempt to defy the trend invest heavily in bulletproof glass, video cameras, industrial-strength locks, vicious dogs, and private security guards, but still find themselves in a losing battle against thugs who intimidate customers and choke commerce.

Drugs are also said to deplete a neighborhood's human capital by ruining once-promising lives and coercing productive members of the community to move elsewhere. As the social life of neighborhoods shrivels up perceptibly, public services also wither: garbage accumulates as side streets become dumping grounds for all manner of refuse, firehouses close as beleaguered firefighters concede ground to the arsonists and drug-addicted "scrappers" who scavenge abandoned buildings, public transportation lines are discontinued as fewer people have reason to come to or leave the neighborhood, taxis are rare, and ambulances careen through potholed streets. As attendance and parental support at school decline, staff are demoralized and children fall further behind developmental milestones. After-school programs are terminated; libraries are not restocked; and swimming pools, basketball courts, and other recreational facilities are made to resemble fortresses that nonetheless do little to insulate residents from the encroaching urban jungle.

The gathering places of the drug culture replace the vanished amenities. Among the institutions of vice and greed that cater to the "criminal underclass subculture" are "shooting galleries (where heroin users can rent equipment and inject drugs), after-hours clubs (where alcohol is sold after closing time and cocaine is snorted or sold), social clubs (for dancing, where illicit alcohol and drugs are frequently consumed), and crack houses (where crack is used or sold)" (Johnson et al., 1990, p. 28).

The focus on drugs as the plague of cities is a new variation on a decades-old theme of blaming the decline of aging industrial centers on newly arrived minority populations. In the older version, the afflictions and miseries associated with inner-city life were said to derive from a "culture of poverty" (Banfield, 1958; Lewis, 1966) or a "deviant subculture" in which poor people sought out, enjoyed, and perpetuated destructive lifestyles. From this angle,

> Neighborhood decline is viewed as a quasi-biotic process, in which the entry of new and alien populations drive[s] out the incumbents and undermines stability. Aging structures, lowered incomes, and the cultural dysfunctions of newcomers combine to accelerate physical decay. In this process, race is like cancer, the darker the invaders, the more virulent the strain. (Greenbaum, 1993, p. 140)

More recently, media accounts have alerted the public to the spread of drug-related urban decay throughout the globe. In Rio de Janeiro, for example, "basuco"-smoking children are said to defy police efforts to control the streets. In response, the latter have formed death squads to eliminate the problem. In Mexico City, sniffing glue has reached epidemic proportions and threatens the tourist industry. In Albania and other newly "free" Eastern European countries, drug trafficking has become a mainstay of their collapsed economies, giving rise to a host of ancillary services like open-air markets for stolen luxury cars. A "Wild West" atmosphere prevails. In Moscow, drug trafficking has exacerbated the widespread corruption of public officials and greatly enhanced the already considerable power of the "Russian Mafia," further retarding efforts to install democratic institutions in a country historically unique in its acquiescence to authoritarian rule. The capital of Somalia, Mogadishu, was nearly demolished by fierce battles between rival paramilitary forces whose zest for war was said to be fueled by incessant khat chewing. The decades-old war in Afghanistan, which ravaged the entire country, was perpetuated by the demand for heroin in the West. Everywhere, it seems, drugs have been responsible for death and decay.

The current image of drugs as the instrument of urban disintegration, however, is new. Indeed, the contrary claim had once been obvious: drugs created wealth and helped to concentrate political power. For example, in the 19th century, the opium trade made Canton, China, one of the busiest ports in the world, and British merchants made enormous amounts of money by trading the substance: "Traders hoping to share in this [opium] prosperity began arriving at Macao like bees to a honeypot. There had in 1832 been twenty-six Britons trading at Canton, apart from [East India] Company men. By 1834 there were sixty-six, and by 1837, 156. Trade became hectic" (Beeching, 1975, p. 42).

Opium was so important to Britain that when China attempted to regulate its internal markets, war broke out between the two countries (see Chapter 1).

Opium was not the only drug to sponsor economic growth and prosperity. Earlier, in the 17th century, tobacco built great southern cities such as Raleigh, Virginia, and Charleston, South Carolina, and was even used in lieu of cash before a monetary system was created. Still earlier, in the 16th century, rum enriched Bristol, London, Halifax, and New England.

In this century, cities such as Cali and Bogotá in Colombia were nourished by cocaine dollars. While the leaders of the cocaine cartels inhabited grandiose villas to accommodate their lavish lifestyles, they also spent on low-income housing, schools, hospitals, playgrounds, and other public facilities. In the Dominican Republic, cocaine revenues magically transformed towns such as San Francisco de Macoris. Spacious, tidy, pastel-colored homes, with cars in the driveway and satellite dishes, sit in the middle of lawns and flowering gardens, where uniform ramshackle shacks with dirt floors and scrappy roofs corrugated with tin had stood. With marijuana and cocaine profits, citizens of Jamaica and Trinidad have significantly improved their homes and communities (Hamid, 1997a).

In and around those American cities that were ravaged allegedly by drugs, there is visible proof that drugs promoted economic growth. The boom in housing construction in south Florida in the late 1980s was underwritten by laundered drug money. In other cities, the suburbs and affluent city enclaves, where higher-level importers and distributors lived, benefited. Middle-class neighborhoods, where extensive use of both legal and illegal psychoactive drugs takes place at nearly double the rate of that in minority neighborhoods (Drug Abuse Warning Network, 1997), were also enriched. Plots to import and distribute drugs in the United States are hatched in comfortable homes sheltered by leafy trees, or in luxury apartments, where the occupants have the resources to realize them. When an op-ed article in the *New York Times* took the Gay Men's Health Crisis to task for sponsoring circuit parties throughout the nation to raise funds for acquired immunodeficiency syndrome (AIDS), although the organizers knew that these partygoers used copious amounts of cocaine, methamphetamine, Ecstasy, and ketamine, no harm was expected to the neighborhoods hosting the parties, such as Miami's Vizcaya Museum and Gardens. Despite the arrival of thousands of gay men bearing drugs on Sunday, August 17, 1997, for the Morning Party, exclusive Fire Island Pines remained the most expensive real estate in the world, its immaculate streets jammed with Porsches and Lexuses. Instead, as was proper, the articles worried about the men themselves: "Every single study that I can find shows that gay men who use more drugs, and who have a higher frequency of drug use, are much more likely to become HIV positive than gay men who hardly use drugs or don't use drugs at all" (Signorile, 1997).

Contradicting scholars who blamed the deterioration of the inner cities on the attitudes and norms of newly arrived minority populations or the drugs they used, another school of social scientists emphasized structural factors (Kasarda, 1992; Peterson, 1991; Portes, Castellis, & Benton, 1989; Wilson, 1987). For them, unemployment was the culprit, not hard drugs. The "destroyers" were those who, following profit maximization and capital accumulation, made economic and political decisions in boardrooms far away from the inner city. The decline in the Northeast was caused by the regional deindustrialization of the 1960s, when manufacturing capital relocated in the nonunionized South and West of the nation, and afterward in Mexico, Chile, and the Pacific Rim. The loss of manufacturing jobs and the worsening of inner-city poverty were concentrated in four northern Frostbelt cities: New York, Philadelphia, Chicago, and Detroit (Peterson & Harrell, 1992, p. 5). "Between 1967 and 1987, Chicago lost 60 percent of its manufacturing jobs, Detroit 51 percent, New York City 58 percent, and Philadelphia 64 percent" (Kasarda, 1992, p. 71). The economies of "sunbelt" cities such as Atlanta, Dallas, Los Angeles, and Phoenix, on the other hand, "were resilient in their earnings across industries during the 1970s. Los Angeles, especially, experienced powerful growth in manufacturing earnings between 1970 and 1980" (Peterson & Harrell, 1992, p. 67).

In a parallel development, "as domestic outlets for profitable manufacturing investment vanished, capital was shifted to the more speculative sectors of finance, insurance and real estate" (Peterson & Harrell, 1992, p. 51). As high-paying, semiskilled factory employment was substituted by office work requiring higher levels of education, the urban labor force was progressively "feminized," until the point was reached when African-American and Latino males were distinctly less employable than even minority females with comparable education. Their choices were thus constricted: "Given rising formal-sector skills limiting their employment in new growth sectors as well as low hourly wages for jobs for which they are qualified, many of the disadvantaged see themselves better off in the underground economy where incomes are actually or perceived to be higher" (Kasarda, 1992, p. 84).

The demographic consequence of this mobility of capital was the population growth of suburbia vis-à-vis both the core cities and the poor rural areas. The tax base of cities and regions shifted. The imbalance created a political consensus militantly hostile to tax increases for public-sector spending on the troubled cities (Phillips, 1990). Cutbacks in budgets for infrastructural repair, schools, and services next terminated many public-sector jobs, which had been, along with manufacturing, another mainstay of modest minority employment during preceding decades. These changes in both labor force composition and the demographic map were in turn reflected in the voting patterns of "an emerging Republican majority," as well as a steadily rightward drift within the Democratic Party itself, such that, in a curious historical irony, President Clinton and his congressional allies now find themselves espousing positions "to the right" of those held by the former Nixon administration in such matters as welfare policy or the proportional allocation of federal drug-policy spending (Kasarda, 1992; Wilson, 1996).

Similarly, the conjoined effect of these structural forces over three decades had affected the availability of housing, real estate values, and money flows, producing the neighborhood contexts for the sorts of drug-using and drug-selling markets described in this book, each of which was accompanied by a different set of psychosocial outcomes (Fagan, 1992, p. 103; Sullivan, 1989). It was within the limits imposed by these larger social forces, then, that some drug distributors and misusers inadvertently "assisted" in the destruction of their communities; they made a bad situation worse.

But the "blighted conditions of urban housing" are only partially explained by the worsening poverty of inner-city residents, and the progressive deterioration of neighborhoods cannot be blamed on their inability or disinterest in maintaining housing conditions (Greenbaum, 1993, p. 143). As European Americans migrated to the suburbs in the 1960s and 1970s, there were, at least initially, simply not enough minorities to fill the vacant housing units they left behind, and abandoned buildings became a common sight in many neighborhoods. The dramatic shift in the demography of urban areas was thus by itself devastating to some neighborhoods:

> Despite losing over 800,000 residents during the 1970s, New York City actually added 266,800 people in households with both poor work history and poverty. Almost all of this increase was due to substantial in-

crements in blacks and Hispanics who were poor and not working regularly. This trend is mirrored in the three other large central metropolitan counties in the North. (Peterson & Harrell, 1992, p. 63)

By the late 1980s, however, large influxes of immigrants from abroad (especially Central America) were repopulating many of the northern Frostbelt cities. By this time, however, many of the abandoned buildings were beyond repair and they were ultimately bulldozed to prevent further decay. The newcomers faced extreme shortages of housing in the late 1980s and 1990s, and were forced to tolerate substandard conditions, or to "double up" and "treble up."

The primarily economic and political, rather than pharmacological or psychological, functions of crack have been described in earlier chapters. The conversion of dwellings into smaller units and single-resident-occupancy units to house more impoverished inner-city populations appeared to be a readily accessible conduit through which some crack profits were laundered, and one that itself generated liquid, illegal dollars. Some real estate in the inner city offered a field in which a few successful crack distributors and real estate speculators/financiers from the corporate world colluded, often through racketeering and abuse of the Minorities Business Act, to determine values and future land use. These rare instances of local reinvestment of crack profits, therefore, furthered neighborhood decline by abusing housing stock and hastening abandonment.

For crack misusers, when kin and neighborhood ties had been exhausted as pools of potential apartment sharers, new acquaintances who met via crack use would adapt to "quadrupling up" and the other uncertainties of poverty. However, the absence of kinship, neighborhood, or other durable ties in these associations heightened the frangibility of makeshift living arrangements and helped to destabilize authority relations within households and in the neighborhood, or the contexts within which the young are to be socialized. When this sort of instability found a home in a neighborhood, it "trashed" it, rendered it useless, and sought out other homes to "trash." Crack users then functioned as a "demolition crew" that completed the destruction of housing stock, and if their crack misuse continued, they ended up homeless. Many homeless persons roaming around a neighborhood marginalizes it more (Hamid, 1990).

The destructive acts of inner-city drug users, therefore, do not result simply from the illegal drugs, but originate in social-structural conditions. Accordingly, a dramatic change in national drug policy is needed that would enable lawmakers not only to refocus the limited resources of the criminal-justice system (now overburdened by the misplaced priorities of the war on drugs) on the more violent and predatory crime in the inner cities, but also to redirect public investment toward the more constructive goals of remedial education, job training, parent education, child care, provision of homes, and community development.

VARIATION BY NEIGHBORHOOD, CITY, OR REGION

Explanations that draw attention to the structural conditions underlying urban decay are an important corrective to those that interpret the problem as one of "deviant" norms, attitudes, or lifestyles. They also account better for variations in patterns of drug use; distributing arrangements; the demographics of users; and effects by age, gender, ethnicity, neighborhood, city, or region. Because these are affected differentially, by structural conditions, drug-related outcomes may also diverge.

Below, the experiences of some neighborhoods and cities in America and abroad are sketched.

Miami

Because Miami was a hub of cocaine importing and distribution in the 1970s and 1980s, crack came to its neighborhoods earlier than in many other cities. However, unlike the Rust Belt cities that continued to experience economic decline and inner-city deterioration during the 1980s, construction boomed in south Florida, requiring a host of ancillary services. As workers arrived to take advantage of expanding economic opportunity, new neighborhoods were created. And yet, even in this boom economy, drugs were just as available—perhaps even more so—than in Rust Belt city ghettoes. "In 1985, few people nationally had ever heard of crack cocaine, but it was already a problem in Miami and Dade County" (Inciardi, 1990, p. 92). But, even despite Miami's storied history with cocaine and its derivatives, it does not have the reputation of a city devastated by crack. The rampant violence of television shows such as *Miami Vice* and movies such as *Scarface* notwithstanding, "crack distribution networks [in Miami were] 'kinder and gentler' than elsewhere" and homicide rates were surprisingly low (Inciardi, 1990, p. 108). Rust Belt cities such as Washington, D.C., Philadelphia, and New York suffered far higher levels of drug-related violence. Furthermore, in contrast with cities such as Los Angeles, Chicago, and Detroit, where gangs often controlled street-level drug sales, "the number of gang members had increased 95 percent to some 3,500, [but the Dade County Grand Jury in 1988] could find no evidence that juvenile gangs had become meshed in drug distribution" (Inciardi, 1990, p. 107).

Even though crack distribution in Miami was not controlled by gangs, however, it was still more organized than the "free-lance" models that were popular in some New York City neighborhoods, and as testimony to their greater organizational sophistication, the Drug Enforcement Administration (DEA) estimated that by 1989 there were "no less than 700 crack houses" (Inciardi, 1992, p. 118) of at least seven different types.

Detroit

Manufacturers staged a virtually complete exodus from Detroit in the post-World War II period. Unemployment skyrocketed, followed by the race riots of 1966, during which "rioters looted many stores in the commercial district and sent the message that it was time to leave. The aftermath of the riots display[ed] a commercial strip devoid of the once prosperous businesses" (Taylor, 1990, p. 9). Institutions of social control exited with businesses. "The church had long been the refuge and anchor for the people of the community, but it too was subject to decline . . . and in 1988, the Archdiocese of Detroit decided to close 35 of 108 parishes in the city" (Taylor, 1990, p. 10). The way was thus cleared for unchecked heroin, cocaine, and crack sales, which flourished in poorer neighborhoods, especially in housing projects.

Because Detroit was evacuated so thoroughly, drug distributors had their pick of neighborhoods in which to do business. Large apartment buildings were frequently targeted by distributors: "One popular locale for selling crack is in older apartment buildings with large foyers, entrances, or commons. Such public spaces provide an arena for sales transactions that, while being sheltered from open public view, allow indoor transactions without the requirement of admitting customers into a dwelling unit itself" (Mieczkowski, 1990, p. 74).

Even more popular were abandoned private houses. Because they were plentiful in Detroit neighborhoods, sellers found it easy to avoid police by continually moving their operation from house to house. The absence of neighborhood institutions facilitated these moves (Mieczkowski, 1990, p. 89).

Crack was brought to Detroit in 1985, but unlike other cities where free-lancers were the first distributors, it served to rally local gangs and other grassroots organizations that had sprouted following the economic, social, and political collapse of earlier decades. A hugely successful organization was "Young Boys Inc.," which, at its height in the late 1980s, "made 7.5 million dollars a week" from drug sales (Taylor, 1990, p. 210). The Los Angeles gangs, such as the Bloods and Crips, which were eager to monopolize crack distribution in the Midwest, feared them and avoided Detroit.

Atlanta

While economic fortunes improved in many Sunbelt cities in the 1980s, especially in comparison with the crumbling Rust Belt cities, Atlanta was very much a "dual city," prospering in high-technology enterprise, but neglected and decaying in more traditional sections of manufacturing. "Employment actually increased in Atlanta by 43,000 jobs between 1980 and 1988, but inner-city neighborhoods benefitted little. Employment decreased in two of the census tracts [we studied] . . . between 1985 and 1991," and with buildings that were constructed before World War II emptying out at an alarming rate (a process that was hastened by the construction of facilities for the 1996 Olympics), "it is . . . a neighborhood which is dying" (Conley & Debro, 1990, pp. 6–7).

The distribution and use of illegal drugs have a long and colorful history in Atlanta, which was a center for "bootlegging" alcohol during Prohibition. The production and sale of illegal alcohol continued apace in Atlanta, even when other drugs were popularized in the 1960s (Conley & Debro, 1990, p. 29). The public housing projects, long neglected, poorly maintained, and leased to tenants who were anxious to escape, were ideally suited for crack distribution in the late 1980s. The organizational structure for marketing the drug was established in the late 1970s by African-American males from south Florida. Although their employees were local, they had no roots in the community and cared little how much violence they unleashed in it (Conley & Debro, 1990, p. 38). Accordingly, drug-related shootings and homicides became so commonplace that Atlanta was dubbed in 1989 "the most violent city in America" (Conley & Debro, 1990, p. 3).

Ironically, by contributing to the demolition of poor Atlanta neighborhoods that had been long-standing eyesores, the owners of crack businesses assisted corporate business interests in redeveloping and reinventing the entire city.

Los Angeles

As the largest city on the West Coast, Los Angeles has a highly complex drug scene that changes over time and varies widely from neighborhood to neighborhood. Since World War II, a series of economic booms have differentially affected its inner-city communities (Moore, 1990, pp. 16–17). The first boom, occurring during and immediately after World War II, was caused by weapons production—airplanes, missiles, and military electronic technology—that required a skilled, professional labor force. It largely bypassed Chicanos and African Americans, but they found other well-paid manufacturing jobs in industries such as "auto assembly, tire, auto parts and steel plants" as well as slightly lower-paid jobs in "garment, shoe and furniture factories" and "food processing plants" (Quicker, Galeai, & Batani-Khalfani, 1990, p. 6).

More economic restructuring took place in the 1970s, with an expansion of high-tech manufacturing and in finance and managerial sectors. Largely excluded again, Chicanos and African Americans were unable to find alternative work this time, as a "Detroit-like decline" afflicted other manufacturing industries. Like the Rust Belt cities, these good jobs were replaced by "very low-wage manufacturing and service industries." Employment patterns during this period were "characterized by unequal growth and class and ethnic differentials" (Quicker et al., 1990, p. 7). Still, most observers agree that Los Angeles did not experience the abject poverty and neighborhood abandonment of many Rust Belt cities (Moore, 1990, pp. 15–16).

While the economic base of Los Angeles was changing and growing more complex in the post–World War II period, the city's drug culture also diversified, but less so in Mexican-American neighborhoods:

> [In the 1950s] heroin did not displace the earlier drugs—marijuana and secobarbital—but created a special "tecato" subculture within the gangs. In the late 1940s the drug was peddled openly in the streets, and El Hoyo Maravilla was one of the major marketing centers. . . . No comparable structures developed in White Fence [where another gang had formed].

> Alcohol, marijuana, barbiturates, and heroin remained the dominant drugs for years. These Chicano gangs rarely participated in the drug fads that flashed through the rest of the city. Psychedelics, for example, never gained much of a foothold nor did Quaaludes—both popular, at times, on the other side of town. (Moore, 1992, p. 468)

Although crack was eventually detected throughout Los Angeles in the 1990s, gaining entrance primarily through African-American neighborhoods, where it was sold and used, police sources maintained that as late as 1990, "they had virtually no crack incidents" in Chicano neighborhoods. Heroin, on the other hand, remained popular:

> Heroin was mostly white or brown: black tar heroin was seen only rarely, and ice virtually never. There was some indication that markets were quite localized. Police argue that the days are long gone when drug users could cross over turf boundaries to buy their drugs. Revitalized gang warfare has driven markets into narrower channels. (Moore, 1990, p. 11)

Crack, meanwhile, had significantly invaded African-American neighborhoods in Southcentral Los Angeles in the mid-1980s (Quicker et al., 1990). Unlike Chicano neighborhoods, where gangs dictated the pace of street life, free-lancers distributed drugs in African-American neighborhoods: "Individualism, doing your own thing, and making a quick dollar, or as many dollars as you need, is the dominant ideology on the street" (Quicker et al., 1990, p. 34). This ethos permitted crack to be diffused briskly, as in New York (Hamid, 1992).

Chicago

Like other large Rust Belt cities, Chicago experienced substantial social and economic disruption in the post–World War II period, particularly during the 1970s and 1980s, when the blue collar industries left (Padilla, 1990, p. 20). The city's European-American population dropped by almost 700,000. Yet the configuration of Chicago's drug problem is quite unique. Compared with Los Angeles, for example, drug distribution is performed largely by gangs, and in a remarkably peaceful manner. Chicago is also singular among major American cities because it resisted crack until after 1990. Cocaine smoking had subsided by then in New York City. An observer explained the relative lack of "turf battles" as follows:

> Since drug use was so widespread, the most rational business decision was to share the market. It was no longer necessary to fight over turfs. This also freed the neighborhood of gang-banging and provided a fairly safe "shopping area" for prospective customers. A neighborhood that was known for its ongoing gang-banging activities tended to scare off customers. (Padilla, 1990, p. 35)

Young, unemployed Chicagoans judged that selling drugs was an acceptable way of pursuing the "American Dream." In many neighborhoods, each gang was permitted to operate its business from a relatively safe turf or marketplace, selling only to those customers who voluntarily frequented there. No free-lancing was allowed, and "individuals who decide to work on their own are fully aware of the severe penalties associated with such behavior" (Padilla, 1990, p. 44). They sold mainly marijuana, followed by cocaine and heroin. But heroin sales and use, mostly of "Mexican brown" until the late 1980s, when the more potent "China White" was offered, were not evenly spread over Chicago (Ouellet, Jimenez, & Wiebel, 1993). On the North Side, a neighborhood where gentrification prohibited curbside dealing, residents preferred to drink alcohol, smoke marijuana, and sniff cocaine. On neighborhoods on the West Side and South Side,

> Outdoor locations often are so crowded that armed men are used to make customers line up and stay in order, and to protect those holding the money or drugs from being overwhelmed by the sheer number of people present, as well as by those who would rob them. . . . In these neighborhoods, it is rather easy to find young heroin users, and they report that heroin is "the in-thing now, it's what everybody be doin." (Ouellet, Jimenez, & Wiebel, 1993, p. 5)

As late as 1990, crack was so scarce in Chicago that the police had seized only one kilo of the drug in the entire previous year (Ouellet, Wiebel, Jimenez, & Johnson, 1993, p. 73). Researchers speculated that the gangs conspired to keep crack out, fearing that their grip on illegal drug markets might be loosened by the introduction of a new drug. Furthermore, unlike many other cities where curbs on drug use by youth had been destroyed, in Chicago, "gangs attempt[ed] to regulate recreational drug use, though specific prescriptions var[ied] from gang to gang" (Ouellet & Wiebel, 1993, p. 5). Thus, gangs determined which illicit drugs would be available in Chicago and when, and they influenced consumption patterns among youth as well.

After 1990, however, crack was first sold and used by gangs in African-American neighborhoods. Soon afterward, the practice moved to the ethnically mixed neighborhoods. Puerto Ricans were the last to accept it. Far fewer "smoke houses" than in other cities such as Miami were organized, and the crack epidemic left a much lighter imprint here (Ouellet et al., 1993, p. 80).

Milwaukee

In many ways, Milwaukee was the prototypical Rust Belt city. Manufacturing jobs and European Americans quitted the city in the same moment as minorities and low-wage jobs were claiming it:

> Even Schlitz, the beer that made Milwaukee famous, has moved, its jobs lost and its Third Street brewery remodeled to accommodate new county social service offices. Perhaps the closing of Schlitz best symbolizes Milwaukee's changes over the past twenty years: a large plant closed and converted to house an expanding welfare bureaucracy. (Hagedorn & Macon, 1988, p. 38)

But economic restructuring and social policies had peculiar outcomes in Milwaukee neighborhoods. When school desegregation was mandated, African Americans were bused from their neighborhoods to schools throughout the city. For African-Americans schoolgoers, their neighborhood "became merely a place to hangout. In contrast, the Hispanic gangs . . . had clearly defined 'turf' where most gang members lived at one time. For the white boys in Punk Alley, the gang and the neighborhood were completely identical" (Hagedorn & Macon, 1988, p. 137).

Researchers expected that, since African-American neighborhoods lacked cohesion, drug entrepreneurs would penetrate them easily. They predicted that, since Milwaukee was a "satellite" of Chicago, its drug gangs would reach out to annex Milwaukee's clientele. But surprisingly, even by the late 1980s, crack and other hard drugs scarcely registered as a problem:

> In Chicago, gangs carved out turf in large high-rise housing projects, where a small organized group could control drug sales and reap enormous profits by simply controlling the housing project elevators by armed force. No such housing projects exist in Milwaukee. Milwaukee gang drug sales, despite the clear intentions of some "entrepreneurs," have largely remained at an individual, "street" level. (Hagedorn & Macon, 1988, p. 104)

Thus, gang members sold marijuana as free-lancers. It was "an easy way to make money" and had "enjoyable fringe benefits"; besides, most of them dismissed selling drugs as "just another low-paying job—one that might guarantee 'survival,' but not much else" (Hagedorn & Macon, 1988, p. 103). Unlike other Rust Belt cities, therefore, where the prospects of drug distribution crazed young men, it had no appeal in Milwaukee until at least the 1990s.

Denver

Neither a Sunbelt nor a Rust Belt city, Denver also transformed socially and economically during the 1970s and 1980s. The city showed a minor increase in industrial employment, but did not qualify as a boom economy for unskilled, entry-level workers, and it was exercised by the same social problems—poverty, gangs, and violence—felt more acutely in other cities:

> [In Denver] there is not an overwhelming sense of poverty or social pathology. Poverty's most visible manifestations are tempered by the small scale of these neighborhoods and by their proximity to more economically stable areas. Substandard, dilapidated housing often shares the same block with the homes of working-class families. The public sector has not broken down; whole neighborhoods are not without basic public services. (Koester & Schwartz, 1993, p. 188)

But although Denver cannot be portrayed as a site of urban decay, crack distribution, controlled by rival organizations of the Bloods and Crips, the Los Angeles gangs, was entrenched in many African-American neighborhoods. Operating from houses, gang members pay crack users minimal wages to sell their product in the street. Differentiating themselves from African Americans, Latinos shunned crack and favored "inhaling or injecting" cocaine. They organized cocaine powder sales in their neighborhoods instead (Koester & Schwartz, 1993, p. 187).

Cities in the United Kingdom

As in the United States, drug distribution and use is not spread evenly across England and have different manifestations in the various neighborhoods studied by researchers. For example, in the Liverpool area, "a large amount of heroin dealing at this low level is done from the user-dealer's own house or flat, although in some towns and cities there are pubs where it is possible to score heroin and other illicit drugs" (Pearson, 1987, p. 123). A striking fact of drug distribution and use in England is that heroin, and to a lesser degree, cocaine—the drugs held responsible for urban decay in the United States—are mainly popular among British (white) users and are sold in their neighborhoods. In Caribbean-African neighborhoods, by contrast, youths avoided heroin and cocaine and their users. "Cannabis dealers operated with a certain degree of freedom within some black communities, [but] they showed little or no interest in heroin" (Pearson, 1987, p. 126).

The cultures of users of hard drugs varied widely in working class white communities to which they were confined. For example, drug availability and use patterns were remarkably different from city to city:

> . . . in the area of South Yorkshire . . . not only have injection techniques been a[n] established part of the polydrug culture for some time, but also a substantial proportion of the opiate drugs locally available consist not of imported "brown" heroin but illicit pharmaceutical products. [By contrast] in the Liverpool area, not only is imported heroin the drug most commonly available, but the pattern of heroin use has so far shown no real evidence of drifting away from the dominant pattern of smoking. (Pearson, 1987, p. 108)

Patterns of distribution and use also varied over time as consumer tastes and the availability of drugs changed. For example, in the Edinburgh area, "heroin became popular [in the 1970s and 1980s] among young people living in council housing estates and was frequently injected among groups of friends" (Ronald & Robertson, 1993, p. 1225). By the 1990s, however, as heroin became slightly more scarce and human immunodeficiency virus (HIV) scared off a new generation of potential users, Edinburgh witnessed the "emergence of a new type of drug user, favouring pharmaceutical drugs and dance drugs, such as Ecstasy, and most often snorting or 'popping' pills instead of injecting" (Ronald & Robertson, 1993, p. 1226).

Cities in Holland

Contrasting starkly with the United States is the relaxed attitude that the Dutch bring to their drug policies. In many cities, marijuana is sold and enjoyed publicly in such calm settings as bars, lounges, and coffee shops. These locations are tolerated as long as they do not cause too much of a nuisance in the neighborhood. Dutch smokers buy marijuana as other goods, taking the time to choose a variety that suits their tastes and pockets.

One benefit of the more tolerant approach to drug control in Holland is that patterns of drug use are much more stable than in the United States. Users are less susceptible to fads that replace one another in quick succession. Far from disenfranchised, the majority of drug users in Holland are integrated into neighborhoods, and they are well known to social service agencies. As a result, the Dutch have much lower rates of risk behaviors and HIV seroprevalence among injecting drug users than most U.S. cities. Furthermore, while some Dutch are poor, neither they nor their drugs are blamed for the misfortune.

NEIGHBORHOOD RENEWAL, DRUGS, AND CRIME

At the peak of the crack epidemic in many large American cities, just as many voters seemed ready to write off the inner cities as hopelessly lost, a remarkable transformation took place. Heralded by red, white, and blue buntings hung from the eaves of rehabilitated apartment buildings, a seemingly improbable revitalization pulled many neighborhoods from the brink of destruction and despair. Even in a global economy, where the gap between wealth and poverty was widening, inner-city neighborhoods defied nearly all expectations and not only showed a heartbeat, but actually began to thrive. In the space of a few years, crime fell to low levels not seen in more than 30 years (Krauss, 1996). Many attributed this astonishing achievement to "innovative policing" (Krauss, 1996), but clearly, something more fundamental was happening because the transformation happened in almost every city throughout the United States, regardless of whether or not new policing strategies had been implemented.

Almost simultaneously, young persons stopped using hard drugs. The decline in crack use in the mid-1990s was dramatic and totally confounded the doomsday prophets who predicted that crack and inner-city life would spawn a generation of morally vacuous "superpredators" (DiIulio, 1995). In Frostbelt cities, crack use tended to peak in the late 1980s and to drop quickly and steeply after that. In Manhattan, for example, "the rate among youthful arrestees went from 70 percent in 1988 down to 31 percent in 1991, where it remained through 1995. It declined further to 22 percent in 1996" (Golub & Johnson, 1997, p. 6). In Philadelphia, "a substantial decline" began in 1989, when the "rate of detected cocaine/crack use among youthful arrestees went from 70 percent in 1988" to under 20% in 1995 (Golub & Johnson, 1997, p. 7). In Detroit, it dropped dramatically among youthful arrestees from 45% in 1987 to only 5% in 1996 (Golub & Johnson, 1997, p. 9). In Chicago, where it started much later than in other cities, it has not declined as precipitously, but fell recently among youthful arrestees from a high of 49% in 1993 to 22% in 1996 (Golub & Johnson, 1997, p. 8).

There were spectacular declines in Sunbelt cities too. In Atlanta, the rate of use among youthful arrestees was low—around 30%—where it has remained since about 1990. In Dallas, "the rate of detected cocaine/crack use among youthful arrestees went from 44 percent in 1988 down to 18 percent by 1993, where it roughly remained through 1996" (Golub & Johnson, 1997, p. 9). In Phoenix, it "has remained at a plateau since 1987, with youthful arrestees testing positive slightly more than 20 percent of the time" (Golub & Johnson, 1997, p. 10). In Los Angeles, the rate among youthful arrestees "declined from 46 percent in 1988 to 25 percent in 1990, where it remained through 1996" (Golub & Johnson, 1997, p. 7).

Precipitous drops in hard drug use have generally followed rather than preceded overall improvements in inner cities. Businesses are reappearing on the main avenues of neighborhoods and there is plenty of new construction. The South Bronx and many other inner-city neighborhoods have been almost totally remade. Block associations, social service agencies, civic groups, and religious institutions were in the forefront of the revitalization.

NEIGHBORHOOD AS THE UNIT OF STUDY

Case studies and comparative analyses—the basic building blocks of anthropological research—have shown remarkable variation between cities and neighborhoods that are differentiated by ethnicity, class, immigrant status, housing patterns, crime, employment opportunities, and many other factors, including the prevalence and tolerance of drug use and distribution. Neighborhood variation shows conclusively that psychopharmacological explanations of drug phenomena are inadequate by themselves.

Neighborhoods should be regarded as the unit of analysis in the investigation of many social problems, such as drug use and distribution. While the macrostructural perspective (see above), greatly illuminates them, it has difficulty accounting for neighborhood variation, and affords individuals little agency:

> The macrostructural thesis . . . suffers from its limited, indeed epiphenomenal, view of culture. Because apparently dysfunctional behaviors are treated as responses to a lack of jobs, underclass behavior is expected to change with improving prospects. This claim, however, asserts causal relationships that run from an economic condition—more employment—to a change in gender roles. Such a linkage is so long and complex that there is substantial room for intervening factors to prevent change. Nor can one simply assume that causality operates in just on[e] direction, such that most members of the underclass will react automatically to economic change. (Greenstone, 1991, p. 403)

Neighborhoods are complex, multidimensional entities where structural constraints and microfactors intersect to form culturally diverse social fabrics. Neighborhoods and communities are important as units for study because, with families, they are the intimate contexts, where people learn to be human. They are the crucible where orientations, outlooks, behaviors, and lifestyles are forged (Arensberg, 1937/1968; Arensberg & Kimball, 1965). The ethnographic method, derived from the investigation of small premodern groups, is particularly well suited to understanding their complexities. In contemporary urban America, there are several excellent examples of how ethnographic methods and techniques can be employed to generate and integrate multiple sources of data to provide a comparative framework for understanding the similarities and differences between neighborhoods. For example, the comparative study by Moore, Garcia, Garcia, Cerda, and Valencia (1978) of three Chicano street gangs in Los Angeles traces their evolution and shows how each gang, in turn, contributed to and was affected by changing local conditions. Sullivan's (1989) ethnographic study of three ethnically diverse neighborhoods in Brooklyn, New York, focused on providing "a sense of the social processes whereby such areas come to have high rates of crime and delinquency":

> The values, cognitions, and choices of individuals are seen as embedded in social interaction. The community is seen as a locus of interaction, intermediate between the individual and the larger society, where the many constraints and opportunities of the total society are narrowed to a subset within which local individuals choose. The local community is also the cultural milieu within which the worth of these specific options is defined. The cognitions and values embedded in community context are not so much fundamentally different from those of the wider society as they are more specific to the actual life experiences of local inhabitants. (Sullivan, 1989, p. 9)

Thus, to appreciate the roles that drugs play in local communities, researchers must have a much more comprehensive view of them as commodities, symbols, and tools. Drug-related activities, economic acts, and indeed all behavior, as the substantivist school of economic anthropology insists (Dalton, 1967; Polanyi, Arensberg, & Pearson, 1957), must be situated in a local community that renders them intelligible. As Sullivan (1989, p. 108) has pointed out with respect to crime, including drug dealing: "criminal economic activity is embedded in community context to a far greater extent than other kinds of economic activity. The risks of regular business activity depend primarily on markets and competition. The risks of criminal activity depend on these factors and on the relative positions of victims and offenders in the community."

Discussion Questions

1. Develop a profile of drug use in the United States. Which regions are affected and to what degree? What are urban-rural differences? Discuss drug use for men and women of different ages.
2. Discuss transformations in the global economy and society over the past three decades and show not only how they have affected local populations in different parts of the United States, but also the drug-producing countries, such as Colombia, Mexico, or Jamaica. Describe the processes by which both inner cities and suburbias formed.
3. Examine the relationship between rates of unemployment and levels of drug use. What neighborhood factors impinge on it? Give reasons why the

neighborhood serves as an appropriate unit for the study of drug use or other social problems.

4. Trace the course of smokable cocaine or other drugs in the cities discussed in the text. Mention the factors that account for the time differentials in onset to the drug. What were some of the consequences of a city's position in the sequence?

5. Review the economic functions of drug economies.

6. How is the reader's community divided? Describe and discuss drug use and distribution in each part. Pay careful attention to class, ethnic, gender, and age differences. Describe the local economy and the structure of opportunity in each part, and discuss how drug use and distribution conform with them.

REFERENCES

Agar, M. (1973). *Ripping and running: A formal ethnography of urban heroin addicts*. New York: Seminar Press.

Anderson, E. (1990). *Streetwise: Race, class, and change in an urban community*. Chicago: University of Chicago Press.

Anthony, J.C., & Helzer, J.E. (1991). Syndromes of drug abuse and dependence. In L. Robins & D. Regier (Eds.), *Psychiatric disorders in America* (pp. 116–154). New York: Free Press.

Arensberg, C. (1937/1968). *The Irish countryman*. Garden City, NY: Natural History Press (American Museum Science Book).

Arensberg, C., & Kimball, S. (1965). *Culture and community*. Gloucester, MA: Peter Smith.

Bachman, J.G., Wallace, J.M., Jr., O'Malley, P.M., Johnston, L.D., Kurth, C.L., & Neighbors, H.W. (1991). Racial/ethnic differences in smoking, drinking and illicit drug use among American high school seniors, 1976–1989. *American Journal of Public Health, 81*, 372–377.

Baldwin, J., & Mead, M. (1971). *A rap on race*. New York: Dell Publishing (a Laurel Book).

Banfield, E. (1958). *The moral basis of a backward society*. New York: Free Press.

Beeching, J. (1975). *The Chinese opium wars*. New York: Harcourt Brace Jovanovich.

Boyle, T.C., & Brunswick, A.F. (1980). What happened in Harlem?: Analysis of a decline in heroin use among a generational unit of urban black youth. *Journal of Drug Issues, 10*, 109–130.

Clayton, R.R., & Voss, H.L. (1981). Young men and drugs in Harlem: A causal analysis. NIDA Research Monograph. Rockville, MD: National Institute on Drug Abuse.

Conley, D., & Debro, J. (1990). The ecology of crime and drugs in a southern city: An ethnographic study of the English Avenue community. Paper prepared for a working group on the ecology of crime and drug use in American cities. New York: Social Science Research Council.

Crane, J. (1991). Effects of neighborhoods on dropping out of school and teenage childbearing. In C. Jencks & P.E. Peterson (Eds.), *The urban underclass*. Washington, DC: The Brookings Institution.

Curtis. R., Friedman, S.R., Neaigus, B., Jose, B., Goldstein, M., & Ildefonso, G. (1995). Street-level drug markets: Network structure and HIV risk. *Social Networks, 17*, 229–249.

Dalton, G. (Ed.). (1967). *Tribal and peasant economics*. Garden City, NY: Natural History Press.

DiIulio, J. (1995). *The truly deviant: Crime, punishment and the disadvantaged*. New York: Simon & Schuster.

Drug Abuse Warning Network (DAWN). (1997). Annual Report. Washington, DC: National Institute of Justice.

Fagan, J. (1990). Introduction. Papers prepared for a working group on the ecology of crime and drug use in American cities. New York: Social Science Research Council.

Fagan, J. (1992). Drug selling and licit income in distressed neighborhoods: The economic lives of street level drug users and dealers. In A. Harrell & G. Peterson (Eds.), *Drugs, crime and social isolation: Barriers to urban opportunity*. Washington, DC: Urban Institute Press.

Gillmore, M.R., Catalano, R.F., Morrison, D.M., Wells, E.A., Iritani, B., & Hawkins, J.D. (1990). Racial differences in availability and acceptability of drugs and early initiation of substance use. *American Journal of Drug and Alcohol Abuse, 16*, 185–206.

Golub, A., & Johnson, B. (1997, May-June). *Research notes*. Washington, DC: National Institute of Justice.

Greenbaum, S.D. (1993). Housing abandonment in inner-city black neighborhoods: A case study of the effects of the dual housing market. In R. Rotenberg & G. McDonough (Eds.), *The cultural meaning of urban space*. Westport, CT: Bergin and Garvey.

Greenstone, J.D. (1991). Culture, rationality, and the underclass. In C. Jencks & P.E. Peterson (Eds.), *The urban underclass*. Washington, DC: The Brookings Institution.

Hacker, A. (1992). *Two nations: Black and white, separate, hostile, unequal*. New York: Ballantine Books.

Hagedorn, J., with Macon, P. (1988). *People and folks: Gangs, crime, and the underclass in a Rustbelt city*. Chicago: Lake View Press.

Hamid, A. (1980). A precapitalist mode of production: Ganja and the Rastafarians in San Fernando, Trinidad. Ph.D. dissertation, Teachers College. Columbia University. Ann Arbor, MI: University Microfilms.

Hamid, A. (1990). The political economy of crack-related violence. *Journal of Contemporary Drug Problems, 17*, 31–78.

Hamid, A. (1992). The developmental cycle of a drug epidemic: The cocaine smoking epidemic of 1981–1991. *Journal of Psychoactive Drugs, 24*, 337–349.

Hamid, A. (1997a). *The political economy of drugs, Pt. I: Ganja and Rastafarians in Trinidad and New York*. Unpublished manuscript.

Hamid, A. (1997b). *The political economy of drugs, Pt. II: The cocaine smoking epidemic in New York City's low income minority neighborhoods, 1981 to 1991*. Unpublished manuscript.

Hughes, M.A. (1988). *The underclass fallacy*. Princeton, NJ: Woodrow Wilson School of Public and International Affairs, Princeton University.

Hymes, D. (Ed.). (1974). *Reinventing anthropology*. New York: Vintage Press.

Inciardi, J.A. (1990). The crack-violence connection within a population of hard-core adolescent offenders. In M. De La Rosa, E.Y. Lambert, & B. Gropper (Eds.), *Drugs and violence: Causes, correlates, and consequences*. NIDA Research Monograph No. 103. Rockville, MD: National Institute on Drug Abuse.

Inciardi, J.A. (1992). *The war on drugs, II: The continuing epic of heroin, cocaine, crack, crime, AIDS and public policy*. Mountain View, CA: Mayfield.

Inciardi, J.A., & McElrath, K. (1996). *The American drug scene: An anthology*. (2nd ed.). Los Angeles: Roxbury Publishing Co.

Jencks, C., & Peterson, P. (Eds.). (1991). *The urban underclass*. Washington, DC: Brookings Institution.

Johnson, B.D., Williams, T., Dei, K.A., & Sanabria, H. (1990). Drug abuse in the inner city: Impact on hard drug users and the community. In M. Tonry & J.Q. Wilson (Eds.), *Drugs and crime*, Vol. 13 (pp. 1–49). Chicago: University of Chicago Press.

Johnston, L.D., O'Malley, P.M., & Bachman, J.C. (1991). *Drug use among American high school seniors, college students and young adults, 1975–1990, Vol. 1: High school seniors*. Rockville, MD: National Institute on Drug Abuse.

Kandel, D.B. (1991). The social demography of drug use. *Milbank Quarterly, 69*, 365–414.

Kandel, D.B., & Davies, M. (1991). Decline in the use of illicit drugs in New York State: Comparison with national data. *American Journal of Public Health, 81*, 1064–1067.

Kandel, D.B., Davies, M., & Davis, M. (1990). New York State youth survey. Albany, NY: New York State Office of Mental Health.

Kandel, D.B., Single, E., & Kessler, R. (1976). The epidemiology of drug use among New York State high school students: Distribution, trends and change in rates of use. *American Journal of Public Health, 66*, 43–53.

Kasarda, J.D. (1992). The severely distressed in economically transforming cities. In A. Harrell & G. Peterson (Eds.), *Drugs, crime and social isolation: Barriers to urban opportunity*. Washington, DC: Urban Institute Press.

Koester, S., & Schwartz, J. (1993). Crack, gangs, sex, and powerlessness: A view from Denver. In M.S. Ratner (Ed.), *Crack pipe as pimp: An ethnographic investigation of sex-for-crack exchanges*. New York: Lexington Books.

Koslofsky, J. (1981). Going foreign: The causes of Jamaican emigration. North American Congress on Latin America, Vol. XV, No. 1.

Krauss, C. (1996, December 20). New York crime rates plummet to levels not seen in thirty years. *New York Times*. A20, p. 20.

Lewis, O. (1966). *La vida*. New York: Random House.

Maddahian, E., Newcomb, M.D., & Bentler, P.M. (1986). Adolescents' substance use: Impact of ethnicity, income and availability. In E. Maddahian, M.D. Newcomb, & P.M. Bentler (Eds.), *Alcohol and substance abuse in women and children* (pp. 63–78). New York: Haworth Press.

Mandel, E. (1980). *Late capitalism* (rev. ed.). Atlantic Highlands, NJ: Humanities Press.

Mieczkowski, T. (1990). The operational styles of crack houses in Detroit. In M. De La Rosa, E.Y. Lambert, & B. Gropper (Eds.), *Drugs and violence: Causes, correlates, and consequences*. NIDA Research Monograph No. 103. Rockville, MD: National Institute on Drug Abuse.

Montgomery, J. (1991, April). Modeling neighborhood effects: Contagion versus selective deprivation. Paper prepared for Urban Opportunity Conference on Drugs, Crime and Social Distress, Washington, DC: Urban Institute.

Moore, D. (1992). Deconstructing "dependence": An ethnographic critique of an influential concept. *Contemporary Drug Problems, 11*, 459–490.

Moore, D., Garcia, R., Garcia, C., Cerda, L., & Valencia, F. (1978). *Homeboys: Gangs, drugs and prison in the barrios of Los Angeles*. Philadelphia: Temple University Press.

Moore, J. (1990). Institutionalized youth gangs: Why White Fence and El Hoyo Maravilla change so slowly. Paper prepared for working group on the ecology of crime and drug use in American cities. Social Science Research Council.

Moynihan, D. (1965). *The Negro family: A report*. Washington, DC: Office of Policy Planning and Research, U.S. Department of Labor.

Murray, C. (1984). *Losing ground: American social policy, 1950–1980.* New York: Basic Books.

National Institute on Drug Abuse (1990). *National Household Survey on drug abuse: Main findings.* Washington, DC: Author.

Ouellet, L.J., Jimenez, A.D., & Wiebel, W.W. (1993, August 11–13). Heroin again: New users of heroin in Chicago. Paper presented at the annual meeting of the Society for the Study of Social Problems. Miami Beach, FL.

Ouellet, L.J., Wiebel, W.W., Jimenez, A.D., & Johnson, W.A. (1993). Crack cocaine and the transformation of prostitution in three Chicago neighborhoods. In M.S. Ratner (Ed.), *Crack pipe as pimp: An ethnographic investigation of sex-for-crack exchanges.* New York: Lexington Books.

Padilla, F. (1990). Getting into the business. Paper prepared for a working group on the ecology of crime and drug use in American cities. New York: Social Science Research Council.

Padilla, F. (1992). *The gang as an American enterprise.* New Brunswick, NJ: Rutgers University Press.

Pearson, G. (1987). *The new heroin users.* Oxford, UK: Basil Blackwell.

Peterson, G., & Harrell, A. (1992). *Drugs, crime and social isolation: Barriers to urban opportunity.* Washington, DC : Urban Institute Press.

Peterson, P.E. (1991). The urban underclass and the poverty paradox. In C. Jencks & P.E. Peterson (Eds.), *The urban underclass.* Washington, DC: The Brookings Institution.

Phillips, K. (1990). *The politics of rich and poor: Wealth and the American electorate in the Reagan aftermath.* New York: Random House.

Polanyi, K., Arensberg, C., & Pearson, H. (Eds.). (1957). *Trade and market in early empires.* Glencoe, IL: Free Press.

Portes, A., Castellis, M., & Benton, L.A. (Eds.). (1989). *The informal economic sector: Studies in advanced and less developed countries.* Baltimore: Johns Hopkins University Press.

Preble, E., & Casey, J.J., Jr. (1969). Taking care of business: The heroin user's life in the streets. *International Journal of the Addictions, 9,* 1–24.

Prendergast, M.L., Austin, G.A., Maton, K.I., & Baker, R. (1989). Substance abuse among black youth. Madison, WI: Wisconsin Clearinghouse, University of Wisconsin, Madison.

Quicker, J.C., Galeai, Y.N., & Batani-Khalfani, A. (1990). Bootstrap or noose: Drugs in South Central Los Angeles. Paper prepared for a working group on the ecology of crime and drug use in American cities. New York: Social Science Research Council.

Ratner, M.S. (Ed.). (1993). *Crack pipe as pimp: An ethnographic investigation of sex-for-crack exchanges.* New York: Lexington Books.

Reuter, P., MacCoun, R., & Murphy, P. (1990). *Money from crime.* Santa Monica, CA: Rand Corporation.

Ronald, P.J., & Robertson, J.R. (1993). Initial and current drug use: How are they related? *Addiction, 88,* 1225–1231.

Sassen-Koob, S., (1989) New York City's informal sector. In A. Portes, M. Castellis, & L.A. Benton (Eds.). *The informal economic sector: Studies in advanced and less developed countries* (pp. 60–77). Baltimore: The Johns Hopkins University Press.

Signorile, M. (1997, August 16). A troubling double standard. *New York Times,* p. 21.

Sullivan, M. (1989). *Getting paid: Youth, crime and work in the inner city.* Ithaca, NY: Cornell University Press.

Taylor, C. (1990). Ecology of crime and drugs in Detroit. Paper prepared for a working group on the ecology of crime and drug use in American cities. New York: Social Science Research Council.

Trimble, J.E., Padilla, A.M., & Bell, C.S. (Eds.). (1987). *Drug abuse among minorities*. DHHS Publication no. (ADM) 87-1474. Washington, DC: Department of Health and Human Services.

Wallace, R., & Wallace, D. (1989). Origins of public health collapse in New York City: The dynamics of planned shrinkage. Contagious urban decay and social disintegration. New York: PISCS, Inc.

Wallerstein, I.M. (1974). *The modern world system: Capitalist agriculture and the origins of the European world-economy in the sixteenth century*. New York: Academic Press.

Welte, J.W., & Barnes, G.M. (1987). Alcohol use among adolescent minority groups. *Journal of Studies on Alcohol, 48*, 329–336.

Williams, T. (1992). *Crackhouse: Notes from the end of the line*. New York: Addison-Wesley.

Wilson, J.Q., & Herrnstein, R. (1985). *Crime and human nature*. New York: Simon & Schuster.

Wilson, W. (1987). *The truly disadvantaged*. Chicago: University of Chicago Press.

Wilson, W. (1996). *When work disappears*. Chicago: University of Chicago Press.

Zabin, L.S., Hardy, J.B., Smith, E.A., & Hirsch, M.B. (1985, March 2). Substance use and its relation to sexual activity among inner-city adolescents. Presented at NIDA technical review on drug abuse and adolescent sexual activity, pregnancy and parenthood. Bethesda, MD.

CHAPTER 9

Addiction, Misuse, and Treatment

Chapter Objectives

Although only a very small minority of drug users suffers adverse psychosocial outcomes as a result of compulsive use or addiction, the lives of several millions, including the children or other family members of the affected person, are compromised by them. Relying solely on psychological and pharmacological explanations of the problem, treatment has had minimal success in rehabilitating patients.

There is a pronounced supraindividual quality about both use and addiction. The same person may alternate between periods of problematic and casual use. These phenomena might be explained if buying drugs is viewed as a species of consumer behavior generally, which is conditioned by the markets in which it takes place. Markets are constituted and driven by social, economic, cultural, and political factors, not chemicals.

Since at least the 1980s, some four million Americans in any given year misuse illicit drugs and suffer manifold adversity consequently (Office for National Drug Control Policy [ONDCP], 1998a). They squander savings and income, lose jobs, betray trust, abuse privileges, commit crimes, alienate friends, traumatize family and kin, disrupt communal harmony, violate norms of seemliness, and fall seriously ill. Each stricken person inflicts immense material and emotional privation on the nonusers linked with her or him.

Their personal misfortune imposes a truly enormous burden on taxpayers. Drug misusers cause accidents on the highway, in the workplace, and at home. They make mistakes or are neglectful at work. They clog law courts, hospitals, and prisons. Some 14,000 die or are killed each year, dissipating capital and withdrawing labor, experience, and skills from the common store. Sometimes citizens have to be protected from them. The total bill exceeds $67 billion a year (ONDCP, 1998a, p. 3). If the costs to society of nicotine and alcohol misuse are added, it rises to $257 billion (MMWR, 1994; Rice, Kelman, & Miller, 1991; Shultz, Novotny, & Rice, 1991. See also Chapter 1). It is argued in Chapter 10, however, that many of these costs may be incurred by drug prohibition rather than drug misuse per se, and that some drug misuse is also a consequence of the punitive policy.

The cost of the government's response is modest in comparison. In the 1998 fiscal year, nearly $2 billion will be spent to prevent youth drug use, $6 billion to reduce drug-related crime and violence, $3 billion on the consequences of drug use, $2 billion to seal the borders, and $4 billion to discourage production (ONDCP, 1998b, p. 11).

The National Drug Control Strategy for 1997 declared that,

> The traditions of American government and democracy affirm self-determination and freedom. While government must minimize interference in the private lives of citizens, it cannot deny security to individuals and the collective culture the people uphold. Drug abuse and its consequences destroy personal liberty and the well-being of communities. (ONDCP, 1998a, p. 3)

In the matter of drugs, if Americans are to respect both the freedoms of individuals and the requirements of national security, the dynamics of misuse, variously labeled "abuse" or "addiction," must be clarified. Sense must be made of baffling data.

HOW USERS DIFFER FROM MISUSERS

Traditional societies exhibited a model for responsible, nonproblematic drug use (see Introduction). A universal requirement was that there should be no ambiguities about the value of using psychoactive drugs. Custom, as well as the favorable opinion of everyone in the contemporary community, justified and cherished the goals of the activity and approved the particular chemicals selected to attain them. Next, its every aspect was heavily governed by rules and ritualized: dosage, occasion, setting, eligibility to participate, expectations, and effects. Usually, a shaman, priest, ritual expert, or elder kin supervised. No detail in the actual moment of intoxication, for example, was left to chance: how a person felt, thought, and acted was rigidly prescribed and orchestrated. As it was communal, drug use harbored no secrets, and its enactment in conformity with group norms was scrutinized by many knowing eyes. A period of debriefing, as it were, followed the drug use session, after which normal life was reassumed.

In the absence of ones furnished publicly by their community, drug users today create their own rituals, which perform regulatory functions such as those of traditional groups. Their drug use, except for its illegality, is consequently nonproblematic. Many Americans drink alcohol only after sunset, beginning with "sundowners." Many others, following the advice of their cardiologists, will drink a 6-oz. glass of wine with meals, but not more. Yet others restrict their alcohol intake to a few beers on weekends or special occasions. Some smoke cigarettes only after meals, or cigars at weddings. Rastafari smoked marijuana within the strictures of a fully developed, indigenous religion (see Chapter 4 and Chapter 5). Heroin use in small daily dosages can persist undetected throughout a lifetime (Hamid et al., 1997).

Drug users are free of compulsion. They take drugs or shun them as they please. If drug taking proves to be a problem at any time by interfering with work, family, personal associations, the purpose of life, or health, they absolutely stop. Since the differences between use and misuse include the social, economic, cultural, and political contexts of the two patterns, the same person may do both as she or he ages, and these contexts evolve and change. They thus have experiences of both using and quitting, usually without professional help or interventions of the state (Waldorf, Reinarman, & Murphy, 1993). Many drug users who were extraordinarily productive and valuable to society have been mentioned throughout this book.

Drug users are sharply differentiated from drug misusers. They are the majority, the latter a burdensome minority. Recently, their social demography changed. While the typical drug misuser in the 1900s was a genteel, middle-class European-American housewife who received drugs from her physician, he or she is more likely to a young minority male since the 1970s (Nurco, Ball, Shaffer, & Hanlon, 1985). Drug misusers are overrepresented in traumatized, marginalized subpopulations, such as male and female sex workers, runaways, and comorbid persons, who either perpetrate or are the victims of domestic violence, spouse abuse, or sexual abuse (see Chapter 1).

The current *Diagnostic and Statistical Manual* of the American Psychiatric Association (APA) has defined 11 classes of drugs that may be part of a substance-abuse disorder and identifies the latter by such criteria as loss of control, continuation despite adverse consequences, obsession or preoccupation, development of tolerance, and withdrawal. It shares some of these with eating disorders, pathological gambling, sect or cult membership, sexual addiction, and collection or accumulation compulsions (APA, 1994).

THEORIES OF ADDICTION

Many theories have been advanced to explain the persistent attraction of drugs and why a minority of persons (but sometimes a substantial absolute number) in every generation and in every culture initiates use. Why a small proportion of these few misuse drugs, sustain injury, and need to be treated also require explanation. Theories of use and addiction, however, are often identical, as their proponents fail to distinguish between the two patterns. For most, any use of an illicit drug is misuse.

These analyses presented drug use and distribution as "diseased" or deviant conduct. They were taken as symptomatic of a more pervasive individual dysfunction:

> At the heart of our current understanding of addiction is the idea that in vulnerable individuals, the disease of addiction is produced by the interaction of the drugs themselves with genetic, environmental, psychosocial, behavioral and other factors, which causes long-lived alterations in the biochemical and functional properties of selected groups of neurons in the brain. In particular, addictive drugs, when taken with adequate dose, frequency, and chronicity appear to commandeer circuits intimately involved in the control of emotion and motivation, thus impairing the insight and volitional control of the addicted person. At the same time, the alterations produced by chronic drug use facilitate the formation of deeply ingrained memories that predispose to drug craving and hence to relapse. (Institute of Medicine, 1997, pp. 37–38)

The history of opiates in Britain illustrates how medical science has "diseased" drug users. Until the closing decades of the 19th century, opium was sold legally in Britain and was widely available, yet there was almost no discussion of "an opium problem" of any kind, much less of a "disease" called "opium addiction":

> Regular opium users or "opium eaters," were acceptable in their communities and rarely the subject of medical attention at the beginning of the century; at its end they were classified as "sick," diseased or deviant in some way and fit subjects for professional treatment. . . . Addiction is now defined as an illness because doctors have categorized it thus. . . . This was a process that had its origins in the last quarter of the nineteenth century. . . . From one point of view, disease theories were part of late Victorian "progress," a step forward from the moral condemnation of opium eating to the scientific elaboration of disease views. But such views were never, however, scientifically autonomous. Their putative objectivity disguised class and moral concerns . . .
>
> "Disease" was generally defined in terms of deviation from the normal. A hybrid disease theory emerged in which the old moral view of opium eating was re-formulated in "scientific" form, where social factors were ignored in favour of explanations in terms of individual personality and biological determination. . . .

Moral values were inserted into this apparently "natural" and "autonomous" disease entity. Addiction, clearly not simply a physical disease entity, was a "disease of the will." It was disease *and* vice. The moral weakness of the patient was an important element in causation; the disease was defined in terms of "moral bankruptcy," "a form of moral insanity." . . . Moral judgments were given some form of spurious scientific respectability simply by being transferred to a medical context. The moral emphasis in causation meant that symptoms were described in terms of personal responsibility, too. It was not the physical or even the mental dimensions of disease which were stressed, but the personal defect of the addict. . . .

This strong moral component ensured a disease theory which was individually oriented, where the addict was responsible for a condition which was somehow also the proper province for medical intervention. Opium eating was medicalized; but failure to achieve cure was a failure of personal responsibility, not medical science. . . .

Addicts were among the "unfit," whose appearance in many areas presaged, it was thought, national decline. . . . Addiction became seen as an exclusive condition rather than, as in the earlier discussions, a bad habit which anyone might fall into. . . . Moderate as much as uncontrolled addicts were equally diseased. Medical intervention was appropriate even if, as many of the case histories demonstrated, the addict lived a normal life in every other respect.

Disease theories, far from marking a step towards greater scientific awareness and analysis of the roots of dependence on narcotics, in many respects marked a closing of avenues, a narrower vision than before. The theories themselves were a hotch-potch of borrowings from developing medical science and established morality. . . . Specialists in inebriety disseminated a confused and illogical series of opinions masquerading as theory. . . . Morality and medical science should apparently have been at odds; yet disease theory was very much a mixture of the two. . . . (Berridge & Edwards, 1981, xxvii, pp. 150–160)

More recent observations are equally perplexed:

The notion of addiction-as-disease, therefore, is a relatively recent social construction, marked by contradictions and confusions since its inception in the late 19th century, and remaining today a rather specious, ill-defined "tangle of medical definition, folk wisdom, legal classification, and social recrimination." (Van Dyck & Byck, 1982, p. 128)

It has invited scathing criticism:

> Our current concept of addiction is an historical anomaly. . . . The narcotic addiction syndrome had not been widely identified in the public mind or by physicians in the nineteenth century or in any other previous era, *although narcotics had been known and used since antiquity*. . . . After all, both alcohol and narcotics have been used widely throughout history. Yet only relatively recently, and then primarily in a few Western societies, did addiction and alcoholism come to be perceived as biological phenomena [sic] . . . The formalization of the addiction concept and of notions of addictive symptoms does not represent a scientific advance, and instead is better understood as a cultural phenomenon that fulfills functional and symbolic needs. . . . This idea of progressive, irreversible, inevitable exacerbation of the habit, causing loss of control of personal behavior and of the ability to make moral discriminations, actually retains strong elements of both colonial and temperance moralism . . . the science of addictionology has become a political, economic, and religious tool . . . It is certainly not the "value-free" view its supporters contend it to be . . . what is declared scientifically "true" depends primarily on *popular opinion*. (Peele, 1990, p. 138)

Nevertheless, the concept of addiction as a progressive, incurable, debilitating disease with an undertone of moral culpability has been strongly endorsed by government-funded drug research since the 1960s (see Chapter 2). The most recent has focused on neurotransmitters such as dopamine, serotonin, and norepinephrine. Administration of cocaine, for example, prevents predrug levels of dopamine from being reestablished in the brain and so retards the activation of the brain's endogenous opiates or endorphins. Robbed of its natural painkilling ability, the body relies on the drug. Amphetamine also strongly stimulates the dopamine pathway leading to the brain reward centers (Hyman, 1996). Recent research has been undertaken to show that long-term drug use causes permanent changes in brain chemistry that produce addiction (O'Brien, 1996). They affect the brain reward circuitry itself (Satel, Southwick, & Gawin, 1991) or may hardwire "emotional memories" in the brain that "people, places and things" associated with a person's drug use may trigger (Institute of Medicine, 1996).

More significantly, the idea was embraced by politicians, policymakers, treatment entrepreneurs, and the media, who were actually its most outspoken proponents. It is fundamental to the policy of punitive prohibition, and calls for total abstinence as the cure. Policymakers have declared one drug after another, from injectable heroin to smokable cocaine, to be instantly "addictive" and have bankrolled steadily more repressive state apparatuses of control.

Addiction has also been the "bread and butter" of sensationalistic journalism and treatment experts. It is the guiding principle of most currently available treatment modalities. For example, an article titled "Kids and Cocaine" portrayed Americans as young as 9 years of age in the grip of the drug peril. It quoted Arnold Washton, a psychopharmacologist at a New Jersey hospital: "Crack is the most addictive drug known to man right now. It is almost instantaneous addiction, whereas if you snort coke it can take two to five years before addiction sets in. There is no such thing as 'recreational use' of crack" (*Newsweek*, 1986). Three years later, drug czar William Bennett, in his Introduction to the National Drug Control Strategy of September 1989, flatly declared that crack is ". . . in fact, the most dangerous and quickly addictive drug known to man" (Office for National Drug Control Policy, 1989a; cited in Belenko, 1993, p. 19). Yet neither authority corroborated this bald assertion with any facts. Some social scientists have lately rallied under the same banner: "Addiction is a physiological phenomenon with a very specific meaning. Addiction is a craving for a particular drug, accompanied by physical dependence . . ." (Inciardi, 1992, p. 62).

Pharmacological and physiological explanations of addiction to drugs have been abundantly refuted. First, addictive behavior may occur without any pharmacological stimulus. For example, compulsive gambling and excessive effort at work or sports are equally dysfunctional in lives as drug addiction. Food obsesses many Americans. Another type remains glued to the television or Internet. Some persons clean their homes incessantly. They love their partners literally "to death." And second, there are numerous instances of people exposed to drugs, including the putatively highly addictive opiates, who do not become addicted—even after prolonged exposure in some cases. The example of returning American veterans of the war in Vietnam has been cited (Robins, 1973). In his 1987 study and review of studies of "recreational" opiate users, Jenike found that roughly 50% of them did not become "addicted." Other studies have also identified "nonaddicted" recreational opiate users (Blackwell, 1983; Faupel, 1987; Hamid et al., 1997). Cocaine smokers used the drug in a restrained, esoteric manner from 1979 to 1981, when it was called "freebase." Renamed crack and spreading rapidly in popularity after 1983–1984, the identical drug next gained notoriety as the most dangerously addictive drug ever. Cocaine smokers exchanged dollars for crack in such a blur, in such an urgency of need, that observers could barely distinguish whether they were inhaling money or drug. But when the latter's appeal faded after 1989, the same users reverted to the earlier pattern of moderating, delaying, and even forgoing consumption (Hamid, 1997). Heroin users too have returned from injecting to sniffing, or do not initiate injecting at all, and find strategies to control their intake of the drug (Hamid et al., 1997).

A genetic difference has been advanced to explain why only a few users become addicted. Thus, Alcoholics Anonymous and some clinicians have argued that some persons are genetically predisposed toward alcoholism and should be compensated or subsidized like other disabled workers (Kendler, Heather, Neale, Kessler, & Eaves, 1992). Additionally, Chinese, Japanese, and Koreans have a "flush reaction" (i.e., facial flushing, rapid heartbeat, headaches, and loss of consciousness) to alcohol that is regarded as a genetic watchdog against its use (Thomasson et al., 1994). Sociocultural theory, however, offers less deterministic and more encompassing explanations for such group or ethnic differences in the incidence of drug or alcohol problems. For example, groups who celebrate festive and ritual occasions with liberal libations of alcohol while abhorring "overindulgence" (such as Jews, Southern European Catholics, or Chinese Americans) have lower rates of alcoholism than those (Irish and Northern Europeans) in whose cultures drunkenness is comprehensible "as a social activity" (Marshall, 1979). The role of "the addict" is available in the cultural repertoire, and recovery from addiction is complicated due to identification with the "addict subculture" (Stephens, 1991; Waterston, 1993).

Personality theorists have found that alcoholics are more prone to exhibit anxiety, depression, and low self-esteem; have difficulty in maintaining emotional intimacy with others; and often felt alone and isolated as prealcoholic adolescents and adults:

> Several studies indicate that alcoholics and drug addicts have an external locus of control: they are easily influenced by environmental factors and do not perceive that they are capable of controlling their drug use. These feelings of helplessness spill over into all aspects of their experience, leaving abusers feeling buffeted by events and emotions that they are powerless to change or even manage. (Mendelson & Mello, 1986, p. 157)

According to this view, alcoholics and drug addicts fall into two subclassifications: the distressed subtype (who uses substances as a form of self-medication to help alleviate feelings of depression and anxiety), and the sociopathic subtype (who uses substances as part of his or her generalized search for instant gratification). These subtypes have been identified among bulimics and anorexics (Mendelson & Mello, 1986).

Experts on the distressed and sociopathic subtype use learning theory to understand their caseload or study population. Thus, compulsive behaviors are

> learned responses that are acquired and maintained because they reduce stress. . . . [They] use these substances because 1.) it helps them to escape their anxiety and 2.) it makes them feel more in control of themselves. . . . If the substance or behavior succeeds in reducing their anxiety and enhancing their sense of self control, it is positively rein-

forcing and the consumer learns to turn to it in times of distress. (Mendelson & Mello, 1986, p. 158)

These personality theorists do not regard the desire for drugs as "hedonistic" but rather as a reduction of dysphoria and emotional distress (Hoch & Loewenstein, 1991). From the consumers' perspective, their actions are rational but after onset, drug use may initiate, or be implicated in, processes that escalate it. Thus, if the individual's emotional state worsens independently as a result of life situations, her or his drug use may rise. More commonly, the consumption of illegal drugs itself results in stigmatization and greater emotional distress, which the person medicates with more frequent administrations of larger amounts of the drug.

Some researchers believe that addiction is mental or psychological, as opposed to "physical" or physiological and pharmacological:

> To avoid withdrawal, a heroin addict needs to use the drug several times daily; however, because of the low potency of heroin bought on the street, some drug experts question whether one can easily become dependent on heroin or other narcotics. If a person is not addicted to heroin but shows signs of addiction, what is that person addicted to? Some people are addicted to the thought of being addicted, to actually "shooting up," and to the lifestyle of an addict. On the other hand, Jenike (1987) noted that if one took regularly increasing amounts of narcotics, dependency could occur in less than two weeks. Jenike (1987) also reports that about half of narcotic abusers become dependent, although there is no valid predictor to determine who will or will not become dependent. . . . (Goldberg, 1994, p. 378)

Khantzian (1975) suggests that dependency develops because one is vulnerable to psychological distress, not to the pharmacological makeup of narcotics themselves. Maddux and Desmond (1982) studied addicts who were abstinent from narcotics for 3 years as a result of being removed from the environment in which they used the drugs. Upon returning to their original environment, however, they relapsed within a month. This proved that addiction is more than a physical phenomenon. Some people turn to opiates to modulate intense feelings of rage and anger. Psychic or inner pain reflecting depression accounts for dependency (Franklin, 1987). Persons dependent on narcotics were found to be depressed at levels significantly higher than occasional narcotics users, who were more depressed than nonusers (Maddux, Desmond, & Costello, 1987).

Although these theories have dominated drug and addiction studies, advocates of the psychological nature of addiction have not decided whether the depression preceded narcotic dependency or vice versa. In a major review and theoretical article of the literature on theories of addiction and dependency, critics found that psychological theories of both negative and positive reinforcement of addiction were incomplete, flawed, and unable to account for all the data (Robinson & Berridge, 1993). Negative reinforcement theories of addiction and dependency posit that drug taking persists because "addicts" are subject to craving and withdrawal, but

> both people and animals will self-administer opioids in the absence of withdrawal symptoms or physical dependence [p. 251]; "relapse" into "addiction" will frequently occur after physical dependence and withdrawal symptoms have disappeared; and, furthermore, there are drugs that produce withdrawal symptoms which are not "addictively" self-administered outside medical contexts, such as, for example, tricyclic antidepressants [p. 253]. (Robinson & Berridge, 1993)

Similarly, a "positive reinforcement theory" of addiction does not account for all the data sufficiently. It argues that "addicted" people (and animals) continue to take drugs compulsively because of the positive affective states, such as euphoria, which are associated with them. Yet very addictive drugs such as nicotine induce no such states. Moreover, persons take opiates and cocaine even in the absence of appreciable euphoric effects and routinely report the disgust they feel toward the drugs that are causing them psychosocial stress (Hamid et al., 1997).

Additionally, a considerable body of evidence shows that other psychological factors—conditioned stimuli—can provoke the major incentive factors of both types of addiction theory: euphoric states, drug craving, and even withdrawal symptoms. Therefore, although the pharmacological properties of the drugs are important in such conditioning, psychological "addictive" properties may then come to play relatively autonomous roles in "addictive syndromes" (Robinson & Berridge, 1993).

It has also been found that, along with conditioning, other forms of closely related psychological factors, such as suggestion and placebo, can produce pronounced druglike effects. Studies have shown that sedatives and hypnotics (exemplified by Valium, chloral hydrate, and others) (e.g., Lyerly, Ross, Krugman, & Clyde, 1964), ethanol (e.g., Platonov & Matskevich, 1933), cocaine (e.g., Stewart, deWit, & Eikelboom, 1984) and other stimulants (e.g., Evans, 1984), hallucinogens (e.g., Reed & Witt, 1965), as well as opiates (e.g., Ludwig & Lyle, 1964), may all be influenced by these psychological factors, individually and collectively (i.e., socioculturally). The form of the influence is as follows: the subjective (phenomonological), physiological, and neuropharmacological effects of the respective substances can be produced in subjects without introduction of the actual chemical substance into the body. In fact, there are examples in each pharmacological category of cases in which the effects of the actual pharmacological substance can be abolished (e.g., see Lyerly et al., 1964; Reed & Witt, 1965; Ludwig & Lyle, 1964; Platonov & Matskevich, 1933) through these psychological means. It has even been demonstrated that effects that are opposite to the usual pharmacological ones can be induced in subjects who have been administered a particular substance. For example, in one study, subjects who ingested a depressant medication (chloral hydrate) reported stimulant effects after receiving suggestions that they were in fact receiving a stimulant drug (Lyerly et al., 1964). The same observations are being made of cocaine and heroin users in the mid-1990s (Hamid et al., 1997).

Psychological, cultural "shaping" or "moulding" of pharmacological effects are not restricted to the acute phase of drug consumption. Not only the effects of a given dose may be simulated, but entire "syndromes" as well. For example, the effects of a drug, followed by aftereffects as well as side effects, may be induced by inert substances, and for considerable periods of time. Hence in his extended review of placebo and related psychopharmacological factors, Evans (1984, p. 12; (see also DeGrandpre & Whit, 1996) concluded that subjects were unable to distinguish reliably between the substances.

Placebo effects can be shown in addiction and withdrawal programs. Boleloucky (1971) found that even after several years of unknowingly using a placebo substitute for morphine, addicts still showed chronic dependence with withdrawal symptoms.

There are other data that must also be considered in any treatment of the concept of addiction. It is not possible simply to equate the addictiveness of drugs with their capacity to produce highly aversive withdrawal syndromes and/or highly desirable affective states. Patients with chronic pain who use opiate narcotics on a daily basis for prolonged periods of as long as decades, often do not experience the "classic" signs of addiction, such as loss of control of drug use, compulsive use despite harm and development of tolerance, when the medication is discontinued (Goldberg, 1994, p. 185). These patients endure withdrawal symptoms—as may "recreational" opiate users—as one of life's unavoidable difficulties, with which they quickly learn to cope and overcome.

Within such a perspective or framework, narcotic drug use—with its attendant costs and benefits—can actually be conceptualized in general "cost/benefit" terms, like other commodities. Indeed, a reanalysis of standard pharmacological studies of drug "reinforcement" (in both animals and humans) utilized this approach and demonstrated that, when narcotic drugs competed with other reinforcers such as food and were subject to negative reinforcers such as heavy required workloads (e.g., multiple lever presses) and/or punishment (e.g., electric shocks), drug ingestion rates actually conformed to a conventional paradigm of standard economic consumption (Bickel, 1995). These studies, utilizing "microeconomics" or "behavioral economics," have forced a reevaluation of basic concepts of "reinforcement" within pharmacological research. Reciprocally, it is very intriguing to note that other studies of consumer behavior (Faber & O'Guinn, 1989; Hirschman, 1992; Rook, 1987), have noted an "addiction-like" nature of certain forms of consumerism.

DRUG USE AS CONSUMER BEHAVIOR

Anthropological investigations during the cocaine smoking epidemic of 1981–1991 revealed that cocaine smokers were distinguished by their spending behavior. For example, consumers of crack showed preferences for different quantities of it: some bought "nickels" ($5 vials), others preferred "dimes" ($10 vials) or "twenties" ($20 vials) and still others would buy only "8-balls" (3.5 grams of crack, or 1/8th of an ounce). These various quantities of the drug were proffered in markets sharply differentiated in terms of risk, the style of the distributors, and use patterns. Although impecunious customers were restricted to the lowliest exchanges, these preferences were to a large extent unrelated to the amount of the user's disposable income or the accessibility of the different markets. Those who preferred to buy "nickels" were called "nickelonians," Kling-ons," or "crackheads" and occupied a lowly status among the drug users in a neighborhood. Bruno, a 35-year-old African-American male user from Flatbush, lost a $50,000 per annum position and then a series of low-paying jobs on account of being one. Finally, he risked losing his wife and children, who had grown disgusted with him. Bruno insisted on purchasing "nickels" at the very exposed open-air crack markets he frequented, although he ran the risks of exposure, assault, robbery, arrest, and buying bogus crack. Indeed, he did lose his job because of a misadventure at one of them:

> Sometimes I go to a block near here where [there are selling] locations: it's just nickels and girls. There are maybe up to ten girls who hang out there regularly. You could offer them just about anything. You tell 'em, "yeah, I got a couple. You want to do a little something." Over there, there are about seven guys selling, a couple of apartments, a little club . . . and they get desperate people over there. They'll give you half a capsule [vial], whatever.
>
> There's another spot like that where I go. It's crazy over there. They'll rob people of anything over there. That's sort of, you know, an off limits type of place. You remember the woman I told you about, the attractive church-going woman I'd seen for years in my [apartment] building, she took me over there.
>
> They cater to the rock bottom over there. They even sell "treys" [$3] and stuff like that. I go over there sometimes. I get fed up with the hanky

panky that people be doing because I get paranoid and I'll go in a different location . . . it's the same old story. Once I went down there and got robbed. I was smoking and I went to get a young lady. Got the young lady . . . and she set me up. We smoked a little bit and then she had some people come and rob me. They took about $100 from me, and the coke that I had.

It was over there that I lost my job too. A guy tried to have his way with me over there. I was inebriated [alcohol], I was walking down the street with a young lady and this guy says "yo, I know where to get this and that" [crack], so he took me to the place and I gave him some money. He brought back the stuff and then he said "let me check it out." Well, I let him have it and he bolted down the stairs with it, and I caught him. I ended up beating him near to death. Damn near to death. And that really scared me. It scared me because I was carrying a firearm, a legal weapon from my job. He ran down into the subway station. Transit police pulled the file on me, and wanted to shoot me, and if I didn't say certain things, he probably would have. I said he tried to rob me and he ended up getting arrested. But I had to take a urinalysis on my job and ended up being terminated when it came back positive. On this job, use, sales, distribution of drugs is illegal. You have to commit a criminal act to obtain them . . . so you're out. (Hamid, 1997, p. 234)

What is puzzling about his case is that, upon examination, Bruno's preference for "nickels" had nothing to do with either his addiction to the drug, or to his interest in risqué sex (he always seeks out a young woman when "beaming up"), or his financial capability. At the time of his first visit to one of the wildest locations he described above, he was robbed of $100 and a quantity of cocaine. On the other occasion he mentioned, he still had the $50,000 per annum job, which afforded a lot of spending money. On both occasions, therefore, he had been financially able to purchase bulk quantities of cocaine or crack, which he could have taken to the former churchgoer's apartment, or to the apartments of other female users. Both his addiction to crack and his craving for sexually charged encounters might have been satisfied at minimal risk; he would have received better weight and drugs of better quality, and he would have avoided the paranoia he blames for driving him from one location to another (and indeed, a paranoia that the locations themselves appear to induce).

What else, therefore, did buying "nickels" offer? Bruno always gravitated toward them, and avoided equidistant locations that offered larger quantities, better prepared drugs, and safer transactions. On one of the days when Bruno was interviewed, he had come home with a $50 tip from the $19,000 per annum job as a manual laborer he had had for the past year. He had performed a task for a homeowner, but instead of billing his company, he had pocketed the money as a private job. He had wanted to "beam up" from the moment he had received the illegal fee, although he had been drug free and attending a Narcotics Anonymous program for the past several weeks. When he got home after work, he said nothing about the tip. He asked his wife to bring in a 40-oz bottle of Ballantine's Ale (a popular beer) from the grocery, thus breaking his record of sobriety. When at length the interview was delayed by half an hour, he went out. He might have gone three blocks from his home to a streetcorner where six or seven abstinent free-lance crack distributors, who had become known as the "Vibrant Posse," sold "dimes" ($10 vials) and "twenties" ($20 vials) to a clientele that it thereby discouraged from making frequent return trips. Or he might have gone an equally short distance to a West Indian restaurant, where a higher-level free-lance crack distributor (who was also a controlled user of the drug) might have sold him half of an "8-ball" [3.5 grams] for $50 (which was the amount of money he had). Either way, he would have made fewer trips more safely for more (and better prepared) crack. Instead, he went an equal distance to a location where "nickels" were sold. He bought two "nickels" and brought them back to his apartment building, where he smoked them in a stairwell; then he went back and bought two more, which he smoked near a friend's motor repair shop. Then he bought three more and went home. At home, his favorite spot for using drugs was the bathroom. On arrival, however, he met the interviewer and came outside of the apartment for the interview. During the interview, which took place in a corner of the building's huge courtyard, he bought and drank another 40-oz bottle of Ballantine's. Afterward, he went again to the location where "nickels" were sold. He probably still had the three vials from the last purchase, and up to $15 from the tip. Why hadn't he satisfied his desire for the drug (and sex) in the least risky, most efficient ways? Clearly, he was not responding only to a desire for cocaine, sex, or even risk taking for its own sake.

Indeed, a profound disgust for these pursuits often characterizes the unfortunate person caught up in them. A theme that emerged in Bruno's accounts, and in the testimony of many other "nickelonians" like him, was their dislike and lack of enjoyment of smokable cocaine after the first few experiences:

> And you know, to tell the truth, the high now, it's a fucked-up head, and I don't know why I keep doing it . . . 'cause it's not really cocaine . . . maybe just a bit. I would think it's more speed or something like that, and I don't know what else they put in that shit, but it's superaddictive and compulsive. You just want to keep doing it no matter what happens, you just want to keep doing it. I would beg Alice for money. Because at this point I cannot manage my money. My whole check goes to her account. I cannot make money at this point in my

life . . . and it's really frustrating . . . a grown man, approximately 35 years old, has been around the world somewhat, and is somewhat educated, has seen career heights, and know better. I absolutely know better. It can't do me any good at all. It can only do me harm, and eventually, if one continues to do it, death is there. But is that a deterrent, actually? No, it's not.

I don't know. It's some kind of speed. It's something that is so addictive that it's ridiculous. I know that it can kill me. I don't know who created this but I think there is a master plan to the whole situation.

It's a fucking nightmare because I don't really enjoy the high any more, it makes me paranoid. I look for this, I'll lose that, I begin to suspect people of ripping me off. It's terrible. How can anybody enjoy feeling like that? I guess it's that initial rush . . . and then you just chasin' air really. (Hamid, 1997)

Why persons "need" any kinds of goods remains a mystery in economics, the science to which one turns for an answer. Why they postpone consumption and save or invest are equally mysterious. Useful for determining in the short term how alterations in income and prices are reflected in a consumer's demand and consumption of goods, the discipline cannot explain why she or he is a consumer in the first place. Viewing us as isolated consumers individually adjusting our personal preferences, economists tacitly agree that we are "material" or "envious" or "greedy" (Hirschman, 1973; Lancaster, 1966; Michael & Becker, 1973) or else they ridicule us for being the dupes of advertising and peer pressure. A customer is justifiably offended by this portrait: more often than not, one has to buy that suit of clothes, resents the obligation, and feels cornered into the purchase (Douglas & Isherwood, 1981).

Anthropologists have viewed the matter very differently. Many of the economic exchanges they have observed have defied "rational" economic explanation: to name a few classics, the three spheres of commodity exchange among the Tiv (Bohannon, 1955), kula objects in the Trobriands (Malinowski, 1922), cattle among the Nuer (Evans-Pritchard, 1940), potlatch in British Columbia (Drucker, 1965), commodities in the early trade empires (Polanyi & Arensberg, 1957), the extravagant spending, in the context of otherworldly beliefs, in Catholic medieval Europe (on cathedrals, clergy, religious services, courtly pomp and circumstance, which included expensive coffee and chocolate drinking—shrewd investments for a few, but as ruinous to many noble families as crack was recently in more plebeian circles) or the Protestant "stinginess," in the context of this-worldly concerns, that followed (Weber, 1905/1958). They have shown, however, that these behaviors were rational and intelligible in their specific social, cultural, and political contexts (Douglas & Isherwood, 1981). Social life is based upon exchange (Ekeh, 1974) and the exchanges involved in the acquisition and consumption of goods illuminate the rational categories upon which social life is based at any given moment (Douglas & Isherwood, 1981). A certain aggregate level of demand for and consumption of all kinds of goods is intellectually and discursively necessary to maintain social life (Baudrillard, 1957, 1981; Barthes, 1972; Forty, 1986; Miller, 1987; Preteceille & Terrail, 1985; Rutz & Orlove, 1989; Veblen, 1953).

Ethnographic research on the demand for smokable cocaine demonstrated that, like the demand for many other commodities, it went through stages, from onset (when it was small) through widespread diffusion (when it peaked) to decline and stabilization (when it fell). Additionally, demand for it was widely differentiated. Distinct types of curbside crack markets formed, such as the free-lance nickels market, the business nickels market, and the crack sellers' coop. In the cultures of these markets, an emblematic style of distributing crack was mirrored by the characteristic way in which buyers used it. Neighborhood, age, gender, and socioeconomic background also complicated the manner in which an individual experienced the drug (Hamid, 1992; Hamid et al., 1997).

Thus, both controlled and compulsive patterns of cocaine smoking have been reported in the cocaine smoking epidemic of 1980–1990, America's most recent drug panic. Many persons experimented with the drug and quickly forswore it. When "the crack vacuum cleaner," or capital depletion at the local level (see Chapter 4), was operating at full force during the heyday of crack (1987–1990), compulsive use-patterns abounded. Yet both before and after this period, the majority of cocaine smokers, and even the same persons who would become misusers, were more restrained in all their behaviors. Others testified that "addiction" is not a progressive disease, but can be arrested decisively by realpolitik considerations, when unfortunates realize that their life of drug misuse is truly only a laboring life, one of unrelenting hardship and incessant work, which is as poorly remunerated as it is heavily stigmatized and criminalized. They conclude that "the white man put drugs in our communities" for exploitative and genocidal reasons and shun them thereafter.

More important, theorists of consumption in postmodern societies have analyzed how contemporary identities are shaped, not simply by kinship, class, nationality, ethnicity, or gender, but more by spending preferences and "styles of life" defined by the acquisition and consumption of commodities (Collison, 1996).

Since the mid-1980s researchers have been examining several manifestations of compulsive and impulsive consumption. For the most part, however, psychological theoretical frameworks have preoccupied them.

Thus, Faber and O'Guinn (1989) examined compulsive consumption and they "identified several characteristics that appeared common across addictive and compulsive phenomena: 1.) the presence of a drive, impulse, or urge to engage in the behavior, 2.) denial of the harmful consequences of engaging in the behavior, and 3.) repeated failure in attempts to control or modify the behavior." These authors believe that compulsive buying is not unlike and conceptually linked to a larger category of compulsive consumer behaviors that include alcoholism, drug abuse, eating disorders, and compulsive gambling. They also noted that these individuals suffered from low self-esteem, had higher scores on general measures of compulsivity, and had a higher "propensity for fantasy."

In a more recent study, Hoch and Loewenstein (1991) focused their investigation on such psychological factors as willpower, the desire for gratification, and self-control in regulating consumption. They argue that "drug addiction bears much in common with other forms of compulsive consumption in both its etiology and consciousness" (Hoch & Loewenstein, 1991, p. 251).

In this perspective, individuals who have low levels of remorse and guilt are more likely to seek out stimulating activities and search for instant gratification and obtain a lower level of secondary process thinking:

> Addicts experience life at the edges of emotion and rational thought. They may even cross over that amorphous boundary that separates sane from insane thought and action. . . Several recovering addicts describe their lives during active addiction as "crazy," "nuts" and "unbelievable." Addicts typically originate from dysfunctional families where the children tend to construct self identities that are incomplete, inadequate or inauthentic. The children typically learn to create a boundary between the self and his/her genuine feelings. Their early identities seem to feel false—an "inauthentic self." As the child grows up they [sic] are introduced to substances that will offer them feelings of comfort and security. . . . [the drugs enable the consumer] to construct a mental-emotional environment that is disconnected from external reality. Their sense of self does not feel authentic because it never grew and developed adequately. Further their self—within their addiction also does not feel authentic because it was constructed from the outside world (the substance). Given this existential state of affairs, it is little wonder that addicts will resort to crime and the deception of others to maintain their addiction, for without the addiction they believe they are nothing.

> Addicted consumers appear to have in common an emotional vacancy that they are compelled to fill with something. They find it very painful to inhabit their own consciousness. Thus, virtually any substance or activity that will alter, numb, or erase that consciousness becomes acceptable, if their preferred drug of choice is unavailable. . . What must be done . . . is to repair the emotional hole in the addict's psyche. (Hirschman, 1992, p. 158)

Compulsive buyers achieve gratification through the buying process itself. According to the American Psychological Association "compulsive behaviors are repetitive and seemingly purposeful behaviors that are performed according to certain rules or in a stereotyped fashion" (APA, 1994, p. 234). They are excessive, ritualistic, and often performed to reduce anxieties that may arise due to obsessional thoughts.

There are two essential definitional criteria that must be present in the various consumption behaviors. Behavior must be repetitive and it must be harmful to the individual. In the early stages of the buying behavior, the individual often perceives the purchase as providing immediate relief from anxiety. This type of short-term positive reward reinforces the behavior and further drives the repetitive compulsions. As the compulsive behavior increases with frequency, the person often feels a sense of grandiosity. This false sensation (and somewhat delusional belief) helps to foster their denial of their problem.

A factor that may be of major significance in this area is arousal. It has been suggested that boredom and high levels of excitement can increase the occurrence of compulsive behaviors. People who suffer from negative affective states may also be more prone to engaging in compulsive behaviors, since it has been found that many of these individuals have low esteem.

In terms of treatment it is very important to distinguish between the types of different compulsive behaviors. Treatment of compulsive behaviors, in general, often involves total abstinence or limited use. Obviously, with compulsive eating or buying these two options are not possible. For these types of compulsions treatment needs to be focused on modification.

Researchers stress that all forms of compulsive behaviors have "normal" aspects. The differences between compulsive and noncompulsive behaviors lie not only with the degree of use but also the motivations and consequences that occur within the context of the compulsive activity:

> Compulsive buyers exhibit a number of personality predispositions commonly included among compulsive consumption behaviors. These include not only shared symptoms and etiologies, but also the presence of a general compulsive trait. This generalized compulsivity trait has been found to be the best predictor of some types of compulsive disorders. This trait is being employed in efforts to develop a general theory of addiction. . . . (Hoch & Loewenstein, 1991, p. 254)

Fantasy may play a major role in compulsive behaviors. Fantastical mechanisms may be involved in reinforcing compulsive behaviors because of their ability to allow the person to "mentally rehearse" the anticipated positive outcomes associated with the activity. Low self-esteem may be of major significance as well. Perhaps the compulsive behaviors are the person's attempt to "block out" or overcome negative feelings toward one's self. The use of fantasy helps the buyer to dissociate the negative consequences from the purchasing activities.

Compulsive buying is often compared or contrasted with impulse buying. Although the latter has been found to have many negative consequences, its effects are often far less severe. The problems compulsive buyers experience economically and psychologically are far more extensive. Their spending habits cause them to suffer extreme debt, low self-esteem and depression, and troubled/damaged interpersonal relationships.

Impulse buying is a distinct and pervasive problem in American society. Nowadays it is enabled by credit cards, 24-hour retailing and banking services, telemarketing, home shopping networks, and "instant credit." The Calvinistic sense of sin about spending is also less severe today than previously.

There is little consensus, however, about what impulse buying actually is. A psychological impulse has been defined as "a strong, sometimes irresistible urge; a sudden inclination to act without deliberation." Impulses are not planned but rather arise immediately when an individual is confronted with a particular stimulus. Once the impulse is suddenly triggered, an immediate action/reaction is encouraged. The idea of an impulse has been the target of philosophical discussion for many years.

Sociologists have studied "deferred gratification," "impulse renunciation," and "instrumental orientation" to describe and analyze impulses. The earliest researchers believed that a failure to learn effective impulse control was more prevalent among the lower classes. These findings, however, have proven inconclusive. Through experimental research, social psychologists have discovered that the ability to delay gratification is highly correlated with increased age, intelligence, social responsibility, and the presence of a father in the home. These researchers also found that individuals who have a high need for achievement have a better ability to delay gratification.

Even though there is much controversy over impulse buying, it is "widely characterized" as unplanned buying. It is considered a reactive behavior that "often involves an immediate action response to a stimulus. Most research has been conducted without the theoretical grounding that descriptive, phenomenological analyses often yield. As a result, we really know very little about what happens when consumers experience the impulse to buy" (Hoch & Loewenstein, 1991, p. 251).

Impulse buying is distinctive and qualitatively different from "unplanned purchasing." It is more spontaneous, more emotional than rational, and more likely to be perceived as "bad" than "good"; the consumer is more likely to feel out of control: "Impulse buying occurs when a consumer experiences a sudden, often powerful and persistent urge to buy something immediately. The impulse to buy is hedonistically complex and may stimulate emotional conflict. Also, impulse buying is prone to occur with diminished regard for its consequences" (Hoch & Loewenstein, 1991, p. 251).

These psychological explanations have not elucidated the origins of this type of compulsive behavior. In constructing his models of the mind and society, Freud explored human impulses extensively. He concluded that they originated from the two competing primal forces, the pleasure principle and the reality principle. The field offers an exciting opportunity for researchers to combine anthropological or cultural, physiological, genetic, social, and psychological models of the mind and society to investigate these phenomena. The resulting conceptualization of consumption must be antireductionist and seek to avoid a simplistic rendering or a dismissal of the importance of consumption. Instead, it must give details of the social character of consumption and address "questions of power through its linkage of ideology and economy" (Rutz & Orlove, 1989, p. 26).

PREVENTION AND TREATMENT

While there are many exceptions, most recently the middle-aged persons who initiated cocaine smoking in the 1980s and the senior citizens who followed them in the 1990s (Hamid, 1992), a consensus is that if a person avoids drug use until 20 years of age, she or he is not likely ever to do so. It follows that preventing drug experimentation at early ages is a desirable goal. In fact, prevention messages are targeted at Americans of all ages, and some are specially tailored for populations deemed at high risk, such as young men whose fathers were alcoholic, or pregnant women.

Drug prevention efforts are of several kinds and have mixed results. School-based drug education programs were discussed in Chapter 2. Training in coping skills is a more recent, better-informed adjunct to them (Bottvin, Baker, Dusenburg, Tortu, & Bottvin, 1990). Evaluation studies found that warning labels on alcoholic beverages were effective in reducing alcohol intake among pregnant women who drank little in the first place, but had no effect on those who were heavier drinkers (Institute of Medicine, 1997). Warning labels on cigarettes have not deterred long-term users. More recently, however, both cigarette smoking and alcoholic beverages have been banned in many locales, and a peculiarly American sight is of workers huddling outside of their workplaces to smoke.

Restrictions on the advertisement of both tobacco and alcohol have tightened recently (see Chapter 1). Both are still widely advertised on radio, TV, in movies, on billboards, at sports or special events arranged by the industries, and on promotional items, such as "Joe Camel" T-shirts, "Newport" caps, sun visors, mugs, and other items. Their ownership puts young persons at greater risk of smoking and drinking (Altman, Levine, Coeytaux, Slade, & Jaffe, 1996). Despite the restrictions, however, the tobacco industry spends nearly $5 billion a year, and the manufacturers of alcoholic beverages $1 billion, to convince Americans that consuming their products is healthy, attractive, and proofs of success and sophistication.

Price manipulation also affects drug seeking and consumption. When taxes on cigarettes were increased in California in 1988, smokers bought fewer packs (Hu, Sung, & Keeler, 1995). When bars offer price reductions, patrons drink more (Babor, Mendelsohn, Uhly, & Souza, 1980). When Chinese restaurants in New York City offered free wine with meals in the early 1990s, a burst of enthusiasm for Chinese food soon waned, and by 1995, restaurateurs had standardized the offer but watered the wine (Hamid et al., 1997).

Other prevention efforts include banning sales to minors, liquor-licensing regulations, zoning laws, and rules applying to the location of vending machines (Kessler et al., 1997). Physicians can warn their patients about drugs. Bartenders could be trained to deny or delay drinks to inebriated customers. These methods, however, may provoke defiance or a backlash, or portray drugs in the glamorous light of the forbidden (Glantz, 1996).

Drug treatment has grown into a substantial industry, and those who earn a living from it often feel they have a vested interest in the concept of addiction, in the conviction that the number of addicted persons is growing, and in the continuation of current approaches to its treatment.

Whether viewed as a means to cure drug abuse or addiction, or as instrumental in the reduction of drug-related crime, violence, or morbidity, drug treatment works, especially in the long term. It compares favorably with the success rates for diseases such as diabetes, hypertension, or asthma, whose sufferers must also change their behaviors to enjoy well-being (O'Brien & McLellan, 1996). Addiction treatment typically proceeds through the three stages of detoxification, rehabilitation, and follow-up care. Relapse is a special vulnerability of the disease, and is therefore a focus throughout treatment (McLellan, Bender, McKay, Janis, & Alterman, 1997).

Treatment takes place in diverse settings. Inpatient facilities are housed in many hospitals, or in public and private clinics. Residential, nonhospital programs and therapeutic communities have also flourished in the past decade. Some are prohibitively expensive, and only a privileged clientele can afford them. At the other end of the scale, some physicians in New York City have been offering to detoxify patients anonymously and cheaply within 24 hours (using naltrexone or other medicines) in their clinics or private apartments (Hamid et al., 1997).

Outpatient services are potentially limitless. Patients may join groups of Alcoholics Anonymous or Narcotics Anonymous; participate in their round-the-clock social, recreational, and therapeutic events; attend seminars and discussion groups organized by churches and other nongovernmental agencies; and access psychiatric services such as individual counseling, behavioral marital therapy, self-control training, social skills training, and stress management. Community supports, such as voluntary organizations from tenants' associations to sports teams, yoga classes, and meditation help maintain sobriety. Brief visits with the pastor, a favorite teacher, or a call to one's AA sponsor can prevent relapse or strengthen resolve. Cigarette cessation programs, voluntarily organized in the community, or part of national commercial enterprises such as Smokenders, are some options for smokers.

Some drugs have been prescribed as antagonists for alcohol, including naltrexone, Antabuse, and acamprosate (O'Malley et al., 1996). They are frequently used in conjunction with antidepressive or antianxiety medications. Methadone is used to maintain heroin addicts (Anglin & Hser, 1992). Nicotine chewing gum and patches are also now available to cigarette smokers (Haxby, 1995; Kornitzer, Boutsen, Dramaix, Thijs, & Gustavsson, 1995). Pharmaceutical companies, coveting the fortunes to be reaped from pharmacotherapy, are sure to develop more. New technologies, using DNA and genetic engineering, are no doubt already being researched in their laboratories.

Discussion Questions

1. Relationships between persons, gambling, buying goods, work, cleaning the home—these are all areas in which persons exhibit compulsions, impulses, and other contradictory emotions and states. Enumerate and discuss them. What conditions of group life produce them?
2. Review theories of addiction and assess how well they explain the available facts. Discuss the rationale and utility of regarding drugs as commodities and misuse as partially aberrant consumer behavior.
3. What factors determine any spending behavior at all? Why do persons spend or save? Do the reasons of the individual consumer make sense when scrutinized, and can they suffice to explain the behavior? How do they resist or give in to impulses to buy? How do different settings, such as department stores, shopping malls, vending machines, credit cards, or ATM machines affect this behavior? How are rates of spending, saving, or investment crucial to the economy? One informant, a crack-misusing New Yorker, declared (see text) that his addiction meant, "I cannot make money at this time in my life!" Consider what this means for a theory of addiction.
4. Draw up a list of measures that the reader might deploy to prevent drug use in her or his community. Identify those currently existing. How effective are they?
5. Describe treatment services that are offered to American drug misusers. How can they be improved? List those offered locally and discuss their adequacy and effectiveness.
6. Give examples of drugs that were prescribed to cure dependence on other drugs. Did they succeed?

REFERENCES

Anglin, D., & Hser,Y-L. (1992). Treatment of drug abuse. In R.W. Watson (Ed.), *Drug abuse treatment, drug and alcohol abuse research*. (Vol. 3) (pp. 393–460). New York: Humana Press.

Altman, D.G., Levine, D.W., Coeytaux, R., Slade, J., & Jaffe, R. (1996). Tobacco promotion and susceptibility to tobacco use among adolescents aged 12 through 17 years in a nationally representative sample. *American Journal of Public Health, 86*, 1590–1593.

American Psychiatric Association (1994). *Diagnostic and Statistical Manual of Mental Disorders: DSM-IV* (4th ed.). Washington, DC: Author.

Babor, T.F., Mendelsohn, J.H., Uhly, B., & Souza, E. (1980). Drinking patterns in experimental and barroom settings. *Journal of Studies on Alcohol, 41*, 635–651.

Barthes, R. (1972). *Elements of semiology*. New York: Hill & Wang.

Baudrillard, J. (1957). *The mirror of production*. St. Louis, MO: Telos Press.

Baudrillard, J. (1981). *For a critique of the political economy of the sign*. St. Louis, MO: Telos Press.

Belenko, S.J. (1993). *Crack and the evolution of anti-drug policy*. Westport, CT: Greenwood Press.

Berridge, V., & Edwards, D. (1981). *Opium and the people: Opiate use in nineteenth century England*. New York: St. Martin's Press.

Bickel, W. (1995). Behavioral economics of drug self administration, I: Functional equivalence of response requirement and drug dose. *Life Sciences, 47*, 1501–1510.

Blackwell, J. (1983, Spring). Drifting, controlling and overcoming: Opiate users who avoid becoming chronically dependent. *Journal of Drug Issues*, 219–235.

Bohannon, P. (1955). Some principles of exchange and investment among the Tiv. *American Anthropologist, 57*, 60–70.

Boleloucky, Z.A. (1971). Contribution to the problem of placebo dependence: Case report. *Activitas Nervosa Superior, 13*, 190–191.

Bottvin, G.J., Baker, E., Dusenburg, L., Tortu, S., & Bottvin, E.M. (1990). Preventing adolescent drug abuse through a multi-modal cognitive-behavioral approach: Results of a 3-year study. *Journal of Consulting and Clinical Psychiatry, 58*, 437–446.

Collison, M. (1996). In search of the high life: Drugs, crime, masculinities and consumption. *British Journal of Criminology, 36*, 428–444).

DeGrandpre, R., & Whit, E. (1996). Drug dialectics. *Arena, 7*, 41–63.

Douglas, M., & Isherwood, B. (1981). *The world of things*. New York: Basic Books.

Drucker, P. (1965). *Cultures of the North Pacific Coast*. San Francisco: Chandler.

Ekeh, P. (1974). *Social exchange theory: The two traditions*. Cambridge, MA: Harvard University Press.

Evans, F.J. (1984, Summer). Unraveling placebo effects: Expectations and the placebo response. *Advances: Institute for the Advancement of Health, 1*(3), 11–20.

Evans-Pritchard, E. (1940). *The Nuer: A description of the modes of livelihood and political institutions of a Nilotic people*. Oxford, UK: Clarendon Press.

Faber, R.J., & O'Guinn, T.C. (1989). Compulsive consumption and credit abuse. *Journal of Consumer Policy, 11*, 97–109.

Faupel, C. (1987). Drug availability, life structure, and situational ethics of heroin addicts. *Urban Life, 15*, 395–419.

Forty, A. (1986). *Objects of desire*. New York: Pantheon Books.

Franklin, J. (1987). *Molecules of the mind.* New York: Dell.

Glantz, S.A. (1996). Preventing tobacco use—The youth access trap. [Editorial]. *American Journal of Public Health, 86,* 156–158.

Goldberg, R. (1994). *Drugs across the spectrum.* St. Paul, MN: West Publishing.

Hamid, A. (1992). The developmental cycle of a drug epidemic: The cocaine smoking epidemic of 1981–1991. *Journal of Psychoactive Drugs, 24,* 337–347.

Hamid, A. (1997). The political economy of drugs, Pt. II: The cocaine smoking epidemic in New York City's low income minority neighborhoods, 1981 to 1991. Unpublished manuscript.

Hamid, A., Curtis, R., McCoy, K., McGuire, J., Conde, A., Bushell, W., Lindenmayer, R., Brimberg, K., Maia, S., Abdur-Rashid, S., & Settembrino, J. (1997). The heroin epidemic in New York City: Current status and prognoses. *Journal of Psychoactive Drugs, 29,* 375–391.

Haxby, D.G. (1995) Treatment of nicotine dependence. *American Journal of Health-System Pharmacists, 52,* 265–281.

Hirschman, A. (1973). The changing tolerance for income inequality in the course of economic development. *The Quarterly Journal of Economics, 87,* 504–566.

Hirschman, E.C. (1992, September). The consciousness of addiction: Toward a general theory of compulsive consumption. *Journal of Consumer Research, 19,* 155–179.

Hoch, S.J., & Loewenstein, G.F. (1991). *A theory of impulse buying.* Chicago, IL: University of Chicago, Graduate School of Business.

Hu, T.W., Sung, H.Y., & Keeler, T.E. (1995). Reducing cigarette consumption in California: Tobacco taxes versus an anti-smoking media campaign. *American Journal of Public Health, 85,* 1218–1222.

Hyman, S.E. (1996). Addiction to cocaine and amphetamine. *Neuron, 16,* 901–904.

Inciardi, J.A. (1992). *The war on drugs, II: The continuing epic of heroin, cocaine, crack, crime, AIDS, and public policy.* Mountain View, CA: Mayfield.

Institute of Medicine. (1996). *Pathways of addiction: Opportunities in drug abuse research.* Washington, DC: National Academy Press.

Institute of Medicine. (1997). *Dispelling the myths about addiction: Strategies to increase understanding and strengthen research.* Washington, DC: National Academy Press.

Jaffe, J.H., & Martin, W.R. (1985). Opioid analgesics and antagonists. In A. Gilman, L.S. Goodman, T.W. Rall, & F. Murad (Eds.), *The pharmacological basis of therapeutics.* New York: Macmillan.

Jenike, M.A. (1987). Drug abuse. In E. Rubenstein & D.D. Federman (Eds.), *Scientific American medicine.* New York: Scientific American Press.

Kendler, K.S., Heath, A.C., Neale, M.C., Kessler, R.C., & Eaves, L.J. (1992). Population based twin-study of alcoholism in women. *Journal of the American Medical Association, 268,* 1877–1882.

Kessler, D.A., Barnett, P.S., Witt, A., Zeller, M.R., Mande, J.R., & Schultz, W.B. (1997). The legal and scientific basis for FDA's assertion of jurisdiction over cigarettes and smokeless tobacco products. *Journal of the American Medical Association, 277,* 405–409.

Khantzian, E.J. (1975). Self-selection and progression, I: Drug dependence. *American Journal of Psychotherapy, 36,* 19–22.

Kornitzer, M., Boutsen, M., Dramaix, M., Thijs, J., & Gustavsson, G. (1995). Combined use of nicotine patch and chewing gum in smoking cessation: A placebo-controlled clinical trial. *Preventive Medicine, 24,* 41–47.

Lancaster, O. (1966). A new approach to consumer theory. *Journal of Political Economy, 74,* 132–157.

Ludwig, A., & Lyle, W. (1964). The experimental production of narcotic drug effects and withdrawal symptoms through hypnosis. *The International Journal of Clinical and Experimental Hypnosis, 12,* 1–17.

Lyerly, S., Ross, S., Krugman, A., & Clyde, D. (1964). Drugs and placebos: The effects of instructions upon performance and mood under amphetamine sulfate and chloral hydrate. *Journal of Abnormal and Social Psychology, 68*, 321–327.

Maddux, J., & Desmond, D. (1982). Residence relocation inhibits opiate dependence. *Archives and General Psychiatry, 39*, 1313–1317.

Maddux, J., Desmond, D., & Costello, R. (1987). Depression in opioid users varies with substance abuse status. *American Journal of Drug and Alcohol Abuse, 13*, 375–378.

Malinowski, B. (1922). *Argonauts of the western Pacific.* London: Routledge & Kegan Paul.

Marshall, M. (Ed.). (1979). *Beliefs, behaviors and alcoholic beverages: A cross-cultural survey.* Ann Arbor, MI: University of Michigan.

McLellan, A.T., Bender, M., McKay, J.R., Janis, D., & Alterman, A.L. (1997). Can the outcomes research literature inform the search for quality indicators in substance abuse treatment? In Institute of Medicine (Ed.), *Managing managed care: Quality improvement in behavioral health.* Washington, DC: National Academy Press.

Mendelson, J., & Mello, N. (1986). *Alcohol use and abuse in America.* Boston: Little, Brown.

Michael, R., & Becker, G. (1973). On the new theory of consumer behavior. *Swedish Journal of Economics, 75*, 378–396.

Miller, D. (1987). *Mass consumption and material culture.* Cambridge, MA: Basil Blackwell.

MMWR (Morbidity and Mortality Weekly Report). (1994). Medical-care expenditures attributable to cigarette smoking—United States 1993. *Morbidity and Mortality Weekly Report, 45*(20), 413–418.

Newsweek (1986, March 17). Kids and cocaine. p. 43.

Nurco, D.N., Ball, J.C., Shaffer, J.W., & Hanlon, T.F. (1985). The criminality of narcotics addicts. *Journal of Nervous and Mental Disease, 173*, 94–102.

O'Brien, C.P. (1996). Drug addiction and drug abuse. In J.G. Hardman & L. Limbird (Eds.), *Goodman and Gilman's the pharmacologic basis of therapeutics* (9th ed.), (pp. 557–577). New York: McGraw-Hill.

O'Brien, C.P., & McLellan, A.T. (1996). Myths about the treatment of addiction. *Lancet, 347*, 237–240.

Office for National Drug Control Policy (1998a). *The national drug control strategy: 1997.* Washington, DC: ONDCP/U.S. Government Printing Office.

Office for National Drug Control Policy (1998b). *The national drug control strategy, 1997: FY 1998 Budget Summary.* Washington, DC: ONDCP/U.S. Government Printing Office.

O'Malley, S.S., Jaffe, A.J., Chang, G., Rode, S., Schottenfeld, R., Meyer, R.E., & Rounsaville, B. (1996). Six-month follow-up of naltrexone and psychotherapy for alcohol dependence. *Archives of General Psychiatry, 53*, 217–224.

Peele, S. (1990). *The diseasing of America.* New York: Simon & Schuster.

Platonov, K., & Matskevich, A. (1933). Hypnosis and the nervous system under the influence of alcohol. *Psychological Abstracts, 7*, 184.

Polanyi, K., & Arensberg, C. (1957). *Trade and market in early empires.* Glencoe, IL: Free Press.

Preteceille, E., & Terrail, J.-P. (1985). *Capitalism, consumption and needs.* New York: Blackwell.

Reed, C., & Witt, P.N. (1965). Factors contributing to unexpected reactions in two human drug placebo experiments. *Confina Psychiatrica, 8*, 57–68.

Rice, D.P., Kelman, S., & Miller, L. (1991). The economic costs of alcoholism. *Alcohol Health and Research World, 15*, 307–316.

Robins, L. (1973). A follow up of Vietnam drug users. Washington, DC: Special Action Office (for drug abuse prevention). Monograph, Series A, Number 2.

Robinson, T., & Berridge, K. (1993). The neural basis of drug craving: an incentive-sensitization theory of addiction. *Brain Research Reviews, 18*, 247–291.

Rook, D. (1987). The buying impulse. *Journal of Consumer Research, 14*, 189–199.

Rutz, A., and Orlove, M. (Eds.). (1989). *The Social Economy of Consumption.* Lanham, MD: University Press of America.

Satel, S.L., Southwick, S.M., & Gawin, F.H. (1991). Clinical features of cocaine-induced paranoia. *American Journal of Psychiatry, 148*, 495–498.

Shultz, J.M., Novotny, T.E., & Rice, D.P. (1991). Quantifying the disease impact of cigarette smoking with SAMMEC 11 software. *Public Health Reports, 106*, 326–333.

Stephens, R.C. (1991). *The street addict role: A theory of addiction.* Albany, NY: State University of New York Press.

Stewart, J., deWit, H., & Eikelboom, R. (1984). Role of unconditioned and conditioned drug effects in the self-administration of opiates and stimulants. *Psychological Review, 91*, 251–268.

Thomasson, H.R., Zeng, D., Mai, X.-L., McGarvey, S., Deka, R., & Li, T.-K. (1994). Population Distribution of ADH2 and ALDH2 Alleles. *Alcoholism: Clinical and Experimental Research* 18:60A.

Van Dyck, & Byck. (1982, March). Addiction. *Scientific American*, 128–141.

Veblen, T. (1953). *The theory of the leisure class.* Glencoe, IL: Free Press.

Waldorf, D., Reinarman, C., & Murphy, S. (1993). *Cocaine changes: The experience of using and quitting.* Philadelphia: Temple University Press.

Waterston, A. (1993). *Street addicts in the political economy.* Philadelphia: Temple University Press.

Weber, M. (1905/1958). *From Max Weber: Essays in sociology.* Oxford, UK: Oxford University Press.

SUGGESTED READING

Caplovitz, K. (1976). *The working addict.* New York: Graduate School of the City University of New York.

Clayton, R. (1981). The delinquency and drug use relationship among adolescents. In D. Lettieri & J. Ludford (Eds.), *Drug abuse and the American adolescent.* Rockville, MD: National Institute on Drug Abuse.

Cloward, R.D., & Ohlin, L.E. (1960). *Delinquency and opportunity: A theory of delinquent gangs.* Glencoe, IL: Free Press.

Gandossy, R., Williams, J., Cohen, J., & Hardwood, H. (1980). *Drugs and crime: A survey and analysis of the literature.* Washington, DC: National Institute of Justice.

Johnson, B.D., Goldstein, P.J., Preble, E., Schmeidler, J., Lipton, D., Spunt, B., & Miller, T. (1985). *Taking care of business: The economics of crime by heroin abusers.* Lexington, MA: Heath.

Kandel, D.B. (1980). Developmental stages in adolescent drug involvement. In M. Lettieri, *Theories on drug abuse: Selected contemporary perspectives.* NIDA Research Monograph No. 30. Washington, DC: Hemisphere-Wiley.

Kaplan, J. (1977). *Marijuana: The new prohibition.* Chicago: University of Chicago Press.

Kaplan, J. (1983). *The hardest drug: Heroin and drug policy.* Chicago: University of Chicago Press.

Lindesmith, A. (1947). *Opiate addiction.* Evanston, IL: Prinapia Press.

Young, J. (1971). *The drugtakers: The social meaning of drug use.* London: MacGibbon & Kee.

CHAPTER 10

Toward an Enlightened Drug Policy for the 21st Century

Chapter Objective

U.S. drug policy, as it now exists, has not relieved drug-related problems and may have even worsened them. Alternative drug policies of the future should aim to bring us closer to a more humane, democratic society.

This book has surveyed how drug use and distribution are implicated in local economies, job markets, the circumstances of persons' laboring lives, consumer behavior, crime, violence, law enforcement, and the ideals of parenthood, motherhood, and femininity. Drug phenomena were reciprocally related with the unique communal life of distinct neighborhoods. In the United States, the public debate about them was obscured by ideological concerns that greatly misrepresented or exaggerated that reciprocal relationship.

The efforts of American policymakers in bringing about this result were also examined. They revealed the tensions and animosities in American society. The drugs that the majority approved were openly marketed; those associated (often exaggeratedly) with minorities were proscribed. It would not overstate the case to assert that antipathy toward minorities frequently dictated the drug policy response. Ruling elites exploited the rhetoric linking drugs with moral decay, the erosion of femininity and motherhood, and endangered family values to reimpose contested regulatory and disciplinary regimens on recent immigrants and the working classes generally.

The evolution of U.S. drug policy demonstrates how the system of punitive prohibition prevailed over a more liberal approach to drug use and attendant problems. The view that drug users were personally to blame for contracting a habit that caused them to become criminal, diseased, or disadvantaged psychosocially had been influential since the colonial period. Medical care and treatment would do nothing for what was essentially a moral depravity. Prison was the only answer.

The system of punitive prohibition was greatly strengthened in the 1920s and 1930s (Reinarman & Levine, 1997). It became the "traditional response to an increase in drug abuse to escalate the penalties for drug offenses through mandatory minimum terms of imprisonment [for possession, use, and small-scale distribution], punishing repeated offenses with greater severity, and making the drug offender ineligible for suspension of sentence, probation and parole" (President's Commission 1967, quoted in Reinarman and Levine, p. 323).

In opposition, liberals in the post–World War II era, relying on sociologists and psychologists, linked drug abuse with juvenile delinquency and other social ills. These persisted, they argued, because government needed to "finish the work of the New Deal." Rising heroin use in the 1960s was a "barometer" of the pressures caused by "poverty, segregation, slums, psychological immaturity, ignorance and misery" (Fort, 1962, p. 41).

Espousing the disease concept of addiction, liberals fought for a greater emphasis on prevention and treatment. Some claimed that the idea of pharmacological duress protected addicts from legal sanctions when buying drugs or even when committing crimes. The liberal cause was shouldered by the legal and criminal justice establishments, which were burdened by the overload of drug cases. Nevertheless, while opposing the heavy penalties drug users faced, liberals disabled them by reducing their autonomy, medicalizing their drug-related problems, and surrendering them to yet other agencies of the state.

While the conservative attitude has triumphed after the postwar gains of liberals, and especially in the past three decades, a temporary truce in the early 21st century may at least restore the balance, if not propel deliberation to a higher, better-informed plane.

THE DEVELOPMENTAL CYCLE OF DRUG EPIDEMICS

It is helpful to remember, for example, that, despite drug-war polemics, drug fashions, fads, or epidemics are finite phenomena that will never entice more than a minority, let alone "all of America" or "the civilized world as we know it."*

Recent declines in New York City's low-income, minority neighborhoods in both crack use and distribution were felicitous for drug researchers because they were such a reminder. The period 1981–1991 also contributed much to under-

---

*The following 18 paragraphs were adapted with permission from A. Hamid, "1992 Developmental Cycle of Drug Epidemic," Vol. 24, No. 4, pp. 337–338, © 1997, *Journal of Psychoacticve Drugs*.

standing why human beings in every known culture have used drugs, and why certain drugs may sometimes become a problem for a small proportion of them. This was so because the period spanned from beginning to end of the entire developmental cycle of a drug epidemic—the "cocaine smoking epidemic." Although opportunities to research the early stages in the cycle were not seized by government funding agencies, there was nevertheless painstaking work done by some scholars (Bourgois, 1989; Hamid, 1990; Maher & Curtis, 1992; Williams, 1989); the later stages were researched as well as reported by the media extensively. Most of the materials for an overall assessment were therefore available.

Ethnographic experience of the complete developmental cycle of the cocaine smoking epidemic enabled researchers to differentiate and describe six stages through which it had progressed. Successive contexts for cocaine use, and especially the six-stage cycle for cocaine smoking, permitted the diffusion of the practice from one social segment to another, erasing social distinctions, creating new ones, and allowing cocaine to acquire new meanings and effects (Hamid, 1992).

Thus, New Yorkers experienced onset to cocaine smoking in 1979–1981 in *after-hours clubs*, after it had resurfaced among former heroin injectors (see also Chapter 6). As marijuana supplies dwindled and cocaine became more available, marijuana distributors were drawn into experimentation with its use and distribution, in *freebase parlors*. When these locales could no longer cater to the demand they had helped to stimulate, and as their proprietors lost viability on account of personal use, they were succeeded by two types of *crack houses*, operated by young minority males who shunned cocaine smoking themselves. The latter also invented a felicitous marketing strategy, of presenting the drug in a ready-to-use form, as crack. A period of *curbside use and distribution* coincided with the most widespread diffusion of the drug and witnessed a proliferation of distributors. Stages of peak, decline, and stabilization followed, in which the number of users and distributors decreased, and use was confined in neighborhoods to *freakhouses* (Hamid, 1992; Hamid et al., 1997).

Many lessons were drawn from an overview of the "cocaine smoking epidemic," which had not been apparent earlier in its course. The concept of the developmental cycle of a drug epidemic taught the following.

A "Cocaine Smoking Epidemic," Not a "Crack Epidemic"

The first lesson to be learned concerned nomenclature. The United States of America, as well as South America (where the epidemic may have originated), Latin America, and the Caribbean islands (which suffered onset earlier than the United States) were afflicted by a "cocaine smoking epidemic," not a "crack epidemic." The periods of freebase smoking, which preceded crack, could not be disregarded, since they shaped further developments.

Drug Epidemics Come to an End

The second lesson is that, indeed, drug epidemics do have developmental cycles, and contrary to the official belief, will not continue rampant unless checked by exogenous factors, such as law enforcement. They have "a beginning, a middle and an end," as Aristotle recommended. The developmental cycle is characterized by periods of initiation, widespread diffusion, peak, and decline. The final stage is stabilization at reduced levels of use (Becker, 1963). For example, in the "heroin injecting epidemic" of 1964–1972, a brief period of initiation was also followed by rapid diffusion among minority males (African American and Hispanic) in their early 20s. From 3% of that age cohort in 1963, the number of heroin injectors climbed to 20% in 1970. By 1973, however, only 13% remained heroin injectors. Reduced still further in number and percentage, and now in their late 40s and 50s, they endure as the only heroin injectors in New York City today; succeeding generations have shunned the drug altogether. Similarly, the crack misusers of the year 2000 will be the lingering survivors of the 1981–1991 epidemic.

A comparison of as many of these cycles for which there were complete data would serve useful scientific ends. It would enable researchers to explore the processes (socioeconomic and political, as well as cultural and psychological) that occur in each and in the transition from one to another. For example, a protracted "incubation period," in which a very few initiates experiment with the drug, weeding out bad effects from the good, appears to be necessary for a drug's most benign introduction to a population. Onset to marijuana, for example, occurred in the early 1960s, but the drug became widely popular only at the end of the decade. It may be critical to an understanding of the effects of smoking cocaine to recognize that it traversed rapidly through five "incubation periods" in 10 years (after-hours clubs, freebase parlors, crack houses, curbside, and freakhouses), in each of which significant features of set and setting were altered.

Alcohol, tea, chocolate, coffee, and tobacco have had cycles of use among European peoples for several hundred years. All are tropical in origin (except alcohol, which was borrowed from the Mediterranean wherever it was not native). These drugs are today fully incorporated into the cultures of European peoples, but their foreign, tropical source is still resisted through recurrent periods of abstinence (see Chapter 1).

Another set of substances, although native to the Old World, like fly-agaric mushrooms or the infamous psychoactives and poisons of Medieval Europe—mandrake root, belladonna, henbane—have fallen into disuse and ill-repute with the passing of time, and are preserved today only in pharmaceutical preparations.

It appears that the more recently introduced psychoactives such as heroin, opium, cocaine, marijuana, and peyote (among others) will suffer the same fate as the latter. Although each has had several cycles over the past 200 years, they were of limited duration, and remain strictly localized, in that they in no way approached the popularity that alcohol, tea, chocolate, coffee, and tobacco enjoyed.

Opponents of the idea of drug legalization who fear that unrestricted access to the members of the second group would result in disastrous drug epidemics should take heart in remembering how selective Western societies have been in the matter of drugs, and that the present age is one in which consciousness of health concerns rather than of altered states is a major preoccupation. Accordingly, even the excessive consumption of alcohol, tea, coffee, chocolate, and tobacco is viewed as dangerously sybaritic.

Do Drug Epidemics Resemble Disease Epidemics or Consumer Fads?

It is important to decide how to picture the developmental cycle of a drug epidemic. For example, does it resemble the course of a disease epidemic? If it does, a suitable terminology would include "contagion," "at risk," or "disease carrier." Suitable policy measures would include: "antidote," "quarantine," or "surgical removal" (i.e., pharmacological and law-enforcement strategies).

In the approach taken in this book, drug epidemics more resemble "spending fads," or consumer fashions. If they do, another set of concepts is needed (see Chapter 9).

Users and Distributors Metamorphose over the Course of the Epidemic

Another lesson is that the characteristics and identities of personnel change over the course of the epidemic. For example, when cycles are first generated, it appears that users initiate distribution among fairly exclusive groups of fellow users. Later, these same distributors gear up to meet increasing demand, but their personal use also increases and eventually destroys their viability in distribution. They are then succeeded by a variety of nonusing distributors. Thus, crack distributors have been correctly described as instantly and fabulously wealthy/instantly impoverished; poor and destitute/earning a middling income; organized in gangs or in tightly hierarchized businesses/individualistic free-lancers; and indoors (freebase parlors? crack houses? freakhouses?)/curbside. The appeal of legitimate jobs as alternatives to crack distribution has been both very weak and very urgent. It depended on the stage in the developmental cycle.

Users and effects have also changed over the course of the epidemic. At first, smoking cocaine was an expensive luxury, and its use was restricted to affluent persons who did not find it instantly addictive. Later, when it had been adopted by a less affluent and more heterogeneous population, and one moreover, that exhibited high consumption periodicities in regard to other (legal and illegal) commodities, variable effects were experienced, including compulsion and "bingeing." Today many users and misusers have simply given up smoking cocaine, even without the benefit of professional help; its appeal has faded for them. While the pharmacology of the drug and the physiology (or mental health status) of its users remained constant, shifting social identities or economic contexts (including the movement of cocaine prices and the conditions of supply) appear to be stronger determinants of the drug's variable effects.

How Drug Epidemics Succeed One Another/Implications for Policy

A further lesson, corollary of the foregoing, is that policy ought to be flexible. For example, while there may have been some meaning in 1987 to the popular, erroneous impression that crack use would entrap all of America, or that neighborhoods had been "invaded" by crack, and needed to be "reclaimed," it makes little sense in 1997, when crack misusers are licking old wounds in indoor retreats (freakhouses where distribution is forbidden), or when crack distributors have been reduced both in number and substance. A "kinder, gentler America" certainly seems more affordable today.

The idea of a developmental cycle of drug epidemics, incorporating distinct stages of initiation, widespread diffusion, peak, decline, and stabilization is a reminder that the dangers and opportunities of a drug are different from stage to stage, and should be met by policy sensitive to change. Perhaps the most critical stage is the one in which crack is now. At this point apparently, policy can be the most effective factor in the cycle, in terms of preventing future epidemics.

The idea also reveals a powerful mechanical control on drug use. Drug fashions, like other consumer trends, progress along a typical developmental cycle of onset and initiation, incubation, widespread diffusion, peak, stabilization, and decline. Left to themselves, they soon run their course and are spent. There seems to be some sort of balancing act that occurs between the forces that encourage drug abuse and those that discourage it. Most likely these agencies are numerous and multidimensional and include drug properties, genetic and biological conditions, learning experiences, neighborhood conditions, family environment, and even global societal and political events.

This inherent limitation in the popularity of any drug argues against reckless fearmongering ("unless we act, soon all Americans will be addicted to . . ."), gives the assurance that drug "fads" have a beginning, a middle, and a definite end, and recommends the flexible adjustment of policy to this progression. Even the legal drugs, such as alcohol, tobacco, or coffee, have not claimed all Americans, despite aggressive marketing and their enormous, sanctioned appeal.

Declines in cigarette smoking and alcohol consumption are testaments to the power of informal controls. Before cigarette smokers were required by law to smoke outside their office buildings, restaurants, and other public places, they had acquiesced to spouses and children and were smoking outside of their homes, on terraces, lawns, or the stoop. Rising indignation against the tragedies caused by drunken driving had spurred partygoers to elect a "designated driver" and impose other safeguards on their drinking. The sharp drop in American alcohol consumption, and the preference for "lite" beer and wines over "hard" liquor, was accomplished entirely at this level of interpersonal negotiation, backed by stiff penalties for injuries or other damage.

Incubation Times

Time itself injects control into a user's consumption pattern. For a drug to be introduced most benignly to a community, a long incubation time is necessary. In this period, users experiment with drugs, discover the best routes of administration, distinguish between good and bad effects, and learn to cultivate the former and expunge the latter before diffusing it to others.

Conditions for a long, successful incubation period are best provided where experimenters are left unmolested. In the case of the Caribbean Africans described in Chapter 6, initiates experimented with marijuana in virtual seclusion for nearly 5 years in the late 1960s and subsequently earned positive rewards from its diffusion. With smokable cocaine in the 1980s, six formats for use rapidly succeeded each other, making it appear as though as many drugs had been introduced and resulting in confusion and regrettable outcomes.

DRUG-RELATED HARM

Drugs are unattractive to the majority of persons in most societies (see Extent of Use, Chapter 1) because, in addition to the pleasurable effects—the droll, merry, or insightful distortions of space, time, and ordinary perceptions, and blissful feelings—they may also have pronounced unpleasant effects. Vomiting, sweating, hot and cold flashes, unquenchable thirst, tremors, constipation or diarrhea, accelerated pulse and heart rate, paralysis, overdosing, poisoning, fright, paranoid or schizophrenic ideation, and other indecorous behavior could be accompaniments.

Drugs are the source of some very substantial concerns for individuals and communities. Although very few young children are interested in drugs, getting drunk or intoxicated interferes with maturation and diverts time from homework and play. Although very few use them in the workplace, drug-impaired airplane pilots or operators of dangerous machinery could be hazards. Illegal street drug markets add to the deficits of the poor neighborhoods that host them. Compulsive drug use, however small, harms not only the individual sufferer, but families and neighborhoods. Health risks, such as human immunodeficiency virus (HIV)/acquired immunodeficiency syndrome (AIDS), and other sexually transmitted diseases (STD), hepatitis, and tuberculosis, should not be countenanced. Persons who excuse their violent behavior by blaming drugs are still a threat to communal peace.

The American experience of legal drugs such as alcohol and tobacco is sobering. Although their consumption has declined steadily, in the case of alcohol since colonial times, for tobacco since the invention of cigarette-making machines, it has nonetheless bequeathed society plenty of problems. Alcohol-related accidents and emergencies, loss in worker productivity, family dysfunction, and hospitalizations for major complaints such as cancer, emphysema, and heart disease and the legal actions that they prompt have absorbed too much of society's wealth and energies.

Drug use in all societies must be regulated. But regulation too may find pathological expressions.

DRUG POLICY IN THE UNITED STATES AND ABROAD COMPARED

The police siege of Bushwick described in Chapter 4 exemplified the system of punitive prohibition that ruled during the crack era and continues to be emblematic of the application of U.S. drug policy. In that situation, it seemed that communities depended upon gangs of disadvantaged youths to reduce levels of violence the state had sponsored through abrasive police tactics.

The unflattering social drama of (mostly) European-American policemen smashing down doors with battering rams in minority neighborhoods and leading off young African Americans, Latinos, or Asians in handcuffs for minor drug offenses (usually the possession of a small quantity of marijuana for personal use) is not replicated anywhere else on earth (or only in the most repressive regimes). In Amsterdam, Edinburgh, Liverpool, or Sydney, for example, the enraged screams, racial slurs, and hateful epithets that fly from officers' mouths in America as they "bust" offenders are replaced frequently by a concerned, caring, solicitous tone of voice, as their counterparts direct or even chauffeur drug users to needle exchanges, hospitals, treatment centers, or social service agencies.

The outrage is compounded when corrupt American policemen execute these aggressions in drug wars. Some themselves misuse the drugs they arrest others for possessing or distributing. The most notorious have not only used drugs but have distributed them brutally and profitably (Gunst, 1997; Hamid et al., 1997; MacAlary, 1990).

Police behave very differently in other countries, especially when they can resist the tremendous American political pressure to emulate the American drug war.

Drugs are not as great a problem in Canada, despite steady bombardment about "drug panics" by the American media. Although Canada relies on the same system of punitive prohibition as in the United States, drug arrests in Canada are never more than two thirds the rate in the United States. Epidemiological surveys of adult and student populations in the United States and Canada show levels of cocaine use in the United States three or four times higher than those in Canada (Cheung & Erickson, 1997).

Although Canada was alerted by U.S. and local media about the "crack plague" that would afflict Canadian cities in the 1980s, only low prevalence rates of crack use and low frequencies of use were subsequently detected. Except for street youths in Toronto, Canadian users did not find crack use compulsive and could refrain from using it for months at a time. Only 9% of a community sample became daily users. They often preferred other drugs, including cocaine powder, over it (Cheung & Erikson, 1997).

Drugs are not as great a problem in Australia. One sociologist was surprised, and enumerated several reasons why they should be. Both Australia and the United States are

> . . . modern, urban, industrial, capitalist democracies (with all the things that all this implies). They share a common language and a similar Anglo-Christian, multicultural tradition. Their polities are remarkably similar—a federation of states with a bicameral parliament. Travel between the two nations is common, and Australia both imports American cultural material (from *CNN News* to the *Cosby Show*) and exports some back (*Crocodile Dundee,* etc). (Mugford, 1997, p. 194)

Yet there was no comparable pattern of crack use in Australia during the 1980s as in the United States (Mugford, 1997).

Drugs are not as great a problem in the Netherlands. Drug-related problems, such as HIV/AIDS transmission through needle sharing or other risky drug use are simply minimal, if not nonexistent. Drug-related property or violent crime is also nonexistent and is not viewed separately from the generally low incidence of crime. Like Australia and Canada, the Netherlands escaped the crack scourge that American policymakers had promised it in the 1980s. Few Dutch persons use it, despite the absence of punitive prohibition (Cohen, 1997).

William Burroughs, a person who was drawn to drugs and heroin use out of a highly intellectual curiosity, concluded in his many writings that the war against drugs is one of the principal strategies by which American "control freaks" dominated the national social and cultural life. They have nearly succeeded in globalizing that hegemony. Many drug-enforcement tactics and sanctions were developed and refined in the United States—including undercover operations, extensive employment of paid informants and electronic surveillance, asset forfeiture laws, farreaching conspiracy statutes, drug testing programs and mandatory minimum and long-term prison sentences. The amount and proportion of police resources and prison space devoted to drug-law enforcement have increased dramatically in virtually every country (Nadelmann, 1993).

DRUGS AND SOCIAL PROBLEMS

What makes American drug problems greater than those of other comparable modern nations, or than those of traditional societies?

Comparisons between drug use in traditional and modern societies must be made with care. The homogeneity of the former affords opportunities for peaceful human organization that are denied in our deeply and complexly divided societies. As a result, while traditional drug use is usually regarded as an integrative positive institution, some modern drug use is problematic.

As Chapter 8 has indicated, one of the great differences between modern European and American cities is the existence in the latter of large inner cities sheltering sizable populations of disadvantaged, disenfranchised citizens.

Another difference is the political consensus. Better-off Americans seem comfortable with the idea that persons who suffer underclass conditions deserve them. If they did not like them, they reason, they would struggle to escape. If they do not escape, they do not really "want" to. Americans blame the poor for their poverty and obscure the link between it and drug abuse or other social problems. They resent the invasion of public spaces like subways and sidewalks by the disadvantaged and their refusal to remain "invisible." Citizens of the industrialized nations of Europe are appalled by these inflexible attitudes and are generally swift to alleviate the suffering of their fellow countrymen.

Thus, the principal reason why the United States is afflicted by worse drug abuse and attendant problems than almost every other industrialized nation is that social justice has been less amply served. Political opportunism, racial division, a vastly unequal distribution of wealth, the intransigence and immaturity of powerful elites, and persistent poverty adversely affects the every behavior—including the drug use—of those who must suffer them.

Drugs are less of a problem in Canada because of Canada's more extensive welfare system, including universal medical care and a national race relations policy of multiculturalism. Together, these social policies prevent the formation of a large, poverty-stricken underclass in inner-city ghettos in which certain racial groups (such as African Americans and Latinos in the United States) are overrepresented. The low level of criminality and the relative lack of inner-city problems mitigate against drug abuse in Canada (Smart, 1983).

Drug are less a problem in Australia because of other sociocultural differences. More Australians live in big cities than do Americans, who tend to cultivate provincial outlooks in the small towns, suburbs, and "rural" cities where they mostly originate. American cities are characterized by residential and lifestyle segregation, with resource-rich suburban areas far distant from decaying inner cities. The former enjoys a rich tax base, while the latter, though in greater need of services, have fewer taxpayers to afford them. In Australian cities, schools, health care, and policing, financed by state rather than local tax boards, are distributed and endowed more evenly. In Australia, the racial minority of Aborigines is not confined to inner cities as in America, but in the "outback." Consequently, their alcohol abuse does not afflict cities. Where small inner-city-like enclaves have grown in Australian capitals in the wake of recent immigration from Southeast Asia, problematic heroin and cocaine use has followed (Maher & Dixon, 1996). Even in this circumstance, however, the emphasis on humane treatment by the police in Australia, a former penal colony founded on the principle of the rehabilitation of prisoners in the 1790s, has slowed the marginalization and immiseration of drug misusers.

Drugs are less a problem in the Netherlands. In a contrast between drug using contexts in Rotterdam and New York, some startling differences were uncovered (Grund, Stern, Kaplan, Drucker, & Adriaans, 1992). Rotterdam had been bombed by the Germans in the 1940s: today, it has been entirely rebuilt, with sparkling new buildings covering the whole city area. There are no stretches of blocks of torched, abandoned buildings and empty, rubble-strewn lots such as those that blight the South Bronx (or Harlem, Flatbush, East New York, and many other sections) in New York City, which has never suffered the ravages of full-scale, modern war. Thus, in Rotterdam, unlike New York City, there are simply no available spaces in which drug users or distributors may "squat" to carry on their activities. Most important, while the South Bronx was an epicenter of the AIDS epidemic in New York, seroconversion rates in Rotterdam were low.

The greater provision of social services and a nonpunitive, harm-reductionist approach to drug regulation have also impacted heavily on the intimate contexts in which drug users and distributors meet, exchange, and use drugs. Beneficiaries of some of the most liberal unemployment, health, and housing policies in the world, Dutch drug users find themselves in contexts quite unlike the squalid, unhygienic ones that their American counterparts must endure. Not subject to police hostility and abuse, but confident that they will receive on request free needles, counseling, and emergency medical services, or even child care if needed, Dutch users have no need to hide, hurry, and mistrust one another. Aside from crackdowns on about 200, mainly Surinamese heroin injectors, "Dutch social policies have made the social and physical situation of most of the addicts in Amsterdam relatively good; mortality is relatively low and most lead relatively normal, inconspicuous lives" (Cohen 1997, p. 212; Korf & Hoogenhoot, 1997; Sluis, Cobelman, & Schrader, 1990). Drug use is nearly nonexistent outside the major cities, and drug-related crime is not considered separately from the general crime problem, which in the Netherlands is a fraction of what it is in the United States (Currie, 1985).

This book has briefly reviewed the problems in America related to local economies, job markets, persons' laboring lives, consumer behavior, race relations, crime, violence, law-enforcement agencies, parenthood, motherhood, femininity, and communities. Unless these are addressed directly, every kind of behavior, including drug use, will remain distorted.

Drugs have by no means left the inner city. Many young people reside there who have the skills and experience required to distribute drugs effectively. Should a new substance gain popularity, there will be no shortage of hands who know how to deliver it to the widest clientele.

The motivation to sell drugs, especially past the initiation stage of use, is wholly economic. If they were offered jobs, most distributors say they would leave distribution altogether. In recently tape-recorded interviews, several distributors (ranging from a college student who sells once a month to "make ends meet" to a street–level user/distributor who lives hand-to-mouth in a pre-homeless condition and sells daily), have complained that they were dissatisfied with this work. They were precise in describing viable alternatives. As a 31-year-old Caribbean-African male immigrant from Grenada put it:

> I am ready for something new. I am a printer by trade and I have family responsibilities, and after hustling [distributing drugs] since I was fifteen and getting nowhere, I would take a steady job. Ain't I-man been working steady [i.e., in drug distribution] all these years? I am ready to work. But not at $5 or $6 an hour! I might as well go and rob instead of that. How could I pay rent, or buy food and clothes, or take care of the children with that? But with $9 or $10 an hour—for that, I-man could work. (Hamid et al., 1997)

The promise of large amounts of cash, and a life of luxury and power, has seduced successive age-cohorts of youngsters into undertaking criminal drug distribution. Frequently, use followed. Appealing to both rich and poor, it competes strongly against the patience that perseverance in school or job training or joining the family firm requires. More generations will be sacrificed in the future unless efforts are made in America comparable to those elsewhere.

DISSATISFACTIONS WITH PROHIBITION

Instead of attending to the social ills that make any behavior potentially problematic, American policymakers have declared war on drugs, as though their misuse was the cause rather than a symptom. Arnold Trebach (1987) ends his book, *The Great American Drug War*, with a reflection on American wars generally. He begins with the small range wars between cattlemen and sheepherders in the American West. They were based entirely on ignorance of basic scientific facts. Sheep and cattle actually like one another, and both species, as well as their human owners, would have thrived far better in one another's company than apart. Excluding World War II and perhaps the Korean War, he finds no compelling reasons for the invasions of the American Southwest, Cuba, or the Philippines. During World War II there was no need for confining Japanese Americans and Italian Americans in concentration camps. Finally, the war in Vietnam, which cost 58,000 young American lives, was also unjustifiable.

The war on drugs is like these conflicts, Trebach finds, in being based on fundamental errors of fact. The most fundamental overlooked truth is that, like cattle and sheep herders, drug users and nonusers can live peacefully side by side and could even profit mutually by doing so.

American drug policy relies on criminal justice bureaucracies and treatment empires. When scrutinized, they prove inefficient and ineffective.

Criminal Sanctions

International drug-enforcement interventions, interdiction, and high-level and street-level domestic drug enforcement efforts are already substantially extended, but have not succeeded in preventing drug abuse. Crop eradication and substitution programs have resulted in "guerrilla farming" methods by producers. Moreover, crops such as marijuana and opium can be grown in many places. Of the 2.5 million square miles of land in South America that can be brought under coca cultivation, only 700 are used so far. "Guerrilla farming" has brought large areas under the control of armed traffickers, who act as rivals to the legitimate government. Although the Coast Guard and U.S. Customs have sophisticated equipment and are busy at the nation's borders, the prices of drugs have fallen steadily while their purity and availability have risen since the mid-1980s (Nadelmann, 1989).

They have been most successful in intercepting the more bulky marijuana, a success that has resulted in the United States itself becoming a major producer of potent marijuanas, and the diversion of marijuana distributors to cocaine (see Chapter 6).

Fears of crack drove government to spend $10 billion on these approaches in 1987 and $20 billion by 1995. Federal expenditures rose from less than $1 billion in 1987 to $8.2 billion in 1995. By 1995, to warehouse more than 400,000 drug law violators in local jails and state and federal prisons, expenditures approached $10 billion. More than 65% of the 95,000 inmates in federal prisons and more than one fifth of those in state prisons and local jails had been put there for drug violations, at a cost of $20,000 to $40,000 per person. The mandatory minimum sentences have sent increasing numbers of nonviolent offenders for long prison terms and have punished minorities overwhelmingly (Reinarman & Levine, 1997).

The direct costs of building and maintaining enough prisons to house this growing population are rising astronomically. These costs are diverted from apprehending and imprisoning more serious criminals, and from other social expenditures. In many cities, urban law enforcement has come to mean drug-law enforcement (Nadelmann, 1989).

Criminal sanctions benefit drug traffickers by inflating the price of drugs. By spending billions on enforcement, government enables traffickers to earn from $10 to $50 billion in illegal profits (Nadelmann, 1989).

It is not clear that drug users commit crime because of their drug use (see Chapter 4), but spending money on prevention and education probably has better results than incarceration. Putting more people in prison would not reduce crimes; putting more policemen on the street to prevent them, and spending more on social services that expunge the criminal urge altogether might.

The impact of the justice juggernaut does not include reduced street crime. The official National Crime Survey reported that in 1985, despite almost two decades of law-and-order politics and get-tough programs, 5 million households were victims of at least one violent crime—rape, robbery, or assault. In 1987, the Federal Bureau of Investigation (FBI) reported more than 20,000 murders (including nonnegligent homicide), a rate of 15% higher than in 1969 (and three times higher than in Canada, if Interpol data for earlier years can be relied upon (Reinarman & Levine, 1997).

Treatment Empires

Large national chains of treatment facilities, as well as an extensive web operated by smaller-scale, local entrepreneurs, are hostile to any diminishment of drug problems, as their livelihoods depend on them, and are unresistant to new developments in treatment philosophy and strategies.

Drug-testing companies have been enriched, and now perform analyses of urine, blood, saliva, and hair, despite the incursions they make on the privacy of individuals and their high fallibility.

The logic of American drug policy has been to produce more users, riskier modes of administration, adulterated drugs, and fear and paranoia about using them. For example, in the most general sense, drug prohibition caused the cocaine smoking epidemic of 1981–1991 (see Chapter 2).

DRUGS AND CIVIL LIBERTIES

The greatest blessings of being American are the protections guaranteed to each citizen by the Bill of Rights. It anticipates that the ideals of personal liberty and empowerment are continuously evolving and never fully attained, but simultaneously commits the nation to support each American in the attempt to reach them. Accordingly, there is, in principle, no "ceiling" on rights in the United States, only a steadily rising "floor" under which none must sink.

The war on drugs, playing on primal fears among Americans, has often seduced them into surrendering their most precious birthright. Terrified by imagined dangers, they are surrendering gains that were won only after protracted and bloody struggle.

> History teaches that grave threats to liberty often come in times of urgency, when constitutional rights seem too extravagant to endure. The World War II camp cases, and the Red Scare and McCarthy-era internal subversion cases, are only the most extreme reminders that when we allow fundamental freedoms to be sacrificed in the name of real or per-

ceived exigency, we invariably come to regret it. (Thurgood Marshall, quoted in Glasser & Siegel, 1997, p. 229)

Drug laws have always harmed minorities, and indeed, were sometimes expressly designed to do so. The crack scare in the 1980s reversed for African Americans and other minorities important victories they had won during the Civil Rights struggle in the 1960s. Drug-law enforcement has restored violations of due process, unusual and cruel punishment, expanded surveillance, search-and-arrest powers by the state, and mandatory minimum sentences, many of which had been revoked.

Because of drug-law enforcement, the United States has the highest known rate of incarceration in the world (Mauer, 1991). In 1991, male African Americans were incarcerated at a rate of four times that of African males in South Africa, which then had "apartheid," an official policy of exclusion, aggression, and terror against the Africans.

INFORMAL CONTROLS

Informal controls work best to prevent and control all kinds of potentially risky behavior (Sampson, 1986). They also conform better with American democratic political ideals. Parents, children, adults, young persons, and communities as a whole negotiate among themselves, through (often imperceptible) cultural and political mechanisms, what is acceptable, for whom, in what manner, and on which occasions.

A new improved drug education campaign, which presents balanced views on drugs and drug-related topics, would be the most important element in such an effort.

LEGALIZATION AND DECRIMINALIZATION

The social and economic costs of drug prohibition laws (see above) have prompted numerous recent calls for the legalization or decriminalization of illicit drugs. These exhortations have come from both conservative and liberal sections of the political spectrum (Buckley et al., 1996). The social and economic benefits of repeal are said to far outweigh the costs of keeping these laws in place. For example, repeal would mean that the possession, consumption, and distribution of drugs would no longer be illegal, and thus criminal justice costs would be substantially reduced. Also, since buying, using, and distributing drugs would no longer be illegal, prices would fall, and this in turn would affect the amount of acquisitive crime committed to fund drug use (Nadelmann, 1989).

Informal controls would have the field if drugs were legalized. "Drug peace" would oblige those who strongly opposed drugs to promote alternatives by giving away organic fruit juices, free meditation training, and information at every street corner. The comely Salvation Army captain would once more rescue the Bowery bum from the debauched life, dispensing with the intervening decades of cursing, violent, corrupt policemen, clogged courts, and millions in prisons.

Several drug legalization scenarios have been suggested. The most radical would appoint the Treasury Department to oversee the cultivation, production, quality control, import, and distribution of drugs. Since the prices of drugs, when legalized, would fall precipitously ($200 per kilo of cocaine, $400 per kilo of heroin, and home-grown marijuana for the cost of production, which could be nothing), the Treasury Department would distribute them free of charge to local groups of subscribers. This would separate the deadly mixture of money and drugs. Attractive, hygienic, medically monitored facilities could be set aside for users, and they could be encouraged to restrict their use to these locales only.

In other scenarios, marijuana would be legalized, while varying degrees of control would be applied to other drugs and perhaps, to special categories of persons. The formula for such regulations would rest on several assumptions. For example, some individuals may be biologically predisposed to drug dependence. There are documented individual differences in genetically influenced personality and temperamental traits: in physiological, metabolic, and biochemical processes and in the body's reactions to drug exposure. Another observable principle is that some drugs are more attractive to some persons than others: they have a "drug of choice." Some drugs may be more addicting than others: nicotine, caffeine, cocaine, heroin, amphetamine, or alcohol. Finally, drug taking is acquired and maintained through learning processes.

In still other propositions, such as those approved in 1996 by voters in Arizona and California, drug use and distribution would be increasingly medicalized. Doctors would prescribe them to persons who needed them for relief or to improve their health.

HARM REDUCTION

Short of drug legalization and still under existing laws, local and national authorities could implement harm-reductionist strategies. Several cities in the world now follow the harm reduction path: Amsterdam, Liverpool, Frankfurt, Madrid, Hamburg, Sydney, San Francisco, New Haven, and Zurich.

How can policymakers reduce the risks that drug users will acquire infections such as HIV, hepatitis B and C, and tuberculosis; suffer an overdose; or develop dangerous abscesses? How can they reduce the likelihood that drug users will engage in criminal and other undesirable activities that harm others? How can they increase the chances that drug users will act responsibly toward others, take care of their families, complete their education or training, and engage in legal employment? How can they increase the likelihood of rehabilitation for drug users who have opted to change their lives? And how, more generally, do they ensure that drug-control policies not cause more harm to drug users and society at large than drug use itself (Nadelmann, 1998)?

Harm reduction is a new name for an old concept (Nadelmann, 1998). During the 19th and early 20th centuries, when potent new drugs became available, drug-control efforts focused less on prohibiting opiates and other drugs and more on ensuring quality, purity, and safe dose levels (Berridge & Edwards, 1981). In Great Britain, the influential Rolleston Report of 1926 formalized the policy of allowing (mainly middle-class) opiate users to obtain their drugs from their physicians (Berridge & Edwards, 1981). Morphine maintenance programs in the United States earlier in this century similarly reflected harm-reduction precepts, as did efforts to persuade drug misusers to switch to safer drugs (Waldorf & Murphy, 1977). During the late 19th and early 20th centuries, many doctors in the United States advised alcoholic patients for whom abstinence did not seem a realistic option to switch from alcohol to opiates (Siegel, 1986).

The modern theory of harm reduction emerges out of community-based, public health interventions that support drug users and their communities in reducing drug-related harm. It was pioneered by the Dutch. It challenges the traditional social service provision and moral/criminal/disease models of drug use by focusing on maximizing individual and community health through participation rather than repression. Harm reduction recognizes that it is the context and situation in which drugs are used that can cause harm, and not necessarily drug use itself. Practitioners of harm reduction distinguish themselves from other service providers by their willingness to engage nonjudgmentally with all people, regardless of personal values, acknowledging the intrinsic value and dignity of all human beings.

Harm reduction is about individual and community empowerment, a sorely felt need in a field dominated by hierarchical interests. A fundamental component of the approach is the reinsertion of the person into an expanding caring network. Agencies inspired by this philosophy commit substantial energies to community organizing, advocacy at community and regional forums, and networking, which gives service providers, outreach workers, drug users, communities, and others opportunities to develop relationships and collaborations with other individuals and agencies working in the field or affected by drug use.

By organizing user groups, harm reduction practitioners impart information on harm-reduction policy, history, politics, legal issues, law enforcement, prison and parole management, philosophy, ethics and theory, art and culture, the mass media, representation of drug users and drug use, art as harm reduction, and the use of culture in harm-reduction strategies. Thus they enable drug users to organize around issues and policies affecting their lives and communities. Issues facing people working in the field of drug-related harm, such as stress management, are also addressed. Sexual health, safer sex, sexual rights, sex work, STD and HIV/AIDS prevention, and mental health are also considered. The aspect of spiritual discovery and reawakening is not ignored. Population-specific harm-reduction strategies for youth, women, communities of color, men, gay communities, runaway adolescents, or homeless colonies are also sought.

Methadone maintenance was an early harm-reductionist strategy. Introduced first in the United States during the 1960s, the practice has since been adopted in dozens of countries. Its central ingredient is the provision of methadone—a long-acting opiate—to heroin and other opiate users who are unable or unwilling to abstain from opiate use. Methadone maintenance programs confronted (and continue to confront) abundant obstacles: accusations that they tolerate, perpetuate, and condone drug addiction, embarrassments when programs are poorly run and depicted unfavorably in the media, and protests from local neighborhoods. Nonetheless, their efficacy in reducing drug-related morbidity, mortality, and criminality, and in facilitating legal employment, better family circumstances, and a general improvement in quality of life are well established. A growing body of evidence also indicates that the negative health consequences of long-term methadone maintenance are clinically insignificant.

Methadone maintenance in the United States, however, could be greatly improved. Although the United States pioneered methadone maintenance, it has fallen far behind developments in other countries. Methadone is the most tightly regulated drug in the pharmacopoeia. It may only be dispensed in licensed clinics subject to strict federal and state regulations regarding dosage levels, pickup times and locations, and other matters typically left to the discretion of doctors where other drugs are concerned. Methadone maintenance programs in the United states are relatively expensive, often punitive, and generally "user-unfriendly."

Drug maintenance and substitution are essential features of harm-reductionist thinking. Greater acceptance of "low-threshold" oral methadone programs, dispensing the drug at police stations and in prisons to opiate users in withdrawal, and eventually maintenance on the opiates of choice—heroin and morphine—are foreseeable gains even in the climate of prohibition.

The acceptance of harm-reduction ideologies was accelerated by the activism of gay men internationally in the struggle to retard the spread of HIV/AIDS. Saving lives, tending the dying, and supplying compassion were imperatives that overrode moral and legal scruples. Prodded by AIDS activists, governments and senior police officials in Great Britain, Australia, and Switzerland declared that the disease posed a greater threat to public health than drug abuse, and designed interventions first to prevent its spread.

Needle-exchange programs and other initiatives to reduce needle sharing among drug injectors were among the first contemporary harm-reductionist strategies to be implemented. They epitomize the notion of harm reduction. They proliferated in most Western countries during the late 1980s as governments sought to stem the relationship between intravenous drug use and the transmission of HIV. Such programs are predicated on the assumption that most people who cannot or will not stop injecting drugs will nonetheless take precautionary measures to reduce the likelihood of contracting HIV. This assumption has since been well substantiated (Nadelmann, 1998).

The availability of clean needles to illicit drug injectors varies substantially, depending on local laws, policies, attitudes, and the personal situations of drug users. Local laws may prohibit the sale of needles without a prescription, as is the case in Washington, D.C., and 10 states—including those where the vast majority of illicit drug injectors live. Even where over-the-counter (or behind-the-counter) sale is permitted, pharmacists may be prohibited or discouraged from selling needles to anyone they suspect of illicit drug use. Drug paraphernalia laws may prohibit possession of needles without a prescription, thereby making drug injectors highly vulnerable to arrest. And even where no laws prohibit the sale and possession of needles, needles may not be readily available to drug users leading impoverished, disorganized, and itinerant lives on the streets.

Efforts to discourage needle sharing among drug injectors have focused on repealing restrictions on the sale and possession of needles and otherwise expanding the infrastructure for needle distribution. Other efforts have focused on distributing containers of bleach, encouraging drug injectors to sterilize their "works," and otherwise educating drug users in harm-reduction methods. Most public health authorities agree that these efforts must be complemented by more active needle-exchange efforts that maximize the availability of sterile needles to injectors, minimize the circulation of used needles, and reach as many drug injectors as possible. Availability is enhanced by both making the needles available at little or no cost and increasing the number of locations where they can be obtained. Circulation of used needles is minimized by encouraging or requiring drug injectors to return used needles for clean ones (Nadelmann, 1998).

The first needle-exchange programs started in the Netherlands in the early 1980s, in response not to AIDS but to a hepatitis B epidemic among drug injectors. These programs were rapidly expanded shortly thereafter in response to the threat of HIV. In Great Britain, political support for needle exchange arose in 1986 in response to strong evidence from Scotland that a shortage of needles had facilitated the spread of AIDS. Needle exchange quickly emerged as the cornerstone of HIV prevention among drug injectors. More than 200 needle-exchange programs now operate in England, and two thirds of all drug agencies maintain some needle distribution scheme. In Australia, needle exchange programs began in 1986 and quickly spread throughout the country. By 1992, seven of Australia's eight juris-dictions provided both needle exchange and methadone. In Switzerland, needle exchange is commonplace in most cities—even though regions differ with regard to the means of distribution. The city with the largest needle-exchange program in the world is Zurich, where between 10,000 and 15,000 needles are exchanged each day. Needle exchanges also operate in most large cities in Germany as well as Vienna, Madrid, Bologna, Dublin, and Oslo, and in many smaller cities. In Lisbon, Copenhagen, Strasbourg, Florence, Milan, and Turin, where no needle exchanges have been established, needles are readily available in pharmacies (Nadelmann, 1998).

Most programs share numerous features in common. They are strongly sup-ported by political and government officials at the national and local level, and by a substantial majority of public opinion. Most law-enforcement officials are also supportive. These programs provide not only needles but also alcohol swabs, sharpsafe containers, medicative ointments, and sterile water. Although injectors are strongly encouraged to return used needles, the 1:1 requirement is not strictly enforced. Condoms are usually provided. Many programs also provide primary health services and more generic advice on maintaining good health. The ethos is "user-friendly." Drug injectors are not harassed about their drug use, although they are informed of, and on request referred to, drug treatment programs and other alternatives. They may be shown how to inject less hazardously so as to avoid local complications such as abscesses, septicemia, and renal thrombosis. Some programs also provide detached or outreach services—such as mobile vans and pedestrian distributors—to provide needles more directly to drug injectors' homes and drug-taking venues. In Zurich, about half of needle exchanges and related services are provided by a van stationed near the open drug scene and by twice-daily foot tours of the scene by two medical staff. In Vienna, needles are exchanged in a mobile *Ganslwirt* bus, which reaches about 10% to 25% of all injectors. In Amsterdam, police stations will provide clean needles in return for dirty ones. One program in northern England employs parents of drug injectors as needle exchangers. Many pharmacists now participate in needle exchange efforts as well. In Liverpool, for instance, over 50 pharmacists sell injecting equipment and 20 operate free needle exchanges (Nadelmann, 1998).

Debates over needle exchange in these countries focus not on whether they are desirable or necessary but on particular tactics and methods. Automated needle-exchange machines—which deliver a clean needle when a used needle is depos-ited—can now be found in Berlin, Bremen, Dortmund, Frankfurt, Nurnberg, Bo-logna, Luxembourg, Easel, Bern, Zurich, Rotterdam, Amsterdam, Sydney, and some smaller cities. These machines are relatively inexpensive, available 24 hours a day, and generally recognized as a useful complement to regular needle-exchange programs. Some public health officials, however, worry that such machines decrease personal contact between drug injectors and health workers, and that public opinion and hard-pressed public health budgets may ultimately favor vending machines over staffed programs. Also controversial is the de facto employment of drug injectors in needle exchange. Some needle-exchange programs limit the number of needles that can be exchanged at one time. Others, however, allow a few injectors to exchange dozens each day. This increases the availability of needles to less-accessible drug injectors and at times (such as at night) when official programs are closed. Opposition arises from the fact that these de facto needle exchangers sometimes take advantage of the overall lack of needles by selling them to injectors in need.

Although the efficacy of needle-exchange programs in reducing HIV transmission has not been proven categorically, abundant evidence points to the effectiveness of these programs and related efforts in the dissemination of information on HIV/AIDS risks, in reducing needle sharing, disposing of used needles, and ultimately reducing the transmission of HIV and other infections by and among drug injectors. The popular assumption (common in the United States) that drug injectors will not alter their behavior to reduce the risks of contracting HIV and other infections is contradicted by abundant evidence. Surveys of drug injectors indicate that substantial and increasing proportions of drug injectors participate in needle-exchange programs and only use sterile needles. In most cities, the rate of HIV infection among those who began injecting drugs since the mid-1980s is dramatically lower than among those who were injecting before needle-exchange programs and AIDS prevention programs began. In Australia and much of the United Kingdom, where needle-exchange programs were instituted quickly and widely in the mid-1980s, rates of HIV infection among drug injectors have remained lower than in most other countries. Fears that increased needle availability would encourage illicit drug injection among new users have proven unfounded. Indeed, the trend in many countries is away from injection toward oral and nasal means of consumption—a result both of greater AIDS awareness and the availability of increasingly potent and inexpensive heroin (Hamid et al., 1997; Nadelmann, 1998).

Other programs that could be instituted include rapid expansion of the number, variety, and quality of oral methadone maintenance programs; repeal of drug paraphernalia laws and prohibitions on the sale and possession of syringes; expansion of needle-exchange schemes; research and development of drug maintenance programs involving drugs other than oral methadone; reform of cannabis policy; toleration of "street rooms," where drugs can be injected in relative safety under the supervision of medical staff; creation of organizations to represent the interests of drug users; integration of police activities with harm-reduction programs; and other initiatives directed at reducing crime and disease (Nadelmann, 1998).

The goal of harm reduction is perhaps best achieved in many minor modifications of the drug-user's life. Switching from heroin to marijuana is harm reduction because one spends less money, commits a misdemeanor rather than a felony, and only slightly disrupts "normal" patterns of behavior. Lowering consumption of either heroin or marijuana is also harm reduction, since one is less at risk of arrest, spends even less money, and deviates only imperceptibly (if at all) from the pre-drug self.

Harm reduction is in essence a continuously evolving orthodoxy. It incorporates whatever each day's practice identifies as beneficial to both drug user and the community of which she or he is a part and with which peaceful coexistence is sought. Some actual and potential principles of the continued advance of the harm reduction philosophy follow (Trebach, 1987).

Recruit the Enforcers as Reformers

In 1997 in New York City, policemen operate under the "quality of life" campaign, which aggresses vigorously against street drug use and distribution. In current studies of heroin in the city, all users and distributors in the city have suffered arrest. Intensive policing has mostly worsened their lives. In some cases, it has caused distributors to employ new technologies (beepers, e-mail), bicycle services, or relay systems (paying at one location, delivery at another) and adaptations among users (switching from injecting to sniffing).

At other times in New York City and in other U.S. cities and abroad, police have operated in a "policy vacuum" (Sutton & James, 1995, pp. 114, 120). For example, a review of Australian drug law enforcement found that street-level activity lacks a foundation in coherent policy: it recommends that such a policy, accompanied by regulation and monitoring, should be developed in which harm minimization should be accorded priority equal to that of "targeting higher level figures" in a structure of drug distribution that does not, in any case, fit the commonly assumed "hierarchical models of organised crime'" (Sutton & James, 1995; p. ix).

Police work is inherently discretionary. Some drug users are arrested, but the power to arrest and charge is a resource used to fulfill a fundamental mandate of public order maintenance. More frequently, other methods are adopted: police disrupt the activity, destroy the drugs, and/or move the user on. These are legitimate uses of discretion; however, under certain conditions, they are harmful to public health and inconsistent with commitments to harm minimization. Police make choices about how and when to enforce the law; minimizing drug-related harm should be a factor that feeds into that choice.

For example, drug laws do not forbid the adoption of harm-reduction ideologies nor the implementation of many specific strategies. Police can reorient their patrol practices by settling

> a natural tension . . . between police tactics which are effective in raising the personal "cost" (to users) of injecting illegal drugs and tactics which are effective in discouraging the use of shared or unsterilized injection equipment. . . . If the goal of policy in this area is taken to be harm minimization then we need to be wary of strategies which purchase a reduction in the number of heroin users at the cost of increased health problems. (Weatherburn & Lind, 1995, pp. 3, 36)

Very often, sheer ignorance is the impediment. In the course of interviews with law-enforcement personnel, researchers found that "very few respondents at the operational level could see health-based strategies and the information they could generate as having any relevance to their work" (Sutton & James, 1995, p. 79). "Operational drug enforcement culture remains typically anchored in a war on drugs conception, in which supply-reduction is considered the key approach to drug problems" (Sutton & James, 1995, p. 114).

To be successful, harm-reduction initiatives require the active and knowledgeable involvement of operational officers. It also requires cooperation with non-police agencies committed to demand reduction and public health; however, "many operational drug enforcers see such agencies and their personnel as either irrelevant to the war on drugs or as anti-drug law enforcement" (Sutton & James, 1995, p. 114). When the latter are overcommitted and underresourced, and consequently limited in their ability to contribute to positive policy development, the police have a particular responsibility. As a well-resourced, politically powerful, and strategically sophisticated organization, they can and should take the lead. In an ideal governmental structure, the police would not take such a role; in current circumstances in Australia, as in the United States, problem-oriented and community policing strategies must be led by the police (Maher & Dixon, 1996).

> The potential for HIV infection, hepatitis C and other complications will be greatly exacerbated if over-vigorous enforcement forces users underground, away from the information, advice, treatment and support provided by community-based health and welfare agencies. . . . It is essential, therefore, that all relevant personnel—not simply those working in specialist bodies—constantly be aware of, and able to work within, the full range of National Drug Strategy guidelines. (Sutton & James, 1995, p. 120)

New York City should dismantle the "quality of life" campaign. It has encouraged hostility toward the very principles upon which harm reduction is founded. Events have proven that to do so, not only is the "hard-line" attitude toward drugs emboldened, but also callous disregard for any "difference" whatever. In August 1997, an Italian-American police officer, declaring that "this is Giuliani time, not

Dinkins time," sodomized a 30-year-old Haitian immigrant with a toilet plunger in the toilet of the 70th precinct, wounding him so grievously that major surgery was subsequently required. He then rammed the plunger into the man's mouth, knocking out several teeth. Coming in the wake of several prior incidents of police brutality, the assault sparked angry protests.

Autonomous action at the local and state governmental levels is critical. In Germany, where the central government opposes harm-reduction initiatives, city officials in Bremen, Frankfurt, Hamburg, and other cities have responded directly to drug abuse problems during the 1980s, and, with the governments of Amsterdam, Zurich, and Frankfurt, created a transgovernmental alliance—the European Cities on Drug Policy (ECDP). The transnational group drafted and signed a "Frankfurt Resolution" calling for a transition to harm-reduction policies. By 1993, the membership of the ECDP included Arnhem, Basel, Hanover, Lucerne, Rotterdam, Zagreb, and other cities, and its annual meeting drew representatives from 58 cities from 14 countries. Efforts were also underway to expand the alliance to North America (Nadelmann, 1998).

Save Our Sick from Humiliation and Pain

If policymakers fear that drug-affected young people will spread disease and moral decay and commit crime and mayhem, they cannot fear bedridden senior citizens. Heroin can rapidly alleviate their pain.

Doctors in California and Arizona (and those throughout the United States who have not yet declared themselves) are convinced that their clinical practices have proven scientifically the substantial medical benefits of smoking marijuana in "joints." Their patients who smoked them fared better than comparable others who did not, in cases of cancer, heart disease, AIDS, and hypertension. Many heroin and cocaine misusers smoke marijuana joints officially or unofficially as they learn to moderate or discontinue use. Such a valuable medicine, endorsed by well-qualified medical practitioners, should be utilized more widely.

The Right to Affordable Treatment as Often as Needed

Drug users are often linked from generation to generation, and tomorrow's drug fashions emerge among drug cultures that are declining today. In the case of the crack misusers now gathered in freakhouses in the inner cities, policy measures should offer a hospitable and humane climate for the passage they must make to rejoin the mainstream world. Their success in achieving that goal will greatly affect how drugs are perceived in future generations, since they will be themselves the most effective communicators of past experiences of drugs.

There is a great danger in condemning and marginalizing disenchanted drug misusers. Denied other avenues of leading satisfactory lives, they are left with no recourse but continued desperate untutored experimentation with drugs. The fate of heroin injectors since 1914 offers an instructive example, showing how frustration with heroin, in the climate of prohibition and hostility, led to incremental experimentation with drugs that culminated in crack (see above).

In New York City, where there is a 50% seropositivity rate for HIV/AIDS, there is space for only 15% in methadone maintenance programs.

Many new categories of users are at special risk. Runaway adolescents and transsexual sex workers are some. Upper middle-class European-American users have also special problems that need to be assessed and analyzed before appropriate responses can be made.

Harm-reductionist treatment providers recognize the right for comprehensive, nonjudgmental, medical and social services for all individuals and communities including users, their loved ones, and the communities affected by drug use. They consider people's relationship to drugs, rather than judging licit and illicit drugs and drug use as good or bad, and appreciate the competency of users to make choices and changes in their lives, including their drug use. Accordingly, they provide options in a nonjudgmental, noncoercive way. In particular, they support expanded and increased low-threshold drug treatment options.

Individuals affected by drug use should be themselves involved in the creation of such harm-reduction strategies and programs.

Love Thy Neighbor Even if He Uses Drugs

Policymakers and opinion leaders should concede that there is a social aspect to drug use and spending on drugs. For example, drug use in modern societies cannot be viewed independently of the multibillion-dollar enterprise of production, distribution, and exchange that it entails. The enterprise comprises several socioeconomic units worldwide, which respond exclusively to economic and political processes. A fashion in drug use channels a specific amount of dollars in a particular direction, and the flow enriches some persons at the expense of others. Traditional explanations of drug use, therefore, which emphasize their psychoactive or symbolic properties, overlook the important functions their production and sale perform in the contemporary world, or the importance that economic motivations play in shaping the drug user's desires, choices, and experiences. The switch from marijuana to smokable cocaine, described in Chapter 6, draws attention to the supraindividual factors, independent of the preferences or motivations of persons that caused it.

Class, socioeconomic background, neighborhood, ethnicity, and gender also influence how a user experiences drugs. A further curb to the style of thinking that finds a drug "instantly addictive" or characterized by some other invariant property, real or imagined, is the painstaking demonstration by ethnographic research of the variability of drug effects.

The Controlled Use of Drugs (Including Smokable Cocaine or Injectable Heroin) Is Possible

Policymakers should forever abandon the thought that any drug is addictive, let alone "instantly addictive." The use of all drugs can be brought under the control of rules, regulations, and rituals, and the example of careful, thoughtful, more experienced users can firmly implant these in initiates. Thus, in the case of smokable cocaine, only a few successful drug distributors and very affluent citizens enjoyed it before 1980, and their use was a model of discretion and control. These virtues were regained in the early 1990s, even after the identical user had lost them in the 1980s (see Chapter 9).

The Benign Use of Drugs (e.g., Marijuana) Is Possible

Some illegal drugs have demonstrably positive effects upon persons, with only a few minor drawbacks. Several studies have reported that marijuana is such a drug (Grinspoon & Bakalar, 1993; Weil, 1972, 1993). Another example of its therapeutic and pacific efficacy was described in Chapter 7.

Marijuana figures largely in the indigenous efforts of drug users to control or terminate their engagements with drugs that have been problematic for them.

Although national drug commissions in many countries during the 1970s recommended the decriminalization of cannabis, only the Netherlands followed through at the national level. The Baan Commission expressed the harm-reduction sentiment, common in other countries as well, that "penalties against possession of a drug should not be more damaging to the individual than the use of the drug itself." It also argued that the tendency of some cannabis users to move on to illicit opiate use could be reduced by separating the "soft-drug" and "hard-drug" markets. In 1976, the Opium Law was revised to increase penalties for heroin and cocaine trafficking and decrease penalties for the sale and consumption of small amounts of cannabis to misdemeanor offenses. Prosecutorial and police guidelines were also revised to deemphasize enforcement of the cannabis laws. The result was the creation of a relatively normalized, essentially noncriminal, and easily accessible cannabis distribution system in most Dutch cities.

Cannabis can be bought in hundreds of Dutch "coffee shops"—some of which are bars serving alcoholic beverages and food as well. Most coffee shops offer a selection of 10 or more types of marijuana and hashish at prices significantly less than current U.S. prices. Advertising is prohibited, open display discouraged, and sale to minors prohibited. The police monitor these shops closely, make no effort to disturb buyers and sellers, and will investigate crimes against house dealers. If police detect sales of heroin or cocaine, they will warn the owner once before ordering the shop closed. The same practice applies to coffee shops that become centers of fencing, late night noise, and hideouts for illegal immigrants.

The Dutch policy appears to have accomplished its objectives. Cannabis consumption among young people has remained relatively low. A national survey in 1989 reported that 17.7% of Dutch 17- to 18-year-olds had smoked cannabis at least once and 4.6% within the last month—approximately half to one third the rates in the United States. Rates of cocaine and heroin consumption among Dutch citizens are similarly modest—although the relatively high quality and low price of the drugs have attracted "drug tourists" from elsewhere in Europe. Dutch authorities express some concern about organized criminal involvement in wholesale production and sales of cannabis, and they must contend with frequent complaints from authorities in neighboring Germany and Belgium—although a few coffee shops opened in Hamburg in late 1993—but by and large the policy is regarded favorably by most Dutch law enforcement and other officials involved in drug control.

In 1987, the South Australian government introduced a Cannabis Expiation Notice system that allows individuals apprehended with small quantities of cannabis (up to 100 grams) to have their offense discharged—with no record of a criminal conviction—upon payment of a fine. A similar scheme was introduced in the Australian Capital Territory in 1992. An analysis of the first 2 years of the expiation system by the South Australian Office of Crime statistics found little evidence of any impact on the number or type of people detected using cannabis. Its principal recommendation was that steps be taken to increase the rate of expiations, since nearly half of the notices had resulted in court appearances for failure to pay the fine.

In August 1991, the Federal High Court of Switzerland decided—in a case involving the sale of eight kilograms of hashish—that penalties for dealing cannabis were unduly harsh and needed to be revised given increasing evidence that the health hazards of cannabis consumption were relatively modest (Nadelmann, 1998).

Organizing Drug Misusers Is Beneficial

Efforts, especially indigenous ones, to organize and educate drug users have affected their lives positively. The antecedents of these initiatives originate in the underground literature of the 1960s and early 1970s, which included such publications as the *International Times* and the *Psychedelic Review*. During the late 1980s, the Lifeline Project in Manchester, England, began publishing *Smack in the Eye*, a comic book targeted at current opiate users that provided harm-minimization information in a user-friendly "style and language." In 1990, it initiated a second comic book series, *Peanut Pete*. Similar publications are produced in the Netherlands, Australia, and Germany. In 1997, two young heroin injectors in California launched *Junkphood*. They warn readers about drug-induced paranoia, the dangers of particular types of drug use, and services of particular interest to drug users (Nadelmann, 1998). These publications also teach drug users to recognize and minimize certain dangers. In the Netherlands, public health authorities recognized that one of the greatest dangers associated with the sudden expansion of the "rave scene" (dance clubs and other gatherings, where young people consume methylenedioxymethamphetamine [MDMA] and other stimulants and hallucinogens, and dance to high-energy rave music) was the sale of adulterated and unexpectedly high potency drugs. They responded by employing drug analysis units at raves, where drugs purchased illicitly could be tested prior to consumption. Such initiatives resemble the Pharmchem program created by the U.S. National Institute on Drug Abuse in 1974, which provided a similar service to illicit drug users who mailed in samples for analysis.

Organized and subsidized self-help groups of illicit drug users play a modest but important role in the formulation and implementation of drug-control policies in the Netherlands, Germany, and Australia, and have begun to exercise some influence in Switzerland. The "junkie union" in Amsterdam was decisive in initiating free needle-exchange programs in 1983–1984 after a major pharmacist in the central inner-city "copping" area refused to sell needles to drug users. Similar groups in Canberra, Rotterdam, Groningen, Basel, Bern, Bremen, and a few other German cities have worked with local public health officials on needle-exchange programs and other harm-reduction initiatives. Most of these groups produce publications targeted at illicit drug users that contain useful information on reducing drug-related harms, kicking the habit, and identifying drug-treatment alternatives. These groups play an important role in articulating the sentiments and perceptions of precisely those citizens who are most affected by local policies. They also offer valuable conduits between local governments and underground populations. But they tend to be short-lived and highly dependent upon one or two highly motivated individuals (Nadelmann, 1998).

Another innovation involves official toleration and even sponsorship of "street rooms," where drug injectors are able to consume illicit drugs in relatively hygienic environments under the supervision of qualified medical staff (O'Hare, Newcombe, Mathews, Buning, & Drucker, 1992). These are regarded as preferable to the two most likely alternatives: open injection of illicit drugs in public places, which is widely regarded as distasteful and unsettling to most urban residents; or consumption of drugs in unsanctioned "shooting galleries" that are often dirty, sometimes violent and frequently controlled by drug dealers, and where needle sharing is often the norm. A few street rooms were quietly tolerated within drug agencies in England during the 1960s. During the late 1970s, a number of "drug cafes" for heroin users were established in Amsterdam—but later shut down when drug dealers effectively displaced social workers from control of the daily course of events. In Switzerland, the first *Gassenzimmer* were established by private organizations in Bern and Basel during the late 1980s. By late 1993, eight were in operation, with most under the direct supervision of city officials: two in Bern, two in Basel, one in Lucerne (in City Hall), and three in Zurich. A number of smaller cities in the German-speaking parts of the country plan to follow suit during 1994. An evaluation of the three *Gassenzimmer* in Zurich after their first year of operation concluded that they had proven effective in reducing the transmission of HIV and the risk of overdose (Nadelmann, 1998).

During the 1980s, open drug scenes emerged in many European cities, often in central areas near train stations, commercial areas, public parks, and tourist attractions. No consensus has yet emerged on whether these scenes should be suppressed and dispersed or tolerated and even regulated. The city of Zurich attracted international notoriety during the late 1980s and early 1990s for its official toleration of an open drug scene in a public park, the Platzspitz, which became known as Needle Park. The initial congregation of illicit drug injectors in the park during the mid-1980s was regarded by most city officials and residents, including the police, as an improvement after years of chasing drug users around the city. The concentration of drug users facilitated the provision of needle exchange, emergency first aid, and other medical and social services.

During the early 1990s, public and official sentiment changed. City residents became upset by the growing numbers of drug injectors flocking to Zurich from elsewhere in Switzerland—about 70% of the approximately 2,000 people entering the park each day were not city residents—and by increases in the number of robberies and car break-ins in the vicinity of the park. Within the park, competition among drug dealers generated rising levels of violence, and general social and sanitary conditions deteriorated. The Platzspitz was closed in February 1992. The open drug scene then flowed into different neighborhoods near the Platzspitz, frustrating police and angering city residents, until city authorities agreed to let it settle on the site of a closed train station a few hundred meters from the Platzspitz. There it remains, still serviced by health and social welfare workers working out of a "contact center," and policed regularly by law-enforcement officials.

No consensus has emerged regarding the lessons of Needle Park. Some police officials believe that the lesson is to adopt more punitive approaches and make Zurich less hospitable to illicit drug users. Proponents of legalization see the failure of Needle Park as evidence of the limits of liberalization within the broader context of drug prohibition. The principal problems in the park, they point out, were all a result of prohibition: the violent behavior and destructive impact of illicit drug dealers; overdoses and other adverse health effects from illicitly produced drugs of unknown potency and purity; robberies and other criminal activities committed by drug users requiring substantial sums of money to buy drugs at prices inflated by prohibition; and the unnatural congregation of many of the country's illicit opiate users in one place as a result of more severe drug policies elsewhere in Switzerland. Still others, including many of the city's public health and social welfare workers, reject the conclusion that Needle Park was a failure. They regard it instead as an experience that made the needs, and the misery, of drug users visible to everyone, thereby generating support for rapid implementation of needle-exchange programs and other harm-reduction measures (Nadelmann, 1998).

Zurich was not the only city to tolerate and attempt to regulate an open drug scene. A much smaller scene—in Bern's Kocherpark—evolved along much the same lines until it too was closed in 1992. In Basel, the open drug scene centered along the river in a smaller version of the situation in Zurich after Needle Park. In Rotterdam, an open drug scene, known as Platform Zero, can be found at the Rotterdam railroad station, where it is closely supervised by local police. Needle-exchange services and a mobile methadone unit are readily available.

In Frankfurt, Germany, open heroin scenes emerged during the 1970s and ended up during the mid-1980s in two adjacent parks, the Gallusanlage and Taunusanlage, when top police officials decided that their decade-long efforts to suppress the local drug scenes had failed to halt their growth and merely shifted them from one neighborhood to another. Working in tandem with Zurich officials, local authorities in Frankfurt established three crisis centers in the vicinity of the drug scenes, stationed a mobile ambulance to provide needle-exchange services and emergency medical assistance, offered first aid courses to junkies, and provided another bus for drug-using prostitutes. Other services were provided in the vicinity of the main train station, where a "pill scene" consisting of a few hundred speed users had formed. The police continued their efforts to apprehend drug dealers but initiated a policy of tolerating an open scene within strictly defined borders within the Taunusanlage Park. These initiatives were combined with efforts to lure drug users away from the drug scene by providing night lodgings, daytime residences, and methadone treatment centers in neighborhoods removed from the city center. In late 1992, following the successful implementation of these measures, the open drug scene in the park was shut down. The entire policy was coordinated and overseen by the "Monday Group"—a group of top city officials, including police, medical, public health, drug policy, and political officials that met each Monday to assess local drug-related developments. By 1993, the new policy was believed responsible for significantly reducing the number of homeless drug users, drug-related robberies, and drug-related deaths in the city (Nadelmann, 1998).

One other innovation worth noting is the "apartment dealer" arrangement, adopted informally in Rotterdam and other Dutch cities, whereby police and prosecutors refrain from arresting and prosecuting apartment dealers—including sellers of heroin and cocaine—so long as they do not cause problems for their neighbors. Both this arrangement and Platform Zero are viewed as part and parcel of broader "safe neighborhood" plans in which police and residents collaborate to keep neighborhoods safe, clean, and free of nuisances.

Toleration and regulation of both open drug scenes and apartment dealers both represent forms of informal zoning controls similar to those employed to regulate illegal prostitution. They also are consistent with the underlying philosophy of community policing in the United States. Law-enforcement authorities recognize that they are unable to effectively suppress most illicit drug use and dealing, and that chasing users and dealers from one neighborhood to another is costly and often counterproductive. Local residents express concern primarily with the safety and cleanliness of their neighborhoods, not with illicit drug use per se. And public health and social welfare officials find it easier to provide essential services when drug scenes are relatively stable and easily accessible. The challenges of maintaining control of such scenes are considerable, given both the illegality of the market and the social maladjustment of many hardcore drug users—but no more so than the quite different challenges of more repressive policies. The greatest challenges, in this domain of harm reduction as in others, primarily involve popular perceptions, media depictions, and public relations (Nadelmann, 1998).

Drug users in the United States for the most part have had to begin some of these activities in the face of public incomprehension and media-fueled hostility. Where they have organized, they have improved their lives. Self-help groups have formed at needle exchanges, sex workers under attack in some neighborhoods have banded together for their own protection, and drug users routinely exchange information in more ad hoc groups, at copping places, or even in holding pens, about alternative medicine and other tips that improve their quality of life.

More Research Is Needed

More research on drugs should be funded. For example, marijuana markets are again thriving while the production and use of heroin continue to rise. Before a heroin epidemic comes, policymakers ought to have proactive knowledge. If heroin consumption climbs in the late 1990s and early 2000s, ethnographic methodologies, tested in the cocaine smoking epidemic of the 1980s, have proved able to assess the development rapidly and accurately. They are an indispensable complement to the usual epidemiological approaches, which, by themselves, have often mistaken the extent of use, how users are initiated, how they switch between drugs or use patterns, how much they use, how they quit, who the drug distributors are, and how they operate (Hamid et al., 1997). Thus, although the Drug Abuse Warning Network (DAWN), Drug Use Forecasting (DUF), the National Household Survey of Drug Abuse (NHSDA), and Monitoring the Future (MTF) are valuably affirming the greater availability and consumption of heroin, they have not grasped the characteristics of new users, plumbed the sources of new demand, or tapped into the emergent rituals and norms that are energizing new use patterns.

The principal drawback, however, and the one that an anthropological ethnography rigorously and systematically corrects, is that surveys cannot apprehend the contexts of social life in which drug use and distribution take place, its complexity and situational aspects, and its economic, cultural, and political dimensions. An ethnographic methodology restores this holistic perspective. Ethnographic procedures are also best suited to access and describe populations and social environments that are withdrawn from public view. Scientific findings—both those that are well founded and those that remain speculative—integrate theories to provide a multidisciplinary perspective, contribute to better informed public opinions, enhance their decision-making ability, increase the potential for the development of effective social policies, provide an update of contemporary treatment strategies, and emphasize need for further research.

The international ramifications of U.S. drug policy must not be overlooked. Just as in the 1950s and 1960s, when the U.S. government sponsored dictators such as Papa "Doc" Duvalier of Haiti and the Shah of Iran because they were allies in the Cold War against the Soviet Union, equally questionable partners have joined the U.S.-directed global war on drugs (Nadelmann, 1993). This area also needs urgently to be researched.

Discussion Questions

1. What should be the aims of a humane, effective drug policy? Make a list and discuss each.
2. Comment on Cohen's remark (see text) that "effective social policy is effective drug policy." What social policies could alleviate the suffering of American drug misusers? What assistance is offered in the reader's community and how could it be increased?
3. What are some obstacles to designing and implementing a more flexible and responsive policy, either locally or nationally?
4. How does drug prohibition, rather than drugs themselves, cause many of the misfortunes afflicting American misusers, such as risky modes of administration, poor hygiene and health, homelessness, unemployment, crime, violence, marginalization, low self-esteem, and other psychiatric problems? Find out about the lifestyles of drug misusers in other countries and compare them with the American experience.
5. If the reader were to devise a harm-reduction program for her or his local community, what would be its main innovations?
6. Could local police be drawn into a harm-reduction approach within the existing laws? Have they taken steps in that direction? Explain.
7. Does it make sense to minimize the penalties for minor drug use, or for the use of less harmful substances such as marijuana, in order to deter experimentation with more problematic ones?

8. How should American authorities deal with drug production, use, and misuse abroad?
9. How could more varied, balanced, and scientific information be brought into national and local debates about drugs?
10. Discuss the cycles of use of various drugs and other commodities. What acts as a brake to further spread, and how can those be strengthened by policy? How can informal controls on behavior be brought to bear on the drug or other social problems?
11. Enumerate the additional information about drugs that future research should provide.
12. What are the reader's recommendations?

REFERENCES

Becker, H. (1963). *Outsiders: Studies in the sociology of deviance*. London: Free Press of Glencoe.

Berridge, V., & Edwards, D. (1981). *Opium and the people: Opiate use in the United Kingdom*. London: A. Lane. New York: St. Martin's Press.

Bourgois, P. (1989). In Search of Horatio Alger: Culture and ideology in the crack economy. *Contemporary Drug Problems, 16*, 1619–1649.

Buckley, W.F., Nadelmann, E., Schmoke, K., McNamara, J., Szasz, T., & Duke, S. (1996, February 12). The war on drugs is lost. *National Review*, pp. 34–48.

Cheung, W., & Erickson, P. (1997). Crack use in Canada: A distant American cousin. In C. Reinarman & H. Levine (Eds.), *Crack in America: Demon drugs and social justice* (pp. 175–193). Berkeley, CA: University of California Press.

Cohen, P. (1997). Crack in the Netherlands: Effective social policy is effective drug policy. In C. Reinarman & H. Levine (Eds.), *Crack in America: Demon drugs and social justice* (pp. 214–224). Berkeley, CA: University of California Press.

Currie, T. (1985). *Confronting crime: An American challenge*. New York: Pantheon.

Fort, J. (1962, September 18). Addiction: Fact or fiction. *Saturday Review of Books*, 30–51.

Glasser & Siegel. (1997). When Constitutional rights seem too extreme to endure: The crack scare and its impact on civil rights and liberties. In C. Reinarman & H. Levine (Eds.), *Crack in America: Demon drugs and social policy*. (pp. 229–248). Berkeley, CA: University of California Press.

Grinspoon, L., Bakalar, J.B. (1993). *Marihuana: The forbidden medicine*. New Haven, CT: Yale University Press.

Grund, M-P., Stern, L.S., Kaplan, C., Drucker, E., & Adriaans, N. (1992). Drug use context and HIV consequences: The effects of drug policy on patterns of everyday drug use in Rotterdam and the South Bronx. *British Journal of Sociology, 87*, 381–392.

Gunst, L. (1997). *Born Fi' Dead*. New York: Henry Holt.

Hamid, A. (1990). The decline of crack use in New York City: Drug policy or natural controls? *International Journal on Drug Policy, 2*(5), 26–28.

Hamid, A. (1992). The developmental cycle of a drug epidemic: The cocaine smoking epidemic in New York's low income neighborhoods, 1981–1991. *Journal of Psychoactive Drugs, 24*, 337–349.

Hamid, A., Curtis, R., McCoy, K., McGuire, J., Conde, A., Bushell, W., Lindenmayer, R., Brimberg, K., Maia, S., Abdur-Rashid, S., & Settembrino, J. (1997). The heroin epidemic in New York City: Current status and prognoses. *Journal of Psychoactive Drugs*, *29*, 375–391.

Korf, D., & Hoogenhoot, H. (1997). *Heroin users: Their experience with and evaluation of the Amsterdam drug treatment system*. Amsterdam, The Netherlands: University of Amsterdam.

MacAlary, M. (1990). *Buddy Boys*. New York: Macmillan.

Maher, L., & Curtis, R. (1992). Women on the edge of crime. *Crime, Law and Social Change*, *18*, 221–258.

Maher, L., & Dixon, D. (1996, November). Policy and public health in a street level drug market. Paper presented at the Annual Meeting of the American Society of Criminology, Chicago.

Mauer, M. (1991). *Americans behind bars: A comparison of international rates of incarceration*. Washington, DC: Sentencing Project, National Institute of Justice.

Mugford, S.K. (1997). Crack in Australia: Why is there no problem? In C. Reinarman & H. Levine (Eds.), *Crack in America: Demon drugs and social policy* (pp. 194–213). Berkeley, CA: University of California Press.

Nadelmann, E. (1989). Drug prohibition in the United States: Costs, consequences and alternatives. *Science*, *245*, 939–946.

Nadelmann, E. (1993). *Cops across borders*. University Park, PA: Pennsylvania State University Press.

Nadelmann, E. (1998, January-February). Experimenting with drugs. *Foreign Affairs*, pp. 111–126.

O'Hare, P., Newcombe, R., Matthews, A., Buning, E., & Drucker, E. (Eds.). (1992). *Reduction of drug-related harm*. London: Whurr.

Reinarman, C., & Levine H. (1997). Punitive prohibition in America. In C. Reinarman & H. Levine (Eds.), *Crack in America: Demon drugs and social justice* (pp. 321–333). Berkeley, CA: University of California Press.

Sampson, R.J. (1986). Crime in cities: The effects of formal and informal social control. In A.J. Reiss & M. Tonry (Eds.), *Communities and crime* (pp. 271–310). Chicago: University of Chicago Press.

Siegel, R. (1986). Alcohol and drug dependence: The Victorian perspective re-examined. *Research Advances in Alcohol and Drug Problems*, *9*, 279–314.

Sluis, T., Cobelens, E., & Schrader, P. (1990). *Overdose deaths in Amsterdam*. Amsterdam: Amsterdam Municipal Health Service.

Smart, E.F. (1983). *Forbidden highs*. Toronto: Addiction Research.

Sutton, M., & James, P. (1995). Evaluation of Australian drug anti-trafficking law enforcement. Payneham, Australia: National Research Unit.

Trebach, A. (1987). *The great drug war*. New York: Macmillan.

Waldorf, D., & Murphy, S. (1977). Cocaine snorters: An ethnography of cocaine snorters. Washington, DC: Drug Policy Council.

Weatherburn, L., & Lind, P. (1995). Drug law enforcement policy and its impact on the heroin market. Sydney: NSW Bureau of Crime Statistics and Research.

Weil, A. (1972). *The natural mind: A new way of looking at drugs and the higher consciousness*. Boston: Houghton Mifflin.

Weil, A. (1993). *Spontaneous healing*. Boston: Houghton MIfflin.

Williams, T., (1989). *Cocaine kids*. Orange, NJ: Addison-Wesley.

Index